The Cambridge Companion to the Declaration of Independence

The Cambridge Companion to the Declaration of Independence offers a wide-ranging and accessible anthology of essays for understanding the Declaration's intellectual and social context, connection to the American Revolution, and influence in the United States and throughout the world. The volume places the document in the context of ideas during the Enlightenment and examines the language and structure to assess its effect and appeal throughout the centuries and across countries. Here are contributions from law, history, and political science, considering such matters as the philosophical foundations of the Declaration, the role of religion, critics of its role in American political development, and whether "Jefferson's handiwork" is still relevant in the twenty-first century. Written by distinguished and emerging scholars, the *Companion* provides new and diverse perspectives on the most important statement of American political commitments.

Mark A. Graber is the Regents Professor at the University of Maryland Carey School of Law, one of only seven professors to hold the highest honor in the University of Maryland system. He has published fifteen books and over 100 articles. In 2023, he received the Lifetime Achievement Award from the Law and Courts Section of the American Political Science Association.

Michael Zuckert is the Nancy R. Dreux Professor of Political Science, Emeritus, at the University of Notre Dame and Clinical Professor at Arizona State University. He has worked extensively in the area of American political thought. He was the founding editor of the journal *American Political Thought* and received the Lifetime Achievement Award from the American Political Thought section of the American Political Science Association. His many books include *The Natural Rights Republic* (1994).

THE CAMBRIDGE
COMPANION TO
AMERICAN STUDIES

This series of Companions to key figures in American history and culture is aimed at students of American studies, history, and literature. Each volume features newly commissioned essays by experts in the field, with a chronology and guide to further reading.

VOLUMES PUBLISHED

The Cambridge Companion to Alfred Hitchcock edited by Jonathan Freedman
The Cambridge Companion to Frederick Douglass edited by Maurice Lee
The Cambridge Companion to Bob Dylan edited by Kevin J. H. Dettmar
The Cambridge Companion to W. E. B. Du Bois edited by Shamoon Zamir
The Cambridge Companion to Benjamin Franklin edited by Carla Mulford
The Cambridge Companion to Thomas Jefferson edited by Frank Shuffelton
The Cambridge Companion to Malcolm X edited by Robert E. Terrill
The Cambridge Companion to Abraham Lincoln edited by Shirley Samuels
The Cambridge Companion to John F. Kennedy edited by Andrew Hoberek

The Cambridge Companion to the Declaration of Independence

Edited by

MARK A. GRABER
University of Maryland

MICHAEL ZUCKERT
University of Notre Dame

Shaftesbury Road, Cambridge CB2 8EA, United Kingdom

One Liberty Plaza, 20th Floor, New York, NY 10006, USA

477 Williamstown Road, Port Melbourne, VIC 3207, Australia

314–321, 3rd Floor, Plot 3, Splendor Forum, Jasola District Centre, New Delhi – 110025, India

103 Penang Road, #05–06/07, Visioncrest Commercial, Singapore 238467

Cambridge University Press is part of Cambridge University Press & Assessment, a department of the University of Cambridge.

We share the University's mission to contribute to society through the pursuit of education, learning and research at the highest international levels of excellence.

www.cambridge.org
Information on this title: www.cambridge.org/9781009692601

DOI: 10.1017/9781009692632

© Mark A. Graber and Michael Zuckert 2026

This publication is in copyright. Subject to statutory exception and to the provisions of relevant collective licensing agreements, no reproduction of any part may take place without the written permission of Cambridge University Press & Assessment.

When citing this work, please include a reference to the DOI 10.1017/9781009692632

First published 2026

Cover image: Gado Images / Alamy Stock Photo. Color magazine cover from *Life* magazine, illustrated by Paul C. Stahr, and published on July 1, 1915

A catalogue record for this publication is available from the British Library

A Cataloging-in-Publication data record for this book is available from the Library of Congress

ISBN 978-1-009-69259-5 Hardback
ISBN 978-1-009-69260-1 Paperback

Cambridge University Press & Assessment has no responsibility for the persistence or accuracy of URLs for external or third-party internet websites referred to in this publication and does not guarantee that any content on such websites is, or will remain, accurate or appropriate.

For EU product safety concerns, contact us at Calle de José Abascal, 56, 1°, 28003 Madrid, Spain, or email eugpsr@cambridge.org

The palpable truth, that the mass of mankind has not been born with saddles on their backs, nor a favored few booted and spurred, ready to ride them legitimately.
      Thomas Jefferson (Letter to Roger C. Weightman)

Contents

List of Contributors		*page* ix
Acknowledgments		xiii
	Introduction Michael Zuckert	1
1	European Antecedents to the Declaration of Independence S. Adam Seagrave	4
2	The Twenty-Six Grievances Woody Holton	19
3	The Process of Writing and Procedures for Adopting the Declaration Peter Charles Hoffer and Williamjames Hull Hoffer	35
4	The Declaration as Political Rhetoric Matthew Crow	46
5	Equality, Liberty, and Rights in the Declaration of Independence Michael Zuckert	61
6	The "Stubborn" Declaration: Less Dissent than Alienation in Black Political Thought and the Declaration of Independence Saladin Ambar	76
7	"Popular Sovereignty" and the Declaration of Independence Sanford Levinson	90
8	Slavery and the Declaration: A Reinterpretation Richard Newman	109
9	A Theological Interpretation of the Declaration of Independence Barbara A. McGraw	123
10	The Declaration versus the Constitution Tom Cutterham	142

11	Getting "the Hang of the Declaration": The Declaration in American Nationalism *Brian Steele*	155
12	Native Nations and Declarations of Independence *Jonathan Todd Hancock*	170
13	The Declaration in Anti-slavery and African American Thought *Thomas J. Davis*	187
14	The Declaration of Independence and Women *Leslie F. Goldstein*	203
15	Aspirational Reliance on the Declaration of Independence: Labor and Woman's Suffrage *Alexander Tsesis*	219
16	Presidents and the Declaration of Independence *Mark A. Graber*	236
	Conclusion: Four Children, Sixteen Essays, and the Declaration of Independence *Mark A. Graber*	251

Bibliography   271
Index   295

Contributors

Saladin Ambar is Professor of Political Science at Rutgers University's Eagleton Institute of Politics. He is the Director of the Democracy Committee of the New Jersey Social Justice Institute for the New Jersey Reparations Council. He also serves as a scholarly advisor to the Lincoln Presidential Foundation and the Woodrow Wilson Presidential Library and Museum. Ambar is the author of six books, including *Malcolm X at Oxford Union: Racial Politics in a Global Era* (Oxford University Press, 2014), *Stars and Shadows: The Politics of Interracial Friendship from Jefferson to Obama* (Oxford University Press, 2022), and *Three Murders on the Mississippi: A Thousand Days That Made Abraham Lincoln* (Diversion Book, 2025).

Matthew Crow is Professor of History at Hobart and William Smith Colleges in Geneva, New York. In addition to several essays and reviews, he is the author of *Thomas Jefferson, Legal History, and the Art of Recollection* (Cambridge University Press, 2017). His second book is titled *Even in the Lawless Seas: Legal Imagination and Oceanic History in the World of Herman Melville* (Cambridge University Press, forthcoming). Beyond that, he is working on books about the history of liturgical texts in the Atlantic world, and on the history of books about the ocean in United States history.

Tom Cutterham is Associate Professor of US History at the University of Birmingham. He is the author of *Gentlemen Revolutionaries: Power and Justice in the New American Republic* (Princeton University Press, 2017), and of essays in the *William and Mary Quarterly*, the *Journal of the Early Republic*, and *American Political Thought*.

Thomas J. Davis, PhD, JD, is Professor Emeritus at Arizona State University, where he taught US legal and constitutional history, and race and the law. A historian and lawyer, he is author of several books published by Greenwood Press, including *Race Relations in America* (2006), *Plessy v. Ferguson*

(2012), and *History of African Americans* (2016), and with Brenda M. Brock, *Documents of the Harlem Renaissance* (ABC-Clio, 2021), among other works.

Leslie F. Goldstein, Morris Professor Emerita of Political Science, University of Delaware, has authored numerous articles and several books in the fields of public law and political philosophy. Her most recent books are *The U.S. Supreme Court and Racial Minorities: Two Centuries of Judicial Review on Trial* (Elgar, 2017) and with co-authors Judith Baer, Courtenay Daum and Terri Fine, *Women's Constitutional and Legal Rights* (West Academic Press, 2019, 4th edn).

Mark A. Graber is the Regents Professor at the University of Maryland Carey School of Law. He is the author, most recently, of *Punish Treason, Reward Loyalty: The Forgotten Goals of Constitutional Reform after the Civil War* (Kansas, 2023), as well as many other books and articles and articles on various dimensions of constitutionalism.

Jonathan Todd Hancock is former Professor of History at Hendrix College. He is the author of *Convulsed States: Earthquakes, Prophecy, and the Remaking of Nations in Early America* (University of North Carolina Press, 2021), as well as essays in Native American and early US history. He lives in Denver, Colorado.

Peter Charles Hoffer teaches history at the University of Georgia. He has a PhD from Harvard University. With N. E. H. Hull and Williamjames Hull Hoffer he was a founding editor of the Landmark Law and American Society Series, and collaborated on histories of the US Supreme Court and the federal courts. He has written numerous other books on topics in legal history, including *The Supreme Court Footnote: A Surprising History* (New York University Press, 2024) and *The Radical Advocacy of Wendell Phillips: Abolitionism, Democracy, and Public Interest Law* (Kent State University Press, 2024).

Williamjames Hull Hoffer is Professor of History at Seton Hall University. His JD is from Harvard University and his PhD is from Johns Hopkins University. He is the author and co-author of several books on US legal history, including, most recently, *The Sick Chicken Case: The US Supreme Court and the New Deal* (University Press of Kansas in February, 2025).

Woody Holton is Professor of History at the University of South Carolina. He is the author of *Forced Founders: Indians, Debtors, Slaves and the Making of the American Revolution in Virginia* (1999), *Unruly Americans and the Origins of the Constitution* (2007), *Abigail Adams* (2009), and *Liberty Is Sweet: The Hidden History of the American Revolution* (2021).

Sanford Levinson is the W. St. John Garwood and W. St. John Garwood Jr. Centennial Chair in Law and Professor of Government at the University of Texas at Austin. He was elected to the American Academy of Arts and Sciences in 2001, and received the Lifetime Achievement Award from the Law and Courts Section of the American Political Science Association in 2010. Levinson is the author of several books on the United States Constitution, including *Our Undemocratic Constitution: Where the Constitution Foes Wrong (And How We the People Can Correct It)* (Oxford University Press, 2008) and *Constitutional Faith* (Princeton University Press, 1988).

Barbara A. McGraw holds joint appointments as Professor of Social Ethics, Law, and Public Life and Professor of Politics, and is the Founding Director of the Center for Engaged Religious Pluralism at Saint Mary's College of California. Her work centers on American identity and its moral and spiritual foundations, the role of religion in public life, and religious liberty. She is author, co-author, and editor of many books, articles, and chapters on religion, law, and politics and on interfaith leadership. Her publications include *Rediscovering America's Sacred Ground: Public Religion and Pursuit of the Good in a Pluralistic America* (State University of New York Press, 2003) and is the editor of the *Wiley-Blackwell Companion to Religion and Politics in the U.S.* (Wiley-Blackwell, 2016).

Richard Newman is Professor of History at the Rochester Institute of Technology. He has served as Distinguished Lecturer for the Organization of American Historians and worked as a historical commentator on various PBS programs, including Dr. Henry Louis Gates' documentary series, *The Black Church: This Is Our Story, This Is Our Song*. Newman is the author and/or editor or seven books in American, African American and Environmental history and reform, including *Freedom's Prophet: Bishop Richard Allen, the AME Church, and the Black Founding Fathers* (New York University Press, 2008) and *Abolitionism: A Very Short Introduction* (Oxford University Press, 2018). His next book is *American Emancipations: The Making and Unmaking of Black Freedom, 1619–The Present* (Cambridge University Press, in press).

S. Adam Seagrave is Associate Professor of Civic and Economic Thought and Leadership at Arizona State University. He received his PhD in Political Science from the University of Notre Dame. Seagrave is the author of *The Foundations of Natural Morality: On the Compatibility of Natural Rights and the Natural Law* (University of Chicago Press, 2014), *Liberty and Equality: The American Conversation* (University Press of Kansas, 2015), and *The Accessible Federalist* (Hackett, 2017), and co-author with Stephanie Shonekan of *Race and the American Story* (Oxford University Press, 2024), and is the author of numerous articles.

Brian Steele is Associate Professor of History at the University of Alabama. He is the author of *Thomas Jefferson and American Nationhood* (Cambridge

University Press, 2012) and is writing a book about how the other "Founding Fathers" remembered George Washington.

Alexander Tsesis is the D'Alemberte Chair in Constitutional Law and Professor of Law at the Florida State University College of Law. He is also the General Editor of the Cambridge Studies on Civil Rights and Civil Liberties and the Oxford Theoretical Foundations in Law. His books include *We Shall Overcome: A History of Civil Rights and the Law* (Yale University Press, 2008), *For Liberty and Equality: The Life and Times of the Declaration of Independence* (Oxford University Press, 2012), and *Free Speech in the Balance* (Cambridge University Press, 2020).

Michael Zuckert is the Nancy R. Dreux Professor of Political Science, Emeritus, at the University of Notre Dame, and Clinical Professor at the Arizona State University. He was founding editor of the journal *American Political Thought* and has written extensively in the area of American political thought.

Acknowledgments

The original editors of this volume were to be Al Brophy and Mark Brandon. They began the editorial process by selecting most of the contributors and settling on a structure for the book and topics for the essays. For various reasons they were unable to complete the task and asked the current editorial team to carry the project forward. We were pleased to take it on and finish the work so well begun. Without their beginnings, this book would surely be different than it is and we are pleased to acknowledge them as our founders. Michael Zuckert would also like to acknowledge Catherine, long-time critic, aid, and love of his life. Mark A. Graber would also like to acknowledge Julia Bess Frank, long-time critic, aid, and love of his life.

Introduction

Michael Zuckert

Abraham Lincoln often spoke of the Declaration of Independence as "the faith of our fathers," as though it were for Americans what the Torah was for God's chosen people. He meant that America was not a nation that grew up willy-nilly from a common tribal past, but one that began in an intentional way, through what he called a dedication to the "proposition that 'All men are created equal.'" Accordingly, America is sometimes called a "propositional nation." We are now approaching the 250th anniversary of the document and the revolution it defended and the Declaration remains so alive that we still have battles over its meaning and significance. Lincoln – or even Thomas Jefferson, its chief author – would surely recognize many of the themes in our discourse about the Declaration as captured in the essays in this volume.

Historian Carl Becker, himself the author of a semi-classic twentieth-century study of the Declaration, once said in a convoluted way something to the effect that every generation rewrites history to suit its needs and according to its perspectives. This twenty-first-century collection of essays on the Declaration in part validates his claim and in part does not. Probably the chief way in which this collection differs from earlier efforts is in its broadened horizons. There is a systematic effort to consider the Declaration in relation to groups and concerns that had largely not been much attended to in the past – women, labor, Native Americans, the international resonances of the document.

But there are familiar themes as well, though mostly treated differently from the past. The intellectual roots of the Declaration is indeed a familiar topic, but the century or so since Becker's book has enriched and deepened our grasp of the intellectual sources and perhaps even more of their meaning. Not often emphasized in previous treatments are the religious and theological influences. Themes like the relation of the Declaration to the political context from which it emerged, the legal basis of the document, its main ideas – these are all topics that have a long history but which receive new treatment here based on new scholarship.

On balance, however, probably more striking than the novelties and the differences and the scholarly advances is the stubborn persistence of major themes – most especially the relation of the Declaration to slavery and its aftermath, to the American nation and its successes, its outright failures, and its shortfalls in living up to the aspirations expressed in the Declaration.

Not everyone involved in the making of the Declaration expected it to be of such lasting import as it has proved to be. John Adams, the acknowledged "colossus" during the debates leading up to the Congressional passed the Resolution of Independence on July 2, 1776, looked at that date as likely to be the most significant in American history, perhaps in world history. It will be, he wrote his wife Abigail, "the most memorable epocha in the history of America." July 2, he predicted, would be "celebrated by succeeding generations as the great anniversary festival," marked by "pomp and parade, shows, games, sports, guns, bells, bonfires, and illuminations, from one end of the continent to the other from this time forward, forevermore." Not July 2, but July 4, the date of the adoption of the Declaration, has been that day of celebration, pomp, and parade. Adams spoke of the Declaration almost as an afterthought: "In a few days," he told Abigail, "a declaration setting forth the causes which have impelled us to this mighty revolution, and the reasons which will justify it in the sight of God and man" would be issued.

From his perspective in 1776, the event the Declaration marked, the actual declaration of independence, an event with immediate practical consequences, seemed far more noteworthy than Congress' words about it. Yet much later, Thomas Jefferson identified his role in preparing the Declaration to be one of the three of his achievements to be memorialized on his tombstone. These were all accomplishments – founding the University of Virginia, and drafting both the Virginia Statute of Religious Liberty and the Declaration – with lasting and ongoing significance. Since Americans celebrate July 4 rather than July 2, it seems that Jefferson had it more right, that the Declaration's future had more abiding import than its immediate purpose. Again Lincoln expresses the point well: "All honor to Jefferson – to the man who, in the concrete pressure of a struggle for national independence by a single people, had the coolness, forecast, and capacity to introduce into a merely revolutionary document, an abstract truth, applicable to all men and all times."

Yet its immediate purpose and circumstances of drafting are of obvious importance as well. The Declaration may have been a "merely [!] Revolutionary document" with a purpose limited to the event it defended, but that event was no small thing. The Declaration was a product of the Second Continental Congress, the governing or coordinating body for the alliance of thirteen colonies then engaged in warfare with the British. By the spring of 1776, most of the delegates, as Jefferson put it in his *Autobiography*, "saw the impossibility that we should ever again be United with Great Britain." Nonetheless, the assemblage was not yet ready, for a variety of reasons, to formalize the decision. It was believed, however, that the member colonies not yet ready to take such a momentous step were "fast advancing to that state." Accordingly, it was decided to postpone the final decision a few weeks until the beginning of July. However, to be ready when and if the moment came, "a committee was appointed" consisting of Jefferson, John Adams, Benjamin Franklin, Roger Sherman, and Robert R. Livingston, a distinguished group indeed.

The committee agreed that Jefferson should prepare a draft that it would review and pass on to the Congress. Hence Jefferson's tombstone inscription, claiming credit as "Author of the Declaration of American Independence." Jefferson's claim to be author was somewhat presumptuous, on several different grounds. First, of course, he prepared his draft on behalf of a committee, which did indeed have input into the draft reported to Congress. Second, Congress itself contributed much of importance to the final version of the Declaration. Finally, in a later reminiscence of his task, he identified the object of the draft as he understood it "not to be to find out new principles, or new arguments never thought of, not merely to say things which had never been said before, but to place before mankind the common sense of the subject, in terms so plain and firm is to command their assent." This common sense might be expected to command assent in America, if not with all mankind, because "it was intended to be an expression of the American mind ... All its authority rests then on the harmonizing sentiments of the day," sentiments Jefferson found "in conversation, in letters, printed essays, or in the elementary books of public right, as Aristotle, Cicero, Locke, Sydney. Etc." That is to say, Jefferson can hardly claim authorship, in the usual sense, of the content of the Declaration.

Yet he can claim responsibility, for the most part, for the concision, clarity, eloquence, and beauty of the final text, though here again Franklin and Adams and Congress deserve some share of the credit. The hand was mostly Jefferson's, but the voice was that of the American people. Acquaintance with the political literature of that age well confirms Jefferson's sense that he was putting into wonderful prose the broad consensus among American Patriots, that is to say, supporters of the movement for independence, of the day. Along this line he might have mentioned his reliance on George Mason's Bill of Rights for Virginia, prepared shortly before he sat down to his drafting task. The Declaration comes to us nearly 250 years later, when it is no longer clear that the consensus that gave it birth any longer holds for us, if any consensus does. It is one task of this volume to probe whether and how it still speaks to us as a nation, whether and in what way, it is still "the Faith of Our Fathers," and of us.

I

European Antecedents to the Declaration of Independence

S. Adam Seagrave

In one way, the Declaration of Independence had no antecedent in human history. Never before had a political community attempted to "declare the causes" for their assuming political independence in such clear, confident, and stunningly universal terms. Neither had any political community ever invoked the companion ideas of natural rights and the laws of nature as composing the substance and justification of these causes. Even if "the Americans did not discover the natural rights/social contract theory adumbrated in the Declaration of Independence," they "were the first to embrace it as the official basis of their most solemn and lasting political actions."[1] The thirteen American states, despite stark differences in other ways, possessed a single "American mind" on basic political principles, which had developed over time in response to unique circumstances and in combination with their predominantly English cultural and intellectual background.[2]

Considered in this way, the Declaration of Independence was *sui generis*, inaugurating the "Novus ordo seclorum" so frequently referenced by the American Founding generation. As unprecedented as the Declaration was, however, it was not without antecedents. The Declaration clearly interacted with and built upon recent expressions of European Enlightenment political philosophy in its focus on "Nature and Nature's God" and in its reliance upon the normative principles of "laws of Nature" as well as natural or "unalienable" rights. These European Enlightenment political philosophers themselves stood in complex and varied relationships with their ancient and medieval predecessors, sometimes adding to, sometimes transforming, and sometimes rejecting ancient and medieval political ideas. The Declaration brilliantly

---

[1] Michael Zuckert, *Natural Rights and the New Republicanism* (Princeton: Princeton University Press, 1994), 15.
[2] Thomas Jefferson to Henry Lee, May 8, 1825, National Archives.

1 European Antecedents

navigates this complex web of intellectual antecedents by treating the ideas of laws of nature, natural rights, the social contract, and republicanism in such a way that the points of tension between their different interpretations are minimized and subsumed within a shared understanding of the importance of nature for political life. In so doing, the Declaration provides an intriguing hint of how the deep fault lines between these political philosophical traditions might ultimately be bridged. Just as American society has always been a "melting pot" for diverse national and cultural backgrounds, so the Declaration's succinct statement of political principles may be viewed as a transformative distillation of a few of its most important European antecedents.

1.1 LAWS OF NATURE

Shortly after invoking "the American mind" in his letter to Henry Lee, Thomas Jefferson lists some of the historical authorities who concur with the "harmonizing sentiments" it contains. Along with the more recent John Locke and Algernon Sidney, he cites two ancient philosophers, Aristotle and Cicero. How, though, could Jefferson claim to have constructed a coherent whole out of such apparently ill-fitting pieces? Besides being separated by more than fifteen centuries in time, the modern pair seem to approach politics from a perspective diametrically opposed to that adopted by the ancient pair. Locke takes the isolated individual in the anarchic "state of nature" as his focus and starting point, while Cicero follows Aristotle in treating the political community as fundamental and basic to the life of the individual. Locke follows Thomas Hobbes in focusing on the minimal condition of self-preservation in deriving the primary goal of politics, while Cicero and Aristotle focus on the ultimate end of happiness or virtue.

According to some well-known interpreters, these differences indicate a tension, contradiction, or incompatibility between modern philosophers like Locke and ancient ones like Aristotle. Modern social contract theories like Locke's are premised, these interpreters argue, upon a rejection of their medieval and ancient predecessors on all of the most important questions for political life.[3] For example, Hobbes – Locke's immediate predecessor and forerunner – describes the philosophy of Aristotle and the medieval Scholastics as "vain" or empty.[4] Locke himself, in his work on the law of nature, flatly denies one of the most important and most recognizable elements of St. Thomas Aquinas' natural law philosophy: namely, that this law can be "known from the natural inclination of mankind."[5] Hobbes and Locke seem to have profound disagreements with philosophers like Cicero and Aristotle and to pit their own political

---

[3] Leo Strauss, *Natural Right and History* (Chicago: University of Chicago Press, 1953).
[4] Thomas Hobbes, *Leviathan* (Indianapolis: Hackett, 1994), xlvi.14, p. 458.
[5] John Locke, *Questions Concerning the Law of Nature*, ed. and trans. Robert Horwitz, Jenny Strauss Clay, and Diskin Clay (Ithaca: Cornell University Press, 1990), Question VI, p. 169.

doctrines against those of their predecessors, making it difficult for succeeding interpreters to see beyond these disagreements.

These difficulties have, moreover, led to divergences in the recent scholarship on the American Founding. Many of the most prominent scholars have tended to emphasize either the "classical republican" side of early American political thought – that represented by Aristotle and Cicero – to the exclusion or downplaying of the modern or "liberal" side;[6] or, on the other hand, to emphasize the Lockean side of early American political thought to the exclusion of the ancient side.[7] Even as sensitivity to the intellectual divide between ancient and modern political philosophy has to a certain extent softened, the hesitancy to grapple simultaneously with these disparate influences has remained.

This hesitancy is an obstacle to attaining a complete understanding of the American Founding in general, and the Declaration of Independence in particular, because Jefferson and the other leading Founders were not troubled by the historical diversity of their influences as their interpreters often are. Jefferson and those who subscribed to the "American mind" he expressed appeared able to see both intellectual historical poles at once and focus on their overlap. In the Declaration, the most important areas of overlap occur in the ideas of laws of nature and of the social contract. Although each of these ideas had changed in various ways by the time they appeared in the Declaration, they remained recognizable versions of their originals in medieval and ancient political philosophy.

The reference to "laws of Nature and of Nature's God" in the Declaration's opening paragraph is a clear reflection of European Enlightenment ideas, and particularly those found in the writings of Locke and Isaac Newton.[8] One of the hallmarks of seventeenth-century Enlightenment thought was a shift in emphasis from the God of religion to the God of nature. For some Enlightenment thinkers, including Jefferson himself, this could take the more radical form of viewing the God of nature as a bona fide alternative to the God of religion. Nature contained the lawlike regularities observable in both the physical world and in the world of animal and human behavior. These lawlike regularities became law simply when they were perceived to issue from a supreme intelligence or Divine Legislator. Nature could be conceived as a branch of divine

---

[6] J. G. A. Pocock, *The Machiavellian Moment* (Princeton: Princeton University Press, 1975); "Between Gog and Magog: The Republican Thesis and the *Ideologica Americana*," *Journal of the History of Ideas* 68 (1987): 325–346; Gordon Wood, *The Creation of the American Republic, 1776–1787* (Chapel Hill: University of North Carolina Press, 1969); Bernard Bailyn, *The Ideological Origins of the American Revolution* (Cambridge, MA: Harvard University Press, 1967).

[7] Louis Hartz, *The Liberal Tradition in America* (Harvest Books, 1991); Michael Zuckert, *The Natural Rights Republic* (Notre Dame: University of Notre Dame Press, 1996); Jerome Huyler, *Locke in America* (Lawrence: University Press of Kansas, 1995); Mark Hulliung, *The Social Contract in America* (Lawrence: University Press of Kansas, 2007).

[8] Carl L. Becker, *The Declaration of Independence* (New York: Alfred A. Knopf, 1948), 35–79.

1 European Antecedents

revelation accessible to human reason, complementing (or occasionally vying with) the rationally inaccessible branch of divine revelation – the Bible.

In the late seventeenth century, though, this idea of laws of nature was not quite the same as it had been in the thirteenth century and before. Cicero, weaving together lines of thought including those of the Stoics, Aristotle, and Plato, had derived the law of nature from the idea of "human nature."[9] For Cicero as for these preceding philosophers, human nature was a stable form or essence that included an inherently teleological orientation. Humanity was an intangible, invisible reality underlying the existence of particular human beings and indicating their proper goals or end. Plato described this situation in terms of participation in the Ideas.[10] Aristotle explained it in terms of formal and final causes.[11] Cicero, the Roman lawyer, derived the idea of "law" from these Greek concepts relating to nature.

Aquinas, centuries later and with the additional influence of Christianity, defined the natural law as "the participation of the eternal law in the rational creature."[12] The "eternal law," according to Aquinas' definition, was "the very Idea of the government of things in God," including the governance of physical things in regular, ordered ways – like the influence of gravity on a falling object.[13] Aquinas combined Plato's notion of separate Ideas – located now in the mind of God – with Aristotle's idea of an essence or nature giving a thing its inherent formal and final causes.

This idea of essences or natures came to be regarded by some during the later Middle Ages and early modern period as misleading. Experienced reality seemed much more particular and concrete. Such thoughts led to a reaction against this idea of nature and the rise of "nominalism" during the latter Middle Ages. Nominalist philosophers, such as William of Ockham, denied the existence of invisible essences or natures entirely, asserting instead only the particular existence of particular things. There were particular beings we called human, but no ethereal "human nature" standing behind each of them.[14]

Ockham's nominalism received support in its undermining of "essentialist" natures two centuries later with the advent of the Protestant Reformation. Theologians such as Martin Luther and John Calvin followed St. Augustine in holding that the Fall had permanently corrupted human and other natures. Because of this, the essences or natures that were originally in the mind of God were, in fact, no longer clearly reflected in Creation. This consideration complicated the derivation of laws of nature from observation – because regularities

---

[9] Marcus Tullius Cicero, *De Re Publica*, trans. C. W. Keyes (Cambridge, MA: Harvard University Press, 1970), bk. 3 § 33, p. 211.
[10] Plato, *Republic*, Bk. VII, 514a–521d.
[11] Aristotle, *Physics*, II.3; *Metaphysics*, V.2.
[12] Aquinas, *Summa Theologica*, Q. 91, art. 2.
[13] Aquinas, *Summa Theologica*, Q. 91, art. 1.
[14] Francis Oakley, *Natural Law, Laws of Nature, Natural Rights: Continuity and Discontinuity in the History of Ideas* (New York: Continuum, 2005), 87–109.

of behavior resulted not only from the edicts of the Divine Legislator but also from His punishments for Original Sin – and helped lead to a revision in the idea of laws of nature during the seventeenth century.[15]

One of the earliest and most significant figures in this revision was Hugo Grotius, the early seventeenth-century Dutch jurist. Grotius' thought is a noteworthy antecedent to the Declaration of Independence for at least three reasons. First, through his famous *etiamsi* argument ("Even if" God did not exist, the natural law would remain), Grotius lent weighty support to the idea that the "laws of Nature and of Nature's God" could maintain their authority even after the Fall and independent of the God of religion. Second, by significantly narrowing the content of the natural law to include primarily respect for individual natural rights, Grotius paved the way for the Declaration's emphasis on "unalienable rights" as the cornerstone of political philosophy. And third, by drawing together international law with natural law in Ciceronian fashion, Grotius prepared European thought for the sort of argument Jefferson would give in the Declaration's opening paragraph.[16]

John Locke and Isaac Newton carried the Grotian revision in natural law thinking forward through the seventeenth century and ultimately into the hands of the American Revolutionaries. In his *Second Treatise*, Locke depicted a "Potter-God" whose legitimate authority over human beings and all of Creation resulted from His original making of things and subsequent ability to annihilate them "at his pleasure."[17] The recurrent biblical image of the "Potter-God" suggests both the source of the natural law's authority – in God's will – and the concrete, physical, mechanistic way in which His laws came to be conceived at this time. Locke joined his paradigmatic definition of the "law of nature" as "reason" with an explanation of its source in the fact that human beings are all the "workmanship" of God; just as, one might add, the clay pot is the workmanship of the potter.

The God standing behind Locke's law of nature is not the God of the Fall and Redemption but the God of Creation – which could be known by reason "even if" one did not possess religious faith. In the "workmanship" argument of the *Second Treatise*, Locke distills the law of nature into a single command regarding the preservation of the individual and the prohibition against harming others. And later in the same chapter of the *Second Treatise*, Locke

---

[15] Michael Zuckert, "The Fullness of Being: Thomas Aquinas and the Modern Critique of Natural Law," *Review of Politics* 69 (2007): 28–47.
[16] Hugo Grotius, *De Jure Belli ac Pacis Libri Tres* (Paris, 1625). James Brown Scott, *The Classics of International Law: De Jure Naturae et Gentium Dissertationes*, 2 vols. (Washington, DC: Carnegie Institution of Washington, [1646] 1916).
[17] Locke, *Questions Concerning the Law of Nature*, fol. 56. See S. Adam Seagrave, "Self-Ownership vs. Divine Ownership: A Lockean Solution to a Liberal Democratic Dilemma," *American Journal of Political Science* 55.3 (July 2011): 710–723; and *The Foundations of Natural Morality: On the Compatibility of Natural Rights and the Natural Law* (Chicago: University of Chicago Press, 2014).

1 European Antecedents

explicitly asserts that "Princes and Rulers" are always in a state of nature with each other, as are two individuals in the "Woods of *America*."[18] In each of these ways, Locke preserves and extends Grotius' revision of the medieval and ancient idea of the law of nature.

The seventeenth century Grotian–Lockean idea of the law of nature received further support and became entrenched in eighteenth-century European minds through the influence of Newtonian philosophy. Newton provided a compelling portrait of a universe governed by the mystical force of gravity with mathematical regularity and precision.[19] His mathematical analysis of nature proved for many at the time that the world in general was governed by laws, and that these laws, being accessible to human reason, must have proceeded from the creative act of an intelligent supreme being.

The Grotian–Lockean–Newtonian law of nature that appears in the Declaration's opening paragraph overlaps significantly with the earlier Ciceronian–Thomistic natural law without being identical to it. The differences lie, first, in the emphasis of the former on the physical, concrete, or empirical manifestations of this law – with Newton's Law of Gravitation serving as the clearest and most paradigmatic example. This difference stems largely from the "nominalist" philosophy of the later Middle Ages in its break with previous thinking about essences or natures. Where Cicero or Aquinas see the natural law reflected in the abstract *telos* or goal of human nature in its ideal form, Newton sees the law of nature reflected in planetary motion and Locke sees this law reflected in individual self-ownership through self-consciousness, and in the legitimate desire for self-preservation resulting therefrom.[20]

This first difference regarding the emphasis on empirical effects of the law of nature as opposed to "formal" or "final" causes leads naturally to a second: a narrowing of the law of nature to include primarily respect for individual natural rights. This shift is present in Grotius' thought but appears even more clearly in Locke's, who retains more general commands of the law of nature such as "the preservation of mankind" but explains the content of this law predominantly in the narrower terms of individual natural rights and the duty to respect and protect these rights.[21]

A third shift lies in the conception of God standing behind the natural law. The ancient and medieval God of the natural law possessed the ideas of things and their governance in His mind, separate from and before creation, and subsequently made the world so that it would participate in and embody these ideas. The modern God of the law of nature, on the other hand, is the

---

[18] John Locke, *Two Treatises of Government*, ed. Peter Laslett (Cambridge: Cambridge University Press, [1689] 1988), II.ii.14, original emphasis.
[19] Isaac Newton, "General Scholium," in *Philosophiae Naturalis Principia Mathematica* (Cambridge, 1713 ed.).
[20] Locke, *Two Treatises*, II.ii–v.
[21] Locke, *Two Treatises*, II.ii.6.

"Potter-God" of Locke's *Treatises* and Newton's *Principia*. This God is the supreme intelligent being whose existence is the necessary presupposition for the empirical regularities governing the physical world.

These differences between the early modern European context and the medieval and ancient contexts are significant. They do not, however, amount to contradictions; and therefore the idea of the "laws of Nature and of Nature's God" that appears in the Declaration of Independence may indeed extend its roots all the way back to Cicero and Aristotle, as Jefferson claimed. The most obvious similarity between the various versions of the law of nature lies in their emphasis on "reason" as comprising the core of this law. Just as Aristotle had defined law as "reason unaffected by desire," Cicero as a "dictate of right reason," and Aquinas as an "ordinance of reason," so Locke identifies the law of nature with "reason" in the *Second Treatise*.[22] The law of nature, according to each of these philosophers, must be accessible to unaided reason. This accessibility is essential both to its being a "law" – since promulgation is essential to the idea of law – and to its being "natural" – since rationality is an element of human nature, and since nature itself is intelligible.

Although nominalism and empiricism did introduce important modifications in understandings of the law of nature, the authors of the Declaration did not view these modifications as invalidating preceding understandings. The shift of focus toward empirical, physical, and particular effects of the law of nature did not necessarily imply a denial of the ideal, abstract, and universal effects of this law. Material and efficient causes, to use Aristotle's terminology, do not imply the absence of formal and final causes. Aquinas, for example, integrates his explanation of the "eternal law," which directs "all actions and movements" in the universe, with his explanation of the natural law, defining the latter as the rational creature's "participation" in the former.[23] The ancient and medieval writers recognize the existence of physical, empirical, and material manifestations of the law of nature, even if they end up focusing on the ideal and moral relevance of this law for human behavior.

Similarly, a narrower emphasis on individual natural rights need not imply a denial of other applications of the law of nature to human behavior and political life. In this connection, the Declaration's reference to "safety and happiness" as goals of political association becomes relevant; the fact that protection of individual natural rights constitutes the primary purpose of government does not necessarily crowd out the importance of typically ancient and medieval concerns relating to the *telos* or goal of human life. And Locke, in an often quoted passage in the *Second Treatise*, goes so far as to say that: "*Law*, in its true Notion, is not so much the Limitation as *the direction of a free and intelligent Agent* to his proper Interest, and prescribes no farther than is for the

---

[22] Aristotle, *Politics*, Bk. III, 1287a 32; Cicero, *De Re Publica*, bk. 3 § 33, p. 211; Aquinas, *Summa Theologica*, Q. 90, art. 4; Locke, *Two Treatises*, II.ii.6.
[23] Aquinas, *Summa Theologica*, Q. 91, art. 1–2.

1 European Antecedents

general Good of those under that Law. Could they be happier without it, the *Law*, as an useless thing would of it self vanish."[24] Although the law of nature is undoubtedly narrowed in its application to human life by modern European Enlightenment thought, it is not narrowed to the point of necessarily excluding the wider and more ambitious aims characteristic of preceding treatments of this law.

The famous reference to the "laws of Nature and of Nature's God" in the Declaration's opening paragraph is, then, both a reflection of recent European Enlightenment ideas, particularly those found in Lockean and Newtonian philosophy, and also of the older Ciceronian–Thomistic tradition of natural law.

1.2 SOCIAL CONTRACT AND REPUBLICANISM

Another and related area of overlap between the Aristotle–Cicero side and the Locke–Sidney side of the Declaration's "harmonizing sentiments" lies in the idea of the social contract. Although we tend to associate social contract theory with the modern triad of Hobbes–Locke–Rousseau, they were preceded by a tradition of popular sovereignty and contract which enjoyed currency among the Scholastics and early Christians.[25] As John Courtney Murray notes, "The principle of consent was inherent in the medieval idea of kingship," insofar as "the king was bound to seek the consent of his people to his legislation."[26] Aquinas asserts that "to order anything to the common good, belongs either to the whole people, or to someone who is the vicegerent of the whole people."[27] The "whole people," in other words, are the original repository of political power, with rulers possessing this power by way of agreement or trust. The *Vindiciae contra tyrannos*, published in 1579, described two separate contracts lying at the foundation of political society, and went so far as to counsel resistance to monarchs who would contravene these contracts.

By refuting Sir Robert Filmer and his account of the divine right of kings in the *Two Treatises*, Locke was partly – though far from simply – returning to the medieval doctrine of social contract. He was also building on the English tradition of liberty embodied in the Magna Carta, by which the nobility entered into a sort of contract with the king for the protection of their rights and freedoms. The Glorious Revolution of 1688 and the accompanying Bill of Rights, which Locke was explicitly writing to defend and justify, fell closely in line with this preceding English and medieval tradition of contract between ruler and subjects. In its listing of grievances against the king, the Declaration echoes this preceding tradition; King George had forfeited his trust and become a tyrant, which justified the American colonists in declaring their

---

[24] Locke, *Two Treatises*, II.vi.57.
[25] S. J. John Courtney Murray, *We Hold These Truths* (Kansas City: Sheed and Ward, 1960), 33.
[26] Murray, *We Hold These Truths*.
[27] Aquinas, *Summa Theologica*, Q. 90, art. 3.

independence from his authority. The Declaration does find an important precedent in this preceding tradition extending at least to the Magna Carta and the early Scholastics.

The doctrine of social contract as it appears in classical and medieval sources is also related to the tradition of classical republicanism. Classical republicanism contains at its core the Aristotelian idea that human beings are "political animals" who find their fulfillment in political life. In this way, it is also closely affiliated with the natural law tradition of Cicero and Aquinas. As Aquinas says in the *Summa*, "since one man is a part of the community, each man, in all that he is and has, belongs to the community; just as a part, in all that it is, belong to the whole."[28]

Classical republicans view the political community as the arena or context within which the individual human being becomes complete, fulfilled, free, and happy. This comports well with the original idea of a social contract that extends to the community level but not beyond to the individuals composing it. The political community, and not the individual, is the level of analysis where the moral components of political life first come into view and become relevant for government's purposes.

These classical republican ideas have been argued to enter into American Revolutionary thinking – and thereby the political philosophy of the Declaration of Independence – most directly through the influence of the British authors John Trenchard and Thomas Gordon, writing under the pseudonym "Cato" in the early eighteenth century. *Cato's Letters* were widely read and immensely influential in American colonial thought in the middle of the eighteenth century, and are therefore an important focal point for unearthing the European antecedents to the Declaration.[29]

Although Cato was initially enlisted by historians in support of the classical republican interpretation of early American political thought, his writings have become the most powerful evidence for the more recent "republican synthesis" interpretation: the idea that American Revolutionary thought combines elements of classical republicanism with modern elements of social contract liberalism and natural rights philosophy. Cato's writings, as Michael Zuckert persuasively argues, put forward a "new republicanism" that included elements of the old or "classical" variant but emphasized human equality and dignity as received from nature or "Nature's God" rather than human fulfillment and completion through participation in political life.[30] These "new" elements of Cato's republicanism are, moreover, remarkably consonant with the natural

---

[28] Aquinas, *Summa Theologica*, Q. 96, art. 4.
[29] John Trenchard and Thomas Gordon, *Cato's Letters, or Essays on Liberty, Civil and Religious, and Other Important Subjects*, ed. and annotated by Ronald Hamowy, 4 vols. in 2, (Indianapolis: Liberty Fund, [1723] 1951), vol. 2. For a discussion of the importance of *Cato's Letters* to the Revolutionary Americans, see Zuckert, *Natural Rights and the New Republicanism*, 297–305.
[30] Zuckert, *Natural Rights and the New Republicanism*, 312–319.

rights philosophy paradigmatically expressed by Locke in his *Second Treatise*; and it is this political philosophy that, more than any other, animates and distinguishes the Americans' distillation of European political thought in the Declaration.

1.3 NATURAL RIGHTS

Although Locke does in one way signal a return to the classical and medieval tradition of the social contract, laws of nature, and republicanism by refuting the absolutist doctrines of Filmer and (less directly and more complicatedly) Hobbes, Locke's doctrine of the social contract in the *Second Treatise* is far from being a simple extension of this preceding tradition.[31] The medieval tradition had conceived of the social contract as occurring between the people as a preexisting community and their rulers. The rulers agree to look after the common good of the society, and the people agree to subjection and obedience. The people were, moreover, depicted not as isolated individuals but as existing in natural society with each other and as forming a natural community. The idea of contract and consent extended to the agreement between people and rulers (or between both and God) but not beyond to the individuals composing the people.

Locke, on the other hand, begins Chapter 8 of the *Second Treatise* by describing how "free, equal, and independent" individuals originally "join and unite into a community."[32] His social contract occurs between individuals rather than between a community and its rulers, or between either and God. The subsequent formation of a government occurs not by way of contract or agreement but rather by way of delegation or trust. Therefore, although the social contract tradition extends into the medieval period, Locke's version differs substantially from its medieval predecessors.

It is Locke's version of the social contract, moreover, that is reflected in the Declaration's second paragraph. The Declaration's "self-evident" truths relate not to communities but to the individuals comprising them: It is individual "men" who are "created equal," who are "endowed by their Creator with certain unalienable rights," and among whom "Governments are instituted" to protect these rights. Governments "derive their just powers from the *consent* of the governed" rather than from a contract or agreement with the governed; political authority is entirely derivative from the original authority of equal and independent individuals.

The Declaration's "consent" is twofold: First, it is the consent to form a political society that will act as a unified body in matters of concern to

---

[31] And so the account I give here differs from that provided, for example, by Brian Tierney in, "Historical Roots of Modern Rights: Before Locke and After," *Ave Maria Law Review* 3 (2005): 23–43.
[32] Locke, *Two Treatises*, II.viii.95.

everyone within the society; and second, it is the consent to submit one's individual authority to judge and punish violations of the law of nature and natural rights to the political authority or government set up by this society. This two-step consent process is clear from the statement of the right of revolution that immediately follows. It is not the original, equally independent, individual "men" who have the right to alter and abolish governments, but the "People" as a unified entity. The "People" possess the right of revolution and the individuals composing it possess the rights to life, liberty, and the pursuit of happiness. The people's right to alter and abolish governments emerges out of the individuals' rights to life, liberty, and the pursuit of happiness by means of their social contract with each other.

All of this comports precisely with Locke's description of the social contract and the corresponding right of revolution in the *Second Treatise*. Locke describes the right of revolution in Chapter XIX of the *Second Treatise* in this way:

> Whensoever therefore the legislative shall transgress this fundamental rule of society; and either by ambition, fear, folly or corruption, endeavour to grasp themselves, or put into the hands of any other, an absolute power over the lives, liberties, and estates of the people; by this breach of trust they forfeit the power the people had put into their hands for quite contrary ends, and it devolves to the people, who have a right to resume their original liberty, and, by the establishment of a new legislative, (such as they shall think fit) provide for their own safety and security, which is the end for which they are in society.[33]

Locke's account here is the exact reverse of his account of the formation of government in Chapter 8. There, individuals with rights to their lives, liberties, and estates originally form a society – contract with one another – with the "end" or goal of providing for the safety and security of these rights. This society with these goals, once formed, has the right to establish a "legislative," that is, a law-making power, in order to codify and enforce observance of the law of nature. The legislative power derives its legitimate authority or "just powers" from the consent of the governed by means of the very process that brings it into existence; no subsequent contract exists between government and governed for Locke.

The hinge upon which the Declaration's Lockean social contract turns is the idea of natural rights.[34] This idea, like the related one of the natural law, has a long and contested history. Some scholars, such as Brian Tierney, Richard Tuck, Cary Nederman, and (at times) Francis Oakley, treat modern invocations of natural rights found in Hobbes or Locke as incremental variations or new applications of a concept whose roots lie in the early medieval period.[35]

---

[33] Locke, *Two Treatises*, II.xix.222.
[34] Zuckert, *Natural Rights Republic*, 24–31.
[35] Richard Tuck, *Natural Rights Theories: Their Origin and Development* (Cambridge: Cambridge University Press, 1979); Brian Tierney, *The Idea of Natural Rights: Studies on Natural Rights: Natural Law and Church Law 1150–1625* (Atlanta: Scholars Press, 1997); Cary Nederman, "Review of Brian Tierney, *The Idea of Natural Rights and Rights, Law*

1 European Antecedents 15

Others, such as Michel Villey, Leo Strauss, Michael Zuckert, and (at other times) Francis Oakley, treat the modern idea of natural rights as entirely different in source and inspiration from its medieval predecessors.[36] The modern idea of natural rights drives the modern doctrine of the social contract found in Locke and the Declaration just as the idea of natural law – and the medieval idea of natural rights corresponding to it – drives the medieval doctrine of the social contract. The fundamental differences between the two social contract doctrines clearly reveal the correspondingly fundamental differences between the two ideas of natural rights standing behind them.

In the case of ancient and medieval political thought, the social contract narrative begins with preformed communities because these communities possess a moral importance founded in natural law. Human beings are "by nature political animals," as Aristotle said, meaning our human nature directs us both to form communities and to regulate these communities by the rule of law.[37] It is only in the context of such a political community, according to Aristotle, Cicero, and the subsequent natural law tradition, that human beings can achieve happiness through virtue. The moral goals of human life as well as the legitimate goals of a political society arise only within the context of human community. The natural rights of individuals are the other side of the natural duties that attach to fundamentally political animals.

For Locke as well as the Declaration, on the other hand, the social contract narrative begins with individuals because these individuals are conceived to possess a moral importance on their own. In other words, the individual has a moral importance or dignity that is not derived from or in any way related to his or her status as a member of a community. As Locke has it, individuals possess this importance in the equal and independent state they "are naturally in"; in the Declaration's phrasing, individuals possess this importance from their very "creation."[38] Either way, the implication is the same: The individual has a certain moral importance or dignity apart from his or her connection to others. Because of this moral importance, the story of legitimate government cannot stop at the community level but has to go all the way to the individuals composing it.

As these disparate ideas of the social contract evidence, the modern idea of natural rights departs significantly from its medieval counterpart. Modern natural rights relate to the unique individual rather than the political or natural community to which the individual belongs. They pinpoint

---

and Infallibility in Medieval Thought," *American Journal of Legal History* 42 (1998): 217–219; "Empire and the Historiography of European Political Thought: Marsiglio of Padua, Nicholas of Cusa, and the Medieval/Modern Divide," *Journal of the History of Ideas* 66 (2005): 1–15; Oakley, *Natural Law*.

[36] Strauss, *Natural Right and History*; Zuckert, *Natural Rights and the New Republicanism*, 169–197; Oakley, *Natural Law*, 106–109.
[37] Aristotle, *Politics*, 1253a.
[38] Locke, *Two Treatises*, II.ii.4.

the moral significance or dignity of the individual as the starting point and legitimate purpose of politics. In all of these ways, the natural rights present in Locke's writing as well as the Declaration derive directly from modern Enlightenment political thought rather than from the medieval and ancient doctrine preceding it.

Although intimately connected with parallel changes in understandings of the natural law or laws of nature and of the social contract, it is the shift in understandings of natural rights that serves as the fulcrum in applying these doctrines to political life. This is why Jefferson asserted in his final reflections on the Declaration that, "All eyes are opened, or opening, to the rights of man."[39] It is the Creator's endowment of human beings with rights that gives urgent practical import to the "laws of Nature and of Nature's God," indicating the primary purposes of political societies and their governments as well as authorizing revolution in reaction to "breaches of trust."[40] By invoking the modern, Lockean doctrine of natural rights as the basis for the Americans' right of revolution, the Declaration of Independence was doing something entirely new. By asserting this natural rights doctrine alongside the "laws of Nature and of Nature's God," and combining the emphasis on individual rights with concerns for the goals of happiness and safety, though, the Declaration embraced the new without abandoning the old.

1.4 NATURE AND POLITICS

Historians of political thought tend to focus their intellectual and scholarly powers on showing how important particular lines of influence were to the Declaration's background at the expense of other, competing lines of influence. This is a useful and often productive endeavor. Jefferson and the other members of the Continental Congress drew self-consciously on many elements of the Western intellectual tradition in fashioning their arguments for independence. But the way in which the Declaration's authors did so is somewhat different from that which many scholars tend to assume. Rather than imbibing abstract political theories from philosophers and books and subsequently applying them to practical political life – as would happen to some extent in Revolutionary France – the Revolutionary Americans came to European political philosophy having already cultivated the seedlings of political philosophy themselves, sprouted through their practical experience of personal, communal, and political life in the New World.[41]

The geographical situation of North America informed and affected the way in which the "American mind," as expressed in the Declaration, processed and viewed its European antecedents. This consideration, combined with the

---

[39] Thomas Jefferson, Letter to Roger Weightman, June 24, 1826, National Archives.
[40] Declaration of Independence.
[41] Becker, *Declaration*, 73.

1 European Antecedents

practical political context of the North American colonies as relatively new, self-governing societies, allowed the Declaration to be new and original, even as it drew upon old and borrowed ideas.

As many scholars have noticed, Europeans in the seventeenth and eighteenth centuries were fascinated by the political possibilities represented by the North American continent. Ideas of a pre-political state of nature gained currency in European political thought at the same time that these ideas were being projected upon and imagined to actually exist in America. Locke, to take the most pertinent example, said that, "In the beginning all the world was America," and frequently used the European experience in America as an example of a state of nature-like situation.[42]

The American settlers themselves had similar ideas. Beginning with John Winthrop's famous speech aboard the *Arbella* in 1630 – more than half a century before the appearance of Locke's *Two Treatises* in England – many American settlers considered themselves to be uniquely positioned to serve as an instructional example to the rest of the world.[43] The combination of their religious and cultural background with the practical and geographical circumstances of their emigration to America would enable these settlers to be a "city upon a hill" relative to their European audience.

The most formative and important political concept that emerged out of this combination, and in continued conversation with European Enlightenment ideas being simultaneously developed across the Atlantic, was that of "Nature." The American settlers experienced and encountered nature in a way most other Europeans could only imagine. From the extremely dangerous and awe-inspiring passage across 3,000 miles of ocean to the entirely new and constantly challenging topography, weather, flora and fauna of the North American continent, the American settlers were impressed from the beginning with the power, beauty, and pressing importance of nature in every aspect of their lives.

The American colonists were situated at the vanguard of a historical movement in favor of resurrecting nature's relevance for political life. Because they had a more direct and pervasive experience of the natural world than their European contemporaries, the American colonists were able to understand the relevance of nature for political life unencumbered by the abstruse philosophical controversies that preoccupied European philosophers. Just as American democracy was able to grow and develop largely outside the shadow of the monarchical and feudal history that haunted European democracies, so American political thinking about nature was able to take form in a manner relatively unaffected by the contentions that drove apart rival camps among its European antecedents.

---

[42] Locke, *Two Treatises*, II.v.49.
[43] See the symposium in *American Political Thought* on the idea of "American exceptionalism," *American Political Thought* 1.1 (2012).

Aristotle and Cicero had each insisted upon the central importance of nature for politics and government. Aristotle prefaced his *Politics* with an extended treatment of human nature in the *Ethics*, culminating in his famous assertion that man is "by nature a political animal." Cicero thought that the civil law and international law derived their legitimacy from the law of nature. Aquinas, too, affirmed that all human laws must be derived from the natural law to be obligatory. Locke reinforces this line of thought when he says in the *Second Treatise* that: "The Obligations of the Law of Nature, cease not in Society, but only in many Cases are drawn closer, and have by Humane Laws known Penalties annexed to them, to inforce their observation. Thus the Law of Nature stands as an Eternal Rule to all Men, *Legislators* as well as others."[44] It is on this point of the relevance of nature for politics, law, and government, more than any other, that Locke, Aquinas, Cicero, and Aristotle agree.

It makes sense, then, that the "American mind" Jefferson claims to have reflected in the Declaration of Independence was, more than anything else, a conviction that nature stands as an "eternal rule" to "all men," King George included. This nature both regulates behavior through "laws" and "endows" human beings with "rights." The "all men" of the Declaration are precisely the same "all Men" Locke claims to be ruled by the "Law of Nature." On the point of nature's relevance for politics, Jefferson's list of historical authorities for the Declaration speak with one voice.

The Declaration thus echoed the united voices of the ancients and moderns on the idea of nature's relevance for politics, and highlighted the constructive character of preceding European political thought. The Declaration is undeniably a document of the modern Enlightenment, of "new republicanism," and of natural rights liberalism. It is also, though, a reaffirmation of the enduring contribution of classical and medieval political thought to modern political life. The Declaration was able to consolidate modern European advances in political philosophy without jettisoning or disparaging crucial insights of prior periods of Western political thought. The "laws of Nature and of Nature's God" maintain their superintendence of the whole, and "safety and happiness" remain the goals of political society, while "unalienable rights" and the consent of the governed come to the fore between and within them.

---

[44] Locke, *Two Treatises*, II.xi.135.

2

The Twenty-Six Grievances

Woody Holton

The Declaration of Independence is a bill of indictment, but whom does it indict? The obvious answer would be George III, since the Declaration repeatedly lambastes the king but never mentions Parliament, at least not by name. Actually, though, the Glorious Revolution of 1688 had all but neutered the English monarch, and if George III were placed on a spectrum with the absolute monarch Charles I at one extreme and the figurehead Charles III at the other, he would land much closer to the figurehead. Seventeen of Congress' twenty-six charges were administrative actions, taken by the king's cabinet, but even these were actually the work of the majority party in Parliament, since without its support, no cabinet could survive. In the late eighteenth century as in the early twenty-first, even the monarch's speeches to Parliament were ventriloquists' acts, penned by the party in power.

If Parliament was Congress' real target – if the American Revolution was really a battle between British and American legislative bodies – why did the authors of the Declaration never use the word *Parliament*? Why did they introduce their list of oppressive British statutes with the awkward claim that George III had "combined with others" – unnamed others – to enact them? Congress' mysterious euphemism was actually a brilliant way of reinforcing its fundamental proposition that the colonies were not declaring independence from Parliament, because they did not need to, because they were already independent of the British legislature and already sovereign states. In the delegates' view, each American colony stood in the same relation to Britain that Scotland had before the Act of Union in 1707: All they shared was a monarch.

The Declaration asserts the right of revolution, but only as a foundation for insisting upon the analogous right of any society participating in an alliance to break out of it whenever it becomes oppressive. By treating Parliament as He Who Shall Not Be Named, Jefferson and his colleagues underscored their message that they had never been subject to its authority. But through this maneuver, the delegates oversimplified the imperial conflict – as they did in other sections of the document as well.

Congress complained about two distinct categories of parliamentary actions: (1) reforms that the House of Commons and its leaders adopted in the wake of the so-called Seven Years' War, which actually ran from 1754 to 1763 and (2) punishments Parliament inflicted on the colonies for resisting its reforms.

2.1 REFORMS

The question addressed in this chapter – "Why did the majority of free North Americans decide in 1776 to declare independence from Britain?" – may actually be the wrong one to ask, since the Americans did not really choose to go. As many of them insisted, independence was imposed on them by others – most notably the British Parliament.

The two essential preconditions for the American Revolution were the Seven Years' War and the February 10, 1763 Paris treaty that ended it. A series of wartime incidents, along with Britain's ultimate victory over Spain and France, convinced the mother country that it needed to drastically reform its relationship with North America. While studies of the origins of the American Revolution typically focus on the colonists' grievances, it is worth remembering that the British government had previously lodged a host of complaints against the Americans. One of Britain's biggest beefs – against molasses smuggling – intensified during the Seven Years' War, when the merely commercial crime of violating Britain's monopoly of American commerce turned into trading with the enemy, verging on treason. The war against France and Spain also prompted several provincial assemblies to undertake new actions that angered the home government; for example, printing paper money. Finally, the war and the subsequent British victory caused the imperial government to completely reverse its attitude toward colonists' encroachment on Native American land.

Out of fear of alienating the colonists, who were indispensable allies in the war against France and Spain, Parliament made little effort to alter its relationship with them while the war continued. But when Britain made peace with France, the dam burst. Statesmen such as George Grenville and Charles Townshend proposed a host of reforms, most falling into four categories that may be conveniently summarized as the four Ts: territory, taxation, treasury bills (currency), and trade.

Given that the one colonial grievance that all schoolchildren learn is "taxation without representation," it is jarring to see that the Declaration of Independence actually mentions taxes once but Indians and their land three times. Two of these territorial grievances targeted policies, both adopted in 1774, that the British viewed as reforms rather than punishments. Previously colonists could obtain western (that is, Indigenous) land for free, paying only government officers' fees.

But on February 3, 1774, the Privy Council instructed colonial officials to begin auctioning western land off to the highest bidder – a policy the Declaration denounces as "raising the Conditions of new Appropriations of Lands." Nearly five months later, on June 22, 1774, George III signed the Quebec Act. As the historian Sydney George Fisher notes, the Quebec bill not only set up "a pernicious example of arbitrary government and the establishment of a hated religion" (Catholicism) but also extended Quebec's borders all the way south to the Ohio River, to encompass much of the region now known as the Midwest.[1] When Jefferson's congressional colleagues edited his draft of the Declaration, they only saw fit to add two grievances; one of these was the Quebec Act.

The Declaration also denounces several other British policies aimed at checking migration from Britain and Ireland to the North American frontier. The Privy Council had vetoed a North Carolina law granting free immigrants a four-year tax exemption, and imperial officials had used instructions and vetoes to prevent the colonies from naturalizing new arrivals earlier than the prescribed seven years.

The one crucial western document that Congress did *not* mention was arguably the most important. On October 7, 1763, the Privy Council prohibited colonial settlement and land speculation west of the divide separating rivers draining east toward the Atlantic from those flowing west into the Mississippi. An imperial ban on westward expansion was already under discussion in the summer of 1763, when London got word that a coalition of Native American Nations had launched a wide-ranging attack against British forts (eight of which they captured) and settlements. "Pontiac's Rebellion" ensured the adoption of the Proclamation of 1763 – a very clear case of Native Americans powerfully if indirectly contributing to deteriorating relations between white colonists and the Crown. The Proclamation Line ran for more than 1,000 miles and could not be enforced against actual settlers, who continued crossing this imaginary boundary and establishing farms in the west. But it did prevent real estate developers from gaining title to Native American land, and without title, the speculators could not profit from its sale. They were furious.

Native Americans even influenced the best known grievance in the Declaration, taxation. Contrary to popular myth, Parliament never tried to compel the British North American colonists to contribute toward paying off the enormous debt it had amassed on its way to winning the Seven Years' War. But Parliament did come out of the war determined to reduce its American expenses – even as it undertook a costly new North American military buildup. At the end of the previous war against France and Spain in 1749, Parliament had brought most of its North American expeditionary force home. But late in

---

[1] Sydney George Fisher, "The Twenty-Eight Charges against the King in the Declaration of Independence," *Pennsylvania Magazine of History and Biography* 31:3 (1907): 257–303, at 292.

1762, Prime Minister John Stuart, the Earl of Bute, and his cabinet decided to leave 10,000 troops in America, even after negotiating peace.

These soldiers' primary mission would be to prevent western settlers and traders from embroiling the empire in another expensive war against the Native Americans. As Thomas Gage, the British commander-in-chief in North America, would explain in 1765, Bute and his team were appalled at the sheer number of "Tribes of Savages who joined the French during the War, and over run our Frontiers." Indeed, in the early years of the global conflict, France and its Indigenous allies had thoroughly dominated the west, annihilating General Edward Braddock's army near modern-day Pittsburgh on July 9, 1755, and capturing Fort William Henry (as depicted in James Fennimore Cooper's *Last of the Mohicans*) two years later. British officials anticipated fighting the French in North America again soon, and they were determined to prevent colonial America's Native neighbors from once again aligning themselves with the French. So they decided to protect the Anglo-Indian frontier with a chain of military outposts. As Gage noted, "The forts were maintained at the Peace for the purposes of keeping the Indians in awe and Subjection." Their garrisons would promote peace along the frontier in another way as well: by preventing western settlers and traders from repeating the abuses that had prompted most Indigenous warriors to side with the French in the Seven Years' War. The *Annual Register for the Year 1763* neatly summed up the government's goal: "awing as well as protecting the Indian nations."[2]

Given that this peacetime army's primary mission would be to protect white Americans – essentially as a human wall – it seemed only reasonable to the Bute ministry to make the colonists pay for it. Narratives of the American Revolution typically begin in 1763 or even 1765. But the reality is that Bute and his cabinet had already laid the foundation for the two highly controversial parliamentary taxes of the mid 1760s – the American Duties Act (known in America as the Sugar Act) of 1764 and the Stamp Act of 1765 – in December 1762, when their concerns about Native warriors caused them to station 10,000 troops in America.

Learning similar lessons from the Seven Years' War, Britain's European rivals adopted similar reforms. Spain was shocked at the British capture of Havana in 1762. After recovering Cuba in the peace negotiations, Charles III and his ministers resolved never to lose it again, and that entailed a massive military buildup throughout Spanish America. Like their British counterparts, Spanish leaders attempted to shift the cost of the new defense establishment onto their American colonists. In October 1763, as the British Privy Council

---

[2] [Thomas Gage], "Report of the Forts in North America ...," enclosed in Gage to William Wildman, second Viscount Barrington, December 18, 1765, in *The Correspondence of General Thomas Gage*, ed. Clarence Edwin Carter, 2 vols. (Hamden: Archon Books, 1969), 2: 319, 321; *TheAnnual Register, or, A View of the History, Politicks, and Literature for the Year 1763* (London: Printed for R. and J. Dodsley, 1764), 21.

announced the Proclamation Line, Charles III created the Junta de Ministros and charged it with increasing American revenues in order to restore and expand the Spanish Atlantic fleet. As in British America, the Spanish government's new colonial taxes prompted often violent resistance.

One of Congress' complaints against Parliament – "cutting off our Trade with all Parts of the World" – covered a wide variety of allegedly anti-American policies. Since the 1650s, the Navigation Acts had given the mother country a monopoly of the colonial market for European manufactured goods and a monopsony (buyer's monopoly) of the most valuable American exports, notably the top three: sugar products, including rum (which could also go to North America), tobacco, and codfish.

Historians typically ascribe mercantilism to a generalized desire to strengthen the empire as a whole. That was certainly one goal, but North American colonists viewed the Navigation Acts in more practical terms, as favoring various interest groups, especially British merchants, at their expense. Britain's tobacco monopoly played a crucial role in provoking Bacon's Rebellion in Virginia in 1676, and nearly a century later, during the Seven Years' War, the travel writer Andrew Burnaby reported that free Virginians considered it a "hardship not to have an unlimited trade to every part of the world." An anonymous Virginia author stated in 1766 that although the British merchants' monopoly of colonial trade had "ever been regarded here as oppressive in many Respects," it was "an Evil we with Patience now must bear, as we have it not in our Power to avoid or Prevent it."[3]

The Navigation Acts were the crucial context in which Americans reacted to the new burdens and restrictions that Parliament tried to impose on them in the 1760s. Many colonists responded to the Stamp Act, tea tax, and other parliamentary levies by saying they already paid their fair share of imperial taxes by submitting to the British monopoly of their trade, which, by reducing their income and increasing their expenses, amounted to a tax. They thus rebutted the popular British characterization of them as wishing to enjoy the benefits of empire without sharing in the costs – but also undermined their own claim that the parliamentary taxes of the 1760s violated precedent.

Free Americans emphasized that they were willing to accept either the mother country's new taxes or its monopoly of their trade but not both. While historians tend to focus on the straws that broke the camel's back in the 1760s, the colonists made it clear that if freed to choose between taxation and trade restrictions, they would have preferred to escape the Navigation Acts. In the spring of 1775, the ministry of Frederick, Lord North, proposed a compromise by which the colonial legislatures could save their constituents from parliamentary taxation by voting annual contributions to imperial defense.

---

[3] Andrew Burnaby, *Travels through the Middle Settlements in North-America in the Years 1759 and 1760, With Observations upon the State of the Colonies* (Dublin: Printed for R. Marchbank, 1775), 44; "A Virginian," Rind's *Virginia Gazette*, December 11, 1766.

But colonists emphasized that they would not agree to North's terms unless Parliament granted them (in the words of the Virginia House of Burgesses) "a free trade with all the world." The burgesses' address, written by Thomas Jefferson, affirmed that Britain's "monopoly of our trade ... brings greater loss to us and benefit to them than the amount of our proportional contributions to the common defence."[4]

Until 1763, the only Americans who truly felt the sting of British commercial restriction were the tobacco planters of the Chesapeake. But starting in that year, Parliament made a move against the trade of the northern provinces: It cracked down on their illegal importation of molasses from French and Spanish sugar colonies in the Caribbean. The principal beneficiaries of the new policy would be Britain's own sugar planters, some of whom sat in Parliament. It was also expected to bring more revenue into the royal treasury.

In tracing the origins of the United States to "the thirteen colonies," we forget that Britain entered the year 1776 not with thirteen American colonies but twenty-six. In addition to the provinces that declared independence later that year and three others in Canada, the empire included Bermuda and the Bahamas out in the Atlantic, along with East and West Florida, and the British sugar islands, which were organized into six provinces. Enslaved workers in the Caribbean were far more valuable to Britain than the North Americans who rebelled in 1776. The mainland's largest export, tobacco, brought in an annual £750,000. But molasses, rum, and sugar had an annual value of nearly £4 million. Say what you want about tobacco, "the brightest jewels in the British crown" were in the Caribbean.[5]

The islands also enriched mainland North America. Most Caribbean planters had long since decided against diverting large numbers of slaves and acres from sugar to food crops – which also had the disadvantage of being even more vulnerable than sugar cane to El Niño hurricanes. Instead, the planters obtained much of their slaves' food from North America, purchasing about half of the grain grown in the American breadbasket: New York, New Jersey, Pennsylvania, Delaware, and increasingly Maryland and Virginia. Colonial New Englanders' largest export was fish. They sent the best of the catch to Southern Europe, where the Catholic Church banned meat on Fridays and saints' days – nearly a third of the year. The remaining two-thirds of North America's high seas harvest – the "refuse" fish – went to enslaved sugar-cane workers in the Caribbean.

In today's Connecticut, equestrians are better known for dressage than roping cattle, but their eighteenth-century forbears annually sent Caribbean slaveholders thousands of horses, oxen, and other livestock. Much of the lumber and other forest products that North Americans harvested also went to the

---

[4] Virginia House of Burgesses, resolutions on Lord North's conciliatory proposal, June 10, 1775, *Founders Online*, https://founders.archives.gov/.
[5] George Wilson Bridges, *The Annals of Jamaica* (London: John Murray, 1828), 1: 134.

West Indies, especially in the form of barrel staves for molasses, sugar, and rum. If, like the mythical island of Atlantis, the sugar islands had sunk beneath the waves, much of North America would have sunk with them. As Daniel Defoe put it, "*no* islands, *no* Continent."[6]

Since 1733, Parliament had used prohibitive taxes on foreign sugar, molasses, and rum to force North American merchants to purchase these commodities only on British islands such as Barbados and Jamaica. But most North American vessels arriving in Caribbean harbors actually dropped anchor at non-British islands such as Cuba and Puerto Rico (owned by Spain), Dutch Surinam, and – most crucially – the French colony of Saint-Domingue (the future Haiti).

The smugglers at least had economic logic on their side. The British West Indies did not need nearly as much grain, fish, livestock, and lumber as the mainland colonists produced. Nor could they meet the North Americans' demands for sugar, molasses, and rum. The largest gap between mainland demand and British Caribbean supply was in the crucial article of molasses. Jamaican and Barbadian planters forced their slaves not only to grow sugar cane and mill it into table sugar and molasses but also to distill most of the molasses into rum, leaving little molasses for export to the more than one hundred rum distilleries in North America, mostly in New England. If the mainland merchants' only desire had been to slake their customers' thirst, Caribbean distillers would have been happy to sell them more rum. Indeed, many North Americans accused the West Indians of trying to shut down the foreign molasses pipeline precisely in order to corner the North American rum market. But mainland colonists wanted molasses, not rum, because they knew that the real profits lay in distilling a sweetener into an intoxicant. And not just for domestic use; stopping the North American provinces' rum exports would saddle them with a chronic and crippling trade deficit.

Even as North American demand for molasses increasingly outstripped the British islands' output, syrupy surpluses piled up on the wharves of French provinces such as Saint-Domingue (which produced more sugar cane than all of the British islands combined), Martinique, and Guadeloupe. Louis XV did not allow French planters to send molasses home to France, either in its original form or distilled into rum, lest it compete with brandy distilled in France from French fruit. Yet sugar refining – which the French government did permit – produces molasses as a byproduct, and the vast French molasses surplus almost inevitably found its way to the North American distilleries, along with cargoes from the Spanish islands and the Dutch entrepôt of St. Eustatius. Less than one-sixteenth of the molasses entering British ports on the American mainland came in from the British islands – which is to say, legally.

---

[6] Defoe, quoted in Richard B. Sheridan, "Formation of Caribbean Plantation Society, 1689–1748," in P. J. Marshall, ed., *The Oxford History of the British Empire, Volume 2: The Eighteenth Century* (New York: Oxford University Press, 1998), 409.

Although the trade between North America and the foreign islands violated French and Spanish as well as British law, it even continued during the late 1750s and early 1760s, as Britain battled France and Spain in history's first world war. Yet imperial officials needed all the allies they could get and hesitated to cross their North American colonists as the war raged.

But then the Peace of Paris gave the British government a freer hand. For more than a century, the Royal Navy had defended not only the realm but the mother country's monopoly of colonial trade. When a naval commander seized and sold a smuggler's ship and cargo, he and his crew split a third of the proceeds. In the spring of 1763, George Grenville helped draft the Hovering Act, which increased the crewmen's share to one half and also allowed them to be deputized as Customs agents. Passed in April, just two months after the peace treaty, the Hovering Act marked the beginning of a grand repurposing of the imperial navy. Benjamin Franklin warned the British that by converting "the brave honest Officers of your Navy into pimping Tide-waiters and Colony Officers of the Customs," they had put their empire in peril.[7] The Sugar Act of 1764 reduced the molasses duty to three pence per gallon but also established an impermeable Customs enforcement system that threatened to shut down smuggling once and for all.

In the spring of 1766, at the same time that Parliament repealed the Stamp Act, it reduced the foreign molasses duty still further, to one penny per gallon, and levied the same amount on British-milled molasses. The 1766 legislation completed the transformation of the molasses duty from mechanism of guaranteeing the British planters' monopoly (its objective in 1733) to unabashed revenue measure. Americans accepted this compromise, though it meant abandoning in practice the distinction they continued to make in print: that Parliament had the authority to regulate their trade but not to tax it.

The controversies over the Stamp Act and Sugar Act clearly showed that the British and colonial Whigs (Patriots) were not the only parties to the imperial conflict. Native resistance during the Seven Years' War had exposed the need for a post-war military establishment, which Parliament wished to finance in part with the revenue from the Stamp Act and the American Duties Act. And the American Duties Act was only the culmination of a multifaceted crackdown on molasses smuggling carried out by the Royal Navy and Customs service at the behest of British West Indian sugar planters.

Another measure that Parliament adopted in the wake of the Seven Years' War, the Quartering Act of 1765, is typically depicted as a civil liberties issue – memorialized in the ban on quartering in the Third Amendment to the US Constitution. Actually, it was a tax. Far from empowering army officers to quarter a single soldier in a colonist's home without the homeowner's consent (it actually banned that for the first time), its real purpose was to shift the cost

---

[7] Benjamin Franklin, "Rules by Which a Great Empire May Be Reduced to a Small One," *Public Advertiser*, September 11, 1773, *Founders Online*, https://founders.archives.gov/.

of feeding and housing redcoats serving in America from British to colonial taxpayers. The Quartering Act thus resembled the Stamp Act not only in being a tax but also in seeking to make American taxpayers share the cost of the 10,000 soldiers left in America at the end of the Seven Years' War.

One of the best known parliamentary taxes of the 1760s was that on tea. When Parliament adopted the so-called Townshend Duties in 1767, it also taxed glass, painters' colors, and lead shipped from the mother country to the American colonies, but these other levies were repealed three years later, leaving only the tea tax. Like the Stamp Act, the Townshend Duties were *not* aimed at reducing the British government's war debt. In fact, the funds were earmarked for expenditure in America, where they were to cover the salaries of high-ranking provincial officials who had previously depended upon the good will of the state assemblies. The taxes were meant to make these officers independent of local legislators and thus more willing to crack down on smugglers and other colonial lawbreakers. In 1773, Parliament allowed the East India Company to ship tea directly to America, in competition with private merchants, and at the same time reduced the taxes the Company had to pay on Chinese tea as it passed through the mother country. The idea was to make Company tea so cheap that Americans would choose it over tea smuggled in from the Netherlands, thus both rescuing the Company from near bankruptcy and accustoming Americans to paying parliamentary taxes. But colonists turned away many of the tea ships and burned others. Most famously, on the night of December 16–17, 1773, Bostonians dumped 342 chests of East India Company tea into their harbor. No one at the time called this incident the Boston Tea Party, but it infuriated the members of Parliament, convincing them to adopt a series of punitive measures known as the Coercive Acts.

Many free Americans were angry at Parliament not only for restricting their trade but also for interfering with their provincial representatives' right to do so. In the first draft of the Declaration of Independence, Thomas Jefferson capped off his list of grievances against George III by claiming that the king had "obtruded" African captives on white Americans. *Obtrude* is a strange word in modern eyes – but not as strange as the notion that free colonists had purchased slaves only because the British government had forced them to. Surprisingly, though, Jefferson's claim contained a grain of truth. When the number of African Americans born each year in any given colony began to exceed the number who died, whites started pushing to reduce transatlantic trafficking of slaves or even halt it altogether. They had several reasons for doing so. The continued arrival of African captives held down the price of those already in the province – a boon for purchasers but a burden for domestic sellers. In addition, the growing population of enslaved workers in the staple colonies swelled tobacco and rice harvests, depressing prices. Whites in colonies that continued to receive large numbers of Africans worried about them scaring off European immigrants. Moreover, slave purchases drained away the colonies' scarce stocks of gold and silver.

There were also other financial reasons to oppose the slave trade, but the motivations that colonists most often mentioned were not economic. Some opposed it on moral grounds. Others were motivated by fear – of the swelling enslaved population in general and especially of slaves who had been born in Africa. Fear prompted reconsideration of the Atlantic slave trade in non-British provinces as well. Louisiana was well on its way to becoming a black-majority colony like South Carolina when numerous Africans participated in the Natchez Indian revolt of 1729, leading the French government to ban further imports.

Slaveowners who wished to halt the forced immigration of Africans encountered opposition from neighbors who feared that doing so would allow them to charge more for their own slaves. But the most effective defense of the African trade came from British merchants who had made their fortunes by it. Occasionally London allowed an American colony to shut out captive Africans temporarily. The South Carolina assembly responded to the Stono Rebellion of 1739 with a tariff of £100 (or more than 100 percent) on every African brought into the province, and the imperial government did not object. But British slave traders often successfully lobbied the administration to overturn provincial moves against the slave trade. In 1767 and 1769, the Virginia legislature voted to double its head tax on every new arrival from 10 to 20 percent, but the Privy Council vetoed both attempts and instructed the governor to block any future slave trade importations. On April 1, 1772, the House of Burgesses unanimously voted to ask the king to withdraw this instruction. The burgesses said they were "sensible that some of your Majesty's Subjects in *Great-Britain*" – the slave merchants – "reap Emoluments from this Sort of Traffic." But ending the forced immigration of Africans into Virginia was the only way of "averting a Calamity of a most alarming Nature," namely a slave revolt.[8]

The apparent author of Virginia's memorial was Richard Henry Lee, who at the time was soliciting a consignment of Africans. John Murray, Lord Dunmore, Virginia's new governor, supported the assemblymen's petition with a warning that any future invader who joined forces with the slaves could make "a conquest of this Country ... in a very short time."[9] In the short space of three and a half years, the governor's dire prophecy would be fulfilled – by Dunmore himself.

Most of the other colonial governors silently complied with their superiors' instructions to safeguard the slave trade. In 1771, when Samuel Adams shepherded an importation ban through the Massachusetts legislature, Governor

---

[8] House of Burgesses, petition against the slave trade, [April 1, 1772], in William J. Van Schreeven, Robert L. Scribner, and Brent Tarter, eds., *Revolutionary Virginia: The Road to Independence*, 7 vols. (Charlottesville: Published for Virginia Independence Bicentennial Commission by the University Press of Virginia, 1973–1983), 1: 87.

[9] Lord Dunmore, quoted in Bruce A. Ragsdale, *A Planters' Republic: The Search for Economic Independence in Revolutionary Virginia* (Madison: Madison House, 1996), 134.

Thomas Hutchinson vetoed it. Of the thirteen North American colonies that would rebel against Britain in 1776, royal officials overturned encroachments on the slave trade in eight.

Especially in Virginia, the North American colony with the largest black population in 1775 – an estimated 186,000 souls out of a total population of 466,000 – whites viewed the battle over forced African immigration as a class conflict pitting them against the British slave merchants, with the British government taking their enemies' side. In *A Summary View of the Rights of British America*, Thomas Jefferson complained that white Americans' "repeated attempts" to halt slave importations had been thwarted by an imperial government that preferred "the immediate advantages of a few British corsairs to the lasting interests of the American states." After the revolution, another Virginian, George Mason, would proclaim the royal government's stubborn support for the slave trade "one of the great causes of our separation from Great Britain."[10]

Congress struck out Jefferson's denunciation of the slave trade, but this complaint was covered by another grievance, against the Crown's prerogative of "disallowing" provincial laws. In denouncing the royal veto in his *Summary View of the Rights of British America*, the sole example Jefferson offered had been the slave trade. There may be no better indication of the complexity that lurks behind the apparent simplicity of the Declaration of Independence than Jefferson's slavery grievance. For more than a century, he and other white colonists had enslaved Africans, who resisted their condition, ultimately prompting their owners to try to halt further importation, raising objections from British merchants, who found a willing ear in the leaders of Parliament. But the document that Congress adopted on July 4, 1776 reduces that multiparty conflict, as well as many others, to the stark contention that King George had oppressed the colonies.

British merchants were also crucial to a colonial commercial grievance that is conspicuous in the Declaration of Independence by its absence. In 1751, Parliament prohibited New England legislators from printing paper money and allowing their constituents to foist it on creditors. Then in the Seven Years' War, most of the remaining assemblies abused their privilege of printing paper money (at least in the British merchants' view), so on April 19, 1764, Parliament shut down their printing presses as well. Angry colonists were not mollified in 1773, when Parliament revised the law to allow the American assemblies to print paper money and accept it in discharge of taxes, so long as they did not require private creditors to take it. Defenders of parliamentary

---

[10] Jefferson, "A Summary View of the Rights of British America" (Jefferson manuscript), *Founders Online*, https://founders.archives.gov/; George Mason, June 15, 1788, in Jonathan Elliot, ed., *The Debates in the Several State Conventions, on the Adoption of the Federal Constitution, as Recommended by the General Convention at Philadelphia in 1787*, 4 vols., 2nd ed. (Washington, DC: Printed for the editor, 1836), 4: 417.

intervention in the colonial money supply accused its critics of trying to skate out of their just debts, which may explain why Jefferson and Congress avoided the issue in the Declaration.

2.2 PUNISHMENTS

The twenty-six complaints in the Declaration of Independence appear in seemingly random order, with two crucial exceptions. Congress' nine grievances against the unnamed Parliament constitute a coherent whole appearing two-thirds of the way through the delegates' seventeen-count indictment of Britain's executive branch. And Congress' final nine grievances also form a coherent whole, in that they all address Parliament's and the king's responses to provincial protests against earlier British policies.

On March 18, 1766, the same day that provincial riots and boycotts forced Parliament to repeal the Stamp Act, the two chambers also insisted upon their right to rule the colonies "in all cases whatsoever." With this sole exception, all of the British responses to American protests enumerated in the Declaration were punishments. For example, when New York legislators refused to comply with the Quartering Act of 1765 by supplying beer, vinegar, and other articles to the redcoats quartered in their capital, Parliament prohibited them from adopting any other legislation until they gave in. And the New York Suspending Act of 1767 was by no means the only imperial punishment of a colonial legislature. Congress also lambasted royal governors for dissolving recalcitrant assemblies and then refusing "for a long time to cause others to be elected." Congress only added one complaint about a British punishment to Jefferson's list: one South Carolina governor and two Massachusetts governors had convened assemblymen beyond the bounds of the provincial capital, supposedly in hopes of "fatiguing them into Compliance" with imperial policy.

Way back in 1544, Parliament had decreed that if English subjects living abroad were accused of treason, they could be brought home for trial. The statute had fallen into disuse, but had never expired, and in 1769, Parliament recommended that the administration use it whenever it feared that American judges and juries would refuse to convict their fellow colonists for crimes such as rioting. Although British officials never acted on this suggestion, Congress denounced them for "transporting us beyond Seas to be tried for pretended Offences."

For the opposite reason – preventing hostile American juries from sending innocent men to the gallows – Parliament in 1774 adopted the Administration of Justice Act, giving government officials accused of murdering Americans the option of being tried back home in England. The so-called Murdering Bill was part of the package – known in Britain as the Coercive Acts and in America as the Intolerable Acts – that Parliament adopted in response to the Boston Tea Party. All through the 1760s and early 1770s, as Bostonians responded to measures such as the Stamp Act and the Tea Act with increasingly violent protests, the Massachusetts countryside had remained quiet. But farmers woke up with a start when Parliament adopted the Coercive Acts, especially the Massachusetts Government Act, which made fundamental changes to their provincial charter. Most crucially, it prohibited the inhabitants' beloved town meetings from assembling more than once a year.

None of the four Coercive Acts applied outside the borders of Massachusetts, but the inhabitants of other provinces believed the Bay Colony was suffering "in the common cause." All of the future rebel colonies except Georgia (which needed royal help for its war against the Muskogee, also known as Creek, Indians) sent delegates to the September–October 1774 First Continental Congress, which proposed a thoroughgoing boycott of British trade.

The Navigation Acts had not given the mother country a total monopoly of colonial commerce. For example, provincials had been permitted to export non-enumerated produce such as wheat wherever they liked. But the two Restraining Acts that passed Parliament in the spring of 1775 closed all of these loopholes, allowing the colonists to trade only with the mother country (and also banning them from fishing the Grand Banks off Newfoundland). Then the Prohibitory Act of December 22, 1775 banned the colonists from trading with the mother country or even with each other, subjecting all colonial vessels to seizure, along with their cargoes and even their crews, which could be drafted into lifetime service in the Royal Navy.

This Prohibitory Act was, properly speaking, a war measure, but it was not the first. Jefferson and Congress interspersed British military maneuvers throughout their bill of indictment – and the five final grievances all addressed ways in which George III was "waging War against us." On August 23, 1775, the king officially declared the colonies to be in rebellion, and in response, Adm. Samuel Graves, the British naval commander in North America, ordered a squadron under Lt. Henry Mowat to attack ports north of Boston. Mowat actually only hit one town, Falmouth, in the Maine District, then part of Massachusetts. On October 18, his cannon crews opened fire, and a landing party completed the destruction of 139 dwellings and 278 other buildings, mostly in the part of Falmouth that would later become Portland, Maine.

Mowat had given Falmouth residents ample time to evacuate, and the subsequent cannonade did not result in a single death or even injury. Moreover, Mowat had spent his wrath on Falmouth. Had he tried to maximize rather than prevent civilian casualties, and if he and other British officers had repeated the process throughout North America, they might possibly have driven the rebels to despair, resignation, and ultimately submission. Britain had successfully deployed that strategy against rebellious Native Americans, slaves, and other people of color the world over – and Irish Catholics closer to home. But these were white Protestants, and in New England, they were of primarily English stock. Had the North ministry carried fire and sword among them, it could not have maintained its majority in Parliament.

When Congress complained George III had "burnt our Towns," it was also referring to the destruction of Charlestown, Massachusetts (a casualty of the battle of Bunker Hill), and Norfolk, Virginia.

At 168 words, Jefferson's capstone grievance against George III – that he had first "obtruded" African slaves on the colonists (as previously discussed) and then incited them to rebel – was more than twice as long as any of the others. Jefferson also indicated in other ways that this was his most pressing grievance. It was the last one on the list, and in the eighteenth century, polemicists knew to save the best for last. It also elicited Jefferson's most passionate language; in no other grievance does Jefferson accuse George III of being a bad Christian or fall back on that ultimate expedient of the amateur author: ALL CAPS.

Congress reduced Jefferson's one hundred and sixty-eight words on slavery to seven: "He has excited domestic Insurrections amongst us." Thus the final draft of the Declaration had something in common with the Constitution adopted in the same room eleven years later: Although it was shot through with slavery, it never used any form of that word.

The euphemistic quality of Congress' indictment of George III for inciting "domestic Insurrections" was not its only deficiency. It implied that African Americans had been quiescent, possibly even contented, until British officials stirred them up. What had occurred over the course of the previous eighteen months was nearly the opposite of that. By September 1774, when most white Americans still hoped for accommodation with the mother country, their slaves began to perceive that the white-on-white conflict could turn violent, providing opportunities for the people who claimed to own them. On September 22, Abigail Adams reported on "a conspiracy of the Negroes" in Boston; they had sent "a petition to the Govener telling him they would fight for him provided he would arm them and engage to liberate them if he conquerd." According to Adams, Massachusetts Governor Thomas Gage, who was also commander-in-chief of British forces in America, "attended so much to it as to consult Pircy upon it, and one [Lieut.?] Small has been very buisy and active." African Americans continued meeting and planning all through the winter of 1774–1775. "In one of our Counties lately," James Madison reported on November 26, 1774, "a few of those unhappy wretches met together & chose a leader who was to conduct them when the English Troops should arrive."[11]

The following April, on the docks of Charles Town, South Carolina, the free black pilot and "very good fisherman" Thomas Jeremiah reportedly advised slaves "to go in to His Majesty's troops when any should arrive, for they were then all to be made free." That same month, reports of slave revolts poured into Williamsburg, the capital of Virginia, from all up and down the James River Basin. On April 21, two African American residents of Norfolk were executed for insurrection. The previous night, Lord Dunmore, Virginia's last royal

---

[11] Abigail Adams to John Adams, September 22, 1774, Madison to William Bradford [Jr.], November 26, 1774, *Founders Online*, https://founders.archives.gov/.

governor, had directed Royal Navy sailors to remove eighteen half-barrels of gunpowder from the hexagonal arms depot in the center of Williamsburg, and white Virginians believed the governor's timing was no coincidence, that he had deliberately taken their gunpowder amid the swirl of servile insurrection rumors in order to abandon them to the fury of their slaves. As "independent companies" of armed volunteers marched toward Williamsburg, the governor seemed to confirm white colonists' fears, threatening that if he or any other British official was harmed, he would "declare freedom to the slaves & reduce the City of Wmsburg to ashes."[12]

Two black Virginians took Dunmore's threat seriously and presented themselves at the governor's palace, offering to fight for him in return for their freedom. He turned them away, but slaves kept approaching Dunmore, and eventually the governor, who found very few white loyalists in Virginia, began to welcome them. They served as soldiers, spies, raiders, and harbor pilots. On November 15, 1775, a detachment of Dunmore's "Ethiopian Regiment" (as he had begun calling them) defeated the Whig militia at Kemp's Landing near Norfolk, and the Whig commander was captured by one of his own former slaves. Later that same day, Dunmore published an emancipation proclamation that resembled in many ways the one Abraham Lincoln would issue four score and seven years later: it applied only to slaves "appertaining to rebels" who were "able and willing to bear Arms" – though about half of the hundreds of black Virginians who made it to the governor's lines in the nine months before he fled the region were women and children.[13]

Given that Dunmore's emancipation proclamation followed an extended period of black activism, Congress' final grievance against the king would have been more accurate if it had stated that the slaves had incited the governor, though that would have reduced its value as propaganda against Britain. Although Dunmore was the only imperial official who made a formal written arrangement with the slaves, by the time Congress approved the Declaration, his counterparts in Georgia and the Carolinas had also welcomed African Americans to their ranks. In the south, the informal alliance between African Americans and the British Empire – or, as one Virginian put it, Britain's policy of "pointing a dagger to their Throats, thru the hands of their Slaves" – was probably the single largest factor pushing already angry whites over the edge and into independence.[14]

---

[12] "Narrative by George Millegen of His Experiences in South Carolina," September 15, 1775, in K. G. Davies, ed., *Documents of the American Revolution 1770–1783*, Colonial Office Series, 21 vols. (Shannon: Irish University Press, 1972–1981), 2: 110; Dunmore, quoted in "Deposition of Dr. William Pasteur in Regard to the Removal of Powder from the Williamsburg Magazine," *Virginia Magazine of History and Biography* 13 (1905), 49.

[13] Dunmore, proclamation, November 7, 1775 [issued November 5, 1775], in Van Schreeven, Scribner, and Tarter, eds., *Revolutionary Virginia*, 4: 334.

[14] Archibald Cary to Richard Henry Lee, December 24, 1775, in Paul P. Hoffman, *The Lee Family Papers 1742–1795* (microfilm, Charlottesville, VA, 1966), unpaginated.

A review of the twenty-six charges against the king in the Declaration of Independence calls into question Congress' depiction of a straightforward conflict between a tyrannical king and his long-suffering colonists. The origins of American independence were actually as diverse as America itself. The break with Britain had ideological origins, as other essays in this volume emphasize, but also practical ones, and the categories often intertwined. The Stamp Act imposed heavy taxes, especially on some of the most powerful people in America: land speculators, attorneys, and newspaper publishers. But the colonists' libertarian arguments against the Stamp Act were sincere, for had it been implemented, it would have established a precedent for taxation without representation. Much the same could be said of Parliament's attempts to crack down on westward expansion, molasses smuggling, and colonial currency. If historians were ever to lodge their own grievances against the Declaration of Independence, my own biggest beef would be with the way it jumbles together the colonists' original grievances – against Britain's fiscal, commercial, and territorial reforms – and their later complaints about Parliament's harsh reaction to their protests. Disjoining the colonists' original and later grievances yields a surprise: In a real sense, free Americans declared independence without ever actually deciding to do so. Like a swimmer breasting successively largely swells, Parliament and the colonists could only react to what was directly in front of them. In 1764 and 1765, when Americans tarred and feathered Customs informers and burned stamped paper, few of them could anticipate that Parliament would assert its right to rule them "in all cases whatsoever," and then, in reaction to additional colonial defiance, seek to enforce its claim militarily. By sending troops to Lexington and accepting enslaved Americans' invitation to an informal alliance, the British infuriated free Americans, and by the final months of 1775, more and more colonials felt they had no choice but to secede from the mother country. Knowing all that, can we really say they chose to declare independence?

3

The Process of Writing and Procedures for Adopting the Declaration

Peter Charles Hoffer and Williamjames Hull Hoffer

As the prospect of full-scale war with Britain became the central concern of the Second Continental Congress, on May 16, 1776, South Carolina's John Rutledge asked outright whether the Congress aimed at independence. Although delegates like Massachusetts' John and Samuel Adams had long made their feelings on this matter evident; other well-regarded members like Pennsylvania's James Wilson and John Dickinson were still uncertain if that was the right course of action. On June 11, 1776, with Virginia's Richard Henry Lee waiting in Richmond for the provincial assembly to answer Rutledge (they would, in the affirmative), Congress created and assigned the task of drafting a declaration of independence to what was, in effect, a committee of lawyers. It featured both Jefferson and Adams, as well as Robert R. Livingston and Roger Sherman, both lawyers, and Benjamin Franklin. He was the only non-lawyer in the drafting process and only entered into its work near its close. When the draft went to the Congress, lawyers like Edward Rutledge of South Carolina, John's brother, had their chance to weigh in. The result was a group effort, although Jefferson had played the most important part. The draft and the final version, unsurprisingly, was a legal document designed to place rebellion on a legal foundation.[1]

3.1 IN THE COMMITTEE

The drafting committee met briefly, Jefferson and Adams taking the lead. Adams recalled that he and Jefferson were named a subcommittee to do the drafting, but that Jefferson actually did the draft and he, Adams, looked it over and

---

[1] Much of the argument herein is adapted with alterations from the authors' *"The Clamor of Lawyers": The Legal Profession and the American Revolution* (Ithaca: Cornell University Press, 2018), and here reproduced with permission.

made suggestions. At least, that is what Adams recalled, told his Massachusetts friend and fellow Federalist Timothy Pickering, and Pickering published. Jefferson saw it, and wrote to his friend and fellow Virginia Republican James Madison that Adams' memory had deceived him. He, Jefferson, had written the entire draft without help, and the committee only made a few, minor alterations. Contemporary evidence suggests that Jefferson's recollection was more accurate than Adams'. In any case, Adams served on a number of committees of Congress, as he was busy enough without having the burden of drafting the document. Finally, the draft and the final version bore the marks of Jefferson's style far more than Adams'. Then again, Jefferson was serving on a number of committees. The difference may have been that Adams often spoke on the floor. Jefferson, a poor public speaker, rarely spoke.[2]

3.2 IN THE CONGRESS

On July 1, Richard Henry Lee offered Virginia's resolution in favor of independence, Congress debated it, and the next day approved. The members then debated Jefferson's draft Declaration. Dickinson, who had great sympathy for the cause of independence, excused himself from the debate and left the hall, recognizing that the die was cast. On July 2, the members began consideration of Jefferson's draft. On July 4, they approved it, with forty changes, cutting its length by one-fourth. The most important emendation is discussed further on. Congress sat as a committee of the whole during its consideration of the Declaration's text. There were thus no formal motions, no formal amendments, but Jefferson obviously acceded to the changes, as did the other members of the committee.[3]

Jefferson later recalled that his draft of the Declaration of Independence merely recombined ideas that had long been discussed, and terminology long adopted, by Congress, on the "harmonizing sentiments of the day." Read as the continuation of his 1775 Declaration of the Causes of Taking Up Arms, Jefferson's apparently bold assumption of an "equal and independent station" for the new nation in 1776 seems to be exactly what he said it was nearly fifty years later: hardly news. As historian David Armitage has demonstrated, sovereignty and independence went hand in hand in the members' understanding of law of nations. In a sense, then, the Declaration assumed independence, otherwise it would have had no foundation. Following this logic, as the members did, surely Jefferson among them, the Declaration was simply stating the reasons – a

---

[2] Pauline Maier, *American Scripture: Making the Declaration of Independence* (New York: Knopf, 1997), 97–104; Carl Becker, *The Declaration of Independence: A Study in the History of Political Ideas* (New York: Knopf, [1922] 1942), 135–141.

[3] Jack Rakove, *Revolutionaries: A New History of the Invention of America* (New York: Houghton Mifflin, 2010), 103–105; Stephen W. Stathis, *Landmark Debates in Congress* (Washington, DC: CQ Press, 2009), 10–15.

justification like the Declaratory Act of 1766 by which Parliament explained its authority over the colonies – for an event already transpired. The United States of America had already taken its place among the sovereign nations of the world (as Jefferson noted at the end of his draft) when he wrote and the committee presented it to Congress. In approving and then signing the Declaration on July 4, Congress approved not independence (they had already voted it on July 2, two days before they officially adopted the Declaration), but merely explained it.[4]

3.3 LITTLE NOVELTY

Jefferson opened with an invitation to the "opinions of mankind" to recognize the reasons for the declaration. He then continued with a paragraph that has over the years swallowed the rest of the draft, that "all men are created equal" and endowed by their creator with the right to "life, liberty, and the pursuit of happiness." It is the insertion of this philosophical justification for rebellion that has caused some modern readers to miss the importance of the Declaration as a legal document. Omitting the phrase would not change the Declaration's authority in context, that is, as part of the Congress' endeavor to put rebellion on a legal foundation, but it did provide an introduction and explanation to the next key text, "laying it's [sic] foundation on such principles & organising it's [sic] powers in such form, as to them shall seem most likely to effect their safety & happiness."

Jefferson, who had already sent a plan for the Virginia Constitution back home, was thinking about that document at the same time as he was crafting the Declaration. Put in the Virginia context rather than the continental context, his next passage makes more sense. "Prudence indeed will dictate that governments long established should not be changed for light & transient causes: and accordingly all experience hath shewn that mankind are more disposed to suffer while evils are sufferable, than to right themselves by abolishing the forms to which they are accustomed."

Congress (and the union of the colonies) had no such government. On the other hand, the royal charter of Virginia, prepared by Crown lawyers and imposed on the colony in 1624, was such a "government long established." It

---

[4] Jefferson to Henry Lee, May 8, 1825, in Albert Ellery Bergh, ed., *Writings of Thomas Jefferson* (Washington, DC: Jefferson Memorial Society, 1907), 15: 118. Assuming for a moment that Jefferson saw the Declaration as a statement of law, was there some formulary with which he was familiar on which he modeled these opening remarks? One obvious source was the jurisdictional part of the pleading in equity, a kind of suit with which Jefferson was very familiar. The jurisdictional statement indicated that the pleading belonged in the court of chancery rather than a court of law. But this assumes that the Declaration was part of ongoing litigation, and as already discussed, Congress regarded the Declaration as a product of a sovereign body. On Jefferson's use of the bill in equity as a model format, see Peter Charles Hoffer, "The Declaration of Independence as a Bill in Equity," in William Pencak and Wythe W. Holt Jr., eds., *The Law in America, 1607–1861* (New York: New-York Historical Society, 1989), 186–209.

was not to be altered lightly, "But when a long train of abuses & usurpations, begun at a distinguished period, & pursuing invariably the same object, evinces a design to subject them to arbitrary power, it is their right, it is their duty, to throw off such government & to provide new guards for their future security."

Thus did Jefferson insert in the Declaration material meant for the independence of Virginia. Seen in this light, "the patient sufferance of these colonies; & such is now the necessity which constrains them to expunge their former systems of government" makes perfect sense, for the travails of Virginia antedated those of the united colonies. He then returned to the subject of the entire colonies:

> The history of his present majesty, is a history of unremitting injuries and usurpations, among which no one fact stands single or solitary to contradict the uniform tenor of the rest, all of which have in direct object the establishment of an absolute tyranny over these states. to prove this, let facts be submitted to a candid world, for the truth of which we pledge a faith yet unsullied by falsehood.[5]

To repeat, the ringing elaboration of the rights of mankind, various borrowings from John Locke, echoes of natural law, and the language of prior resolves and declarations, were not really pertinent to a declaration for the independence of a continent, but make sense in the more limited framework of Virginia constitutional change. For this reason, that opening portion of the Declaration was not particularly important to the generation that made the Revolution. What was important to the heirs of the Founders was that the Declaration explained why the colonies had to be independent. Consequently, the long train of abuses, already rehearsed at some length in earlier documents, was the meat and potatoes of the 1776 document.

These complaints were familiar in pleadings as the stating part of the complaint in equity, explaining in plain language what the complainant had suffered. If one were to reimagine the Declaration as part of some ongoing litigation in a court of chancery, this list would have been essential. If, as argued here, the Declaration was the explanation of independence already assumed, the list did not have to be so long or so detailed. What happened was that the process of amendment of the document in committee and then on the floor of Congress added items to the list – except in one case.[6]

---

[5] First "Rough" Draft of the Declaration in Julian P. Boyd, ed., *Papers of Jefferson* (Princeton: Princeton University Press, 1950), 1: 243–247; Jefferson's admission that little was original in the Declaration: Garry Wills, *Inventing America: Jefferson's Declaration of Independence*, rev. ed. (Boston: Houghton Mifflin, 2002), 171–172, 230–231. On the Virginia connection, see Richard Beeman, *Our Lives, Our Fortunes, and Our Sacred Honor: The Forging of American Independence, 1774–1776* (New York: Basic, 2013), 396–397. Our emphasis on the "government long established" and subsequent text is not quite the same as Beeman's on the synchronicity of the two drafting projects.

[6] Beeman, *Our Lives*, 387, "There has been considerable speculation – and disagreement – about the extent to which Jefferson's drafts [for a Virginia constitution] influenced the final version of Virginia's frame of government," and also on how they influenced his draft of the Declaration.

3 Adopting the Declaration

One of the accusations in the draft was not a fact at all, at least in a legal sense. It was a repetition of Jefferson's moral outrage at slavery. In a way, it, too, like the middle parts of the opening passages, was directed to the framers of the Virginia Constitution working in Williamsburg. Note that the offense is against both human nature and law. The Crown had refused to intervene against the slave trade: "He has waged cruel war against human nature itself, violating it's most sacred rights of life & liberty in the persons of a distant people who never offended him, captivating & carrying them into slavery in another hemisphere, or to incur miserable death in their transportation thither."

Under international law, slavery was legal, but piracy was not, a point Jefferson emphasized: "This piratical warfare, the opprobrium of infidel powers, is the warfare of the CHRISTIAN king of Great Britain." The final count of this indictment was the Crown's negative on attempts in the colonies to suppress the overseas slave trade. He "determined to keep open a market where MEN should be bought & sold, he has prostituted his negative for suppressing every legislative attempt to prohibit or to restrain this execrable commerce." But Jefferson's strictures in this regard were undercut by his condemnation of Virginia Governor Lord Dunmore's offer of freedom for slaves who aided the royal cause: "he is now exciting those very people to rise in arms among us, and to purchase that liberty of which he has deprived them, & murdering the people upon whom he also obtruded them." Slavery's tentacles were so many and so far-reaching in Virginia that Jefferson could not pull free of them. The last passage once again suggests that the Declaration was as much meant for his home colony as for the united colonies.[7]

With the exception of Jefferson's own views on slavery, at the time not the common sense of the matter save for James Otis', Dickinson's, and a few Quaker abolitionists, the language of this rough draft Declaration was not innovative. It rested instead on fifteen years of revolutionary lawyering. The important point is that the initial draft he prepared demonstrated the relationship between the evolution of the opposition legal argument and the drafting committee's charge.

---

[7] Alan Taylor, *The Internal Enemy: Slavery and War in Virginia, 1772–1832* (New York: W. W. Norton & Company, 2013), 23–27 (Dunmore's offer and Virginia leaders' fears). When it came to places other than Virginia, for example, Jefferson's opposition to the expansion of slavery into the Northwest Territory in 1784 was genuine. While not overseas slave trade, forcibly taking men and women from their homes in Africa, the internal slave trade broke up slave families and carried members far from their homes in the eastern portion of the country. Jefferson was not the first to propose a ban on slavery in the territory, that honor went to Massachusetts politician Timothy Pickering. But Jefferson's own contributions to the debate over slavery in the territory would have been a major blow to Virginia masters' interests in selling surplus slaves west. An older Jefferson denied that he had this intent. See, e.g., Garry Wills, *Negro President: Jefferson and the Slave Power* (Boston: Houghton Mifflin, 2003), 21–25.

3.4 A NATION IN BEING?

It cannot be emphasized too often that Congress had already engaged in diplomatic, military, and financial business that showed it to be a governing body. Although it was not sovereign in the sense of having power over the various colonies, it attempted to exert power over the affairs of the united colonies in waging war and diplomacy. In addition, Congress laid down the rules for its own proceedings, for the colonies to send representatives to it, and for its operations. These were the essential functions of any independent government. Finally, for at least a year, Congress addressed the Crown as if Congress were an autonomous governing body. As such, its declarations, like its instructions to the Continental Army, were legal documents.

The final version of the Declaration differed somewhat from the original, the key difference being the excision of Jefferson's condemnation of the slave trade, and by inference, of slavery itself. In one sense, the revision brought the Declaration even more closely into accord with existing colonial law – for slavery was legal in the colonies. Thus the change Congress imposed, no matter how obnoxious it may appear to modern readers, was itself within colonial legal precedent.

A reminder of the contemporary legal status of the Declaration will be useful before one parses the text of the final version. Although elements of the Declaration were part of the revolutionary bar's elucidation of a constitution of rights, the Declaration itself was not just a part of or the conclusion of a long conversation on rights. It was a legal document. Such documents are the product of sovereign states. One disobeys them at one's peril, as the Loyalists in the American Revolution discovered. Scorn might follow the loser in a constitutional quarrel, but there was nothing like the loss of property, status, domicile, and even freedom that disobedience to the Declaration and the various state and confederate legislation that it fostered.

3.5 BACK TO THE PREAMBLE

The Preamble to the final version of the Declaration, along with the Preamble to the federal Constitution, speaks to an ideal future. Aspirations can be part of legal documents, and preambles are often aspirational. Jefferson set his Preamble in the long stream of history, "in the course of human events," although historical precedents for such a preamble would have been hard to find. Rebellions there were, and a handful had led to successful separation of a part of an empire from the whole. History did not, however, provide the "necessity" for "one people to dissolve the political bands which have connected them with another, and to assume among the powers of the earth, the separate and equal station to which the Laws of Nature and of Nature's God entitle them." Jefferson here adopted a theory of history along the lines of the natural sciences so popular in this Age of

3 Adopting the Declaration 41

Enlightenment. If history had laws that necessitated human action, then independence was not the act of a people too long abused by their distant masters, but was instead dictated by some force beyond human control. None of this makes any more sense as political theory or philosophical reasoning than it does as history.

What did make sense was that Jefferson needed a reason to place the Declaration on a sounder legal ground than mere declaration of a pre-existing fact. He could have begun that "a decent respect to the opinions of mankind requires that [a people declaring that they were independent] should declare the causes which impel them to the separation." As a matter of legal draftsmanship that would have done the job. But "necessity" was one ground in common law for the non-performance of a contract. If the colonial tie to Britain was a kind of contract, that is a voluntary agreement into which the British government and the colonists had entered – as Jefferson's resolves of 1774 and John Adams' *Novanglus Essays* of 1775 insisted – then necessity was a legitimate legal ground for breaching the contract. Necessity required Americans to "dissolve the bond," that is, to terminate the contract for British nonperformance of its terms.[8]

The draft then continued with the words that have become part of American civil scripture: "We hold these truths to be self-evident, that all men are created equal, that they are endowed by their Creator with certain unalienable Rights, that among these are Life, Liberty and the pursuit of Happiness." As we have noted, this aspiration had little legal weight in theory or practice, but the next lines, however, stood on far firmer legal ground than "we hold." The right of a people to form a government and to dissolve that government was analogous to the right of a private person to form the legal "trusteeship," and if that trusteeship was illegally or improperly administered, or the beneficiaries of the trust were bilked, to dissolve that trust:

That to secure these rights, Governments are instituted among Men, deriving their just powers from the consent of the governed, – That whenever any Form of Government becomes destructive of these ends, it is the Right of the People to alter or to abolish it, and to institute new Government, laying its foundation on such principles and organizing its powers in such form, as to them shall seem most likely to effect their Safety and Happiness.

---

[8] The idea of government originating as a contract appeared in numerous works, including John Locke's *Second Treatise on Government* (London: Awnsham Churchill, 1690). Jefferson read it, as did the other revolutionary lawyers. Bernard Bailyn, *The Ideological Origins of the American Revolution*, enlarged ed. (Cambridge, MA: Harvard University Press, 1994), 28, finds much of the citation of Locke to be "superficial," but Thad Tate, "The Social Contract in America, 1774–1787: Revolutionary Theory as a Conservative Instrument," *William and Mary Quarterly* 3rd ser. 22 (1965): 376–378, finds the idea much more influential. For our purposes, however, the key notion is not the general one, but the specific grounds for declaring that a contract had been breached: John Philip Reid, *Constitutional History of the American Revolution, Volume 3: The Authority to Legislate* (Madison: University of Wisconsin Press, 1991), 121–122.

To repeat, "we hold" is an aspiration without legal foundation; "secure these rights" stands on the firm foundations of trust law, a body of law that occupied Jefferson for much of his legal career. It would have been familiar to any colonial or English lawyer.[9]

True, the expression of these familiar legal forms in the Declaration has a certain excess, but then during the time he practiced law, Jefferson himself was wont to add "eloquent" flourishes to his formal legal writing, including "poetic perorations" and displays of erudition. His mentor, Wythe, was even more given to lavishly embroidered legal writing, a show of learning that made him the foremost teacher of law in the colonies.[10]

3.6 CLAIMS AGAINST THE KING

Jefferson continued, "Prudence, indeed, will dictate that Governments long established should not be changed for light and transient causes; and accordingly all experience hath shewn, that mankind are more disposed to suffer, while evils are sufferable, than to right themselves by abolishing the forms to which they are accustomed." How different this was in tone and empirical verification than "all men are created equal." Whether "all experience" had shown anything, certainly an over-generalization if not an unprovable assertion, Jefferson was right that most people would rather suffer the devil they know than one they have not met: "But when a long train of abuses and usurpations, pursuing invariably the same Object evinces a design to reduce them under absolute Despotism, it is their right, it is their duty, to throw off such Government, and to provide new Guards for their future security." This would have sufficed without the laundry list of offenses that followed.

The middle part of the Declaration was a cumulative list of all the accusations the revolutionary lawyers had gathered and in various situations pronounced. It was a grab bag of sorts, but almost all of it concerned explicit legal, or some combination of legal and political, matters. The very first of these accusations were entirely legal, directed at the empire's chief executive officer: the king:

---

[9] David Thomas Konig, in his forthcoming study of Jefferson's law practice, has told the authors of the present piece that he will emphasize these connections. Jefferson himself was familiar with the political version of them, for example in the Virginia Declaration of Rights of 1776, to which he contributed, "that magistrates are their trustees and servants and at all times amenable to them." See also Maier, *American Scripture*, 57.

[10] Maier, *American Scripture*, 167–170; Julia Rudolph, *Common Law and Enlightenment in England, 1689–1750* (Woodbridge, UK: The Boydell Press, 2013), 164–200; Edward Dumbauld, *Thomas Jefferson and the Law* (Norman: University of Oklahoma Press, 1978), 85, 102; Thomas Hunter, "The Teaching of George Wythe," in Steve Sheppard, ed., *History of Legal Education in the United States* (Pasadena: Salem Press, 1999), 1: 159.

3 Adopting the Declaration

He has refused his Assent to Laws, the most wholesome and necessary for the public good. He has forbidden his Governors to pass Laws of immediate and pressing importance, unless suspended in their operation till his Assent should be obtained; and when so suspended, he has utterly neglected to attend to them. He has refused to pass other Laws for the accommodation of large districts of people, unless those people would relinquish the right of Representation in the Legislature, a right inestimable to them and formidable to tyrants only.

Other counts were quasi-legal, that is, they lay in the overlap of lawmaking and political autonomy or regarded the administration of laws and the adjudication of lawsuits:

He has called together legislative bodies at places unusual, uncomfortable, and distant from the depository of their public Records, for the sole purpose of fatiguing them into compliance with his measures. He has dissolved Representative Houses repeatedly, for opposing with manly firmness his invasions on the rights of the people … He has endeavoured to prevent the population of these States; for that purpose obstructing the Laws for Naturalization of Foreigners; refusing to pass others to encourage their migrations hither, and raising the conditions of new Appropriations of Lands.

Even more strikingly, legal clauses were complaints about royal interference in the judicial process itself:

He has obstructed the Administration of Justice, by refusing his Assent to Laws for establishing Judiciary powers. He has made Judges dependent on his Will alone, for the tenure of their offices, and the amount and payment of their salaries … For depriving us in many cases, of the benefits of Trial by Jury: For transporting us beyond Seas to be tried for pretended offences.

The rest of the list of abuses concerned more recent events, condemning the royal declaration of rebellion, the Crown's responsibility for hostilities, and "transporting large Armies of foreign Mercenaries to compleat the works of death, desolation and tyranny, already begun with circumstances of Cruelty & perfidy scarcely parallelled in the most barbarous ages, and totally unworthy the Head of a civilized nation." One of these counts touched slavery: "He has excited domestic insurrections amongst us." Another reflected the loyalty that many Native peoples had for the Crown, "endeavoured to bring on the inhabitants of our frontiers, the merciless Indian Savages, whose known rule of warfare, is an undistinguished destruction of all ages, sexes and conditions."

3.7 A NATION IN BEING

The final portion of the Declaration provided a legal remedy for the unlawfulness of the Crown and Parliament. Most of the colonies had already prepared declarations of independence. These elided the long list of grievance that Congress included, instead citing only the ills of a tyrannous English government. They did not explore at any length the legality of separation.

For purposes of revolutionary lawyering precedent, thus, they were of little importance. The key question, as a matter of law, by what authority did the Congress sever the colonies from the home country, was however answered in the congressional Declaration. The answer was: "by the authority of the good people of these colonies: We, therefore, the Representatives of the united States of America, in General Congress, Assembled ... and by Authority of the good People of these Colonies, solemnly publish and declare, That these United Colonies are, and of Right ought to be Free and Independent States." Note that the Declaration had simply borrowed the argument of the *Causes and Necessity*, 1775, the work of Jefferson and Dickinson, and *Novanglus* that the true source of public law was the consent of the governed.

The Declaration here seemed to straddle the issue whether it was simply a statement of the causes of an independence already existing (the references to "United *States* of America" [italics added] and "are ... free and independent *states*" [italics added] or created independence (the reference to "United *Colonies*" [italics added]). For a document that was read and edited by some of the foremost lawyers in the Congress, the confusion of colony and state was bad drafting at best. Taking it at face value, however, one must assume that Congress was hedging its bets. This part of the Declaration was both a purported statement of a fact – the states were already independent, and the Declaration was explaining why; and a legal document which, when voted up by the representatives of the people, created independence. Apparently, the committee and the body of the delegates felt they could have it both ways. Nor was this some quirk of drafts. On July 15, Josiah Bartlett of New Hampshire reported back to John Langdon in Portsmouth that "the colony of New-York have fully acceded to the Declaration of Independence, so that it now has the sanction of thirteen united states" terming New York both a state and a colony in the same sentence. Throughout July, in his private correspondence, Adams continued to refer to the American colonies as if the Declaration had not been voted up and sent out to the new states. The ambiguity in the references to colonies and states shows that the Declaration occupied a crucial transition in political and legal history from colonies to states. Calling the states colonies suggested that the breach was still very new.[11]

The penultimate passage of the document contained an extended explanatory clause that continued to reflect ambiguity of independence: "that they are Absolved from all Allegiance to the British Crown, and that all political connection between them and the State of Great Britain, is and ought to be totally dissolved." Is dissolved or ought to be dissolved? Had it happened, or should it? Jefferson had left the question hanging, but Congress did not stop here, and the next clause of the Declaration may well have been its most

---

[11] Josiah Bartlett to John Landon, July 15, 1776, in Frank C. Mevers, ed., *The Papers of Josiah Bartlett* (Hanover: University Press of New England, 1979), 95; see, e.g., John Adams to Abigail Adams, July 10, 1776, Adams Family Papers, Massachusetts Historical Society.

important insofar as the legal impact of the document. In it, the ambiguous status of the revolutionary establishments was finally resolved: "that as Free and Independent States, they have full Power to levy War, conclude Peace, contract Alliances, establish Commerce, and to do all other Acts and Things which Independent States may of right do." The "as" was the key word, attaching the local statement to the definition of sovereignty in the law of nations.[12]

3.8 A FIRST NATIONAL CONSTITUTION

Even if the Declaration were a legal document announcing the independence of the United States, according to oppositionist constitutional theory no independent state could exist without fundamental law, in this case a constitution of some sort that was ratified by the people. The Revolutionaries agreed that constitutions must precede and empower governments, or the fundamental rule of consent of the governed could not be followed. Congress did not have such a foundation. The last paragraph of the Declaration thus served as a miniature prototype constitution until such time as a more substantial document could be prepared and ratified. The powers that the Declaration gave to the United States, to wage and conclude wars, regulate commerce, and all the other powers that independent states "may of right do" were the very definition of sovereignty.

The Declaration was signed late in the morning of July 4 by John Hancock, then president of the Congress. The rest of Congress signed either on August 2, or shortly thereafter. Pauline Maier, the foremost student of this specimen of American Scripture, offered no definitive reason for it to be signed at all. Other congressional documents went out to the states or to the Continental Army without signature. But some resolves were signed by all the delegates if they "bound themselves" as individuals to pledge themselves to the documents' purposes. The signatures also signified to the newly self-constituted states that their delegates in Congress agreed to this momentous step. But the most obvious reason, not included in Maier's otherwise persuasive analysis, is that legal documents were always signed by the parties responsible for their execution. The Declaration was no exception to that rule.[13]

---

[12] Maier, *American Scripture*, 78–87.
[13] Maier, *American Scripture*, 152–153.

4

The Declaration as Political Rhetoric

Matthew Crow

That the Declaration of Independence could usefully be studied as political rhetoric may well strike the reader as self-evident. It was after all a declaration, and it declared the dissolution of bonds connecting one set of political bodies to another. So, the Declaration *was* political rhetoric, but is it today? Yes, but not on Jefferson's terms, and not just on ours, either. To take up the question of the Declaration as political rhetoric is to take up the question of its status in the polity it cleared the way for creating. If the United States is a nation that began with what Rev. Martin Luther King, Jr., called a "promissory note,"[1] then while the Declaration might not be all of the promise, it is definitely the note, and it follows from its historical existence as political rhetoric, and as material for more political rhetoric, that past and present are mutually implicated in each other's fate. Today, the Declaration of Independence is the product of substantive and consequential reflection from many people in many different contexts on the power of language to summon available historical experience in the service of politics in the present. That was how Jefferson thought about it, and there still are good reasons to think about it that way.

Now this too might sound rather obvious: Nothing about the wider world of words and deeds that created the United States – or the study of those words and deeds – can or should be so simple as what Jefferson would have wanted people to take away from his own role in framing and interpreting them. Jefferson listed himself as the author of the Declaration on his tombstone, and one could argue he has paid for that authority in recent years. Most notably in the work of historian Annette Gordon-Reed on Jefferson's relationship with Sally Hemings, the stark contradictions inherent in the enslaving society that dared declare itself dedicated to freedom and equality has come to be seen

---

[1] Martin Luther King, "I Have a Dream," 1963, www.archives.gov/files/press/exhibits/dream-speech.pdf.

ever more clearly through the changing study of his life.[2] Indeed, any study of the early modern imperial world of the Declaration confronts the modern researcher with an uncomfortable fact: The reality of slavery and continental expansion, paired with the language of liberty, was not just a contradiction gradually overcome by the blessings of the liberal tradition passed down by the Declaration or its authors and readers. It would not be merely ideological or inherently cynical to read the Declaration as chiefly the authorized press release of a white settler colonialist revolt on behalf of the freedom to own other bodies and lands and things and to clear some space in which to own some more. What else was it, if anything, and what else could it be?

4.1 THINKING ABOUT THE DECLARATION AS POLITICAL RHETORIC

In its immediate context, the Declaration was certainly a political text, and one with a variety of explicitly political goals. As Eliga Gould has demonstrated, the representatives assembled in the Second Continental Congress from 1775–1776 and beyond were under a series of pressures to unite the fractious colonial interests they purportedly represented, and perhaps even more importantly, to provide legitimacy to a state entity so that it could claim to be possessed of at least enough popular support and lawful power to make foreign policy, and to make war.[3] The audience of the Declaration, then, is less the newly declared "one people" or their posterity than foreign governments understandably anxious about open conflict with the British Empire and about the ability of the new government to make alliances, collect taxes, and pay back international loans. Even so, acknowledging the more pragmatic and immediate purposes of the text does not necessarily foreclose the Declaration as a source of political ideas.[4] For many of its subsequent readers, the Declaration's insistence on equality has made it a potential building block of a radically egalitarian and democratic politics that has yet to be fully realized.[5]

The Declaration of Independence is political because it is rhetorical; it is political because it is not in any meaningful sense philosophical. It has its origins and its life in the art of persuasion as opposed to the quest for accuracy and knowledge, in negotiated questions of perspective, right, and interest rather

---

[2] Annette Gordon-Reed, *The Hemingses of Monticello: An American Family* (New York: W. W. Norton & Company, 2008).
[3] Eliga H. Gould, *Among the Powers of the Earth: The American Revolution and the Making of a New World Empire* (Cambridge, MA: Harvard University Press, 2010).
[4] Gordon S. Wood, "Rhetoric and Reality in the American Revolution," *William and Mary Quarterly* 23.1 (January 1966): 3–32.
[5] See Richard K. Matthews, *The Radical Politics of Thomas Jefferson* (Lawrence: University Press of Kansas, 1986); Michael Hardt, *Thomas Jefferson: The Declaration of Independence* (London: Verso, 2007); Danielle Allen, *Our Declaration: A Reading of the Declaration of Independence in Defense of Equality* (New York: Liveright, 2014).

than nonnegotiable absolutes. Hannah Arendt recognized as much when she argued in her book *On Revolution* that the action in the words "we hold these truths to be self-evident" was not in ancient or modern theories of nature, truth, self, or evidence but in the actual activities of speaking, holding, and declaring: in the very plurality and so the shared and contestable quality of the truths that are said to be held.[6] Again, it is in the saying that the text assumes its political character, and in the saying that it opens itself to a world and a history of political argument. The Greek *polis*, which for Arendt was the source of political thought and experience in the West, consisted "of the organization of the people as it arises out of acting and speaking together."[7] This deeply humanist understanding of politics, rooted in the assumption of the human being as a political animal, *zoon politikon*, unique in creation for its capacity for speech, for rhetoric, was characteristic of the kinds of political thinking available in the world of the Declaration. It was certainly a tool in Jefferson's kit, and Jefferson, for Arendt, was uniquely aware of the importance and the fragility of this understanding of politics as in large part the organization and the security of remembered words and deeds, of the art of recollection. In time, the Declaration becomes part and parcel of such practices.

For Arendt, the Declaration was a model, or what in the classical rhetorical tradition would be an exemplar, a recorded and recovered event that clarifies by historical example what an orator or writer and their audience might want to understand or supposedly need to know about politics, language, or history. One of the key things that makes the Declaration and with it the American Revolution exemplary for Arendt is the lack of a fundamental reliance on an absolute sovereign source of legitimate political power: In the "we hold," the Declaration recovers just enough of its rhetorical nerve from the apparent need to fall back on the endowing powers of the "Creator" and the "Laws of Nature and Nature's God." This distinctively political and historical self-awareness, the refusal to totally rely on an absolute or to speak on behalf of universal humanity, for Arendt, distinguishes the American case from more prevalent French, communist, and Bolshevik examples, for whom laws of Nature and History were, according to Arendt, respectively and absolutely fundamental.

For the philosopher Jacques Derrida, by contrast, the introduction of Nature's God into the text is a necessary part of what the text accomplishes: the performative creation of a new people in a new state.[8] This is a rhetorical move that papers over the work of at once drawing on and bringing into existence a sovereign people seizing the right to be recognized as such, and on no other possible ground than a cosmic authority outside of that people's recorded historical experience. Derrida's Declaration is an act of founding, and

---

[6] Hannah Arendt, *On Revolution* (New York: Penguin, [1963] 2006), 21–24, 121–124, 184–186.
[7] Hannah Arendt, *The Human Condition* (Chicago: University of Chicago Press, 1958), 198.
[8] Jacques Derrida, "Declarations of Independence," *New Political Science* 15 (Summer 1986): 7–15.

4 The Declaration as Political Rhetoric

for political theorist Bonnie Honig, Derrida provides a corrective to Arendt's account. The "rhetorical force" of the Declaration, she observes, "derives in large measure from this unclarity" about what the principles held really are and on whose or what authority they are being declared and put to work.[9] Jefferson felt he needed a god or something like a god in there somewhere, so he made one in the Declaration of Independence, and Arendt felt she needed a model for political action that did not rely on a god or something like a god anywhere, so she made one out of the Declaration of Independence. Honig's insight is an important one, and it provides a useful jumping-off point for taking a look at the political and rhetorical stakes of the Declaration itself.

This chapter takes up the rhetoric of the Declaration less as a sacred founding moment and more as an important site in the history of politics for contesting and remaking histories. Whether the Declaration retains that importance in a fractured present and if so in what ways and for whom might be open questions, but that it has had that importance, and emerged from a world where similar questions were front and center, is clearer. Derrida's argument notwithstanding, the Declaration was not in its moment of declaring a founding document. It was made and remade as one later. A good deal of writing across the various drafts of the Declaration does not found so much as unfound, criticizing and severing as it goes, justifying less a new order than the moment in time when it was judged possible and even necessary to pull out of an old one, come what may. Perhaps counterintuitively, that is a big part of what makes it relevant today. Just so, and Arendt's argument notwithstanding, in the "we hold" of the Declaration, the "we" is doing at least as much work as the "hold." As historians Peter Silver and Robert Parkinson have demonstrated, the very possibility of a "we" in the construction of a national identity from the Seven Years War and through the imperial crisis was predicated on drawing more rigid racial boundaries around that emerging identity.[10] Jefferson himself devoted a good deal of attention to those boundaries, and the Declaration is an example of that attention.

4.2 JEFFERSON'S RHETORICAL POLITICS

If the Declaration of Independence has been "American Scripture," it did not start out that way. Jefferson's drafts emerged out of an explosive terrain of political speech and circulating print. Over the course of the imperial crisis, Americans who resisted British policy, did so by fusing distinctive stands of legal, political, and religious argument of the nearly two centuries of antecedent constitutional politics. The Declaration was a compromise, not only among

---

[9] B. Honig, "Declarations of Independence: Arendt and Derrida on the Problem of Founding a Republic," *American Political Science Review* 85.1 (March 1991): 105.

[10] Peter Silver, *Our Savage Neighbors: How Indian War Transformed Early America* (New York: W. W. Norton & Company, 2007); Robert Parkinson, *The Common Cause: Crafting Race and Nation in the American Revolution* (Chapel Hill: University of North Carolina Press, 2016).

the men who worked on it but also among available vocabularies for making declarations. It contains pieces of common law and natural jurisprudential legal arguments, political commentary, religious authority, and on close inspection, deeply emotional appeals to the declared loss of a certain kind of dependence and the beginnings of a confrontation with what independence on a collective and an individual level would mean.

The indictment in the Declaration targets the Crown, but that it did so was the result of a previous decade of rhetorical transformation in American political thought. Parliament exercised the powers of sovereignty, of making and defining law for the empire, and so Parliament passed colonial legislation like the Stamp Act, the Tea Act, or the Townshend Duties, and it was in reference to Parliament that pamphlet-authoring lawyers like James Otis, John Adams, and James Wilson had constructed their arguments against these policies.[11] The first volume of William Blackstone's *Commentaries on the Laws of England* in 1765 made it clear that the colonies were distinct but dependent dominions within the empire, and the Declaratory Act of 1766 insisted on the powers of Parliament to pass binding legislation not only for Britain and the empire as a whole but also for Britain's colonies. Acts of declaration never take place in a vacuum, nor indeed it would seem without other declarations. In her book *American Scripture: The Making of the Declaration of Independence*, historian Pauline Maier demonstrated how important acts of declaring rights in the constitutional struggles of early modern England, most notably in the Declaration of Rights of 1689, would prove to be for later colonial history.[12] To the extent that the two can be separated at all, much of the argument and the language of the Declaration of Independence percolated in less celebrated council resolutions, instructions, and declarations of the previous year. "When dissensions first arose, we felt our hearts warmly attached to the King of *Great Britain* and the Royal family," freeholders of Buckingham County, Virginia stated in the *Address and Instructions* to Congress in May of 1776, "but now the case is much altered. At that time we wished to look upon the Ministry and Parliament as the only fountains from which the bitter waters flowed, and considered the King as deceived and misguided by his counsellors."[13] In shifting their attention

---

[11] See Bernard Bailyn, *The Ideological Origins of the American Revolution* (Cambridge, MA: Harvard University Press, 1967); Pauline Maier, *From Resistance to Revolution: Colonial Radicals and the Development of American Opposition to Britain, 1765–1776* (New York: Knopf, 1973); Brendan McConville, *The King's Three Faces: The Rise and Fall of Royal America, 1688–1776* (Chapel Hill: University of North Carolina Press, 2006); Craig M. Yirush, *Settlers, Liberty, and Empire: The Roots of Early American Political Theory, 1675–1775* (Cambridge: Cambridge University Press, 2011); Eric Nelson, *The Royalist Revolution: Monarchy and the American Founding* (Cambridge: Harvard University Press, 2014).

[12] Pauline Maier, *American Scripture: Making the Declaration of Independence* (New York: Knopf, 1997).

[13] "An Address and Instructions of the Freeholders of the said County," quoted in Maier, *American Scripture*, 226.

to the king, and in instructing their representatives to do the same, colonists charted the course of what would prove to be a chartered independence.

That instructions had to come before declarations was certainly a sign of the felt need for a legal and constitutional framework, but daring to instruct in the first place was an inkling of a genuinely revolutionary moment. This was not lost on Jefferson, whose own path to drafting a declaration had proceeded along similar lines. "Not only the principles of common sense, but the common feelings of human nature" would have to be given up for colonists to "believe they hold their political existence at the will of a British parliament, Jefferson had written in his *Summary View of the Rights of British America*, published in 1774.[14] The *Summary View* was styled as an address to the Crown, laying out the constitutional case for royal intervention in an extended crisis of parliamentary overreach, but it stuffed an emotive and personal tension into the formality of elite and learned legal disputation at the same time that it clothed an alternative settler-centered history of near complete constitutional independence of the British North American colonies. Against a "systematical plan of reducing us to slavery," and the possible implication that George III himself wished the Americans to become "the absolute slaves of his sovereign will," Jefferson offered counsel and instruction to the king, positing the legislative sovereignty of the colonies as derived from their independent settlement, occupancy, later possession, and so recognized title to the land. Speaking with what he called "that freedom of language and sentiment which becomes a free people claiming their rights, as derived from the laws of nature, and not as the gift of their chief magistrate," Jefferson put the American colonists on equivalent jurisdictional footing with their British counterparts, reconstituting the Crown as a common sovereign or "chief magistrate" of a confederated empire. He continued: "Let those flatter who fear; it is not an American art."[15] Disavowing flattery, Jefferson put rhetorical performance at the center of what he thought was at stake in the conflict.

The Declaration of Independence proceeds from the noted failure of that performance, and tensions between Jefferson's sense of himself and his own identity on the one hand and the wider political purpose of the text on the other mark both his original submitted draft and the version publicly released by Congress. While the *Summary View* packaged a logic of jurisdictional independence and a growing resentment on the part of the patriot elite in lawyerly prose, the Declaration had to deal with its status as a public text – to be heard and read – and it had to do so in the aftermath of the publication of Thomas Paine's more populist *Common Sense*. Still, in his drafting, Jefferson felt compelled to try and maintain the implicit assertion of the cultural and

---

[14] Thomas Jefferson, "Summary View of the Rights of British America," in *Jefferson: Writings*, ed. Merrill D. Peterson (New York: Library of America, 1984), 111.
[15] Jefferson, "Summary View," 117, 120–121.

institutional development of the British North American colonies, largely by presenting evidence of the intellectual cultivation of colonial leaders. Consider Jefferson's draft of the concluding passage of the second paragraph with the final version:

Draft:

The history of the present king of Great Britain is a history of unremitting injuries & usurpations, among which appears no solitary fact to contradict the uniform tenor of the rest but all have in direct object the establishment of an absolute tyranny over these states. To prove this let facts be submitted to a candid world for the truth of which we pledge a faith yet unsullied by falsehood.

Declaration:

The history of the present king of Great Britain is a history of injuries & usurpations all having in direct object the establishment of an absolute tyranny over these states. To prove this let facts be submitted to a candid world.[16]

The improvement is pretty obvious, as is the case with many of the other changes, but it is interesting that Jefferson would later feel the need to insist on releasing his "original" as part of his autobiography, composed in 1823 and left with his papers when he died in 1826. Jefferson remained wedded to his condemnation of the slave trade as an imposition on the colonies enforced by the power of the Royal African Company from 1660 as part of the restoration of the Stuart monarchy under Charles II.[17] Indeed, he would insist to the end of his life that his repeated rhetorical opposition to slavery would have had real policy implications if only the selectively and carefully placed evidence of that opposition across his career as a legislator had been allowed to go forward and take effect.[18] But there is more at stake in the drafts for Jefferson than his desire to be remembered as an abolitionist.

4.3 THE RHETORIC OF NATURAL HISTORY

What drove Jefferson's self-conscious effort to perform rhetorically was his felt need to contest the European idea of American degeneracy. Expressed most vividly, and for Jefferson most upsettingly in George Louis LeClerc, Comte de Buffon's voluminous *Natural History*, the idea held that natural history had at some point in the distant past ceased to develop in the Americas on the path enlightened observers noted in Europe. American fauna, according to Buffon, was inferior in size and biological complexity to European counterparts.

---

[16] Jefferson, "Autobiography," *Writings*, 19–20.
[17] Holly Brewer, "Slavery, Sovereignty, and 'Inheritable Blood': Reconsidering John Locke and the Origins of American Slavery," *American Historical Review* 122.4 (October, 2017): 1038–1078.
[18] Peter S. Onuf, *The Mind of Thomas Jefferson* (Charlottesville: University of Virginia Press, 2006), 213–214.

Landscapes and life forms alike had degenerated as a result of the interaction of natural and historical forces over the course of deep time. Human beings were not spared in this analysis: For Buffon, the Native inhabitants of the Americas lacked all but the most rudimentary forms of law and language.[19] They were savages more than they were barbarians, the latter of whom were thought to possess at minimum static cultures and constitutions, not unlike the constructed image of Persians and Goths against which ancient Greek and Roman thinkers had measured their societies. Perhaps most crucially, in addition to the cataclysmic events evidenced in the great mountains and canyons of the Americas, Native Americans by Buffon's lights had not cultivated and developed the soil, leaving the land, the people, and natural history itself in a state of ruin and decay. Even the populated and bustling settlements of the British North American colonies, in this analysis, had yet to produce evidence of a truly cultivated culture and society, although Buffon held out the prospect of empire guiding natural and civil history in the new world on its proper path.

In his *Notes on the State of Virginia*, Jefferson would go on to contest Buffon's thesis, but he did so in a way that relocated historical agency from Europe to the white anglophone settler populations of what would become the United States.[20] Jefferson needed to incorporate the idea of Native Americans as having failed to cultivate the land because it confirmed for him that they had not established sufficient legal title to challenge the superior claim of settlers. At the same time, he needed to suggest that natural and civil history in America stood ready to accept and benefit from further settler cultivation, and that this process was already underway in the rapid development of a new nation led by men with impressive libraries, fossil collections, and rhetorical abilities. There is a kind of "check this out" going on in the Declaration's language as Jefferson balances performing his own learning and capacity to play ball in the big leagues of an enlightened republic of letters with his depiction of a national character defined by its contempt for courtly flattery and unmoved by European standards of high culture.

Resolutions sent to Congress from the Cheraws District of South Carolina described Americans as "a people, born and bred in a land of freedom and virtue, uncorrupted by those refinements which effeminate and debase the mind, manly and generous in their sentiments, bold and hardy in their nature."[21] These were not simply matters of individual egos and national pride. The thesis of American degeneracy and the carefully gendered construct of the creole

---

[19] George Louis LeClerc, *Comte de Buffon, Natural History: General and Particular, by the Count de Buffon, Translated into English*, trans. William Smellie (London: William Strahan and Thoams Cadell, 1781), 5: 130–131. On Jefferson and Buffon, see Gordon M. Sayre, "Jefferson and Native Americans: Policy and Archive," and Timothy Sweet, "Jefferson, Science, and the Enlightenment," in Frank Shuffleton, ed., *The Cambridge Companion to Thomas Jefferson* (Cambridge: Cambridge University Press, 2009); 61–72, 101–113.
[20] Jefferson, *Notes on the State of Virginia*, in *Writings*, 175–192.
[21] Quoted in Maier, *American Scripture*, 229.

settler meant to combat it had real economic and jurisdictional implications for the colonies as they declared their new identities as states. What was at stake for the colonists in their disputes with British policy included questions of access to natural resources like western land and coastal fisheries. The ability of American statesmen to convince their continental European counterparts of the feasibility of independence and credit trustworthiness would have to be tied to positive evaluations of American economic potential. Eighteenth-century jurisdictional conflict between colonial elites and imperial officials had been driven by questions of the adequacy of colonial legal institutions to exercise the full powers of the English legal system in support of the mercantilist political economy of the empire. As a Virginian who immersed himself in that history, Jefferson was no stranger to these disputes. A fundamental part of his concern in the *Summary View* and the Declaration was not only to put forward himself as evidence of colonial learning and development, but also to defend a history of legitimate provincial jurisprudence and constitutionalism.

In his *Discourses on the Public Revenues, and on the Trade of England*, published in 1698, Charles Davenant had suggested a common colonial government as one way to bring the plurality of economic and political cultures in the North American colonies under regular metropolitan governance. Likewise, Sir William Keith would go on to suggest in the eighteenth century that colonies existed to serve the imperial state, and that it was imperative for metropolitan officials to bring colonial courts and legislatures under more centralized control. At stake was the jurisdictional structure and commercial profitability of empire. It was plain to Keith that "none of the *English* Plantations in *America* can with any Reason or good Sense pretend to claim an absolute legislative Power within themselves," no matter what various charters, declarations, or customary practices had been assembled and asserted by colonials to suggest otherwise.[22] Especially problematic was the pretension inherent in colonial courts exercising chancery powers, or the more discretionary judicial authority of equity jurisprudence: for Keith an indefensible localization of powers historically tied to the royal prerogative as an institution of the conscience of the Crown. For colonial elites, centralization threatened their localized power to protect their own interests and the distinctive social orders that had developed in economically diverse albeit interconnected polities. Perhaps just as importantly, and nowhere more intensely than in Virginia, arguments for greater imperial control threatened the historical self-understanding of men who fashioned themselves as a cultivated governing elite directing a history of institutional development according to English principles. In theory, this

---

[22] William Keith, *A Collection of Papers and Other Tracts Written Occasionally on Various Subjects, to Which Is Prefixed, by Way of Preface, An Essay on the Nature of a Publick Spirit* (London: J. Mechell, 1740), 175. See David Thomas Konig, "Virginia and the Imperial State: Law, Enlightenment, and 'the Crooked Cord of Discretion,'" in David Lemmings, ed., *The British and Their Laws in the Eighteenth Century* (London: Boydell, 2005), 206–229.

allowed for differences of context, not the least of which were the cultures of colonial economies built on slavery, but all within a British Atlantic imperial world that allowed for the balance of British identity and the legitimacy of provincial distinctions.

Across the spectra of various social orders and in so many different ways, it would be a grave mistake to underestimate the psychological power of this felt need for acknowledgment of one's status or experience from others. A good deal of the colonial rhetoric in the transatlantic constitutional debates of the imperial crisis was a plea for acknowledgment of these legitimate legal histories. The Declaration of Independence is a recognition of the failure of that plea, but it bears the markers of those previous efforts all the same. The extended legal indictment of the crown that follows from the preamble tells a story of dissolution, and the work of declaring that dissolution to be a simple, necessary fact depends on telling that story in a particular way. The king had "refused his assent to laws" necessary for the public good, "forbidden his governors to pass laws of immediate & pressing importance," called legislative bodies into assembly "at places unusual, uncomfortable, and distant from the depository of their public records," the very stuff of the history of lawful settlement, planting, and governance; he had "obstructed the administration of justice by refusing his assent to laws for establishing judiciary powers," and made "judges dependent on his will alone," and in refusing to intervene on behalf of the colonists in their dispute with Parliament, he had "combined with others to subject us to a jurisdiction foreign to our constitutions & unacknowledged by our laws."[23] These are matters of constitutional significance to be sure, but it is important to note that these are issues of access to law, of disruptions to regular, expected, and equitable proceedings in private law as much as wider public law questions of sovereignty and representation. Questions of jurisdiction and the location of judiciary powers within the imperial constitution are paramount here, and so it is the specifically legal powers of the Crown that are at the center of the argument. The Declaration as a piece of legal rhetoric is a big part of what makes it political rhetoric.

Jefferson took to making that argument like the lawyer that he was, but the recourse to natural law in the preamble and the passionate denunciation of corruptions in the imperial constitution suggest that the rhetoric of the Declaration breaks out of many of the normal parameters of both civil and international legal argument in its day. Jefferson's own voluminous commonplace books in both common law and equity jurisprudence attest to the importance of rhetoric to legal practice: to the ability to call on precedents

---

[23] Jefferson, "Autobiography," in *Writings*, 20–21. See John Philip Reid, "The Irrelevance of the Declaration," in Hendrik Hartog, ed., *Law in the American Revolution and the American Revolution in the Law* (New York: New York University Press, 1981), 46–89; Jack P. Greene, *The Constitutional Origins of the American Revolution* (Cambridge: Cambridge University Press, 2010).

and principles of British constitutional history and European philosophy in oral argument and drafted text.[24] Arendt notes a "slightly comical erudition in political theory" among the Founding Fathers as a crucial part of their felt need to gather a history that would make sense of the action they were taking.[25] Like his *Summary View*, Jefferson's Declaration concerns itself with the Crown as a legal office, one that makes and unmakes other offices; but if the earlier pamphlet was a plea to the conscience of the Crown as the guarantor of a law-governed empire, the Declaration departs from the plea and makes a case to a global forum of equally judging consciences, and in doing so, it lists a series of wrongs that allow the judicious observer to imagine these wrongs in reality, making abstract notions of justice concrete in the illustration of particular cases.

In one sense, this is all entirely appropriate and predictable as the product of a legal mind and legal culture, one that understood the necessity of carefully balancing forms of discretionary authority, and that grappled with the embodiment of these forms in multiple locations across the jurisdictional space of the imperial constitution. But in another sense, the Declaration is far more radical than its reduction to one legal or intellectual tradition or another allows. In shifting its rhetorical audience from the Crown to the world, and in delivering the argument in the way that it does, the Declaration performs a break from the centralization of discretionary judgment. At its most radical and unsettling, in the end, the Declaration makes judges of us all. It does not just replace one center in the form of a royal decider with another in the form of a sovereign people, and in that sense to its lasting credit it was not – and perhaps is not – a founding document. The Declaration of Independence undoes sovereignty and distant, centralized, and incontestable powers of decision and judgment, and leaves it at that. The world of the Declaration is an existential one where we are left responsible for politics and justice, where no power of heaven or earth but our own can reliably promise much of anything in so far as our lives together in politics are concerned. That Jefferson originally concluded his draft with a mutual pledge of "our lives, our fortunes, & our sacred honor," and that the committee felt the need to add "a firm reliance on the protection of divine providence" to the final text would seem to suggest that Jefferson felt deeply the severity of the step they were taking, and that even the other signers, after reading it, felt themselves departing from one history and entering others over which they might have even less control, and so were profoundly uncertain about the implications of what they were declaring, on whose authority, and of who else would be reading, listening, and declaring, too.[26]

---

[24] Matthew Crow, *Thomas Jefferson, Legal History, and the Art of Recollection* (Cambridge: Cambridge University Press, 2017).
[25] Arendt, *On Revolution*, 112.
[26] Jefferson, "Autobiography," in *Writings*, 24.

4.4 THE POLITICS OF RHETORIC

Jefferson himself had anxieties about his own rhetorical abilities and the rhetorical performances of others. He cited the widely publicized violence in western territories between settlers and Native Americans, indicting the Crown for its encouragement of "the inhabitants of our frontiers, the merciless Indian savages, whose known rule of warfare is an undistinguished destruction of all ages, sexes, & conditions."[27] While he fretfully reinforced the idea of the frontier as a racial line, putting expansionist desires at the heart of the Declaration, he was also compelled to confront Native American resistance and diplomacy as part of the rhetorical universe that would constitute life in and around the new empire. Taking the original peoples of the North American continent as a group, in his *Notes on the State of Virginia* he contested the implications of Buffon's depiction of them, with rhetorical performance as the primary evidence. Painting a picture of Native life as blissfully free of law and force, Jefferson suggested that they are called to their duties to one another "by personal influence and persuasion." Their "eminence in oratory" was the product of their tribal councils, and Jefferson singled out the address of the Mingo Chief Logan in response to the violence visited on Native families by settler forces at the end of the Seven Years' War as a worthy challenge to the "whole orations of Demosthenes and Cicero," or indeed all of the European rhetorical tradition. "I appeal to any white man to say, if he ever entered Logan's cabin hungry, and he gave him not meat; if ever he came cold and naked, and he clothed him not," Jefferson recorded, giving the lie to the displacement of responsibility for conflict in the west onto Native savagery that he performed in the Declaration.[28]

As Anthony F. C. Wallace and others have argued, Jefferson's portrayal of Logan's address and his wider, lifelong interest in Native American language and history served an ideological purpose.[29] It was a persistent theme of eighteenth-century reflections on rhetoric that modern print culture and the growing volume and sophistication of law and government in particular had dramatically undermined the necessity of training in the *ars rhetorica* that had been at the center of civic humanist learning in the past.[30] For lawyers in particular, technical command of specific areas of law threatened to supersede excellence in the art of persuasion that the collection of legal and political commonplaces had been meant to support. It was an equally persistent theme

---

[27] Jefferson, "Autobiography," in *Writings*, 21.
[28] Jefferson, *Notes on the State of Virginia*, 187–189.
[29] Anthony F.C. Wallace, *Jefferson and the Indians: The Tragic Fate of the First Americans* (Cambridge: Harvard University Press, 1999); Sandra M. Gustafson, *Eloquence Is Power: Oratory and Performance in Early America* (Chapel Hill: University of North Carolina Press, 2000).
[30] See David Hume, "On Eloquence," Eugene F. Miller, ed., *Essays: Literary, Moral, and Philosophical* (Indianapolis: Liberty Fund, 1985), 102–103.

of European and American Enlightenment thinking about Native Americans that their collective lives in confederated tribes and nations made them living examples of ancient republicanism, possessed of the rhetorical abilities and the martial spirit that some thinkers then living on the cusp of modernity had begun to mourn.[31] In his own career as an active theorist of history and politics, Jefferson was often one of these thinkers, but his depiction of Native Americans as comparable to the great classical orators served to render their way of life as he perceived it incompatible with the progressive and expansionist spirit of the empire of settler liberty for which he would go on to become a figurehead.

Jefferson drafted the Declaration sitting at the center of a political upheaval and a rhetorical one, too. As a neoclassical culture of constituting a self for appearance in legal and political affairs gave way to an increasing desire for an immediacy of authentic and genuine expression, an uneasy public speaker like Jefferson was particularly ill-suited to join in a shift toward what was felt to be more natural public speech. We can certainly read his treatments of the rhetorical abilities of other Virginians as driven in part by some jealousy, in addition to a discomfort with emotive politics. Of George Mason, whose Virginia Declaration of Rights in June of 1776 had begun with the principle that "all men are by nature equally free and independent," Jefferson wrote in his autobiography that "his elocution was neither flowing or smooth, but his language was strong," and he was "a man of the first order of wisdom among those who acted on the theatre of the revolution."[32] How central an awareness of theatricality was to these men and to Jefferson in particular was even more apparent in his recollections of Patrick Henry, whose eloquence, Jefferson recalled to Daniel Webster, "was peculiar, if indeed it should be called eloquence; for it was impressive and sublime ... His pronunciation was vulgar and vicious, but it was forgotten while he was speaking."[33] Henry bothered Jefferson, who in his own attempt to straddle what Jay Fliegelman recognized as a conflict between decorum and expression, was deeply unsettled by a figure whose rhetorical brilliance appeared to stem from not being anchored to the weight of deep and extensive reading.[34]

George Mason and Patrick Henry, of course, were not the only Virginians whose appearance on the political stage of the revolution troubled Jefferson to his core: Free and enslaved African Americans did that, too. Of the many reasons that Jefferson invented in his *Notes on the State of Virginia* not to

---

[31] Cadwallader Colden, *The History of the Five Indian Nations, Depending on the Province of New-York in America: A Critical Edition* (Ithaca: Cornell University Press, 2017); see Martin Thom, *Republics, Nations, and Tribes* (London: Verso, 1995).

[32] Jefferson, "Autobiography," 36.

[33] Recollection of Daniel Webster, quoted in Jay Fliegelman, *Declaring Independence: Jefferson, Natural Language, and the Culture of Performance* (Stanford: Stanford University Press, 1993), 94–95.

[34] Fliegelman, *Declaring Independence*, 95.

4 The Declaration as Political Rhetoric 59

give enslaved black Americans a path to citizenship in the new state, perhaps the most telling was his appraisal of racially specific rhetorical abilities; for Jefferson, an "immoveable veil of black" in the faces of these men and women rendered a shared polity of mutually acknowledged deliberation and discourse unthinkable.[35] While he contrasted African Americans negatively with Native Americans on the grounds of rhetorical and so political capacity, in both cases, as was the case with all women for Jefferson, what we get from him is a commitment to drawing boundaries around his idealized and self-possessed concept of a white settler citizen, around the fragility of his own sense of himself as an actor in the theater of revolutionary political time. Perhaps he knew at some level that political language does not work like that, that it does not provide protection from the exercise of historical and political judgment on words and actions to anyone, and that the Declaration is a good example of why it does not.

Later "in the course of human events," the Declaration as political rhetoric would continue to open space for action, speech, and judgment. As early as 1776, as Eric Slauter has pointed out, a mixed-race former indentured servant by the name of Lemuel Haynes used the preamble to begin his essay on the "illegality" of slavery.[36] And as Thomas Jefferson neared the end of his life in 1826, Elizabeth Cady Stanton, Frederick Douglass, and Abraham Lincoln had just begun theirs, each life a memorial of sorts to the kind of tough and civic work the Declaration can perhaps still be made to do. Just down the road from me as I try to polish off my own rhetorical performance here, in Seneca Falls, New York, there is a memorial that honors Stanton, Douglas, and others who participated in the drafting of the Declaration of Sentiments in 1848, linking women's suffrage to the foundational promise of the polity. The Women's Rights National Historical Park is a museum of powerful people and personalities, but it is also, and perhaps more fundamentally, a museum and a memorial of words, and their power. "All honor to Jefferson," Lincoln reflected in a letter of 1859,

who, in the concrete pressure of a struggle for national independence by a single people, had the coolness, forecast, and capacity to introduce into a merely revolutionary document, an abstract truth, applicable to all men and all times, and so to embalm it there, and in all coming days, it shall be a rebuke and a stumbling-block to the very harbingers of re-appearing tyranny and oppression.[37]

We might no longer share all of Lincoln's honoring of Jefferson or even his faith in Jefferson's Declaration, but we would do well to recover some of his appreciation for what words can do in politics, for good and for ill, and in

---

[35] Jefferson, *Notes on the State of Virginia*, 264–265.
[36] Eric Slauter, "The Declaration of Independence and the New Nation," *The Cambridge Companion to Thomas Jefferson*, 12–34.
[37] Abraham Lincoln to Henry L. Pierce, April 6, 1859, *Abraham Lincoln: Selected Speeches and Writings* (New York: Library of America, 1992), 216.

doing so, maybe recover something of both men's rather incredible faith in us. To borrow some more words from Lincoln on Jefferson, "soberly, it is now no child's play" to save the project of democratic equality in this nation.[38] Even so, we miss something of the Declaration's vibrancy and relevance when we try and turn it into a vehicle for doctrine. There are strands of American constitutional discourse that see the founders as sacred lawgiving patriarchs, and the democratic people in all our messy plurality as mostly faithless children. But that misses Jefferson's own embrace of the imagination and playfulness necessary for a free political life, lived together, and so it misses Jefferson's profoundly rhetorical sense of politics as a game, even one with often very high stakes. What the Declaration as political rhetoric shows us is not some sacred origin point to which we must recommit, but rather a fragile, persistent, democratic, and revolutionary hope, Jefferson's hope: that the children have not forgotten how to play.

[38] Lincoln to Pierce, April 6, 1859, 216.

5

Equality, Liberty, and Rights in the Declaration of Independence

Michael Zuckert

Strictly speaking, the document we call the Declaration of Independence is misnamed. The actual or official declaration of independence occurred on July 2, 1776, when the Second Continental Congress adopted the resolution for independence introduced a month earlier by Virginian Richard Henry Lee. The relevant part of Lee's resolution was incorporated in the July 4 document near its end: "That these United Colonies are, and of right ought to be Free and Independent States; that they are Absolved from all Allegiance to the British Crown, and that all political connection between them and the State of Great Britain, is and ought to be totally dissolved." What then is the Declaration of Independence, so called? The opening sentence of that document announces its aim: Acting with "a decent respect to the opinions of mankind," the Americans propose to "declare the causes which impel them to this separation." A better title for our document then would be, "The Declaration of the Causes Which Impel the Americans to Declare Independence."

5.1 THE STRUCTURE OF THE DECLARATION

As a declaration of causes meant to both explain and justify the Americans in the eyes of the world in terms of "The Laws of Nature and of Nature's God," the Declaration (let us stick to its traditional title) intended to show the "causes," in the sense of the impelling reasons for the Americans' actions, as well as the "causes" in the sense of moral justification for their action. The Declaration thus contains not only much historical information relating to the recent relations between Britain and the colonies but also a general theory of political right that is meant to show the colonists to be justified even in the eyes of "The Supreme Judge of the world."

This justificatory intention dictates the general structure of the Declaration. It takes the form of a long but very recognizable syllogism. After an opening paragraph announcing their intention in the document, the Declaration proceeds to lay out the major premises of its argument, presented here as "truths" held to be "self-evident" by the colonists, the final one of which proclaims that "whenever any Form of Government becomes destructive of these ends [for which government is instituted], it is the Right of the People to alter or abolish it, and to institute new Government." Following this major premise is a series of "facts submitted ... to a candid world," purporting to show that the government under which the British held the colonies was one that was indeed "destructive of these ends." If that is so, then the conclusion, introduced by the word "therefore," "that these United Colonies are, and of Right ought to be Free and Independent States," follows with the logical necessity of a geometric proof. Contrary to the opinion of some scholars that the parts of the Declaration are disparate and of unequal importance, the main parts – the theory of rightful government contained in the major premises of the second paragraph, and the list of grievances comprising the minor premise – are integrally connected and equally essential to accomplishing the aim of the document.[1]

I begin with the syllogistic character of the Declaration, for too often this is missed and the various ideas present in it, especially in its second or theoretical paragraph, are taken as separate nuggets and interpreted in a free-floating way, independently of the rest. This is particularly true of such resonant ideas as the first of the so-called self-evident truths: "all men are created equal." Throughout American history, this phrase has been treated as especially important, and many of the hopes and aspirations of various political movements have been projected onto these five words. Most notable, probably, has been Abraham Lincoln's quotation of them in his best known speech, the Gettysburg Address of 1863: "Four-score and seven years ago our fathers brought forth upon this continent, a new nation, conceived in liberty and dedicated to the proposition that all men are created equal." This was a prelude to his call for a "new birth of freedom," to be effected through the liberation of the enslaved persons he had begun to achieve in his Emancipation Proclamation. But the equality clause has been appealed to on many more occasions than that, often with quite different applications. Sometimes, as with Lincoln, it is taken as a call for natural equality, that is to say, for recognition of a universal human status that rules slavery out of court; sometimes, as with the early women's movement, as a call for full civil equality, that is to say, for recognition of a civil status contrary to the various disabilities from which women suffered. Sometimes it is taken to be a call for economic equality, or equality of condition, such as

---

[1] See, e.g., David Armitage, *The Declaration of Independence: A Global History* (Cambridge: Harvard University Press, 2007); John Phillip Reid, "The Irrelevance of the Declaration," in Hendrik Hartog, ed., *Law in the American Revolution and the Revolution in Law: A Collection of Review Essays on American Legal History* (New York: New York University Press, 1981); John Phillip Reid, *Constitutional History of the American Revolution: The Authority of Rights* (Madison: University of Wisconsin Press, 1986).

is held to be inconsistent with great social and economic inequalities. Ripped from its context as part of the major premise of a great syllogism, the equality proposition is rendered quite indeterminate in meaning and becomes subject to this great variety of interpretive and political appropriations. One recent study even found "five facets" of equality in the Declaration, a lot of work for one small word.[2]

5.2 THE TRUTHS: PREMISES OF THE ARGUMENT

As part of the major premise of the Declaration's syllogism and as part of a general theory of rightful government, it is unlikely that the main ideas in the Declaration's second paragraph exist as separate, free-floating nuggets of indeterminate meaning. My task in this essay is to reconstruct the theory of rightful government contained in that paragraph in order to progress toward fixing meaning for those ideas – equality, rights, liberty, and others – that have been so important to the self-understanding and political aspirations of Americans from 1776 on.

Contributing in no small degree to the notion that the big ideas in the second paragraph are separate nuggets is the way the text introduces them: "we hold these truths to be self-evident," a clause then followed by a list of six identifiable truths that, so introduced, might appear to be just six independent, separate truths. But if we set aside the claim about self-evidence for a moment, we can readily see that the six truths are not separate and disconnected. We can paraphrase the six in the following shorthand manner:

1. All men are created equal.
2. They are endowed with unalienable rights, among which are life, liberty, and pursuit of happiness.
3. Governments are instituted among men in order to secure these rights.
4. Governments derive their just powers from the consent of the governed.
5. If governments fail at their instituted purpose of securing these rights, the people have a right to alter or abolish them, that is, a right of revolution.
6. The people then have a right to institute new governments, which in their judgment will succeed better in providing the security of rights for which they made government in the first place.

The list appears to have a distinctly temporal character. It begins by announcing how things are at the beginning, at creation: At the beginning human beings are equal, and they possess certain rights. The next two truths tell of the sequel – human beings institute government to "secure" these rights with which that they are born. Government is necessary because in the conditions at the beginning the rights are insecure. So the second set of truths

---

[2] Danielle Allen, *Our Declaration: A Reading of the Declaration of Independence in Defense of Equality* (New York: Liveright Publishing Corporation, 2014), 309.

tells us why governments exist and how they rightfully come to have their powers – via "consent of the governed." The governed are particularly central to the enterprise of government, for it is the securing of their rights that serves as the purpose of governmental institution, and their consent is the means by which rightful government comes to be. So, we can draw a conclusion about the relations among the first four truths: The second two tell of the formation of government as a remedy to a deficiency of the pre-governmental situation. The first two truths, therefore, must refer to a situation where there is no government, and thus where rights are insecure.

The last two truths speak of a situation subsequent to the institution of government. The mere existence of government does not guarantee the security of rights for the sake of which government is desired. Government can fail at its appointed task. When it does, the people have the right to change or even throw off their government. Since they would then find themselves with no government, and therefore once again with the insecurity of rights, they have the same right to make new governments that they had at the beginning, which we can now see need not mean some absolute beginning, but the beginning of a cycle of no-government – government instituting – government altering or abolishing and back to the beginning. This last set of truths is particularly important, as Pauline Maier has pointed out, for it is the altering or (in this case) "abolishing" that the Americans are attempting to explain and justify in their Declaration.[3] Given the temporally sequential character of the list of rights, it is obvious that the fifth truth affirming a right to "alter or abolish" is connected to, and could even be said to follow from, the truths that precede it. Indeed, we can look at the list of truths as an argument in which each set of two truths follows logically (not just temporally) from the truths ahead of them on the list.

5.3 EQUALITY

To understand the logic of the second paragraph, we must put aside for the moment the temporality of the sequence of truth claims that we have so far been using to make sense of the text. The first two truths clearly speak of something original – how men were at the beginning ("created equal") and what they possessed at the beginning ("endowed by their creator with unalienable rights"). On reflection, these claims cannot refer to a strictly temporal beginning or origin, for they are said to refer to "all men," that is to say, not just to those who stand at the very beginning, literally before government was instituted. All men, whether born into a society already possessing government or somehow not, are "created equal," and possess rights not deriving from or dependent for their existence on government.

---

[3] Pauline Maier, *American Scripture: Making the Declaration of Independence*, 1st Vintage Books ed. (New York: Vintage Books, 1998).

5 Equality, Liberty, and Rights

The claim that governments are instituted via consent of the governed gives a clue as to how to understand these puzzling claims: Governments derive their "just powers," that is to say, their rightful power to command and expect obedience not from any inherent right they possess, but only from the consent of the citizens subject to that government. So far as that is so, one can translate the claim that all men are created equal into the claim that no man is born naturally or originally subject to government or owing obedience to government. We are all originally equal in that nobody possesses inherent authority over us. This is the same claim that political philosophers of the age stated in terms of the idea of an original "state of nature." John Locke defined that state as one "that is ... [a] *State ... of Equality*, wherein all the Power and Jurisdiction is reciprocal, no one having more than another" (original emphasis).[4] The equality in question is equality in "power and jurisdiction," that is, in authority, or the right to command others. In authority all are by nature equal, and they are equal in having no authority over others, for it is "a *State of perfect Freedom* to order their Actions ... as they think fit, ... without asking leave, or depending upon the Will of any other Man" (original emphasis).[5]

Placing the first truth about equality within the context of the political theory outlined in the Declaration's second paragraph leads us to see that equality there has a quite precise and even radical meaning: Human beings are not *naturally* subject to the authority of any other human being. Whatever the ultimate implications of this natural equality may be, we can see that the Declaration is not invoking a loose concept ready to be filled in as we please, as it has sometimes been treated. Nonetheless, the affirmation of natural equality immediately raises two urgent questions. First, on what basis is this equality affirmed? It is clearly not the result of immediate empirical observation, because most are born under government and are thought to be subject to the authority of that government, an observation that has led many political thinkers, like Aristotle in particular, to pronounce political authority natural. The second urgent question arises from the observation that this natural equality, this situation of non-subjection to any human authority, does not persist, for the text of the second paragraph quickly moves on to affirm the existence of "rightful powers" of government. But just how does the original non-subjection transform into subjection?

In attempting to answer these two questions, we must remind ourselves of the kind of text the Declaration is – and is not. The purpose of the text, you may recall, is to "declare the causes" for the Americans' separation from the authority to whom they have heretofore owed obedience. It is a giving of reasons, not a mere assertion of will. That is why it takes the form of an argument. But it is still a political document; it is not a treatise in political philosophy. The Declaration presents an argument to justify the deeds of the Americans, but it

---

[4] John Locke, *Two Treatises of Government*, ed. Peter Laslett (Cambridge: Cambridge University Press, [1690] 1988), 269.
[5] Locke, *Two Treatises*, 269.

is a truncated presentation of an argument that perhaps would require a treatise to make its case fully. We must tailor our expectations of the Declaration accordingly. Among other things, that means one has to do some real work to expand the very concisely expressed elements of the Declaration's argument.

5.4 RIGHTS

In the pre-governmental situation human beings are equal, and they also possess rights. One very common way to put together these two ideas is to claim, as Abraham Lincoln did, that the Declaration is affirming equality of a certain sort – equality in rights.[6] No doubt, since all human beings have the same rights, this is correct, but it misses the particular sense of equality affirmed. There is another and more promising way to connect these two aspects of the original situation, which at the same time provides an answer to our question of the grounds for the affirmation of human equality.

The Declaration lists three rights as among the inherent or natural rights human beings possess in a state of nature: rights to life, liberty, and pursuit of happiness. There are clearly others, such as the "right to alter or abolish" governments affirmed a bit later in the paragraph, or the right to liberty of conscience as frequently affirmed by members of the founding generation, or the right to property, also universally affirmed. Why are these three rights singled out for mention? It is difficult to give a definitive answer to that question, but it is plausible to say that these, along with "the right to alter or abolish," were the most relevant to the task of justifying American independence.

In any case, we can see a kind of coherence and deep complementarity to the list of rights presented. The right to life is a right to what is most one's own, one's life. Given the nature of a human life, it is difficult to see how it could be anything other than one's own, how it could in any sense belong to others. Given the dependence (or base) of life in or on the body, the right to life must contain a right to bodily immunity, the right not to have one's body seized, invaded, assaulted, or controlled by others.

The right to liberty extends the right to life: Not only does one possess a rightful immunity against depredations by others on one's body, but one also has a right to the use of one's body. We can take control of our bodies, or of parts of our bodies, to produce voluntary motion. We can invest our body's movements with our intentions and broader purposes. The natural right to liberty affirms the prima facie rightfulness of active, intentional use of the body. This is to say that the right to liberty contains more than the narrow right not to be imprisoned, through it surely includes that. There is something more positive as well to the right to liberty – the right to exercise our faculties as we see fit – always with the caveat that the same right in others must be respected.

[6] Abraham Lincoln, *Speeches and Writings*, ed. Don E. Fehrenbacher (New York: Literary Classics of the United States, 1989), 1: 398.

5 Equality, Liberty, and Rights 67

5.5 PROPERTY

The text does not directly affirm the right to property, often conjoined to the rights to life and liberty in common lists of rights. Its absence from this list has led to speculation that the authors of the Declaration did not mean to affirm a natural right to property. This seems doubtful in light of all the documents of the age, including many by Thomas Jefferson, the chief draftsman of the Declaration, that do affirm the natural right to property.[7] Moreover, the natural right to property is implicit elsewhere in the Declaration's text when the Americans complain of the attempt by the British to tax them without their consent. This concern, well known to be one of the most significant of the colonial grievances, as is captured in the slogan, "No taxation without representation," implies the recognition of a natural right to property, for it is that status that leads the Americans to conclude that they must themselves be represented in the body that lays taxes on them. That is to say, the Americans interpreted the no taxation without representation requirement of the traditional English Constitution differently from the way the English themselves did because they clearly and unequivocally saw property to be a natural right.[8] The tacitly present right to property involves an extension of rights from the spheres of one's own life, body, and actions to the external world. It proclaims the rightful power of human beings to make the external their own in the same way that they can make their bodies their own.

5.6 PURSUIT OF HAPPINESS

The three basic rights together amount to the affirmation of a kind of personal sovereignty, rightful control over one's person, actions, and possessions in the service of one's intents and purposes. When seen as an integrated system of immunities and controls, the specific rights sum to a comprehensive right to pursue a shape and way of life self-chosen. The comprehensive or summative character of the right to pursuit of happiness both extends and subsumes the other rights. The comprehensive character of the system of rights, as summed up in the right to pursuit of happiness, implies a kind of individual sovereignty and there with a way to understand the ground for the affirmation of natural equality. If there is by nature a personal right to pursuit of happiness, that is, a right to pursue a shape of life for oneself and one self-chosen (within the boundaries of the parallel rights of others and the needs of society), then human beings must be equal in the sense affirmed: The personal right to pursue

---

[7] On the right to property, see Michael P. Zuckert, *Launching Liberalism: On Lockean Political Philosophy* (Lawrence: University Press of Kansas, 2002), 220–224.
[8] See Zuckert, *Launching Liberalism*, 221, 274–293; Michael Zuckert, "Natural Rights and Imperial Constitutionalism: The American Revolution and the Development of the American Amalgam," 22 *Social Philosophy and Policy* 27 (2005): 27–55.

happiness is incompatible in its very nature with natural subjection to another. Natural equality is thus a correlate or even a derivation from the natural rights specified in the Declaration. The two first truths are thus tightly and logically linked. If we push our inquiry about grounds for equality to rights, we reach something like a dead-end. The Declaration itself does not tell us how we know that human beings are rights-bearers or how we know just what rights to include in the list of natural rights. Perhaps we can learn more when we examine the overarching claim that these truths are, or rather, are held, to be "self-evident."

5.7 EQUALITY OF WHOM?

Before we move on to our second question of how the theory of the Declaration gets from a state of no-authority to an institution that has "just powers" and which thus abrogates the original equality, we must pause to interrogate the equality claim at somewhat greater length. A frequently raised objection to the Declaration in the twentieth and twenty-first centuries is that the Declaration may say equality of all, but it does not really mean it – that it means, for example, equality of white men only, excluding persons of other races and genders. The assertion that the Declaration's proclamation of equality excludes persons of other races was forcefully raised in the years leading up to the Civil War as a response to abolitionist appeals to the "created equal" phrase in their attacks on slavery. The most notorious denial of the inclusion of the slaves and all blacks from the equality claim in the Declaration came in the *Dred Scott* case in the Supreme Court opinion by Chief Justice Roger B. Taney, who concluded that neither the language of the Declaration nor the protections in the Constitution applied to the black race: blacks, he said, "had no rights which the white man was bound to respect."[9] (*Dred Scott v. Sandford* 1857, 701). Taney attributed this view to the authors of the Declaration – how could they affirm the natural rights of the blacks and at the same time hold so many in slavery? Thomas Jefferson, a slaveholder to be sure, did not agree with Taney. In his draft of the Declaration, he condemned the king for having "waged cruel war against human nature itself, violating its most sacred rights of life and liberty in the persons of a distant people who never offended him, captivating them and carrying them into slavery in another hemisphere." Jefferson added that the king was "determined to keep open a market where MEN should be bought and sold" (original emphasis). There is thus no doubt that Jefferson considered the blacks to be men and thus within the meaning of the language of the Declaration. So Jefferson the slaveholder could write of American slavery in his *Notes on the State of Virginia*: "I tremble for my country when I reflect that God is just: that his justice cannot sleep forever." He feared a coming race war, of which he observes that, "The Almighty has no attribute which

---

[9] *Dred Scott v. Sandford*, 60 U.S. 393, 407 (1856).

can take side with us in such a contest."[10] Some years later he spoke again of slavery of the blacks. "The love of justice and the love of country plead equally the cause of these people, and it is a moral reproach to us that they should have pleaded it so long in vain, and should have produced not a single effort ... to relieve them & ourselves from our present condition of moral & political reprobation."[11] Jefferson and other American declarers of independence may have been slaveholders, but they were guilty reprobates in their own eyes. How best to understand the simultaneous condemnation and continuance of slavery is a worthy question, the answering of which goes beyond the possibilities of this essay, but there can be little doubt that the Americans understand the blacks to be included in the "all men" who are "created equal."

And women? Are they included in "all men?" It is sometimes doubted that women were included, in part because of the use of that ambiguous term "men," but even more because of the various civil and political disabilities under which women suffered in 1776: Could the authors of the Declaration mean to pronounce women equal when they were denied the right to vote, the right to serve on juries, to hold political office, to pursue certain professions? Without denying the importance of these civil and political disabilities, it is necessary to note the bearing of the Declaration's affirmation of universal human equality: It applies to a pre-political or perhaps nonpolitical situation. It is an attempt to consider the human endowment outside of, irrespective of, and ultimately constitutive for, the political. Note that none of the rights listed in this part of the Declaration are political rights, which makes perfect sense because these are rights held independently of the existence of government. They are natural as opposed to civil or political rights. Understood in this way, it is difficult to deny that women are included, for their basic natural rights are indeed recognized in 1776. The law, for example, recognizes women as possessing a right to life in so far as it forbids the taking of a woman's life as much as it does a man's. Now it remains an important question, unsettled within the Declaration itself or by the founding generation, what the original equality and possession of rights implies about civil and political rights. This is a question that has been and still is being worked out within the American political tradition.

5.8 EQUALITY AND RIGHTS INSECURITY

As we move to the second set of truths, those that sketch the why and the how of the institution of government, we are forced to notice that there is a suppressed or underdeveloped premise in the argument. The text tells us: "in order to secure these rights, governments are instituted among men." This implies that without government, the natural rights are insecure, but we are given no

---

[10] Thomas Jefferson, *Writings* (ed. Merrill D. Peterson) (New York: Library of America, 1984), 289.
[11] Jefferson, *Writings*, 1344.

further information on why that is so. In the political-philosophic literature that the Declaration's theory so closely resembles, much space is devoted to discussing why the state of equality, the state of human life without government, would render rights insecure. The chief philosophers agree on the fact but disagree on the reasons for rights insecurity. The Declaration takes no sides on whether Hobbes or Locke, to take two important examples, is more correct on the reason for the unviability of the state of nature. The Declaration, however, agrees with the philosophers in the chief point they extract from thinking about human life without government and thus of coming to understand why government is needed. The point they all agree on can most perspicuously be restated as follows: Even though all human beings are endowed by nature or God with natural rights, these rights will tend not to be respected by others absent the existence in society of an institution armed with legitimate coercive authority, with which it can pass laws to protect and exercise the muscle to see that these laws are enforced. They agree, in a word, that the state of strict equality as a state of no-rule is not a viable human condition; neither a situation in which no one can rightfully coerce others, nor one where all can rightfully coerce produces a situation where the rights of all are respected. So, a specialized institution to exercise coercion on behalf of rights, government, is needed.

5.9 CONSENT

Thus, the tight logic of the Declaration continues into the second set of truths, so long as we note the underdeveloped premise of rights insecurity in the condition of equality. The government instituted among men derives "its just powers from the consent of the governed." The way in which this claim follows from the precedent truths is evident when we take seriously the implication of the original equality: That men are created equal means that there is no natural basis for political authority; contrary to a long tradition that held otherwise, the Declaration is affirming that neither God nor nature has ordained or appointed government or governors. Since there is no natural or divine source of authority, the people forming the government must be the source of its rightful powers. Only they can remove themselves from their primitive condition of non-subjection to one of subjection to government. This action by the governed is described as consent, but exactly how this consent is expressed is not stated. The reason for this silence is relatively easy to discern: The immediate goal of the document is to justify the act of rebellion that is the declaring of independence. This is an act not of giving but of withdrawing consent. In a sense, the act of rightfully withdrawing consent is nothing other than refusing to recognize the existing authorities as legitimate and withholding obedience to their laws and other actions. Conversely, the act of consenting to government must involve at least recognizing government and governmental authorities and willingly obeying their laws and other actions.

5 Equality, Liberty, and Rights

It is often thought that the truth about consent implies the sole legitimacy of democracy as the rightful form of government. That conclusion is certainly understandable, but it is not well supported by the Declaration's text. As the last of the Declaration's six truths pronounces, the people in the post-revolutionary situation, having altered or abolished the existing government, have "the Right ... to institute new government, laying its foundation on such principles and organizing its powers in such form, as to then shall seem most likely to effect their safety and Happiness." The theory of the Declaration does not commit to one form of government as solely legitimate, but is quite open-ended in leaving it up to each people to decide for themself, in light of their own situation and traditions. Indeed, the text even proclaims an openness to monarchy, the kind of government the Americans were in the process of throwing off. After listing the grievances against the king, the text concludes that "a Prince whose character is thus marked by every act which may define a tyrant, is unfit to be the ruler of a free people." It follows then that a prince who is not a tyrant, a prince who respects and secures the rights for the sake of which government exists, could well be a fit and legitimate ruler. Nonetheless, the American themselves and others like the French who endorsed a philosophy like that of the Declaration opted against monarchy and in favor of democratic republics. This, of course, is an option validated in the text, but over time the consent requirement has come to be interpreted in a much more democratic way than it is understood in the Declaration itself.

5.10 REVOLUTION

Again, we must notice that the argument of the Declaration is tightly logical – the second set of truths follows deductively from the first set. This same is true and readily shown for the third set. If, as the text tells us, governments exist for a given purpose – "to secure these rights" – and if it is instituted via consent of the governed in order to achieve this purpose and in no other way, then it follows that the people may withdraw their consent from governments that fail through malevolence or incompetence to achieve their purpose. Thus, the so-called right of revolution follows logically from the truths already announced. And as we have seen, the last truth follows also: So far as withdrawing consent leaves the people with no legitimate authority, they have a right to make new government. That is, back in the condition of original equality, they have the same right, and the same need, to institute new government.

5.11 SELF-EVIDENT TRUTHS

We have so far passed over one of the most striking claims in the second paragraph of the Declaration: "We hold these truths to be self-evident." This claim about self-evidence has been among the most controversial features of the text. The assertion about self-evidence is often taken in modern times as evidence of the intellectual and political innocence of the simpler days of the Founding. As historian Henry Steele Commager put it, "There was indeed a simplicity in the moral standards and in political faith – a simplicity reflected ... in the language of the time: 'we hold these truths to be self-evident.'"[12] "We would not today," says Commager, "assume a body of 'self-evident truths,' certainly not in the arena of government or politics."[13] Sanford Levinson, political theorist and law professor, puts it even more strongly: "It is simply not open to an intellectually sophisticated modern thinker to share Jefferson's world."[14] On the other side, Danielle Allen, in her study of the Declaration, disagrees strongly with the self-evidence skeptics. She finds the truths affirmed in the second paragraph to be, indeed, self-evidently so,[15] and a sign of the authors' intellectual sophistication rather than the reverse.

The disagreement over self-evidence is important not only as part of a contest over the level of intellectual development of the American founding generation but more importantly also for the attempt to judge the truth or falseness of the theory of government propounded in the Declaration. This task is of preeminent importance if we are to take the Declaration as something more than a historically interesting document. Since the Declaration as a whole constitutes one long syllogism, and since the second paragraph itself constitutes a tightly argued theory in which succeeding claims follow logically from antecedent claims, the truth value of the whole depends on our ability to affirm the truth of the initial premises. In the document as a whole, the minor premise, as provided by the long list of grievances, rests on empirical instances of kingly actions and inactions. But what does the major premise, supplied by the theoretical section, rest on? The text seems to say: These claims are self-evidently true. Their self-evidence would vouch for the truth of the theory as a whole.

Now it is evident that these allegedly self-evident truths are not self-evident in the sense of being obvious or clearly true to all readers. The Declaration put forward a controversial theory of the origin and nature of political life; it put forward a way of looking at politics that failed to correspond to the theory and practice of nearly all nations and individuals in the world at the time. It was an innovation. Perhaps the assertion of self-evidence should be taken not only as in indication of intellectual naiveté, as Commager and Levinson would, but also as a sign of American insularity in the eighteenth century.

To judge better of the self-evidence of the claims in the Declaration demands that we reject the "obvious-to-everyone" interpretation of self-evidence, for the concept of self-evidence was a major theme in the philosophic literature of the

---

[12] Henry Steele Commager, *Jefferson, Nationalism, and the Enlightenment* (New York: George Braziller, 1975), xi.
[13] Commager, *Jefferson*, 82.
[14] Sanford Levinson, "Self-Evident Truths in the Declaration of Independence," 57 *Texas Law Review* 847 (1979).
[15] Allen, *Our Declaration*, 160–166.

5 Equality, Liberty, and Rights

age, literature in which Jefferson and others of the generation that produced the Declaration were well versed. Particularly important is the fact that John Locke, one of "the three greatest men that have ever lived, without any exception," according to Jefferson, devoted an entire chapter of his masterwork *An Essay Concerning Human Understanding* to the topic of self-evident truths.[16] Allen comes to a more favorable conclusion regarding the self-evidence and therefore truth of the Declaration's claims just because she takes more seriously the philosophic meaning of self-evidence.

In order to judge well, one must first identify exactly what claims are identified with self-evidence. The text leaves little doubt on this score: All six truths are "held" to be self-evident. The list of six is introduced by the clause, "we held *these truths* to be self-evident," with all six standing in an exactly parallel construction, governed by that introductory clause. The text does not warrant the view, sometimes put forward, that only the first (equality) or the first two truths are held to be self-evident.

The separate and equal denomination of all the truths as held to be self-evident takes on special significance when we consult the definition of self-evident that Locke put forward: "*Knowledge* ... consists in the perception of the agreement or disagreement of *Ideas*: Now where that agreement or disagreement is perceived immediately by it self [sic], without the intervention or help of any other [idea], there our *Knowledge is self-evident*" (original emphasis).[17] The most obvious example of such an immediate agreement of ideas would be a proposition of simple identity, like "*whatsoever is white is white*," or "*Red is not Blew*" (original emphasis).[18] Or, a somewhat more subtle but equally self-evident proposition: "*the Whole is equal to all its Parts taken together*" (original emphasis).[19]

Several important points about the Declaration follow. Since the perception of agreement or disagreement of ideas is immediate, self-evident propositions neither require nor can depend on demonstrations or chains of reasoning of any kind.[20] A chain of reasoning, or a syllogism, involves the "intervention or help" of other ideas than those present in the original proposition. Self-evident are propositions that contain their evidence within themselves, not in their connections to other ideas. Thus, Allen is mistaken when she claims that all conclusions derived in arguments beginning with self-evident truths are themselves self-evident.[21] The bearing of this observation on the Declaration should be clear: The six truths are related to each other as steps in a deductive argument, and therefore at least the last four of them cannot be self-evident,

---

[16] Jefferson, *Writings*, 939; John Locke, *An Essay Concerning Human Understanding*, ed. Peter H. Nidditch) (New York: Oxford University Press, [1690] 1979), 591–608.
[17] Locke, *An Essay*, 591.
[18] Locke, *An Essay*, 592–593.
[19] Locke, *An Essay*, 596.
[20] Locke, *An Essay*, 607–608.
[21] Allen, *Our Declaration*, 161–163.

since they are derived from other truths or ideas. But all are equally held to be self-evident. Does this mean that none are?

In fact, not one of the truths in the list of six is self-evidently true. There is no immediate agreement of ideas between the idea of man and the idea of equality as no relation of authority as there is between whole and part. One can say without contradiction, as Robert Filmer did in his theory of divine right monarchy, that all men are subject to Adam and his heirs. True or false, this is not a claim that is self-evidently one or the other. Likewise, the claim that all men are endowed with the right to the pursuit of happiness is not self-evident. It may be true, but it is not evidently so. As we have seen, the claim about rights serves as the first premise for the theory of legitimate government sketched in the Declaration's second paragraph, but it is not a self-evident starting point. We are entitled to ask the authors of the Declaration for their reason for holding their claims about rights to be true, which we would be foolish to do to someone who proclaimed "red is red." All that person could do in reply is say, "look." This would not be an appropriate answer to a query about the reasons for affirming natural rights.

So, none of the six allegedly self-evident truths is in fact self-evident. Does this mean the authors of the Declaration were ignorant, inept, or ultra-naive? To answer that question, one must look at what the text actually says. We and most students of the Declaration have been proceeding as if the text said: "These are self-evident truths." But it actually says: "*We hold* these truths to be self-evident." This is not equivalent to saying "these are self-evident truths." There is no room in the recognition of self-evidence for "holding." A self-evident is perceived directly to be such, and there is no room for a "we" who "holds" or a "holding." One way to understand or translate the "we hold" clause is to say, "we deem these truths to be self-evident." Judgments of "deeming" have no place in recognizing self-evidence.

The authors of the Declaration are therefore not claiming the actual status of self-evident truth for the six truths that together justify the American actions, but are saying something more like this: These are the basic premises for our political action. For us as a people, they serve the function self-evident truths or axioms can be taken to serve in demonstrations: They provide the first principles for our political reasoning and acting. We are not speaking of the epistemic status of these truths, but of their political status. Their epistemic status is, as Jefferson said in a letter written late in his life, a matter of the "light of science."[22] But political communities are not composed of scientists or philosophers. One can no more expect a people to possess the philosophic ground for affirming natural rights than one can expect it, as a people, to grasp string theory. But political life requires that the fundamental political truths be held, held as deep convictions, if not as truths in the full sense. The fundamental truths must be held *as if* self-evident, as if their truth were as evident as "red

---

[22] Jefferson, *Writings*, 1517.

5 Equality, Liberty, and Rights

is red." It is not necessary that the people as such hold the truths (or theories) of physics in this way.

Since the truths are not said to be truly self-evident, we are left wondering what argument might actually ground them. Jefferson himself and Locke both put forth arguments for the truths, especially the primary truths of rights and equality, but not in the Declaration. This merely brings us back to an observation with which we began: The Declaration is a giving of reasons, but it is a political document, not a philosophic treatise.[23] The Declaration leads us to the threshold of political philosophy but does not go there itself.

---

[23] On Jefferson, see Michael P. Zuckert, *The Natural Rights Republic: Studies in the Foundation of the American Political Tradition* (South Bend: University of Notre Dame Press, 1996), 56–89. On Locke, see Michael P. Zuckert, *Natural Rights and the New Republicanism* (Princeton: Princeton University Press, 1994), 275–286.

6

The "Stubborn" Declaration

Less Dissent than Alienation in Black Political Thought and the Declaration of Independence

Saladin Ambar

For all the recent controversy over the alleged teaching of Critical Race Theory (CRT) in American public schools (and the theory's purported animosity towards the American Founding), neither CRT, nor most other branches of Black Political Thought, are effusive in their condemnations of America's defining document, the Declaration of Independence. On the contrary, if there is a thread of discourse among black political thinkers concerning the Declaration, it is one of alienation, rather than dissent. Take Derrick Bell, the late Harvard law professor *The New Yorker* called "The Man behind Critical Race Theory."[1] The publication of a collection of his works in *The Derrick Bell Reader* (2005) includes but one passing reference to the Declaration – and it is to praise it – at least Thomas Jefferson's original draft, well known for its condemnation of slavery.[2] Ironically, it is this lauded first draft of the Declaration that critics of CRT point to when objecting to CRT's approach to American history.

The shared admiration for the Declaration's original draft by both CRT scholars and their critics goes some way in illustrating the complexity of CRT's view of the founding. Bell and other CRT scholars point to Jefferson's original draft to demonstrate America's founding hypocrisies; CRT's critics highlight Jefferson's original draft to demonstrate the Founder's best intentions.[3] With respect to Bell, what then is his criticism or dissent from the Declaration, if

---

[1] Jelani Cobb, "The Man behind Critical Race Theory," *The New Yorker*, September 20, 2021.
[2] From his "Black Faith in a Racist Land," (1971) Bell emphasized that most school "texts neglect to mention that a first draft of the Declaration of Independence written by Thomas Jefferson criticized the King of England for having introduced slavery to these shores." See Derrick Bell, *The Derrick Bell Reader*, ed. Richard Delgado and Jean Stefancic (New York: New York University Press, 2005), 128.
[3] For example, see David Azerrad's "What the Constitution Really Says about Race and Slavery," December 28, 2015, bit.ly/4fzN7bi.

one is to be had? It is not to be found in the document itself, but in his rebuke of Chief Justice Roger B. Taney's infamous interpretation of the Declaration in the Dred Scot decision (1857), a hardly controversial position, even among CRT's most ardent critics.[4]

To be sure, black scholars and thinkers, not all of whom are identified with CRT, find parts of the Declaration objectionable. These objections center around the document's infamous grievance rebuking King George III for inciting the "merciless Indian savages," against the colonists, as well as the unnamed black "domestic" population threatening insurrection.[5] There are other critiques inveighing against the gendered language of the Declaration, and other class-based analyses that have found the document objectionable. Nevertheless, the great expanse of Black Political Thought – at least since Benjamin Banneker's exchange of letters with Thomas Jefferson in 1791, has found fault with the Declaration's racial exclusivity, not with its underlying principles – and certainly not its most hallowed idea that "all men are created equal."[6] While today, "men" is often exchanged for "people" or "humans" by scholars to reflect a non-gendered value for human life, there is no, has been no, and can be no, replacement for the word "equal." Indeed, it is the fundamental egalitarianism of the Declaration that makes it less a document that Critical Race Theorists have dissented from, than one they have critiqued for its limited applicability.

Part of the trouble with the trouble over race and the Declaration has to do with failures to see the complex array of thought found within Black Political Thought, including CRT. For if there has been any great intellectual assault on the Declaration by black scholars and thinkers historically, it has not come preeminently from CRT scholars, but rather black nationalists and or black separatist movements in America. Even here, there are shades of gray, for the Declaration's core ethos has made it stubbornly immune from attack. Where it is embattled is in its list of grievances, its racial exclusivity – which has bound it to white supremacy temporally, if not ideationally – and in its racialist defenders over the centuries. "We hold these truths to be self-evident, that all men are created equal, that they are endowed by their Creator with certain unalienable Rights, that among these are Life, Liberty and the pursuit of Happiness," speaks a political objective so profound, and so universal, that voices as distinct as the radical black socialist writer, Hubert Harrison ("a splendid truth"),[7] to

---

[4] Bell, *The Derrick Bell Reader*, 129.
[5] These grievances are the final ones listed in the document. See the National Archives site for the Declaration, www.archives.gov/founding-docs/declaration-transcript.
[6] For Banneker's criticism of Jefferson's about-face on slavery in the Declaration, see Saladin Ambar, *Stars and Shadows: The Politics of Interracial Friendship from Jefferson to Obama* (Oxford: Oxford University Press, 2022), 7–10.
[7] "Take the Declaration of Independence, for instance," Harrison wrote. "That seemed a splendid truth. But the black man merely touched it and it became a splendid lie." See Hubert Harrison, *A Hubert Harrison Reader*, ed. Jeffrey B. Perry (Middletown: Wesleyan University Press, 2001), 54.

Frederick Douglass ("the ringbolt to the nation's redemption"),[8] have praised it. We therefore start from that basic fact of Black Political Thought's assent to the Declaration's creed, before venturing into the myriad and diverse forms of critique it has occasioned – though less from its content, than the alienation it has confirmed in black lives since its birth.

6.1 BLACK NATIONALISM AND THE DECLARATION

The Nation of Islam (NOI) is the oldest and perhaps most influential black nationalist organization in US history. That its newspaper, *The Final Call* runs a column on or near the fourth of July every year, rebuking the American Founding by the organization's former leader, the Honorable Elijah Muhammad, is no surprise. But the column, "Independence Day," upon closer inspection, is revelatory in its reverential treatment of the Fourth, albeit for very different reasons. For it was on July 4, 1930, according to the organization's history and religious cosmology, that the NOI's founder, Wallace Fard Muhammad, believed to be Allah in the form of a man, presented himself to the black race in America. "The significance of His coming to us, on the Independence Day of the White man, is very great," Muhammad wrote. "It is their day of great rejoicing. As with former peoples and their governments, their destruction took place when they were at the height of their rejoicing."[9]

Muhammad does not engage the text of the Declaration, but rather, underscores it as a separatist-inspired document in its own right. "Now, the history of the 4th of July shows that it is the Independence Day of the American White man. They wrote the Declaration of Independence for themselves. The White man did not put anything in the Declaration of Independence for the benefit of the Black Man, who was the servitude-slave of the White man at that time."[10] Thus the "coming of Allah in the person of Master Fard Muhammad" on the Fourth serves as a form of instantiation – a reversal of America's independence, but also a bestowal of sorts, for black independence from America. For even in its disavowal of America, the NOI does so by substituting one undeniable and universally accepted political (and in its own right, spiritual) founding for another.

---

[8] Frederick Douglass, "What to the Slave Is the Fourth of July?" in *The Frederick Douglass Papers, Series One: Speeches, Debates, and Interviews, Volume I: 1841–46*, ed. John W. Blassingame (New Haven: Yale University Press, 1979), 363–364, quoted in Melvin L. Rogers and Jack Turner, eds., *African American Political Thought: A Collected History* (Chicago: University of Chicago Press, 2021), 137.

[9] "Independence Day," originally was published as part of Muhammad's 1973 book, *The Fall of America*. See Elijah Muhammad, *The Fall of America* (Chicago: Secretarius Memps Publishing, 2006). The column can be found online at: www.finalcall.com/artman/publish/Columns_4/article_8979.shtml.

[10] Muhammad, *The Fall of America*, 68.

6 The "Stubborn" Declaration

Theological considerations aside, black nationalist renderings of the Declaration have not been very different from Muhammad's. They, too, have been less oriented towards critical deconstructions of the text and more inclined to reading in the Declaration a right to separation for African Americans and black people throughout the diaspora. Take the United Negro Improvement Association founder and Jamaican-born leader of America's Back to Africa movement, Marcus Garvey's "Declaration of the Rights of the Negro Peoples of the World" (1920). The document's first demand in its declaration of rights quotes directly from the Declaration of Independence:

Be it known to all men that whereas all men are created equal and entitled to the rights of life, liberty and the pursuit of happiness, and because of this we, the duly elected representative of the Negro peoples of the world, invoking the aid of the just and Almighty God, do declare all men, women and children of our blood throughout the world free denizens and do claim them as free citizens of Africa, the Motherland of all Negroes.[11]

This black right to return is thus prefaced upon human equality, an equality that Garvey pronounced in the language of the Declaration. What the Declaration did not intend in its time for black people, Garvey understands as belonging to Africans everywhere. Moreover, by so explicitly borrowing from the Declaration, Garvey implicitly confirms the document's credibility. No improvement on language is necessary as the Declaration's authority –indeed, the components of its most famous line – is proof positive of the righteousness of the cause of Africans.

Garvey was only echoing the sentiment of earlier black political thinkers, such as Martin R. Delany, who, as a contemporary of Douglass, found the Declaration of Independence an irrelevancy to the liberation of African Americans. Delany supported emigration to Latin America or the Caribbean for America's black population, arguing in 1852 that, "We have speculated and moralized much about equality – claiming to be as good as our neighbors, and every body else – all of which may do very well in ethics –but not in politics. We live in societies among men, governed by rules and regulations."[12] However noble and true Jefferson's words, they amounted to merely that – words. Delany's dissent was ultimately from American hypocrisy – not the Declaration's essential truths. By contrast, Douglass' historic and fiery denunciation of the Declaration delivered the same year as Delany's essay calling for expatriation, was the invective of someone committed to the black freedom struggle in America.

Before Delany and Douglass, David Walker in his pamphlet, *An Appeal to the Colored Citizens of the World* (1829), represented a proto-nationalist

---

[11] Marcus Garvey, *Selected Writings and Speeches of Marcus Garvey*, ed. Bob Blaisdell (Mineola: Dover Publishing, 2004), 18.
[12] See Martin R. Delany, *The Conditions, Elevation, Emigration and Destiny of the Colored People of the United States* (Amherst: Humanity Books, 2004), 67.

orientation, one that saw in the Declaration of Independence the right for black self-government and equality. Walker's nationalism is not that of the separatist, but rather that of the prophetic and scathing critic; his denunciations of the Declaration are tied to its cruel ironies. Moreover, Walker's nationalism is rooted in black pride with respect to history, aesthetics, and culture. Indeed, Walker spends more time in his Appeal addressing Jefferson's white supremacist theories found in *Notes on the State of Virginia*, than he does the Declaration.[13]

The Declaration, in a sense, needs no refutation – it is the hypocritical conduct of whites that earns Walker's wrath, not the language of Thomas Jefferson. Speaking to the prohibition of the Appeal's circulation in the South, Walker writes, "the Americans do their very best to keep my Brethren from receiving and reading my 'Appeal' for fear they will find in it an extract I made from their Declaration of Independence, which says, 'We hold these truths to be self-evident, that all men are created equal.'"[14] In this light, Melvin Rogers and Jack Turner's direction for us to "Think of David Walker's reinterpretation of the Declaration of Independence as a warrant for black emancipation and coequal citizenship," is well founded. Indeed, as Peter Thompson has argued, "David Walker is more properly considered black nationalism's Thomas Jefferson rather than abolitionism's Thomas Paine."[15] For it is the radicalism of Jefferson's call to "alter or abolish" government that does not recognize one's fundamental rights that speaks most pointedly to the enslaved. That many black political thinkers would follow Walker down this path only serves to underscore the Declaration as an ironic and, therefore, highly effective tool for articulating a rationale for black liberation, however prescribed.[16]

In the end, the black nationalist critique of the Declaration draws attention to the distance between the aspirations for human equality it implies and its application at the time of its drafting. The "are" and "ought" that observers such as Jacques Derrida scrutinized in the Declaration's closing lines referencing the right of the then colonies to become "free and independent states," remain at the core of nationalist critiques, for invariably, those two words hold up a mirror to the Declaration's promises as alien to African Americans.[17] As Malcolm X put it in one of his scathing attacks on the American Founding:

---

[13] Thomas Jefferson, *Notes on the State of Virginia*, ed. Robert Pierce Forbes (New Haven: Yale University Press, 2022).
[14] David Walker, *An Appeal to the Colored Citizens of the World*, introduction by Sean Wilentz, rev. ed. (New York: Hill and Wang, 1995), 72.
[15] Peter Thompson, "David Walker's Nationalism – and Thomas Jefferson's," *Journal of the Early Republic*, 37.1 (Spring 2017): 62–63.
[16] Rogers and Turner, eds., *African American Political Thought*, 12.
[17] See Derrida's "Declarations of Independence," *New Political Science* 15 (Summer 1986): 11–12, www-personal.umich.edu/~alisse/PDFs/Derrida.pdf.

6 The "Stubborn" Declaration

Yes, when they wrote, how does that thing go – about "all men created equal"? – that was later on. Who was it wrote that – "all men created equal"? It was Jefferson. Jefferson had more slaves than anybody else. So they weren't talking about us. When I see some poor old brainwashed Negroes – you mention Thomas Jefferson and George Washington and Patrick Henry, they just swoon, you know, with patriotism. But they don't realize that in the sight of George Washington, you were a sack of molasses, a sack of potatoes. You – yes – were a sack of potatoes, a barrel of molasses, you amounted to nothing, in the sight of Washington, or in the sight of Jefferson, or Hamilton, and some of those other so-called founding fathers. You were their property. And if it was left up to them, you'd still be their property today.[18]

Even so, when Malcolm X references the extremism of Patrick Henry at the Oxford Union debate in late 1964 ("give me liberty or give me death") – it is an extremism he supports.[19] And it is one that comes directly out of the Declaration's radical premise of a people's right to seek revolutionary redress after "a long train of abuses." One might add, by any means necessary.

6.2 THE DECLARATION AND BLACK LIBERALISM

The first direct assault on Jefferson by an African American related to the Declaration came from Banneker, the free black man from Maryland whom Jefferson selected while secretary of state to be part of the team of surveyors in 1791 that would lay the boundary stones for what would become Washington, DC. Upon returning to his farm in Maryland, Banneker decided to use his newfound notoriety to write Jefferson – not to thank him, but to challenge him on the racist views he had espoused ten years earlier in his *Notes on Virginia*. And Banneker did so by using Jefferson's own words against him. Noting Jefferson's embrace of liberty during the American Revolutionary War, Banneker wrote:

This Sir, was a time in which you clearly saw into the injustice of Slavery, and in which you had just apprehensions of the horrors of its conditions, it was now Sir, that your abhorrence thereof was so excited, that you publickly held forth this true and invaluable doctrine, which is worthy to be recorded and remember'd in all Succeeding ages. "We hold these truths to be Self evident, that all men are created equal, and that they are endowed by their creator with certain unalienable rights, that among these are life, liberty, and the pursuit of happiness."[20]

Banneker's critique scarcely touched upon the document itself, other than to hold a mirror up to Jefferson's acceptance of slavery. His letter of August 19, 1791 invoked Christianity, an appeal to Jefferson's scientific expertise (he sent an almanac he wrote, along with the letter, as proof of the intellectual

---

[18] Malcolm X, *Malcolm X on Afro-American History* (New York: Pathfinder, 1990), 44–45.
[19] Saladin Ambar, *Malcolm X at Oxford Union* (Oxford: Oxford University Press, 2014), 87.
[20] See my discussion of Banneker's exchange of letters with Jefferson in Saladin Ambar, *Stars and Shadows: The Politics of Interracial Friendship from Jefferson to Obama* (Oxford: Oxford University Press, 2022), 1–24.

capabilities of African Americans), and the Declaration itself, as evidence in support of black liberation.[21] In short, Banneker chastised Jefferson on liberal terms, appealing to his Enlightenment sensibilities and failing that, to a (presumed) shared religious faith.

Again, Banneker offered no dissent from the Declaration per se and decades later, when Douglass (who was a great admirer of Banneker) took up the cudgel against the hypocrisy of Independence Day, in his famous address, "What to the Slave Is the Fourth of July," he, too, offered a scathing invective towards the hypocrisy found in the behavior of whites, not the Declaration itself. As Douglass' biographer David W. Blight has written about his 1852 address, "Douglass loved the Declaration of Independence, but since its principles were natural rights, like the precious ores of the earth, he refused to argue for their existence or their righteousness against the claims of proslavery ideologues."[22]

Again, the spirit expressed is one of alienation rather than dissent. "I shall see, this day, and its popular characteristics, from the slave's point of view," Douglass told his audience:

Standing, there, identified with the American bondman, making his wrongs mine, I do not hesitate to declare, with all my soul, that the character and conduct of this nation never looked blacker to me than on this 4th of July! Whether we turn to the declarations of the past, or to the professions of the present, the conduct of the nation seems equally hideous and revolting.[23]

Neither "declarations" nor "professions" can take the place of actions for Douglass – but in and of themselves, they are not the source of his opprobrium.

Banneker and Douglass offer harsh critiques of national hypocrisy – and both do so on liberal terms. That is to say, they accept a rights-based formulation of personal sovereignty, and both men evince total support for the language of the Declaration. Indeed, Douglass goes even further, arguing for a broader, anti-slavery reading of the Constitution in his fourth of July oration, something that white abolitionists such as William Lloyd Garrison did not do. As we will see, Critical Race Theorists, owing to the craft of their trade – namely the deconstruction of language – have been more inclined to find fault with the Declaration (though even this is qualified). Black liberals and nationalists are on similar ground, however, with respect to the Declaration. They are revolted by its exclusivity, not its content. Their differences are related

---

[21] "To Thomas Jefferson from Benjamin Banneker, August 19, 1791," *Founders Online*, National Archives, https://founders.archives.gov/documents/Jefferson/01 22-02-0049. [Original source: *The Papers of Thomas Jefferson*, vol. 22, *August 6, 1791–31 December 1791*, ed. Charles T. Cullen (Princeton: Princeton University Press, 1986), 49–54.]

[22] David W. Blight, *Frederick Douglass: Prophet of Freedom* (New York: Simon & Schuster, 2018), 233.

[23] Frederick Douglass. "What to the Slave Is the Fourth of July?" Speech, July 5, 1852, from *Teaching American History*, bit.ly/46Y8wZv.

6 The "Stubborn" Declaration

to solutions. Douglass could never countenance expatriation, as his friend, Delany, unapologetically did.

In *The Souls of Black Folk* (1903), W. E. B. Du Bois echoes this spirit. "We the darker ones come even now come not altogether empty-handed," Du Bois wrote. "[T]here are to-day no truer exponents of the pure human spirit of the Declaration of Independence than the American Negroes."[24] Even in 1955, when Du Bois' disenchantment with the United States had reached its heights, he nevertheless found the language and political sentiments of the Declaration to be ineluctable. Denied by the US State Department the right to travel to attend the Bandung Conference, the anticolonial gathering of developing nations from Asia and African, Du Bois sent a short statement, entitled, "A Proposed Declaration of Independence for the Peoples of Africa," in which he asserted the right to "Freedom of Self-Government," along with the right to "Food and Shelter, Education and Health."[25] To be sure, this is a far more radical Du Bois than the young scholar who penned *Souls* (he closes his Bandung statement thusly: "Let the white world keep its missionaries at home to teach the Golden Rule to its corporate thieves.").[26] Nevertheless, the premise of a right to self-government and its attachment to the Declaration remained solid ground for him decades later.

One strains to find examples of true dissenting views from the Declaration of Independence among black intellectuals and activists, historically. While this may be less surprising when considering black liberals such as A. Philip Randolph, their admonitions against white supremacy are no less fervent when employing the Declaration in asserting their claims for racial equality. Writing of Randolph, Michael McCann notes the then young activist's fiery assault on American hypocrisy: "[W]e find that at the very beginning of our national existence the Declaration of Independence, with all of its lofty rhetoric, was signed by slave holders, thereby placing the stamp of hypocrisy on the brow of the new-born nation." The problem for Randolph was "how to work out a constructive answer to the question of the relation between democracy expressed in the Declaration of Independence, the Federal Constitution, we now have, and the change in our social and economic system we now need."[27] The lamentations of black liberals and their engagement with the Declaration of Independence are perhaps best expressed by Dr. Martin Luther King, Jr., in his final speech delivered on April 3, 1968, in Memphis. "All we say to

---

[24] W. E. B. Du Bois, *The Souls of Black Folk* (New York: W. W. Norton & Company, 2007), 7.
[25] See Gerald Horne and Mary Young, eds., *W.E.B. Du Bois: An Encyclopedia* (Westport: Greenwood Press, 2001), 24.
[26] For the Bandung statement, see W. E. B. (William Edward Burghardt) Du Bois, 1868–1963, A Proposed Declaration of Independence for the Peoples of Africa, April 1955, W. E. B. Du Bois Papers (MS 312), Special Collections and University Archives, University of Massachusetts Amherst Libraries.
[27] See Michael McCann, "A. Philip Randolph: Radicalizing Rights at the Intersection of Class and Race," in *African American Political Thought*, 304 and 308.

America is, be true to what you said on paper," King intoned.[28] And there can be little doubt that it was the Declaration that King was referring to.

6.3 BLACK RADICALISM AND THE DECLARATION

On the evening of November 16, 2016, at the New York Public Theater, Bobby Seale, former co-founder of the Black Panther Party, explained how the Panthers' ten-point Program came to be. "We wrote this program piece by piece ... and then I ran into this Declaration of Independence, and I read it, and re-read it – and the first two paragraphs," Seale began, before reciting the opening lines of the Declaration from memory, drawing applause from the audience.[29] The two paragraphs referenced by Seale appear in the tenth point of the Panther program, under the heading, "What We Believe." The testimonies of Seale, the Panther platform, and the audience that evening are each, in their own way, reflections of the Declaration's stubborn, if not hallowed place within black political thought – including that of the black Left.

The Black Panther Party's politics was drawn from a number of intellectual traditions, chief among them socialism, Marxism, black nationalism, and Pan-Africanism – all predicated upon an anti-colonial orientation. Not only was the Declaration not seen as at odds with this braided set of ideologies, it seemed right at home. That the American Founders themselves were constructors and protectors of a racist and imperialist-driven political framework, was not the problem of those seeking liberation. It was up to whites who wanted to be part of a new, revolutionary system, to deconstruct their own racist personae. The Declaration, however, was good enough to be enshrined in Panther founding history – word for word.[30]

Among the brightest lights of the black political Left in America was Hubert Harrison, whose writings and work in the early twentieth century became highly influential in African American intellectual circles. It was Harrison's work in Harlem that most influenced Garvey; and it was his uncompromising disposition that would distinguish him from the black liberalism of his and later times. As the *New York Times* reported on Harrison's organizing efforts in the aftermath of the 1919 East St. Louis Race Riots, "They are saying a great deal about democracy in Washington now," [Harrison] said, "but while they are talking about fighting for freedom and the Stars and Stripes, here at home the whites apply the torch to the black men's homes, and their bullets, clubs, and stones to their bodies."[31] Harrison's advocacy of black self-defense,

---

[28] Cited in Clayborne Carson and Kris Shepard, eds., *A Call to Conscience: The Landmark Speeches of Dr. Martin Luther King, Jr.* (New York: Warner Books, 2001), 213.
[29] See Seale at the Public Forum, 2016, www.youtube.com/watch?v=U16UQ9VWG4Y.
[30] Cited in Joshua Bloom and Waldo E. Martin, Jr., *Black against Empire: The History of the Black Panther Party* (Oakland: University of California Press, 2016), 72–73.
[31] "Liberty League President Advises Negroes to 'Defend Their Lives,'" *New York Times*, July 5, 1919.

along with his socialist beliefs, marked him out as a radical outside of the intellectual bounds of the early and "long" civil rights movement.

In his 1911 speech, "The Negro and Socialism," Harrison argued that, "Politically, the Negro is the touchstone of the modern democratic idea. The presence of the Negro puts our democracy to the proof and reveals the falsity of it. Take the Declaration of Independence, for instance. This seemed a splendid truth. But the black man merely touched it and it became a splendid lie."[32] Here, Harrison is referencing the removal of Jefferson's condemnation of slavery from the original draft – by which the "black man's touching" it made it a work of deception. As Alexis de Tocqueville claimed a need to depart from the precepts of democracy in America once he introduced race into his discussion, so, too, did Harrison – and many other black thinkers – feel the need to qualify the power of the Declaration's truths.[33]

While Cedric J. Robinson's conclusion that the "Declaration of Independence ... [was an expression] of the interests and creed of the American bourgeoisie" reflects a basic tenet of the American Left, black Marxists and socialists thinkers have found the Declaration a useful source for contextualizing the black freedom struggle in America, for both its promises and the nation's shortcomings in living up to them.[34] Movement politics in America invariably involved asserting claims to citizenship and rights, and those claims were most pointedly founded upon the premises of the Declaration's assertion of universal equality. Indeed, Bayard Rustin's biographer, Jerald Podair, has called the Declaration's language the "basis of [Rustin's] political and economic philosophy," a powerful illustration of the Declaration's influence on the one-time member of the Communist Party, and highly influential confidante of Dr. King.[35]

Angela Davis, whose writings and activism have bridged the black radical tradition and critical legal studies, offered a different, albeit oblique critique of the Declaration than others decrying its inapplicability to African Americans historically, when in 2015, she criticized Hillary Clinton's use of the expression "all lives matter," in a speech near Ferguson, Missouri, site of the police killing of Michael Brown. "Does she not realize," Davis asked, "the extent to which such universal proclamations have been clandestinely racialized? Any critical engagement with racism requires us to understand the tyranny of the universal."[36] While

---

[32] Harrison, *A Hubert Harrison Reader*, 54.
[33] "These objects, which touch on my subject, do not enter into it: they are American without being democratic; and it is above all democracy that I wanted to portray," wrote Tocqueville. "I therefore had to turn away from them at first; but in ending I have to come back to them." See Alexis de Tocqueville, *Democracy in America*, trans. and ed. Harvey C. Mansfield and Delba Winthrop (Chicago: University of Chicago Press, 2000), 303.
[34] Cedric J. Robinson, *Black Marxism: The Making of the Black Radical Tradition* (Chapel Hill: University of North Carolina Press, 2020), 186.
[35] Jerald Podair, *Bayard Rustin: American Dreamer* (Lanham: Rowman & Littlefield, 2008), 2.
[36] Angela Y. Davis, *Freedom Is a Constant Struggle: Ferguson, Palestine, and the Foundations of a Movement* (Chicago: Haymarket Books, 2016), 87.

not directly referencing the Declaration, Davis' point speaks to the Declaration's failure to specify black rights as a form of acquiescence to racial inequality. "All men are created equal" – like "all lives matter," obfuscates an historic truth – and thus confers benefits and penalties, accordingly, on those who enjoy, or suffer from the fruits of such denialism. Toni Morrison explained this phenomenon in literary terms:

> For reasons that should not need explanation here, until very recently, and regardless of the race of the author, the readers of virtually all of American fiction have been positioned as white. I am interested to know what this assumption has meant to the literary imagination. When does racial "unconsciousness" or awareness of race enrich our interpretive language, and when does it impoverish it?[37]

The search for an anti-racist politics that critiques and yet preserves the egalitarian and universal claims of the Declaration have been part of the black intellectual endeavor since the American Founding. As Harold Cruse wrote when considering Black Power theorists' prospective solutions to racial inequality in America: "Despite their vaunted anti-Americanism, they are more American than they think."[38] The same may be said for the radical left tradition – though the arguments from this school of thought begin to introduce more class analyses, the absence of which is something Cruse, in his *The Crisis of the Negro Intellectual* (1967), critiques among black nationalists. Yet, the fervor over the Declaration today, if one is to be had, has been most inspired by those scholars writing within the tradition of CRT – a loosely bounded intellectual school, yet one that has produced a backlash of intellectual, legislative, and political counterassaults over the American Founding that are truly remarkable.

6.4 CRT AND THE DECLARATION

In 2011, Kimberlé Williams Crenshaw wrote a retrospective piece for the *Connecticut Law Review*, "Twenty Years of Critical Race Theory: Looking Back to Look Forward."[39] In the article, Crenshaw, who has been widely credited with coining the phrase, "intersectionality" and is one of CRT's prominent founding voices, wrote of the challenges CRT faced in 2011 (as they related to those it confronted in 1989, the generally accepted birthdate of the school):

> Then, as now, racial constituencies were confronting doctrinal and political retreats that severely limited the scope of civil rights advocacy. Then, as now, both liberal visions of race reform and radical critiques of class hierarchy failed in different ways

---

[37] Toni Morrison, *Playing in the Dark: Whiteness and the Literary Imagination* (New York: Vintage Books, 1992), xii.
[38] Harold Cruse, *The Crisis of the Negro Intellectual* (New York: New York Review of Books, 2005), 560.
[39] Kimberlé W. Crenshaw, "Twenty Years of Critical Race Theory: Looking Back to Move Forward," 43 *Conn. L. Rev.* 1253 (2011), https://scholarship.law.columbia.edu/faculty_scholarship/2864.

to address the institutional, structural and ideological reproduction of racial hierarchy. Then, as now, the collapse of racial barriers convinced many advocates and laypersons alike that fundamental transformation was at hand. Then, as now, racial progress was associated with an accommodationist orientation to the terms of racial power rather than a sustained collective contestation of it.[40]

This assortment of trials came ironically enough at a time of relative decline in familiarity with CRT. Indeed, Google Ngram's chart shows a precipitous decline in the frequency of "critical race theory" in publications in 2011 from its apex in 2000.[41] That has since changed rather dramatically, as CRT has become, if not better understood, certainly more widely discussed, as a source of debate in America's culture wars over education, race, and the future of American democracy. As the 2022 midterm elections approached, it was one of the leading talking points among Republican candidates who have identified the movement with an assault on American values and the founding of the country. Florida Governor Ron DeSantis, for example, touted his signing into a law the limiting of the teaching of CRT and discussions of race in places of businesses and schools, in a late-October 2022 debate with his Democratic opponent Charlie Crist.[42] For all of the furor, what has been this legal school's engagement with the Declaration of Independence?

Take Joe Feagin and Eileen O'Brien's discussion of reparations for African Americans. The two sociologists, associated with CRT, make their case based on the Declaration's creed. "Economic, political, and perhaps other forms of reparations for African Americans are essential if the United States is to begin to approach the equality long enunciated in the Declaration of Independence's opening premise, 'All men are created equal and are endowed by their creator with certain unalienable rights,'" they wrote in 1999.[43] This scarcely counts as a dissent from the document.

Something similar may be said for Columbia University Law School's Professor Patricia J. Williams, who is described on Columbia College's Core Curriculum web page as "one of the early proponents of Critical Race Theory (CRT)."[44] In her classic work, *The Alchemy of Race and Rights*, Williams sees the Declaration as a potential vessel for racial justice:

If one looks at the Declaration of Independence and the Constitution, one can see how they marry aspects of consent and aspects of symbology – for example, concepts like the notion of freedom. On the one hand there is the letter of the law exalted in these

---

[40] Kimberlé Williams Crenshaw, "Twenty Years of Critical Race Theory: Looking Back to Move Forward Commentary: Critical Race Theory: A Commemoration: Lead Article," *Connecticut Law Review* 117 (2011), https://opencommons.uconn.edu/law_review/117.
[41] Online: bit.ly/41L1l3k.
[42] Online: bit.ly/46TDhig.
[43] Cited in Roy L. Brooks, ed., *When Sorry Isn't Enough: The Controversy over Apologies for Reparations for Human Injustice* (New York: New York University Press, 1999), 421.
[44] www.college.columbia.edu/core/content/patricia-williams.

documents, which describes a specific range of rights and precepts. On the other hand there is the spirit of the law, the symbology of freedom, which is in some ways utterly meaningless or empty – although at the same time the very emptiness provides a vessel to be filled with possibility, with a plurality of autonomous yearnings.[45]

It is hard to imagine high school students radicalized by such an equanimous passage, if in fact CRT were taught in America's public schools. To be sure, CRT is more asserted in political arguments than it is a field in which most have widely read. Perhaps this places it in good company with the Declaration, whose creed of equality is amplified, but grievances largely skimmed over.

Here Feagin and co-author Ried E. Mackay take on the Declaration in its most widely criticized grievance against the king. It reads, "He has excited domestic insurrections amongst us, and has endeavoured to bring on the inhabitants of our frontiers, the merciless Indian Savages, whose known rule of warfare, is an undistinguished destruction of all ages, sexes, and conditions." If there is a dissent from the Declaration to be had, it is most closely associated with this passage. As Feagin and Mackay argue,

This passage reflects, and potentially generates, white emotions of fear and anger toward Native people ... The Declaration racially frames Native Americans as savages lacking in human values and willing to blindly destroy white Americans. White self-victimizing in the Declaration allows elite and ordinary whites to rationalize their anti-Indigenous violence as virtuous and necessary actions to secure their safety and right to lands they invaded.[46]

As the historian Robert Parkinson has argued, "This talk that was intended to generate racial fear was a key factor in the march toward independence."[47]

Still, CRT scholars have not dispensed with the Declaration as a purely racist or antidemocratic document. More often than not, they have juxtaposed it with the Constitution for the latter's countenance of slavery. In the words of CRT scholar, Devon Carbado, asserts "[t]he drafters of the Constitution took a sober second look at the rhetoric of radical egalitarianism in the Declaration of Independence, and they blinked."[48] One might say Lincoln's sleight of hand at Gettysburg was just this – the implicit eclipsing of the Constitution with the Declaration's highest aspirations. As Alvin B. Tillery, Jr., put it, in explaining the complex accounting of race by the nation's Founders: "Many of the authors

---

[45] Patricia J. Williams, *The Alchemy of Race and Rights: Diary of a Law Professor* (Cambridge: Harvard University Press, 1991), 16.

[46] R. E. Mackay and J. Feagin, "'Merciless Indian Savages': Deconstructing Anti-Indigenous Framing," *Sociology of Race and Ethnicity*, 8.4 (2022): 518–533, doi-org.proxy.libraries.rutgers.edu/10.1177/23326492221112040.

[47] See Robert G. Parkinson, "You Can't Tell the Story of 1776 without Talking about Race and Slavery," *Time*, July 4, 2021, https://time.com/6077468/united-states-1776-racism-slavery/.

[48] Devon W. Carbado, "Critical What What?" *Connecticut Law Review*, 43.5 (July 1, 2011): 1593, UCLA School of Law Research Paper No. 11-28, available at SSRN: https://ssrn.com/abstract=1919716.

6 The "Stubborn" Declaration

conservatives want students to read actually agree with critical race theory's core argument: Systemic racism is a cornerstone of the U.S. republic."[49]

6.5 CONCLUSION: LIVING IN IRONY

In Alex Haley's novel *Roots*, American independence is translated to enslaved African Americans through black intermediaries able to travel with their white masters who are exposed to national events beyond the plantation. They hear "Somethin' bout some Decoration a Ind'pen'ence" and the recruiting of black "drummers, fifers, or pioneers." When one slave asks for the meaning of "pioneers," he is told, "It mean git stuck up front an' git kilt!"[50] Such is the tragicomic sense of alienation captured by black writers surrounding American Independence and the Declaration. Ralph Ellison's "Liberty Paints" chapter in *Invisible Man*, does likewise. The very creation of whiteness, Ellison suggests, is tied to notions of liberty and racial purity. As explained to the nameless black protagonist when he asks, "Why the white [paint] rather than the others?": "Because we started stressing it from the first."[51]

To remove "all men are created equal" from the Declaration would be to remove irony from the American experience – and also its greatest source of hope. CRT has understood this all too well – but so have other black intellectual traditions. There is no deep, discernible break or dissent from the Declaration within black political thought in America, as such. Even black separatists and nationalists who have proffered a better life for African Americans in a separate state have done so not in opposition to the Declaration, but in opposition to the greater lie it has represented. The Declaration has been a stubborn yet largely welcome reminder of what a multiracial democracy might look like. That black scholars, activists, and everyday people of all backgrounds have proven even more stubborn in their efforts to bring this about suggests the historic *pas de deux* with the Declaration and its message of universal equality, is one we will long see performed.

---

[49] "Alvin B. Tillery, Jr., "Would the Founding Fathers Support Critical Race Theory," *Washington Post*, June 30, 2021, https://wapo.st/46YgP7K.
[50] Alex Haley, *Roots* (Boston: Da Capo Press, 2014), 360.
[51] Ralph Ellison, *Invisible Man* (New York: Vintage Books, 1995), 217.

7

"Popular Sovereignty" and the Declaration of Independence

Sanford Levinson

7.1 INTRODUCTION: LO THE "SOVEREIGN PEOPLE"

There are many ways to approach the Declaration of Independence. One way is to don the robes of the professional historian dedicated to reconstructing the thought, inasmuch as possible, of those who authored, signed, or simply affirmed the Declaration in July 1776 and thereafter. There is an impressive phalanx of such historians who have been, for example, interested in figuring out what was meant at the time by such concepts as "inalienable rights," "the creator," or, for that matter, government by "consent of the governed." All of these are important questions, but they are not really my questions. I am not a professional historian, and my primary interest in the Declaration concerns its continuing place in contemporary political argument and rhetoric. Almost necessarily, one is far more likely to find appeals to ostensible "plain meaning" instead of historically sophisticated inquiries that are often based on the premise, which I in fact accept, that the past is indeed a different country. I agree that it is often problematic to assume that any given old text can be read without the aid of an historical dictionary in hand (and the guidance of historically trained adepts). The extent to which this is true about the Declaration itself raises important questions.

In any event, most "contemporary" readers tend to focus either on the theme of equality, as Danielle Allen notably did in her extended meditation on the Declaration,[1] or the myriad of books that look to the phrase "life, liberty, and the pursuit of happiness" to provide an underpinning for a basically libertarian reading of the American ethos. Both are important and, no doubt, appear in many of the other essays in the present collection. I am,

---

[1] Danielle Allen, *Our Declaration: A Reading of the Declaration of Independence in Defense of Equality* (New York: Liveright Publishing, 2014).

however, interested in a key concept that does not appear overtly within the Declaration – "sovereignty." The same omission, incidentally, is true of the foundational document that was drafted in Philadelphia eleven years later. One has to infer from both a theory of sovereignty with regard to governmental powers and the limits to those powers, if any. Yet that term remains, for better or worse,[2] very much present within our contemporary discourse.

Americans lack canonical sentences similar to that found in the Declaration of the Rights of Man and of the Citizen by the National Assembly of France in 1789: "The nation is essentially the source of all sovereignty; nor can any individual, or any body of men, be entitled to any authority which is not expressly derived from it."[3] Or consider the opening words of the Declaration of Sovereignty on June 25, 1992, by the Confederated Tribes of the Warm Springs Reservation of Oregon: "Our people have exercised inherent sovereignty, as nations, on the Columbia Plateau for thousands of years, since time immemorial. Our Sovereignty is permeated by the spiritual and the sacred, which are, and always have been, inseparable parts of our lives, for the Creator leads us in all aspects of our existence."[4] After several pages, there are then the closing words:

We recognize that this declaration may not perfectly state the full and complete extent of our sovereignty. Our sovereignty is based, not on the laws of human beings, but on natural laws given to us by our Creator; these natural laws are as they are, not as human beings may define them. In addition, these natural laws are best expressed in our traditional languages and not in the language brought here by newcomers. In spite of these limitations, and without waiving any additional attributes of sovereignty that may not be expressly described in this document, we make this declaration in order to inform all who deal with us, and future generations of tribal members, of the essential nature of our national sovereignty ...

Political theorists may be interested in exploring the implications of the notion that sovereignty is based "not on the laws of human beings, but on natural laws given to us by our Creator." Compare in this regard the declaration in the 1975 Papua New Guinea Constitution that proclaims, "WE, THE PEOPLE, do now establish this sovereign nation and declare ourselves, under the guiding hand of God, to be the Independent State of Papua New

---

[2] I much admire Don Herzog, *SOVEREIGNTY, R.I.P.* (London: Yale University Press, 2019), which basically argues that the term, whatever its utility at the time of its creation among political theorists at the turn of the seventeenth century, is basically useless – and misleading – for us today. The original concept required the triune attributes of absolute power, non-accountability at least to any earthly authority, and indivisibility. None distinguishes so-called sovereigns today. Still, one can hardly ignore the fact that the term continues to be very much present within both contemporary political and legal discourse. It is not going to disappear simply because it has become increasingly incoherent for rigorous thinkers.

[3] https://shorturl.at/5B4YE.

[4] https://warmsprings-nsn.gov/treaty-documents/declaration-of-sovereignty/.

Guinea."[5] If one believes, as I do, that all theories of sovereignty have their origin in submission to God (or gods), then it is no small matter to substitute "the people" for the Divine as the source of authority. The Declaration does, of course, notably refer to a "Creator," not to mention "self-evident truths," but, at the very least, one might believe that they have not been treated as its most important messages, especially to national liberation movements around the world who have been inspired by the document.

One may or may not take either the French, Papua New Guinean, or the Warm Springs declarations with complete seriousness, at least with regard to what is thought to follow from these thundering statements. In the last case, one can be confident, for better or, quite possibly, for worse, that the United States government (and even more certainly, the United States Supreme Court) will feel no duty to recognize the claims asserted.[6] Sovereignty is a claim rather than a necessarily successful performative utterance. Whatever the importance of the declaration to the person or group making it, it requires acceptance and recognition by the onlooking audience. No one could possibly understand the Declaration as a political phenomenon without being fully aware that it was intended to be read by (and to inspire) by not only fellow "Americans," but also foreign audiences, particularly in France and the Netherlands, who were being asked to support the would-be Americans by loans that would require political and military success in order ever to be repaid. To be sure, even unacknowledged claims can have political importance for those asserting them, but that is different from according them juridical significance. "Declarations

---

[5] Preamble to the Papua New Guinea Constitution. It is worth setting out the Preamble in full:

WE, THE PEOPLE OF PAPUA NEW GUINEA – united in one nation pay homage to the memory of our ancestors – the source of our strength and origin of our combined heritage acknowledge the worthy customs and traditional wisdoms of our people – which have come down to us from generation to generation pledge ourselves to guard and pass on to those who come after us our noble traditions and the Christian principles that are ours now. By authority of our inherent right as ancient, free and independent peoples WE, THE PEOPLE, do now establish this sovereign nation and declare ourselves, under the guiding hand of God, to be the Independent State of Papua New Guinea. AND WE ASSERT, by virtue of that authority·that all power belongs to the people – acting through their duly elected representatives that respect for the dignity of the individual and community interdependence are basic principles of our society that we guard with our lives our national identity, integrity and self respect that we reject violence and seek consensus as a means of solving our common problems that our national wealth, won by honest, hard work be equitably shared by all Preamble WE DO NOW THEREFORE DECLARE that we, having resolved to enact a Constitution for the Independent State of Papua New Guinea AND ACTING through our Constituent Assembly on August 15, 1975 HEREBY ESTABLISH, ADOPT and GIVE TO OURSELVES this Constitution to come into effect on Independence Day, that is September 16, 1975. (www.parliament.gov.pg/images/misc/PNG-CONSTITUTION.pdf)

[6] See Justice Thomas' concurring opinion in *U.S. v. Lara*, 541 U.S. 192 (2004) for his trenchant comments on the incoherence of the Supreme Court's application of the notion of "sovereignty" to Indigenous Nations.

7 "Popular Sovereignty"

of independence" without the recognition of a relevant audience, even if only one relatively important actor in the international system, generates only pathos, if one is sympathetic to the declarants, or condemnation of their hubris if one is not.[7]

In any event, one looks through the roughly 1,337 words of the Declaration, one will not find the "magic" words of "sovereign" or "sovereignty." Still, one does find the crucial argument that provides the central basis for this essay: "Governments are instituted among Men, deriving their just powers from the consent of the governed." This appears to suggest that the foundation of government – and, therefore, sovereignty? – lies in the freely given consent of those who are governed. Without their consent, there is no legitimate government. With their consent, however, legitimacy is conferred. More importantly, perhaps, all things may become juridically possible, depending on what we think of the theory of "inalienable rights" protected from any and all governmental limitation. If, as Jonathan Gienapp has powerfully argued, the Declaration should be understood as establishing a robust right of "the people" to govern in the common good (more on this further on), then governmental *power* seems more impressive than the oft-cited notion of *limited government*.[8]

There are, however, two obvious problems with the theory of "popular sovereignty" (or, beyond that, the theory of "sovereignty" more generally) that provides the basis for this essay. The first involves exactly who is imagined as part of the presumptively "sovereign people"? To adopt Benedict Anderson's meme-like phrase, who are within the "imagined community" in whose name government speaks and acts?[9] Does the Declaration provide a helpful answer with regard to defining the *demos* presumably underlying any given democratic government? But the second question goes to the heart of the very notion of "sovereignty" itself: What limits, if any, must be recognized by a "sovereign people" with regard to any existing form of government? Do *all* "democratic" governments rest on the contingency of ongoing consent, that is, on the "awakening" of a perhaps "sleeping sovereign" who asserts the power to "alter and abolish" any and all existing forms? I shall consider these in turn.

---

[7] It is worth reading the opinion of the International Court of Justice upholding the right of Kosovo to declare its independence from Serbia but carefully refraining from according it any sweeping juridical significance. It is also worth noting that many countries have refrained from recognizing Kosovar independence, either on pure political grounds or because of fear of secessionist independence movements in their own countries. The most prominent example of the latter is surely Spain, which is adamantly opposed to any inklings of Catalan independence. See "International recognition of Kosovo," Wikipedia, https://shorturl.at/QS36J.

[8] I am much indebted to Jonathan Gienapp, "In Search of Nationhood at the Founding," *Fordham Law Review* 89 (2021): 1785–1786 at 1783.

[9] See Benedict Anderson, *Imagined Communities: Reflections on the Origin and Spread of Nationalism* (London: Verso, 1983).

7.2 DEFINING THE *DEMOS*

So let us turn to the first sentence of the Declaration and its presentation of what lawyers might call the "facts of the case." The very first sentence of the Declaration makes an astonishing declaration: There exists "one people" who not only wish, but are also presumptively entitled, "to dissolve the political bands which have connected them with another, and to assume among the powers of the earth, the separate and equal station to which the Laws of Nature and of Nature's God entitle them ..." The next paragraph is, in some sense, even more radical, for it asserts the "right of the People to alter or to abolish" any government whenever it has become destructive of the stipulated ends of protecting rights. Still, at no point does the Declaration offer any explicit description of the "one people" who are attempting, at least in the Declaration itself, to justify what Harvard (and British-born) historian David Armitage labels the "secession" of the various colonies from the existing framework of the British Empire. Whatever complexities were presented by seventeenth- and eighteenth-century disputes about the relative powers of parliament and monarchy with regard to their ability to speak for the collectivity of the British people, there was surely no agreement that settlers sent at the behest of the Crown to colonize the "new world" could throw off their loyalties and strike out on their own.

So the first task facing any serious reader of the Declaration is to figure out who in the world (quite literally) the authors are referring to in making their remarkable, even grandiose, claim of sovereign power. One possibility, especially for those readers who readily skip the first several paragraphs and immediately focus on the "long train of abuses" set out against King George III and his minions, is that "the people" are (or should it be "is"?) the set of all individuals who have suffered one or another oppression from the existing government. There are, however, two immediate problems with such a response. The first is that many – most? – of those suffering such oppression were enslaved persons, and the Declaration can scarcely be read, especially with an historically informed eye, as a declaration of their own freedom from oppression.

The second is that it may be quite a stretch to regard all of the "American patriots" as in fact being "oppressed." For starters, is "oppression" an "objective" or a "subjective" condition? The existence of many "Loyalists" who pledged their own fortunes and sacred honor to defending British sovereignty is certainly evidence, one might presume, for their own failure to feel oppressed.[10] Perhaps we are inclined to view this as a form of "false consciousness," for surely they *ought* to have felt oppressed? But then consider the fact that many enslaved persons and free blacks, whom we might well

---

[10] See, for example, the wonderful book by Maya Jasanoff, *Liberty's Exiles: American Loyalists in the Revolutionary World* (New York: Alfred A. Knopf, 2011).

assume *did* view themselves as oppressed, cast their lot with the British rather than those they might have perceived as slave owning aristocrats. This is also the case, incidentally, with many members of America's Indigenous Nations, who plausibly believed that the British settlers, if set free, would be even more rapacious than was the case under British rule. As already noted, however, it is not logically entailed, at least by the early paragraphs of the Declaration, that the perception (or reality) of oppression is a necessary – even if it is arguably a sufficient – condition to "alter and abolish" an existing political framework; Nonetheless, it surely helps, especially if one is looking for support from onlookers for the inevitable destabilization that attends even non-secessionist alteration and abolition.

But what may be most interesting about an emphasis on "oppression" alone is that it may be entirely orthogonal to any appeal to "nationhood" or "national identity" of the kind of sees evoked by both the French and the Warm Springs Reservation or, in fact, almost all "national liberation" struggles whose partisans might quote the Declaration. Libertarians like Randy Barnett are happy to read the Declaration, however controversially and even dubiously, as endorsing *individual* sovereignty quite devoid of membership in larger all-embracing communities.[11] That would be "methodological individualism" to the nth degree! All individuals presumably are entitled to imagine their own mode of achieving "life, liberty, or the pursuit of happiness." Perhaps that will require joining one or another community, but it is not clear how much loyalty is due any overarching polity or, more to the point, especially in contemporary terms, whether individuals view their own identity as fundamentally linked to the group making claims for independence (other, perhaps, than as victims of arbitrary oppression).

Gienapp quotes John Adams' argument that "the first 'collection' of authority" was an "agreement" among individuals "to form themselves into a *nation, people, community, or body politic.*"[12] But is not it obvious that the italicized words can have very different connotations, especially to a modern sensibility? Is a "people" necessarily a "nation" (or even a "community"), let alone a "body politic"? This, of course, is a key question for "multinational" polities, where the key question that must be resolved in order, perhaps, to avoid civil war, is how to blend disparate nations and communities into a single body politic.

It is conceivable that the only way of identifying a relevant "people" is territorial, that is to say, the set of individuals, whatever their backgrounds and attributes, who inhabit a given territory. Even here one obvious problem is that

---

[11] See Randy E. Barnett, "We the People: Each and Every One," *Yale Law Journal* 123 (2014): 2576.
[12] Gienapp, "In Search of Nationhood at the Founding," at 1791, quoting John Adams, A DEFENCE OF THE CONSTITUTION OF GOVERNMENT OF THE UNITED STATES OF AMERICA 6 (emphasis in original).

"territories" are not self-defining and often require reference to some political entity that claims "possession" of the land in question. Perhaps, for example, it is the pope, who in 1493 purported to determine which "explorers could claim foreign territory in the name of Christian monarchs and that such claims were legitimate because the inhabitants of the 'discovered' lands lacked European civilization."[13] One might doubt that the British explorers post-dating Henry VIII paid much attention to papal decrees, but certainly the American "settlers" all presented various "authorizations" from existing European rulers, even if the "New World" often featured conflict as to whose claims would dominate. Consider in this context the transformation of New Amsterdam – and Dutch origins – to New York with its celebration of the Duke of York. This was not the result of what might be viewed as a "free-will offering" by the Dutch; rather, as was so true of colonial America, it represented the triumph of British military power over a variety of hapless opponents, including other European rivals and, of course, numerous Indigenous Nations.[14] As John Marshall suggested in *Johnson* v. *M'Intosh*,[15] dealing with the conquest of Indigenous Nations by European settlers, the decisive principle could be summarized as "might makes legal right." The Nations certainly did not give their consent to what at times could be described as genocidal displacement. It did not matter.

The Declaration speaks only for those living within the thirteen colonies about to become states of the new United States of America, but, as the above paragraph makes clear, not for *all* territorial inhabitants. One can easily argue that most inhabitants of the territory did not, under any plausible theory, offer their active "consent." So the immediate issue then becomes whether (and how) a *portion* of those who are governed can claim to speak for the whole and bind those who did not (and, as a matter of fact, almost certainly *would* not) offer their consent to, for example, being enslaved or subjected to the limitless jurisdiction of "settlers" encroaching upon existing indigenous peoples with their own conceptions of sovereign authority. Or one can simply recall Abigail Adams' plaintive appeal to her husband to "remember the ladies" while imagining a presumptively new form of government and the brute fact that her appeal was wholly unsuccessful. Of course, males at the time were happy to offer theories of "virtual representation" that they believed should assuage any complaints offered by their wives, mothers, sisters, nieces, or, possibly, any other women. Similar theories could be offered, with greater plausibility, to explain the lack of participation rights by youngsters. But no one seriously offered theories of virtual representation to explain the subordination

---

[13] Mahmood Mamdani, *Neither Settler nor Native: The Making and Unmaking of Permanent Minorities* (Cambridge: Belknap Press, 2020), 5.
[14] See, for example, Bernard Bailyn's all too aptly named *The Barbarous Years: The Conflict of Civilizations, 1600–1675* (New York: Alfred A. Knopf, 2012).
[15] 21 U.S. 543 (1823).

of enslaved persons or Indigenous Nations. If they appeared in the Declaration at all, it was far more as perceived threats than as future members of the independent "nation" or "community."[16]

One can frame this problem within the context of the "constituent power" that frames any given "constituted" political order. Who shares in the "constituent power" and who does not?[17] Political theorists now regularly refer to the "boundaries problem" when discussing "democratic" political theory. Who is within a given set of boundaries and who, on the other hand, remains outside them? Even if one emphasizes only "literal" territorial boundaries, problems quickly emerge, as was obvious with regard to the controversy over how to count the 2020 census in the United States: Were noncitizens, let alone undocumented aliens living within the boundaries of the United States, to be counted as part of the population of "the United States"? The Trump administration was rebuffed on this point by a split decision of the United States Supreme Court, but the grounds were more technical than substantive. Similarly, the Court earlier rejected a claim by private citizens that the Texas legislature should not, when apportioning seats in the state legislature, count noncitizens as part of the basis of representation, given the fact that they have no vote for any public office in Texas. The Constitution itself, after all, sharply distinguishes between those who are counted as "full" residents and those who are not, including "Indians not taxed" and, most importantly, enslaved persons.

Justice Alito wrote a concurring opinion agreeing that Texas could not be forced to leave noncitizens out of their count when computing the number of represented Texans in any given district. But he left open the possibility that the state might nevertheless be constitutionally authorized to do so if it wished. The Constitution can easily be read as silent on this important question, as is true of so many other fundamental questions of what might be meant by "self-government" (or a "Republican Form of Government"). Why, then, should "sovereign states" not be able to decide this issue for themselves, free of interference from a federal judiciary claiming to enforce the Constitution? As I phrased the problem several years ago, however inelegantly, "Who Counts? (Sez Who?)."[18] *All* communities, from a local chess club to a mighty

---

[16] King George is accused of having "excited domestic insurrections amongst us, and has endeavoured to bring on the inhabitants of our frontiers, the merciless Indian Savages, whose known rule of warfare, is an undistinguished destruction of all ages, sexes and conditions." Is it really unlikely that the "domestic insurrections" are a reference to the possibility of slave rebellions, encouraged, perhaps, by British promises of freedom to those who will join them in trying to repress the American secessionists?

[17] There is, of course, an enormous literature on the notion of "constituent power." A useful short introduction is Martin Loughlin's chapter on the concept in *Against Constitutionalism?* (Cambridge: Harvard University Press, 2022), 77–86. For a fuller introduction, see Jose Colon-Rios, *Constituent Power and the Law* (Oxford: Oxford University Press, 2020).

[18] Sanford Levinson, "Who Counts? (Sez Who?)," *University of St. Louis Law Journal* 58.4 (2014): 937–987.

nation-state, can be conceived of as entities with their own membership committees. The one thing that can be said with confidence is that one cannot join simply by asserting one's desire to do so. That is to say, as an empirical reality there are almost never truly "open borders." They may be "thinkable" in the confines of a seminar room, but they are seemingly completely absent within the political and even social worlds that we in fact inhabit.

To be sure, political territory is not irrelevant for the Declaration's authors. It was issued in the name of the discrete colonies along the Atlantic Coast, the brand new "United States of America" (though the word "united" was left uncapitalized in at least some texts of the time), but common residence in a territory is quite different – or so one might think – from a genuinely shared sense of membership in a common sociocultural (and ultimately political) enterprise. Both John Adams and Thomas Jefferson viewed themselves, respectively, primarily as citizens of Massachusetts and Virginia, at least in 1776. Perhaps, according at least to Lin-Manuel Miranda, Alexander Hamilton, a nineteen-year-old immigrant from the West Indies, absent from the Convention that endorsed the Declaration, was already subordinating his New York identity to that of being an "American," but he would probably have been an anomaly. Was "independence" truly declared by a singular United States of America or, instead, by the delegates of the distinctly different colonies (now "states") joined in an alliance against the purported British tyrant? It is surely not irrelevant that the "first Constitution" of the new country was named the Articles of Confederation, treated in terms of most political theory of the time as announcing an alliance, almost always for military or economic reasons, against powerful outside threats.

One of the most powerful arguments against the Constitution of 1787 was offered by "Agrippa": "It is impossible, for one code of laws to suit Georgia and Massachusetts." He was one of those "Anti-federalists" described by Gienapp, who rejected the idea of an "American nation" and feared the "consolidated government" that he saw as being proffered by the cosmopolitan Philadelphians: "the idea of an uncompounded republic, on an average, one thousand miles in length, and eight hundred in breadth, and containing six millions of white inabitants [sic] all reduced to the same standard of morals, or habits, and of laws," complained James Winthrop ("Agrippa"), "is in itself an absurdity, and contrary to the whole experience of mankind."[19] One suspects that Agrippa's reservations would find a receptive audience today among many residents of the United States.

Twentieth-century America is, for better *and* worse, often linked to the specifically Wilsonian idea of "*national* self-determination," which surely referred to more than a common residence in a given land. Indeed, one cannot ignore the fact that Wilson was very definitely a Southerner in terms of his own personal

---

[19] Agrippa, No. 4, December 3, 1787, in Philip Kurland and Ralph Lerner, eds., *The Founders' Constitution* (Chicago: Chicago University Press, 1987), 1: 268.

background. His father, a Presbyterian minister, was an avid supporter of secession, and Wilson, probably the most white-supremacist president following Andrew Johnson (and until Donald Trump), certainly had his own nostalgia for the Lost Cause. Claims of the "nation" to "sovereign" independence, whether within the boundaries of the United States or in the various imperial systems dissolved by the consequences of world wars, was often linked to attempts to achieve ethnic homogeneity and hegemony, coupled not infrequently by ethnic cleansing or other transfers of population thought conducive to achieving the proper new identity as a self-governing people. Devotees of Wilsonianism should be reminded that another important theorist of national self-determination at the time was Carl Schmitt, who proclaimed that "democracy requires ... first homogeneity and second – if the need arises – elimination or eradication of heterogeneity."[20]

The most obvious – and brutal – example within the United States involves the fate of Indigenous Nations first exiled and then placed on "reservations." One should also consider in this context the fantasy of many sincere "anti-slavery" politicians, including Abraham Lincoln, that freedom would quickly be followed by the decision of freed blacks – who could not really be imagined as genuine "African Americans" – to accept the entreaties of the American Colonization Society to move abroad, an early version of what Mitt Romney, in the context of undocumented aliens, would call "self-deportation." Who is fit to join the club of true Americans has never been, shall we say, a "self-evident truth" even if one subscribes to a theory of equality regarding those who *are* let inside the club.

The Constitution claims to be "ordained" by the collective action of "We the People," but to this day there is no genuine consensus as to who comprises "the American people."[21] One possibility is ideological: Anyone (and everyone) can become American who is, in the language of American naturalization law, "attached to the principles of the Constitution." To be sure, it is not self-evident what these principles are. This was illustrated in the 1943 case *Schneiderman* v. *U.S.*,[22] where a bitterly divided Court held that a committed communist could at the same time manifest such "attachment." But the point is that any such discussion requires a focus on abstract principles and whether, for example, support of the "dictatorship of the proletarian" is congruent with the idea of a "Republican Form of Government." Nor are things made any easier if one says that "American identity" is achieved by ardent embrace of the "thin principles" enunciated in the Declaration, which one might well see as referring to "essentially contested concepts" that promote disputation and even war rather than serving as the basis of political settlement.

---

[20] Carl Schmitt, *The Crisis of Parliamentary Democracy*, trans. Ellen Kennedy (Cambridge: MIT Press, 1985), 9. I was reminded of this statement by Mark Tushnet (unpublished review, 2022).

[21] See especially the invaluable book by Rogers Smith, *Civic Ideals: Conflicting Visions of Citizenship in Us History* (New Haven and London: Yale University Press, 1999).

[22] See Sanford Levinson, *Constitutional Faith*, 2nd ed. (Princeton and Oxford: Princeton University Press, [1988] 2011), chapter 4.

There is no logical end to the number of persons who could plausibly claim to be attached to the principles of the Constitution (or the Declaration) and, therefore, eligible to join the American political community. That is, of course, not how we arrange our naturalization process. Not only must one spend five years first as a noncitizen presumably compliant with all relevant laws; far more important is that the United States in fact imposes quite stringent limits on the number of people who can enter the country in the first place. It is altogether irrelevant that supplicants for entry profess their devotion to what we would like to believe are our central ideological principles. First they must be let in, and anyone reading contemporary newspapers knows how arduous a process that can be. It is hornbook constitutional law that the Executive has great discretion over both the number of persons allowed entry in any given year; moreover, residents of specific countries can be selected out for special (dis)favor. The United States is certainly not exceptional in this regard, but it may be more difficult to justify immigration restrictions if one emphasizes more universalistic readings of the Declaration when defining "the people" in whose name secession (and independence) is being justified.

7.3 A "NEW AMERICAN NATION"

As Gienapp demonstrates, many important architects of the Declaration and, even more so, of the Constitution, were ardent nationalists, very much concerned with creating a "new American nation."[23] They recognized that sentiments like Agrippa's could prove fatal to any hopes for a flourishing United States of America, and they wanted to head them off at the pass. The Declaration only proclaims that we are "one people." It does not offer anything by way of argument as to why this should be thought to be true, other, of course, than the common oppression "we" are said to have suffered under King George. So consider in this context what is perhaps the most ambitious attempt to provide an answer to the question of national identity, John Jay's *Federalist* 2, which in 1787 described thusly the American polity:

Providence has been pleased to give this one connected country to one united people – a people descended from the same ancestors, speaking the same language, professing the same religion, attached to the same principles of government, very similar in their manners and customs, and who, by their joint counsels, arms and efforts, fighting side by side throughout a long and bloody war, have nobly established general liberty and independence.[24]

---

[23] I borrow this term from the distinguished series, *The New American Nation*, 42 vols. (New York: HarperCollins, 1957–2015), written by many of our most distinguished historians.
[24] Compare Jay's description of the basis of the American Union with that of his successor, Chief Justice Salmon P. Chase, in *Texas* v. *White* (1869), where he rejected the constitutional right of Texas to secede from the Union. According to Chase, the Union "grew out of common origin, mutual sympathies, kindred principles, similar interests, and geographical

Jay speaks, to be sure, of "attach[ment] to the same principles of government," but there is so much more that he asserts as well when defining what might be termed "Americanness." I have frequently quoted this passage, almost always to ridicule its central assertion that we were indeed a "united people" along the lines Jay is suggesting. To take the easiest example, the New Yorker was surely aware even by the time he was penning his essay that the Constitution issued by the Convention on September 17, 1787, had quickly been translated into Dutch in order that it be understood and intelligently voted upon by the descendants of settlers of the fittingly named New Amsterdam, whose English was apparently still imperfect.[25] A German-language translation was distributed to the roughly one-third Pennsylvanians who were still primarily German speakers. (Benjamin Franklin, who wanted English as the national language, was presumably not amused by this.)

It is also worth noting in this context that the American secessionists of 1776 very much hoped to enlist Quebec, added to the British Empire only in 1763 as a result of the Seven Years' (or French and Indian) War and therefore, presumably, open to entreaties by their abutting neighbors. Benedict Arnold, an important "patriot" before his decision to return to the Crown in 1777, led American troops in an attack on Quebec City in 1775, presumably a substitute, or at least a supplement, to efforts at "reasoned deliberation." Had the French living in Canada succumbed to the American invitation, that would obviously have immediately put on the table the issue of bilingualism, a central reality of modern Canada's public life, not to mention even broader questions of multiculturalism. Mark Anderson in his history of the episode suggests that one reason for resisting the Americans was the perception that the New Englanders especially were ravingly "anti-Papist" and scarcely likely to be accommodating to the Catholics living across the border. Perhaps Jay had some firm idea in mind of what he meant by the "same religion," but surely as the descendant of French Huguenots he was aware that Christianity itself was scarcely united and that different branches of Christianity were more than happy to exile (or to kill) one another in the name of the "one true faith." Nor, of course, did he pay any attention to the fact that there were actually some non-Christian settlers, not to mention those Indigenous Nations that were resistant to missionaries trying to elicit their conversion to Christianity.[26]

---

relations." 74 US 700, 725. One might ask, of course, if the Civil War demonstrated such commonalities or, instead, the proposition that the Union was always quite dicey because "the people" were never really "one."

[25] See Sanford Levinson, "What One Can Learn from Foreign-Language Translations of the U.S. Constitution," *Constitutional Commentary* 31 (2016): 55–70.

[26] See Mark R. Anderson, *The Battle for the Fourteenth Colony: America's War of Liberation in Canada, 1776–1776* (Lebanon: University Press of New England, 2013); Thomas A. Desjardin, *Through a Howling Wilderness: Benedict Arnold's March to Quebec, 1775* (New York: St. Martin's Griffin, 2007).

But focusing on language is simply the first step in "deconstructing" Jay's effort at describing the American people. Are readers supposed to think that Providence "gave" the so-called New World to the agents of the various European countries attempting to displace the Indigenous Nations who, after all, amply filled the territory? And, of course, Jay paid no attention to those people whose lot in life was to submit to the arbitrary rule of their "masters" who might, at any time, sell them – or perhaps even lose them while gambling – along with any children that enslaved parents might have. Ironically or not, Jay, as Chief Justice, would pen one of the great paeons to "popular sovereignty" in his opinion in *Chisholm* v. *Georgia*, which, among other things, sharply dismissed any claims to "sovereignty" by the state of Georgia itself. As every legal academic knows, however, Chisholm itself was overruled by the first post-Bill of Rights Amendment, and the current majority of the Supreme Court appears to believe not simply that "the American people" overturned a decision they (or "it") did not like, but also that *Chisholm* itself was wrongly decided. If one agrees, then Jay (and James Wilson, one of the most prominent Framers in Philadelphia before being named to the Court by Washington) were simply mistaken in their theory of "sovereignty" within the American setting, leaving one to wonder how they could make such an error (if error it was).[27] More likely, of course, is that the controversy over *Chisholm* simply reflected that there was in fact a deep cleavage among political elites – and, one assumes, the "American people" as well – as to the nature of their political identities. There was, one might suggest, no truly common "original public meaning" as to what it meant to be "an American" at any point during the "Founding period."

There was no singular "people" occupying the existing "American" territory that in 1776 stretched from Maine (still part of Massachusetts) to the southern border of Georgia, and that was more true almost literally every mile that one moved away from the Atlantic Coast. After all, one reason that many Indigenous Nations joined Great Britain in trying to suppress the American secessionists was that the "tyrannical" King George III had in 1763, as part of the Treaty of Paris ending the Seven Years' War, declared that there would be no British settlement beyond the Alleghany Mountains. To be sure, this was not intended to be a permanent recognition of firm borders between the British colonies and "sovereign" Indigenous Nations, but it was far better, or so many of the Nations believed, than the relentless move westward generated in part by land speculators like George Washington himself. Although almost never seriously taught, especially within American law schools, the United States had its own version of a "hundred years war" with

---

[27] I have elaborated my own doubts about the utility of the Court's use of "sovereignty" language in Sanford Levinson, "The Confusing Language of McCulloch v. Maryland: Did Marshall Really Know What He Was Doing (or Meant?)," *Arkansas Law Review* 7 (2019): 7–33.

7 "Popular Sovereignty"

a variety of Indigenous Nations who were not willing simply to submit to "American" hegemony.

Generally speaking, the Declaration is taught as part of the Whig tradition of American history. That is, it is supposed to encapsulate the very best of what we might even call the "American project," that is to say, a commitment to "life, liberty, and the pursuit of happiness" coupled with vigorous opposition, and attempts to hold accountable, would-be "tyrants" antagonistic to achieving the *telos* thought to be embedded in the words of the Declaration. Barack Obama was extremely fond of the trope "this is not who we are" when discussing one or another failing actually found in America today. He was not delusional: He did not deny, for example, that the United States engaged in torture in Iraq or that millions of Americans could not get life-saving medical care because of their economic circumstances. Rather, he suggested that there was an "ontological" America, so to speak, that would, if properly educated and motivated, come to realize that these defects violated our "essential" definition as Americans and, therefore, should be sloughed off.

This, of course, is part of the endless debate about slavery and its relationship to the Declaration. How, after all, could a slaveowner have penned the words of the Declaration without recognizing that the institution was simply incongruent with the description being offered? Most of us presumably want to reject Chief Justice Roger B. Taney's attempt to "save" Jefferson and his colleagues in *Dred Scott* by suggesting that they of course did not mean to include enslaved persons (or even the descendants of enslaved persons) in the category of "the People." It was, after all, a discrete group of "people" who were seceding (or rebelling). Unlike, say, Napoleon or Lenin, Washington and Jefferson were not engaged in a self-conscious project to conquer the entire world in behalf of the new ideology being set out in Philadelphia. What was wanted, after all, was *independence*, not the right to take over the entire British Empire and rule it, presumably in a far more enlightened fashion, from London. That limited aspiration is precisely what defines the project of "national self-determination." We are really not all alike, as some of the more naive descriptions of the "international human rights project" might sometimes suggest. If we were, then we would be aspiring to a single world government, with suitable degrees of subsidiarity that might allow us to confront such problems as global warming and the consequences of inequality. But that has, alas, become a utopian aspiration, not least because few people actually believe that we can (or even *should*) overcome our profound cultural differences.

Nations, defined in part by their idiosyncratic cultural attributes, do exist in the world we inhabit, even if not in what logicians call "all possible worlds." Indeed, I am often tempted to suggest that, as with many drugs and guns, we would all be better off without them. The costs of nationalism, demonstrated in so many different ways, may simply outweigh whatever putative benefits are thought to be attached to it. This is, after all, at the heart of critiques of "patriotism" offered by thinkers like Martha Nussbaum,[28] and George Kateb,[29] at least if "patriotism" requires commitment to anything beyond a broad set of universalistic ideas. Should one learn to celebrate the Fourth of July, assuming one *does* want to celebrate it, as simply the forerunner of a move toward universalistic solidarity and, ideally, world government? Or should it continue to be celebrated as the birthday of our *own* polity, cherished for its differences from many others around the world even as we might regard those other polities as legitimate and worth respect in their own right because that is just what pluralism requires?

But then we approach a central paradox: If the United States is a distinct polity on the basis of something other than the universalistic values seemingly endorsed by the Declaration, then how exactly, and with what justification, did that come about? One plausible answer is simply to endorse the view that Carl Lotus Becker and others presented of the Declaration during the Progressive Era. That is, it was written as carefully conceived propaganda to elicit support for a venture that would have perhaps appeared less enticing had it frankly been presented as an attempt to shore up the economic interests of colonial elites or, even more so, of slaveowners worried about certain trends in the mother country concerning the legitimacy of the "peculiar institution"? This, of course, is at the heart of the acrimonious controversy over the "1619 Project,"[30] and the suggestion by Nikole Hannah-Jones that at least a partial explanation for the willingness of some Virginians to join in the secessionist movement was the perceived protection of slavery that independence would provide. Far better to proclaim a universalistic ideology and ignore potentially uncomfortable realities (though it is certainly possible that France would have supported the nascent United States in any case once it was persuaded that the "patriots" actually had a chance of prevailing against the British enemy).

This is simply to return to the classic distinction between "home rule," described in the language of "popular sovereignty," and "who should rule at home," which makes sense as a controversy only if one recognizes that there was in fact no "united people." Independence would bring in its wake multiple conflicts over the actualities of "popular" rule. *Federalist* 10 is in its own way a response to the optimistic (or Schmittian) account set out in *Federalist* 2. Instead, James Madison sets out extremely vividly all of the

---

[28] Martha Nussbaum, "Patriotism and Cosmopolitanism," *Boston Review*, October/November 1994, available at: www.oneworlduv.com/wp-content/uploads/2011/06/patriotism_cosmopolitanism.pdf. See also the collection later published, which included a number of responses to Nussbaum's essay, Martha Nussbaum, "Patriotism and Cosmopolitanism," in *For Love of Country: Debating the Limits of Patriotism* (Boston: Beacon Press, 1996), 2–20.
[29] George Kateb, "Is Patriotism a Mistake?" *Social Research* 67 (2000): 901–924.
[30] See generally, Nikole Hannah-Jones, ed., *The 1619 Project: A New Origin Story* (London: One World, 2021).

ways that "the people" were in fact divided into factions defined by their antagonism to one another. It is well to be reminded at suitable length of our de facto heterogeneity, beyond the "latent causes of faction" that are "sown in the nature of man." Instead of Jay's reference to a common religion, we read of "[a] zeal for different opinions concerning religion" and, of course, the relationship between religion and government itself. There are always likely to be "different leaders ambitiously contending for pre-eminence and power" and therefore contribute to "divid[ing] mankind into parties, inflam[ing] them with mutual animosity," and therefore making it ever more likely to "vex and oppress each other than to co-operate for their common good. So strong is this propensity of mankind to fall into mutual animosities," Madison asserts, "that where no substantial occasion presents itself, the most frivolous and fanciful distinctions have been sufficient to kindle their unfriendly passions and excite their most violent conflicts."[31]

But then Madison goes on to offer an analysis that has led some to identify him as a proto-Marxist: "But the most common and durable source of factions has been the various and unequal distribution of property. Those who hold and those who are without property have ever formed distinct interests in society." Class struggle is a constant: "A landed interest, a manufacturing interest, a mercantile interest, a moneyed interest [antagonistic to debtors], with many lesser interests, grow up of necessity in civilized nations, and divide them into different classes, actuated by different sentiments and views." The assertion that we are "one people" seems analogous to what Gerald Rosenberg, in another context, labeled a "hollow hope." Indeed, Madison was obsessed by the reality of factional division, and we are to this day debating the plausibility of his ostensible "solutions," whether the "extended republic" or his seeming faith that federal elections, unlike state ones, would elect leaders with sufficient civic virtue to govern in the common interest rather than mirror the selfish desires of many (most?) of their constituents. It is hard at this time to place much credence in the Madisonian nostrums. Instead, "polarization" has become the most operative word to describe the American polity; by definition, that denies the existence of "one people" save in the most limited territorial sense that would treat the Hatfields and the McCoys as "one people" albeit involved in endless deadly feuding with one another. And it is perhaps telling that Madison's list of contributions to our heterogeneity and factionalism did not include race or ethnicity. One can easily suspect that it did not occur to him that the United States would, at least on occasion, become an entry point for those who might even be described as "the wretched refuse" of all of Europe, let alone the other continents.

[31] Alexander Hamilton, James Madison, and John Jay, *The Federalist Papers*, ed. Clinton Rossiter (New York: New American Library, 1961), 79, and https://avalon.law.yale.edu/18th_century/fed10.asp.

7.4 THE SOVEREIGN PEOPLE(S)

But recall once more that the claim of the Declaration is not only that the "one people" of the British colonies have a right to secede and to enter the international system as a new "United States," but also that "the people" retain a right to "alter and abolish" any existing system of government whenever that is thought to be conducive to their overall happiness. "Americans" were quick to act on that ostensible promise. Vermont applied in 1777 to join the new Union, but, perhaps not surprisingly, the states of New York and New Hampshire were considerably less enamored of secessionism when applied to their own polities, and Vermont was not accepted into the Union until 1791. Christian Fritz's *American Sovereigns: The People and America's Constitutional Tradition Before the Civil War* (2007) is an invaluable reminder of the attraction that "starting over" had for many Americans imbued with their understanding of the Declaration. Sometimes this meant, as in Kentucky, that new "conventions," whether or not specifically authorized by the state's constitution, could be summoned into being and rewriting the fundamental law for the state. Other times, as with Vermont, one could see unsuccessful efforts to create brand new states, including Franklin and Transylvania. It is simply a mistake to assume that the Constitution stilled all dreams of further exercises of popular sovereignty. Our fixation on the single national Constitution has often blinded us to the valuable insights to be gained from looking closely at what John Dinan calls *The American State Constitutional Tradition*, not to mention what might be learned from taking "popular constitutionalism" seriously.

William Lloyd Garrison not only burnt the Constitution. He also called for "no Union with slaveholders," which implied seceding from the Union established on the basis of a "Covenant with Death and Agreement with Hell" and starting over again. At the other end of the spectrum, of course, were the secessionists of 1860–1861, but they, too, could claim to be loyal followers of the Declaration. Consider only the statue that graces (if that is the proper word) the south entrance to the Texas State Capitol even today and memorializes both the Confederate dead and their leader Jefferson Davis:

DIED FOR STATE RIGHTS GUARANTEED UNDER THE CONSTITUTION
THE PEOPLE OF THE SOUTH, **ANIMATED BY THE SPIRIT OF** 1776, TO PRESERVE THEIR RIGHTS, WITHDREW FROM THE FEDERAL COMPACT IN 1861. THE NORTH RESORTED TO COERCION. THE SOUTH, AGAINST OVERWHELMING NUMBERS AND RESOURCES, FOUGHT UNTIL EXHAUSTED.[32]

---

[32] See generally Sanford Levinson, *Written in Stone: Public Monuments in Changing Societies*, 2nd ed. (Durham: Duke University Press, 2018), on the attempts of all political regimes to use public space in order to inculcate regime loyalty and a particular version of relevant history (emphasis added).

It is obvious that "the Constitution," for the devotees of the Lost Cause, included the Declaration and its instantiation of "the spirit of 1776." One might be tempted to describe the Southern invocation of it as a desecration, but, as Samuel Johnson and other skeptics about American independence suggested, it is not clear that the Confederate argument was, so to speak, "unprecedented."[33] To be sure, Alexander Stephens articulated what James Madison and others did not, whether out of conviction or simply prudence, a commitment to white supremacy and consequent black subordination.[34] It is tempting to say that Stephens did not represent "who we are," and it is certainly true that Stephens did not speak for *all* Americans, including, most importantly, the 16th President of the United States. But that is simply to repeat the empirical truth that the United States, in 1861 as in 1776, could scarcely be described as "one people" in a way that erased painful questions about the actual meaning of "popular sovereignty" as implied, even if not always clearly indicated, in the Declaration.

7.5 CREEDAL FAITH (AND ITS ABSENCE)

It is often suggested that what constitutes American exceptionalism is the emphasis "we" place on certain creedal documents and commitments in lieu of other unifying characteristics commonly found in more typical "nation-states." As someone who avidly wishes a new constitutional convention to engage in radical reform of what I consider to be significantly defective Constitution, I am often met with the riposte that it is the only thing that is holding our fragile country together and, therefore, we must continue to generate "constitutional faith," whether truly merited or not.[35] It is precisely because Madison – and not Jay – is a better guide to the actualities of American society that we sometimes desperately search for what might unify us. If Jay were truly correct, either then or now, then we could surely return to cultivating our own gardens and not feel the need to engage in anguished conversations about the very survival of the United States as a functioning constitutional republic. Madison seemed ultimately to suggest, in *Federalist* 49, that "veneration" for the Constitution could save us – and one of the things we needed to be saved from was the Jeffersonian support for new conventions or even significant movements directed to constitutional "reform" on the basis that the existing Constitution is in some ways radically defective. Is "the Constitution" enough? It was not for Lincoln, notably, who ostentatiously dated the formation of the Union in 1776 and not 1787, and, Noah Feldman

[33] "How is it that we hear the loudest *yelps* for liberty among the drivers of negroes?" wrote Johnson in *Taxation: No Tyranny* (1775), available at: www.samueljohnson.com/tnt.html.
[34] See Alexander Stephens, "Cornerstone Speech," 1861, available at: www.battlefields.org/learn/primary-sources/cornerstone-speech.
[35] See Levinson, Constitutional Faith.

suggests,[36] came to the ultimate realization that the Constitution was irredeemably "broken" and that the American nation (or, at least, Lincoln's conception of it) had to be saved by going beyond constitutional limits. The Constitution was a frame around the true "apple of gold," which was the Declaration to which he frequently recurred.

But it should be obvious that the Declaration does not solve the problem of deep pluralism any more than does the Constitution itself. If we are to be a "light unto the nations," it will be because we will in fact figure out a way to achieve a functioning, stable, and even inspiring way that a quite wildly diverse set of peoples can live with one another peacefully and even with mutual respect. It is not at all clear that the Declaration itself will provide any real help in attaining that goal, especially if one reads the emphasis on "equality" and protection of "rights" to apply to the various groups that in fact compromise the constitutional order. We are on our own, having to forge a future that could not possibly have been envisioned by any but a true utopian (or, possibly, dystopian) in 1776.

---

[36] Noah Feldman, *The Broken Constitution: Lincoln, Slavery, and the Refounding of America* (New York: Farrar, Straus and Giroux, 2021).

8

Slavery and the Declaration

A Reinterpretation

Richard Newman

Perhaps more than any other document in American history, the Declaration of Independence captures both the triumph and trauma of the nation's perennial struggle against racial injustice. While it was once viewed by Americans (including abolitionists) as the liberating heartbeat of freedom in the United States, recent generations of both scholars and citizens see the Declaration through the prism of slaveholding hypocrisy. How could so many American Founders proclaim freedom as a national value while maintaining slavery after 1776? Indeed, it is hard to imagine a time when the Declaration stood as an unsullied ode to American liberty. But when Cornell historian Carl Becker wrote his classic study of the Declaration in 1922, racial slavery rated only brief analysis. In fact, Becker viewed slavery as a sidelight to the Declaration's ultimate importance as a vehicle of national independence and individual freedom.[1]

Even as scholars offered more sophisticated examinations of the Declaration through much of the twentieth century, Becker's perspective hovered over them. The Declaration and its era could still be understood apart from deeper meditations on race, slavery, and black struggles for freedom. As Thad Tate has noted, when Benjamin Quarles published his seminal book *The Negro in the American Revolution* (1961), "the idea of a book length treatment of the subject" took mainstream "white reviewers somewhat by surprise."[2] A decade later, Kurtz and Hutson's seminal collection, *Essays on the American Revolution*, contained no chapters on race, slavery, or African Americans. With contributions by Bernard Bailyn, Edmund Morgan, William Mcloughlin,

---

[1] Carl Becker, *The Declaration of Independence* (New York: Harcourt, 1922).
[2] See Tate's "Forward" to the 1996 edition of Benjamin Quarles classic work, *The Negro in the American Revolution* (Chapel Hill: University of North Carolina Press for the Institute of Early American History and Culture, 1961).

and other luminaries, the book ranged over such key topics as ideology, religion, and violence but offered no new insights on the Founders and slavery.[3]

To be sure, the modern Civil Rights struggle inspired a dissenting tradition of scholarship about American racial sins dating back to the Revolution. Scholars ranging from Quarles to David Brion Davis looked anew at the Declaration as an apt embodiment of America's Janus-faced founding.[4] Yet the nation's Bicentennial in 1976, and America's final Cold War struggles against the Soviet Union afterwards, mitigated such critiques in mainstream scholarship. Even as they acknowledged slavery's importance, both Garry Wills and Jay Fliegelman agreed that the Declaration still served as a powerful expression of American liberty.[5]

However, in the twenty-first century, it has been virtually impossible to study the Declaration (or the broader Revolutionary era) without confronting slavery. Take Eric Foner's monumental *Give Me Liberty!*, perhaps the leading textbook for American undergraduates, which features an entire section on the single question: "What was the impact of the Revolution on slavery?" Though Foner highlights the Declaration's significance in looming anti-slavery struggles, he concludes that radical dissent by black activists and white reformers may have been more important in pushing abolition forward.[6] Other distinguished scholars echo this view. Robin Kelley and Earl Lewis' well-regarded text *To Make Our World Anew: A History of African Americans*, highlights black struggles for freedom as perhaps the most "revolutionary" part of the founding era.[7]

This notion seems more entrenched than ever. As Ibram X. Kendi has recently argued, the Declaration offered soaring rhetoric about human freedom, only to "criminalize" black activists who sought it (as runaways seeking liberty under British rule).[8] Kendi is hardly the last word on the matter – other scholars have continued to picture the Declaration as a ramifying document through time and space.[9] Yet Kendi's interpretation speaks to the powerful sense of racial

---

[3] Stephen G. Kurtz and James H. Hutson, *Essays on the American Revolution* (Chapel Hill: University of North Carolina Press, 1973).

[4] David Brion Davis, *The Problem of Slavery in the Age of Revolution, 1770–1823* (New York: Cornell University Press, 1976).

[5] Garry Wills, *Inventing America: Jefferson's Declaration of Independence*, reprint ed. (New York, Knopf, 2018); and Jay Fliegelman, *Declaring Independence* (Palo Alto: Stanford University Press, 1993).

[6] Eric Foner, *Give Me Liberty!*, 5th ed. (New York: W. W. Norton & Company, 2017), 223–229.

[7] See Robin D. G. Kelley and Earl Lewis, eds., *To Make Our World Anew: A History of African Americans to 1880, Volume One: A History of African Americans to 1800* (Oxford: Oxford University Press, 2000), quotes at 102–103.

[8] Ibram X. Kendi, *Stamped at the Beginning: A Definitive History of Racist Ideas in America* (New York: Nation Books, 2016).

[9] For worldwide impacts of the Declaration, see David Armitage, *The Declaration of Independence: A Global History* (Cambridge: Harvard University Press, 2008); for enduring cultural impacts in America – and efforts to reimagine the Declaration – see Danielle Allen's trenchant *Our Declaration* (New York: Liveright Publishing, 2014).

reckoning that has reverberated throughout the historical profession in recent years, compelling scholars to re-examine the entire foundation of American history. Indeed, in the era of Black Lives Matter, it is no longer possible to read the Declaration without focusing directly on the "glaring double-standard," as Leslie Alexander and Michelle Alexander put it in *The 1619 Project*, of both slavery and racism in the nation's founding. Drawing on recent scholarship on slave rebellion in the Caribbean during the Age of Revolutions, they argue that "the Haitian act of independence [in 1804]" was a more powerful expression of human liberation because it "radically upended the basic premise of white supremacy" undergirding Western culture.[10]

As we approach the 250th anniversary of the Declaration, just where does this leave us? What was the Declaration's relationship to slavery and emancipation in its own time and beyond? Somewhat ironically, the word "slavery" does not actually appear in the final Declaration's roughly 1,300 words. Yet as this essay shows, slavery played a critical role in nearly every aspect of the Declaration's creation and reception in Revolutionary American society. It also inspired generations of abolitionist struggle after 1776. For black as well as white Americans, it was a powerful statement about human liberty. Still, the Declaration remained a fraught document precisely because it promised a brand of freedom and equality that many (white) Americans were reluctant to endorse. That included the Declaration's main author, Thomas Jefferson, who continued to meditate on (and even oppose) the deeper meaning of an American egalitarianism he thought was self-evident. Down to the Civil War, the Declaration signified America's struggle against slavery and racial oppression – as well as the backlash against taking its grand words literally.

8.1 SLAVERY AND THE DECLARATION: AN OVERVIEW

When the Continental Congress created a committee to craft the Declaration on June 10, 1776, it hoped that the five men given the charge would build an unimpeachable case for American independence. The committee (John Adams, Ben Franklin, Thomas Jefferson, Robert R. Livingston, and Roger Sherman) ultimately produced a document that captured slavery's complex and shifting place in American politics and society. It could hardly have been otherwise. A super-majority of men in the Second Continental Congress were slaveholders – including northern as well as southern representatives – and three of the five people on the Declaration's committee owned human beings before the Revolution began: Jefferson inherited several dozen enslaved people from his father and then acquired well over a hundred more bonds people after

---

[10] Leslie Alexander and Michelle Wallace, "Fear," in Nikole Hannah-Jones, et al., eds., *The 1619 Project,* rev. ed. (New York: One World Publishers, 2021), especially 100–102 and 108–110. On the Haitian rebellion, see also Laurent Dubois, *Avengers of the New World* (Cambridge: Belknap, 2004).

marrying Martha Wayles in 1774; Franklin owned five enslaved people during his lifetime (never liberating any of them, even as he gravitated towards abolition); and Robert R. Livingston was one of the largest slaveholders in colonial New York.[11] While neither Adams nor Sherman owned enslaved people, human bondage was not far from their lives either: Adams' wife, Abigail, came from a slaveholding Massachusetts family, while Sherman had several slave-trading colleagues in Connecticut.[12] Racial slavery was often in full view of the men making the Declaration. As Jefferson wrote about human liberty in Philadelphia, he was waited on by Robert Hemings, an enslaved teenager he brought from Virginia.[13]

But slavery framed the Declaration in myriad other ways, too.[14] Indeed, the list of British "oppressions" and grievances outlined in the main body of the Declaration extended critiques about American "enslavement" to Great Britain dating back over a decade. By the time Jefferson began crafting the Declaration, he and other colonists were well versed in the rhetorical uses of slavery discourses in transatlantic politics. As Jefferson argued in his 1774 *Summary View* pamphlet, there was little doubt in colonial minds that British officials had undertaken a "deliberate and systematical plan of reducing us to slavery."[15] The Declaration told a candid world that colonists' right to rebellion against imperial slavery was not merely justified but self-evident.

Colonial opposition to imperial slavery flowed not just from imperial politics but racial realities evident across American society. For rebelling colonists saw the effects of chattel slavery on a daily basis – the oppressive power of one individual over another, the lack of agency associated with racial bondage, and the sense that servile beings were literally tools of slaveholders. Thus, in their critiques of empire, patriot leaders referred to the palpable qualities of racial bondage – chains, shackles, and other instruments of physical oppression they hoped to avoid. The Suffolk Resolves, adopted by Massachusetts representatives in September 1774 and then rushed to the First Continental Congress, argued that removing the "shackles" of imperial bondage was essential to American freedom. Such allusions only made sense in a world where enslaved

---

[11] On Jefferson's lifelong link to slavery, see most recently John Boles, *Jefferson, Architect of American Liberty* (New York: Basic, 2017); on the Founders and slavery, among other books see David Waldstreicher, *Runaway America: Ben Franklin, Slavery, and The American Revolution* (New York: Hill and Wang, 2004).

[12] By one count, thirty-four of forty-seven people who signed the Declaration were slaveholders. See Douglas Egerton, *Death or Liberty: African Americans and Revolutionary America* (New York: Oxford University Press, 2009).

[13] On the Hemings family, see Annette Gordon Reed's epic book, *The Hemingses of Monticello* (New York: W. W. Norton & Company, 2008).

[14] Bernard Bailyn, *The Ideological Origins of the American Revolution* (Cambridge: Belknap Press of Harvard University Press, 1967).

[15] Jefferson, *Summary View Summary View of the Rights of British America* (Williamsburg and London, 1774), 18.

people themselves were shackled and chained in bondage.[16] As the Declaration boldly asserted, this was the captive condition colonists revolted against. It is hard to imagine the Declaration without the foils of racial and imperial bondage as a backdrop.

Enslaved peoples' uprisings in the Atlantic world may also have framed the Declaration. While Jefferson's call to revolution as a just remedy for human oppression had many intellectual antecedents in British and European thought (from Locke to Rousseau), there were more specific models in his world. Indeed, the Age of Revolution began in the 1760s with major slave rebellions in British Jamaica and Dutch Berbice. Reported on widely in the Atlantic press, these uprisings frightened slaveholders across imperial regimes. They also offered a vivid picture of the human struggle for liberty in the face of imperial slavery.

That became clear in the wake of Tacky's Rebellion.[17] Launched in Jamaica in the Spring of 1760, the uprising was led by interconnected groups of freedom fighters who attacked hundreds of British sugar plantations over a six month period. News reports circulating across Atlantic society (including papers in colonial Boston, New York, and Philadelphia) noted that rebels wanted an end to slavery itself. Jamaican masters rejected any truce that would end both the uprising and Caribbean bondage. Though the British military eventually defeated the rebels, the threat of slave uprisings continued in Jamaica and other parts of the British Caribbean into the 1770s.[18] If one lesson of Tacky's revolt was that British officials were ruthless supporters of racial bondage, another was that black rebels had shown the vulnerabilities of the empire to colonists around the Atlantic world. In this way, we can read the Declaration of Independence not just as the culmination of American efforts to end imperial bondage but also as a nod to the impact of slave rebellion as a liberating force in Atlantic society.

This brings us to the third way that slavery impacted the Declaration. For Jefferson's alarms about black flight at the start of the war served as a further justification of independence from Great Britain. As he noted in his list of grievances, British officials had encouraged enslaved people to flee bondage as a way to undermine the American cause. Far from a lone complaint, Jefferson and others returned to the problem of black restiveness throughout the war. Why did so many African Americans run to British forces? (Jefferson believed that thousands of enslaved people fled bondage, though scholars estimate that 60,000–100,000 African Americans ran away during the war.)[19]

---

[16] See the Massachusetts Resolves in the "Supplement" to the *Massachusetts Gazette*, September 15, 1774.
[17] Vincent Brown, *Tacky's Rebellion: The Story of an Atlantic Slave War* (Cambridge: Belknap Press of Harvard University Press, 2021).
[18] Trevor Burnard, *Jamaica in the Age of the American Revolution* (Philadelphia: University of Pennsylvania Press, 2020).
[19] Cassandra Pybus, "Jefferson's Faulty Math: The Question of Slave Defections in the American Revolution," *William and Mary Quarterly*, Third Series, 62.2 (April 2005): 243–264.

By interrogating black allegiance in wartime, Jefferson and other Founders tripped over the idea at the center of the Declaration: that freedom was a principle oppressed people would risk their lives to achieve. Jefferson's great friend James Madison worried about black uprising at the start of the war after hearing from one correspondent that enslaved people in Charleston, South Carolina, planned to revolt for their freedom. As still another Virginian explained, enslaved people "entertained ideas that the present contest was for obliging us to give them their liberty."[20]

Thus, in a roundabout way, the Declaration actually recognized African Americans as "Revolutionary Citizens," as Earl Lewis has put it: freedom-seeking figures who could both alter the fate of American Independence and clarify the broader moral and philosophical meaning of the American Revolution.[21] Over and against many white patriots' opposition, blacks charted their own path to liberty. African Americans' alliance with British soldiers and generals symbolized their effort to turn the war into a battle over black freedom. Responding to Lord Dunmore's freedom proclamation of November 1775, African Americans flooded British lines. A former royal governor in Virginia, Lord Dunmore (John Murray) knew well colonial whites' fear of black restiveness. When he raised the Ethiopian Regiment, a black military unit comprised of several hundred former enslaved people, Dunmore stuck a revolutionary motto on the front of black soldiers' uniforms: "Liberty to Slaves." White Virginians warned blacks away from British forces and set up patrols to capture African Americans attempting to flee from slavery. But this hardly stopped black flight. By war's end, roughly 12,000 African Americans served with British forces and several thousand black Loyalists escaped with departing Redcoats. As soldiers and freedom fighters, former enslaved people made clear that they saw liberty very much as Jefferson did: a birthright condition.[22]

On the American side, too, African Americans used the war to win freedom. Even before British officials offered liberty to enslaved people in the colonial South, black New Englanders used Revolutionary rhetoric to earn liberty from patriot slaveholders. By June 1775, nearly 10 percent of the colonial forces facing British regulars at the Battle of Bunker Hill in Boston were black, including several soldiers who had been promised freedom by their Massachusetts masters. Though enslaved blacks were soon barred from Continental forces, some state regiments linked emancipation to African American military service. In 1778, the First Rhode Island Regiment included perhaps 200 enslaved people who had been promised freedom for joining the war effort. By war's

---

[20] William Bradford to James Madison, July 10, 1775, in *Founders Online*: https://tinyurl.com/59kad3r6.

[21] Lewis, "Revolutionary Citizens," chapter 3 in Kelley and Lewis, eds., *To Make Our World Anew*, 103–168.

[22] On Dunmore's Proclamation and black troops in British forces, see Egerton, *Death or Liberty*.

8 Slavery and the Declaration

end, roughly 5,000 African Americans had joined American forces, using their military service as an egalitarian claim on the new nation.[23]

Which brings us to a fourth way that slavery collided with the Declaration: In his initial draft, Jefferson attacked British officials who rejected colonial efforts to curb the overseas slave trade. Jefferson accused the King and his minions of *"suppressing every legislative attempt to prohibit or to restrain this execrable commerce" in various American colonies*. This section of the Declaration was deleted by the Continental Congress, much to the chagrin of Jefferson (Adams also lamented its absence). Some leaders in the Continental Congress thought that Jefferson's accusation was too harsh – and, coming from slaveholder like Jefferson, that it would harm the American cause globally.

Yet the draft paragraph on the slave trade illuminated rising American concerns with British attacks on the hypocritical nature of the patriot cause. Stung by British accusations that colonial slaveholders did not sanction African American liberty, Americans lashed out at British support of slavery in the first place. Jefferson wondered how the British King could justify the "cruel" slave trade in African captives. This was not the first time that Jefferson or American colonists broached the idea of ending the slave trade. In December 1774, the Continental Congress suspended the trade as part of a boycott of British trade.[24] Individual colonies-cum-states followed suit. In doing so, they heeded calls by Atlantic reformers such as Anthony Benezet and Benjamin Rush, who believed that slave-trade abolition was a necessary precursor to domestic emancipation. In his widely circulated 1773 pamphlet *An Address to the Inhabitants of the British Settlements* on the rising anti-slavery cause, Rush urged colonial legislatures to ban slave trading as the opening salvo in a war on slavery itself. "The first thing I would recommend to put a stop to slavery in this country," he observed, "is to leave off importing slaves."[25] When British officials opposed such bans, Rush, Franklin, Jefferson, and others attacked the empire as hypocritical. Jefferson hoped to use British support of the slave trade as a way to undercut imperial standing in the Revolutionary world.

But Jefferson and other colonists had ulterior motives in espousing slave-trade abolition. During the 1760s and 1770s, as slave uprisings swept across the Atlantic world, whites claimed that African people were inherently rebellious. Some American slaveholders thought that reducing the number of African captives would reduce rebellions (some anti-slave-trading advocates also believed that a shortage of slaves would boost the value of human chattels in colonial America). Thus Jefferson's deleted paragraph on the slave trade was

---

[23] On black troops in American forces, see especially Judith L. Van Buskirk, *Standing in Their Own Light: African American Patriots in the American Revolution* (Norman: University of Oklahoma Press, 2017)
[24] Christian McBurney, "The First Efforts to Limit the African Slave Trade," *Journal of the American Revolution* (September 15, 2020), online at: https://tinyurl.com/k5zb6hrz.
[25] Benjamin Rush, *An Address to the Inhabitants of the British Settlements, on the Slavery of the Negroes in America* (Philadelphia, 1773), 19.

much more than an indictment of British hypocrisy. It flowed from American slaveholders' longstanding fears of black uprising.

8.2 ANTI-SLAVERY SENTIMENT AND THE DECLARATION

Here we come to the Declaration and American slavery itself. As Jefferson's deleted paragraph on the slave trade showed, he and other American leaders were well aware of anti-slavery arguments circulating throughout Atlantic culture. This sense of awareness framed not just the rhetorical uses of (anti-) slavery discourses in the Revolutionary era – for instance, condemning British officials for "enslaving" American colonists – but the deeper meaning of liberty to the American cause. Indeed, the Declaration was aimed not only at rationalizing revolution (or separating from the empire); it also valorized a new type of republican governance based on universal human liberty. According to the Declaration, freedom was part and parcel of American national identity and could never be separated from it.

Many Americans (black as well as white) saw the Declaration as an anti-slavery and egalitarian document. When James Forten, a free black teenager, first heard the Declaration read out publicly at the Pennsylvania statehouse in July 1776, he thought the words applied to him, too. Forten volunteered for the American Navy as a powder boy. After the war, he became a leading abolitionist (eventually influencing William Lloyd Garrison in the 1830s). Throughout his life, he fought to bring the principles of the Declaration – "all men are created equal" – to fruition in American society.[26] In this way, Forten spoke for many reformers who saw the Declaration as an elegant statement about the nation's highest ideals: Freedom and justice for all.

If one thinks of the Declaration in this way, it is not merely because of Jefferson's felicitous phrasing but because it drew from the same stream of ideas about human freedom circulating across Revolutionary society. As Jefferson famously put it, the Declaration was an "an expression of the American mind."[27] But that collective mind included black as well as white commentary on liberty. For instance, enslaved people in Massachusetts petitioned colonial officials for universal freedom in 1773 and 1774, prefiguring some of the same broad claims about birthright liberty that Jefferson would make. One freedom petition to Massachusetts Governor Thomas Gage asserted boldly that enslaved Bostonians had "in common with other men, a natural right to be free, and ... that no person can have any just claim to their services unless by the laws of the land they have forfeited them."[28] Caesar Sarter,

---

[26] On Forten, see Julie Winch, *A Gentleman of Color: The Life of James Forten* (New York: Oxford University Press, 2002).
[27] See Boles, *Jefferson*, 27.
[28] See the petition to Thomas Gage in June 1774, reprinted at the Massachusetts Historical Society website: https://shorturl.at/y8DPq.

8 Slavery and the Declaration

an enslaved man in Newburyport, Massachusetts, made similar claims, castigating Americans for the "gross heinousness of reducing to ... slavery a free people." Only when Americans embraced universal freedom, Sarter asserted, would their cause fully justified.[29]

Abolitionists made similar arguments. Before the Revolution, Anthony Benezet linked the freedom struggles of American colonists and enslaved people.[30] "At a time when the general rights and liberties of mankind, and the preservation of those valuable privileges transmitted to us from our ancestors, are become so much the subjects of universal consideration," he began his 1766 pamphlet, *A Caution and Warning to the Great Britain and Her Colonies*,

can it be an inquiry indifferent to any, how many of those who distinguish themselves as the Advocates of Liberty, remain insensible and inattentive to the treatment of thousands and tens of thousands of our fellow-men, who, from motives of avarice, and the inexorable degree of tyrant custom, are at this very time kept in the most deplorable state of slavery, in many parts of the British Dominions.[31]

Here and elsewhere, Benezet anticipated ideas that ended up in the Declaration.

Indeed, by 1776, the distance between the world of anti-slavery protest and the world of colonial protest narrowed considerably. Leaders of the revolutionary cause – John Adams, Ben Franklin, Patrick Henry, Benjamin Rush – were quite familiar with black calls for liberty and abolitionist appeals for universal human freedom. Unsurprisingly, Jefferson nodded towards anti-slavery ideas in the draft Declaration, using words and phrases that had long been part of Benezet's lexicon. In his widely circulated 1771 pamphlet on slavery, Benezet argued that England was not an *"enlightened Christian country"* but rather a perpetrator of heinous crimes against a *"distant"* people in Africa who were subjected to the most "cruel methods used in carrying on ... the Slave trade." "When, and how, have these oppressed people forfeited their liberty," Benezet demanded to know? "Does not justice loudly call for its being restored to them? Have they not the same right to demand it, as any of us should have, if we had been violently snatched by pirates from our native land?"[32] Similarly, Jefferson's draft Declaration argued that *"the CHRISTIAN king of Great Britain"* had *"waged cruel war against human nature itself, violating its most sacred rights of life & liberty."* As he put it in terms Benezet would have recognized, the slave trade operated on *"a distant people who never offended him, captivating & carrying them into slavery in*

---

[29] Caesar Sarter, *Essex Journal*, August 17, 1774.
[30] On Benezet's activist life, see Maurice Jackson, *Let This Voice Be Heard* (Philadelphia: University of Pennsylvania Press, 2009).
[31] Anthony Benezet, *A Caution and Warning to the Great Britain and Her Colonies* (Philadelphia, 1766), 1–4.
[32] Anthony Benezet, "Some Historical Account of Guinea" (Philadelphia, 1771), introduction, chapter 11.

another hemisphere." *Once again,* while such language was stripped from the final Declaration, it informed Jefferson's broader claim that human freedom was the foundation of American nationhood.

8.3 THE DECLARATION AND ABOLITION AFTER 1776

Though Benezet died in 1784, other abolitionists agreed with his assessment that the Declaration abetted their cause by linking the concept of human freedom to national identity. Leading Quaker reformer John Parrish still saw it as a key part of American abolitionism decades later. In his 1806 pamphlet, *An Essay on the Slavery of Black People*, Parrish credited the first Congress – meaning the Second Continental Congress that signed the Declaration of Independence – with establishing human freedom as a national standard. In a draft version, he went further, wondering if the Declaration had already liberated enslaved African Americans across the land. Though he toned down such rhetoric, Parrish saw the Declaration as eternally relevant to the abolitionist cause.[33]

Yet the Declaration ultimately remained words on paper. The task of turning its broad promises into abolitionist reality fell to state-level politicians in the new nation. Vermont's 1777 constitution included a broad-based "Declaration of Rights" that prohibited adult bondage – the first anti-slavery constitution in America.[34] As Amani Whitfield has trenchantly noted, there were important gaps in Vermont's anti-slavery constitution (including the maintenance of childhood bondage).[35] Still, Vermont mirrored the Declaration of Independence by picturing slavery as out of place in a new republican society.

In 1780, Pennsylvania legislators passed the world's first gradual abolition law, which also nodded to the Declaration.[36] Crafted in the same assembly hall as the Declaration, Pennsylvania's emancipation edict flowed from a sense that slavery violated the tenants of human liberty enshrined in America's founding. The lead sponsor, Irish émigré George Bryan, guided the law through political opposition because he believed that bondage must be eliminated, first in Pennsylvania and then around the nation. Still, the law was truly gradual, liberating enslaved Pennsylvanians born after 1780 at the age of twenty-eight. In addition, it did not apply to the roughly 6,000–7,000 enslaved people born before the law took shape. Nevertheless, the abolition act served as an abolitionist accelerant. Not only did African Americans in Pennsylvania work

---

[33] Richard Newman, "John Parrish, 'Notes on Abolition,' Circa 1805," Quakers and Slavery website, Swarthmore College, at: https://shorturl.at/Ehm49.

[34] Constitution of Vermont, July 8, 1777, at Avalon Law Project, https://avalon.law.yale.edu/18th_century/vt01.asp.

[35] Harvey Amani Whitfield, *The Problem of Slavery in Early Vermont, 1777–1810* (Barre: Vermont Historical Society Publications, 2020).

[36] Gary Nash and Jean Soderlund, *Freedom by Degrees: Emancipation in Pennsylvania and Its Aftermath* (New York: Oxford University Press, 1991).

8 Slavery and the Declaration

with abolitionists to bargain down perpetual slavery to terms of indenture (by running away and pursuing freedom) but enslaved people from Delaware, Maryland and Virginia fled to the Quaker State with claims that they had been liberated by merely touching the free soil of Pennsylvania. By the early 1800s, Pennsylvania was an anti-slavery borderland where African Americans and abolitionists used the emancipation law to undermine bondage as a national institution.[37]

In Massachusetts, a more emphatic end to slavery occurred in 1783 when the state Supreme Court declared bondage null and void, though here, too, the Declaration framed early American anti-slavery policy. Ruling on the freedom suit of Quock Walker (who sued his alleged master Nathaniel Jennison for violating a manumission agreement), Chief Justice William Cushing argued that the Massachusetts Constitution (crafted largely by John Adams) did not sanction slavery. In his trial notes, Cushing cited the Declaration as well, noting that in the new nation "all men are born free and equal" (whereas colonial law said otherwise).[38] The ruling liberated nearly 2,000 African Americans in one fell swoop. Even before that decision, a county court in western Massachusetts declared an enslaved woman named "Mum Bett" free on similar grounds. That case flowed from Mum Bett's idea that the Revolutionary language of the Declaration applied to her, too. A white jury agreed and she (and her sister) were liberated.[39]

Though no southern state adopted gradual abolition laws or constitutional strictures on bondage after 1776, Delaware, Maryland, and Virginia eased manumission codes in ways that also reflected the Declaration's impact on anti-slavery policy. In 1782, the Virginia assembly responded to a wave of anti-slavery petitions by enabling private manumission without legislative pre-approval – a major change in its slave code.[40] Since the 1720s, Virginia law dictated that all manumission deeds must meet the strict standard of "meritorious service," which legislators defined narrowly (meaning that African Americans had protected slaveholders' interests). Not only did the 1782 law allow slaveholders to liberate bondspeople without political approval but it also enabled acts of conscience to justify black freedom. This enhanced the ability of African Americans to shape and exploit freedom deals. Now they

---

[37] On black runaways and Pennsylvania abolitionists, see Richard S. Newman, *The Transformation of American Abolitionism* (Chapel Hill: University of North Carolina Press, 2002), especially chapter 3.

[38] See William Cushing's "Legal Notes" on the case transcribed online at the Massachusetts Historical Society: www.masshist.org/database/viewer.php?item_id=630&br=1.

[39] See the summary of the case of *Brom and Bett* v. *Ashley* in the Massachusetts Historical Society's "The Legal End of Slavery in Massachusetts," online at: www.masshist.org/features/endofslavery/end_MA.

[40] See Eva Sheppard Wolf's excellent book on Virginia, *Race and Liberty in the New Nation: Emancipation in Virginia from the Revolution to Nat Turner's Rebellion* (Baton Rouge: LSU Press, 2006).

could shame slaveholders into upholding the ideals of the Declaration of Independence. Even before this, African Americans used the Declaration in such savvy ways. In 1780, a free black man named Benjamin Bilberry petitioned the Virginia legislature for his enslaved wife's freedom on the grounds that African Americans were "equal by nature" and could claim their "freedom" just as surely as any white person. The legislature agreed.[41]

Manumission deeds proved how deeply the Declaration had infiltrated some slaveholding minds in Virginia (where roughly 6,000–10,000 African Americans won freedom by the early 1800s). In one sample from the Charles City region – located between Richmond and Norfolk – several slaveholders used the Declaration's words to rationalize private emancipation. For instance, in 1791, a man named Samuel Hargrave proclaimed "that freedom is the natural right of all mankind" when crafting a deed liberating five African Americans. Hargrave issued several more manumission deeds over the next few years, each noting that "freedom is a natural right." Similarly, a slaveholding woman named Mary Leadbetter liberated five people on the grounds that "freedom is a natural right."[42] In Maryland and Delaware, too, liberalized manumission laws allowed slaveholders to manumit thousands of African Americans via acts of conscience. As one Delaware slaveholder put in a manumission agreement in 1800, slavery was simply "indefensible" in a post-Revolutionary world celebrating human freedom as a natural right.[43]

8.4 THE LIMITS OF THE DECLARATION AFTER 1776

Despite such anti-slavery breakthroughs, it is the failure of southern (and thus American) abolition that stands out between the Revolution and Civil War. While it enshrined liberty as a human birthright, the Declaration did not dictate abolition as national policy. In fact, generations of slaveholders used the Declaration's ode to personal liberty to rationalize human bondage. Even if they saw slavery as morally wrong, most southern slaveholders viewed bondage as a sanctified property right in the United States. That became clear not only at the Constitutional Convention of 1787 – which compromised on southern slavery's essential status in the new federal union – but also in the entrance of several slave states during the early republic. Although the Northwest Ordinance prohibited slavery in federal territories along the Great Lakes, new southern states put slavery beyond the reach of any government

---

[41] See Benajmin Bilberry's memorial "To the Honorable Speaker and Gentlemen of the Assembly," November 11, 1780, in Race and Slavery Petitions Project files, at: https://library.uncg.edu/slavery/petitions/details.aspx?pid=2201.

[42] See Michael Nicholls and Lenaye Howard of Utah State University, "Slaves Freed after 1782," at: www.freeafricanamericans.com/virginiafreeafter1782.htm.

[43] "To All the Christian People to whom these presents may concern," Manumission of Cudjoe Thompson by William Armour, January 1, 1800, in "Slavery Papers," Delaware Public Archives, online, https://shorturl.at/jNEAo.

emancipator. Thus, while Kentucky's 1792 constitution declared that "all men ... are equal," it also stated that the legislature "shall have no power to pass laws for the emancipation of slaves without the consent of their owners."[44]

Slaveholders' opposition to emancipation also channeled new forms of anti-black racism that emerged after the Revolution. Here, the Declaration played a role, too, compelling white as well as black Americans to think more deeply about racial equality in the new nation. Was everyone truly created equal? While abolitionists often answered with a resounding yes, a steady stream of anti-abolitionists North and South responded in the negative.

Anti-abolitionists found inspiration in Jefferson, who meditated publicly on black inequality in the new nation. Having long worried about the stability of republican society, Jefferson believed that universal emancipation and the corresponding push for black equality would create social divisions that would undo American nationhood. Though he initially favored gradual abolition in Virginia, Jefferson soon made black expulsion a necessary follow-up to emancipation. Drawing on early racial science, he argued that black and white Americans occupied different social stations in American society: racial superiors (whites) and inferiors (blacks). Emancipation would only pit them against each other. Unless liberated blacks could be removed from Virginia, he saw emancipation as a worse problem than slavery.

Jefferson published these concerns in his only major treatise, "Notes on the State of Virginia," which was initially produced for a French diplomat but then turned into a published book by the mid 1780s.[45] *Notes* was widely republished and excerpted in American culture down to the Civil War. While African Americans like Benjamin Banneker challenged Jefferson's essentialist claims about black inferiority, anti-abolitionists used them to reject both domestic emancipation and racial equality. Even in the North, anti-black racial scientists saw Jefferson as a visionary. New York publisher John Van Evrie used Jefferson's words about racial inequality as an epigram to his pro-southern, pro-slavery, and viciously anti-black book, *Negroes and Negro Slavery* (1861). Arguing that slavery was the natural condition of African-descended people, Van Evrie skewered abolitionists as fanatics. But the first thing readers saw when they opened Van Evrie's treatise was Jefferson's words from *Notes*: "I advance it, therefore, as a suspicion only, that the blacks, whether originally a different race, or made distinct by time and circumstances, are inferior to the whites in the endowments both of mind and body."[46]

As much as the Declaration remained an inspiration to abolitionists, then, Notes became its cultural doppelganger: a counter-declaration of inequality.

---

[44] Article IX of the 1792 Kentucky Constitution, transcribed and reprinted online at: https://images.procon.org/wp-content/uploads/sites/48/1792_ky_constitution.pdf.
[45] See Robert Forbes' excellent version, *Notes on the State of Virginia: An Annotated Edition* (New Haven: Yale University Press, 2022).
[46] John Van Evrie, *Negroes and Negro Slavery* (New York, 1861), front page.

No less a figure than Roger Taney read the Declaration through the prism of Jefferson's *Notes* in his (in)famous Dred Scott decision of March 1857. Arguing that Revolutionary Americans like Jefferson saw African Americans as "beings of an inferior order and unfit associates of the white race," Taney rejected black citizenship and claims to equality. Citing the Declaration and not simply the Constitution, he claimed that America's founding document had assigned blacks to a completely "separate" class as slaves and underlings.[47]

New generations of anti-slavery politicians howled in protest. The Republican Party pushed back firmly against Taneyism, or the idea that both the Declaration and Constitution were arraigned against black freedom and citizenship.[48] As Abraham Lincoln put it as a Republican candidate for the U.S. Senate in 1858, African Americans were "entitled to all the natural rights enumerated in the Declaration of Independence," including "the right to life, liberty and the pursuit of happiness."[49] This did little to persuade ardent southern slaveholders, who began using the Declaration more explicitly to justify separation from the United States in the lead-up to the Civil War. Significantly, when the Confederacy proclaimed independence to the world, its supporters rewrote Jefferson's Declaration by arguing that the southern nation "rests upon the great truth that the negro is not equal to the white man," in the words of Alexander Stephens.[50]

It would take a brutal Civil War to repudiate such views and re-establish human freedom as an essential foundation of the Declaration of Independence. Even then, generations of Americans divided over the ultimate meaning of the Declaration as a vehicle of equality and justice for all. Centuries later, we are still having that debate.

---

[47] The "Dred Scott Case," reprinted partially in the *Richmond Daily Dispatch*, March 11, 1857; see also Donald E. Fehrenbacher, *Slavery, Law and Politics: The Dred Scott Case in Historical Perspective* (New York: Oxford University Press, 1981).
[48] James Oakes, *Freedom National* (New York: W. W. Norton & Company, 2012).
[49] See Lincoln's Speech at Ottawa, Illinois, August 21, 1858, in the digital compendium of the Lincoln–Douglass Debates at Northern Illinois University: https://digital.lib.niu.edu/islandora/object/niu-lincoln:34803.
[50] Alexander Stevens, "Cornerstone Speech," March 21, 1861, reprinted online at the American Battlefield Trust: www.battlefields.org/learn/primary-sources/cornerstone-speech.

9

A Theological Interpretation of the Declaration of Independence

Barbara A. McGraw

9.1 INTRODUCTION

Popular political culture in the United States is so imbued with the belief in liberty and equality that most Americans just take it for granted – as a fact. But where does this "fact" come from? And why is it ingrained in our psyches, institutions, and politics?

Certainly revolutionary Americans were not all of one mind – not even all those who joined the cause for separation from Britain. Still, they converged under the banner of the Declaration of Independence's "self-evident" truths "that all men are created equal, that they are endowed by their Creator with certain unalienable Rights, that among these are Life, Liberty and the pursuit of Happiness," in order to make a new nation "to which the Laws of Nature and of Nature's God entitle them." And belief in those truths has become the foundation of American self-identity, even when we disagree vehemently about how best to realize them.

Yet what many people across the political spectrum in the United States either do not know or do not think is important today is that at the founding, the Declaration placed the whole reason for establishment of the nation, and therefore the answer to our question, squarely in the natural law tradition. And that tradition's influence on the Declaration can be, and I would argue ought to be, interpreted theologically. As I have written elsewhere, our nation has a "sacred ground."[1]

The author acknowledges and is grateful for the financial support of, and visiting fellowship with, the Pluralism and Civil Exchange program of the Mercatus Center, George Mason University, and for the Luce-AAR Advancing Public Scholarship grant from the American Academy of Religion, which made scholarly leave possible. Also acknowledged is previous support from the Institute for Humane Studies, George Mason University.

[1] Barbara A. McGraw, *Rediscovering America's Sacred Ground: Public Religion and Pursuit of the Good in a Pluralistic America* (Albany: State University of New York Press, 2003).

9.2 LOCKE, HUMAN NATURE, AND GOD'S NATURAL LAW

The Americans who decided to separate from Britain were in agreement that there was a profound justification for asserting their rights and resisting arbitrary authority. They found that justification in natural law discourse generally, but in particular in the writings of John Locke (1632–1704).

Locke's England was a time and place of innovative inquiry. As the hold of Church dogma and authority had cracked and eventually eroded in the centuries after the Protestant Reformation began (c. 1517), philosophers turned to nature to understand the universe and humanity's place in it. Locke entered that discourse in correspondences with colleagues and friends and in published works: *The Two Treatises of Government* (1689), *An Essay Concerning Human Understanding* (1689/1690), *A Letter Concerning Toleration* (1689), and his writings on education (1693, 1706).[2] Believing that truths about the universe could be discerned by investigating God's handiwork, Locke focused a lens on human nature. His work challenged the bleak Hobbesian and Calvinist assessment of human nature as being inherently sinful, which justified an absolutist government to contain and direct it.[3]

While others took a more scientific, or more "secular," approach to the natural law, Locke's speculation and discovery began with theological inquiry. In Locke's understanding, the natural law is God's law, and the moral law is founded in the natural law through its source – God, or more precisely God's will – and it is discernable through human reason.

In his pivotal work *An Essay Concerning Human Understanding*, Locke relied on the cosmological argument for the existence of God as his "central proof" that there must be a Creator of the universe and that everything and everyone are dependent on that Creator,[4] because otherwise none would have come into being.[5] It is significant that in Locke's understanding, the universe that God created is full of purpose, God's purpose, which Locke maintained is the preservation of God's creation – humankind.[6] That purpose is the reason

---

[2] John Locke, *Some Thoughts Concerning Education*, ed. John W. Yolton and Jean S. Yolton (Oxford: Clarendon Press; and New York: Oxford University Press, [1693] 1989); and *Of the Conduct of the Understanding*, ed. Francis W. Garforth (New York: Teachers College Press, Columbia University, [1706] 1966).

[3] W. von Leyden, "Introduction," in *John Locke: Essays on the Law of Nature*, ed. W. von Leyden (Oxford: Oxford University Press, [1954] 1988), 37, hereafter, Locke, *ELN*.

[4] James Tully, *A Discourse on Property: John Locke and His Adversaries* (New York: Cambridge University Press, 1980), 37.

[5] For a comprehensive summary discussion, see Bruce Reichenbach, "Cosmological Argument," in *Stanford Encyclopedia of Philosophy*, rev. 2022, https://plato.stanford.edu/entries/cosmological-argument.

[6] John Locke, *Second Treatise of Government*, in *Political Writings of John Locke*, ed. David Wootton (London: Mentor, 1993), chapter 11, ¶135, 330. Even in his early unpublished work, Locke made clear what became salient in his later work: God "has not created this world for nothing and without purpose. For it is contrary to such great wisdom to work with no fixed aim"(Locke, *ELN*, 157).

for human beings' natural faculties (senses and reason). God intends human beings to use those faculties to live according to the natural law. As Locke said, "*Reason* is natural *Revelation*,"[7] and "*the Voice of God in him [man]*,"[8] with scripture as the other part of what Locke held is the divine law. Neither of them contradicts the other, in Locke's understanding, when scripture is understood through the lens of natural theology.[9]

Natural laws for human beings can be determined by looking to what end our natural faculties are designed to achieve. That is to say that for Locke, some natural laws are "self-evident" because they follow from the nature of human being, while others are discovered through the application of logic.[10] The natural laws, then, can be discovered by man in nature by nature – human beings' nature. So it is that human beings "have Light enough to lead them to the Knowledge of their Maker, and the sight of their own Duties."[11] Consequently, Locke famously maintained in the *Essay* that human beings do not have innate knowledge. All knowledge is gained through sense experience of the natural world, which is then submitted to human beings' reasoning – their own ability to exercise their deductive faculty as well as through argument and debate with others, including matters concerning God.[12]

In that regard, it is significant that the ability to deliberate is central to Locke's understanding of human personhood; moreover, deliberation is inextricably

---

[7] John Locke, *An Essay Concerning Human Understanding*, ed. Peter H. Nidditch (Oxford: Oxford University Press, 1975), Book IV, chapter XIX, ¶4, 698, hereafter, Locke, *ECHU*.

[8] John Locke, *First Treatise, Two Treatises of Government*, ed. Thomas I. Cook (New York: Hafner Publishing, 1947), chapter 1, ¶86. See also Locke, *ELN*, 111: "[T]his law of nature can be described as being the decree of the divine will discernable by the light of nature and indicating what is and what is not in conformity with rational nature, and for this very reason commanding or prohibiting it."

[9] Locke, *ECHU*, Book IV, chapter XIX, ¶4, 698; ¶11, 702.

[10] Locke, *ECHU*, Book I, chapter IV, ¶22, 99:

> To conclude: some *Ideas* forwardly offer themselves to all Men's Understandings; and some sorts of Truths result from any *Ideas*, as soon as the mind puts them into Propositions: Other Truths require a train of *Ideas* placed in order, a due comparing of them, and deductions made with attention, before they can be discovered and assented to. Some of the first sort, because of their general and easy reception, have been mistaken for innate.

Locke, *ECHU*, Book I, chapter II, ¶21, 59:

> This cannot be deny'd, that Men grow first acquainted with many of these self-evident Truths, upon their being proposed: But it is clear that whosoever does so, finds in himself That he then begins to know a Proposition, which he knew not before; and which from thenceforth he never questions: not because it was innate; but because the consideration of the Nature of the things contained in those Words, would not suffer him to think otherwise, how, or whensoever he is brought to reflect on them.

See also Locke, *ECHU*, Book IV, chapter III, ¶18, 549.

[11] Locke, *ECHU*, Book I, chapter I, ¶5, 45.

[12] Locke, *ECHU*, Book IV, chapter X.

joined to human liberty.[13] As James Tully observes: For Locke, "[d]eliberation is not only necessary to free agency; it is the duty and perfection of man's intellectual nature."[14] Locke maintained that through human beings' deliberative capacities, including with other seekers, "truth" can "shift for herself" by making "her way into the understanding by her own light," which is not the case when coercion ("force to procure her entrance into the minds of men") is applied.[15]

God has not made human beings as God's puppets. Rather, liberty serves God's purpose. As Locke said, "the end of law is not to abolish or restrain, but to preserve and enlarge freedom."[16] Discovery of what conduces to our happiness through the deliberative process of human beings' reason is "the end and use of our *Liberty.*"[17] And it is directed to the common good: "[Natural] law, in its true notion, is not so much the limitation as the direction of a free and intelligent agent to his proper Interest, and prescribes no farther than is for the general good,"[18] and through such means, God guides us to what will preserve and benefit human beings and their society, having "joined *Virtue* and publick Happiness together."[19]

Importantly, liberty is equal liberty. For Locke, human beings' equal creation is more than a right; it is a fact of existence: "equal one amongst the other without subordination or subjection"; all are equal "by nature" and have an "equal right … to natural freedom."[20] Because human beings are "all the workmanship of one omnipotent and infinitely wise maker," they are "made to last during his [God's], not one another's pleasure."[21] Countering those who argue for subjection of some by others, Locke centers human beings' natural right in God's right as the giver of life to whom we owe our duties: "remember God who is 'the author and giver of life; it is in Him alone we live, move, and have our being.' [Acts 17:28]"[22] Moreover, liberty is not for liberty's sake alone. Liberty's purpose is not merely to serve one's own selfish desires, as that would be against God's purpose of general flourishing.[23] Consequently, liberty is not only for

---

[13] See Locke, *ECHU*, Book II, chapter XXI, ¶¶48–52, 264–267.
[14] Tully, *Discourse on Property*, 106–107, citing *ECHU*, Book II, chapter XXI, ¶¶47–50. See also, *ECHU*, Book II, chapter XXI, ¶52: "For the inclination, and tendency of their [human beings'] nature to happiness is an obligation, and motive to them … [which] necessarily puts them upon caution, deliberation, and wariness, in the direction of their particular actions, which are the means to obtain it."
[15] John Locke, *A Letter Concerning Toleration*, trans. William Popple (1685, published 1689), in *Political Writings*, 420–421.
[16] Locke, *Second Treatise*, chapter 6, ¶57, 289.
[17] Locke, *ECHU*, Book II, Ch XXI, ¶48, 264.
[18] Locke, *Second Treatise*, chapter 6, ¶57, 288–289.
[19] Locke, *ECHU*, Book I, chapter III, ¶6, 69.
[20] Locke, *Second Treatise*, chapter 2, ¶4, 263, and chapter 6, ¶ 54, 287–288, respectively.
[21] Locke, *Second Treatise*, chapter 2, ¶6, 264.
[22] Locke, *First Treatise*, chapter 6, ¶52.
[23] Locke, *Second Treatise*, chapter 2, ¶7, 263–264. "Everyone … when his own preservation comes not into competition, ought he, as much as he can, preserve the rest of mankind[.]"

one's own preservation and comfort; it is also for the preservation and comfort of others.[24] As Locke concluded, it is for everyone's "pursuit of Happiness."[25]

The constant desire of Happiness, and the constraint it puts upon us to act for it, no Body, I think, accounts an abridgment of *Liberty*, or at least an abridgment of *Liberty* to be complain'd of. God Almighty himself is under the necessity of being happy; and the more any intelligent Being is so, the nearer is its approach to infinite perfection and happiness.[26]

We see, then, that in Locke's natural theology, human beings' duties are grounded in their relationship with God and with each other. Locke maintained that, otherwise, man "would be a god to himself and the satisfaction of his own will the sole measure and end of all his actions."[27] Without such sacred obligations beyond the self, egoism would lead to confusion as everyone would assert their own interests, and God's purpose would not be realized.

Further, human beings not only have a duty to adhere to the natural law to sustain themselves and others in the here and now, but their duties have a view to the afterlife. Locke is clear: "there is a possibility of another state when this scene is over, and that the happiness and misery of that depends on the ordering of ourselves in our actions in this time of our probationership here."[28] Consequently, the freedom to be and do according to conscience is sacrosanct, as it is only through free will, not coercion by church or state, that human beings can be held responsible and therefore our actions can be deemed worthy by God.[29] That is why Locke advocated for religious tolerance, recognizing a wide spectrum of religious orientations, including those in all sects of Protestant Christianity (naming the most controversial of his day), Catholics, Jews, Muslims, or "Mahometans," Native Americans, and pagans,[30] as well as "idolatry, superstition, and heresy" and "heathens."[31]

---

[24] Locke, *Letter Concerning Toleration*, 422:

> [T]he necessity of preserving men in the possession of what honest industry has already acquired, and also of preserving their liberty and strength, whereby they may acquire what they farther want, obliges men to enter into society with one another, that by mutual assistance and joint force they may secure unto each other their properties in these things that contribute to the comfort and happiness of this life.

[25] Locke, *ECHU*, Book II, chapter XXI, ¶59, 273, and cf., ¶51, 266: "[W]e are by the necessity of preferring and pursuing true happiness as our greatest good, obliged to suspend the satisfaction of our desire in particular cases."

[26] Locke, *ECHU*, Book II, chapter XXI, ¶50, 265.

[27] John Locke, "Law," Bodleian MS Locke c.28, fo. 141 (c. 1693), Oxford University, in *Locke Political Essays*, ed. Mark Goldie (Cambridge: Cambridge University Press, 1997), 328–329.

[28] John Locke, "Understanding," Bodleian MS Locke, fo. 2, 42–55 (February 8, 1677), Oxford University, in *Locke Political Essays*, 263.

[29] Locke, *Letter Concerning Toleration*, 421. See discussion at McGraw, *America's Sacred Ground*, 45–50.

[30] Locke, *Letter Concerning Toleration*, 400, 412, 416, 417, 420, 431.

[31] Locke, *Letter Concerning Toleration*, 402, 420.

It is not surprising that Locke repudiated predestination and its corollary unequal creation – the view that human beings are designated for heaven or hell, even before they are born; that is, the idea that some are worthy and others are not. In that view, only those chosen for heaven have God's grace and are saved from damnation; whatever we do in our lives will not change that. That view was influential among the English Dissenter Christian sects in Locke's time. In contrast, Locke maintained that we are all responsible to fulfill our duties through our liberty and answer to God individually, and what we do in this life matters as we all have the opportunity through our freedom to choose to fulfill God's purpose. "[O]ur main duty is ... to doe our dutys in all our callings as far as the frailty of our bodys or mindes will allow us."[32] As Locke said in *Of the Conduct of the Understanding*,

> There is indeed one science (as they are now distinguished) incomparably above all the rest, where it is not by corruption narrowed into a trade or faction for mean or ill ends and secular interests; I mean theology; which, containing the knowledge of God and his creatures, our duty to him and our fellow-creatures and a view of our present and future state, is the comprehension of all other knowledge directed to its true end, i.e., the honour and veneration of the Creator and the happiness of mankind.[33]

Many in Locke's time were influenced by philosophers who argued that the natural law dictates the absolute authority of the monarch as the beneficiary of the "divine right of kings."[34] That view had become "the new orthodoxy."[35] Locke's contemporary, Robert Filmer (1588–1653), relied instead on his reading of historical precedent and tradition. He eschewed the natural law as being an unworkable source for political theory and claimed not only the absolute authority of the king, but also a justification for the entire patriarchal order by analogy to the patriarchal head of the family. However, Locke concluded that mutual preservation and contentment of the people are the only legitimate purposes of government; all political authority, wherever it is vested, is rightly limited to just that. Human beings are not mere sheep destined to follow the

---

[32] John Locke to Denis Grenville, c. March 1677, *The Correspondence of John Locke*, ed. E.S. de Beer (Oxford: Clarendon Press, 1976–1989), 1: 472–475.

[33] Locke, *Conduct of the Understanding*, 77. For the considerable influence of Locke's educational works during the founding era, see Jay Fliegelman, *Prodigals and Pilgrims: The American Revolution Against Patriarchal Authority 1750–1800* (Cambridge: Cambridge University Press, 1985).

[34] For a brief summary discussion of the development of the doctrine of the divine right of kings, see Barbara A. McGraw, "Church and State in Context," in Ann W. Duncan and Steven L. Jones, eds., *Church and State Issues in America Today* (Santa Barbara: Greenwood Publishing), 5–7. That view was an extension of the reasoning of Hugo Grotius and others, whose works lent legitimacy to authoritarian governments. See, e.g., Hugo Grotius, *The Rights of War and Peace*, trans. A. C. Campbell, with an introduction by David J. Hill (New York: M. Walter Dunne, [1625] 1901). Liberty Fund, I.III.viii, https://oll.libertyfund.org/title/grotius-the-rights-of-war-and-peace-1901-ed.

[35] Tully, *Discourse on Property*, 157.

precepts of their supposed betters. Rather, human beings' inherent capacity for reason, understanding, and knowledge make possible their ability to contribute to the betterment of themselves and others.

Thus, for Locke, government is not by divine right, but is a human artifact – one that ought to enable human beings to serve God's purpose. Consequently, it is appropriate to resist, and even reject and overthrow, any authority that overreaches in violation of that purpose. This conclusion was so central to Locke's project that it has been referred to as "Locke's primary ideological task."[36]

That was also the American Founders' primary task. In particular, that was Thomas Jefferson's task when he drafted the Declaration of Independence. But declaring a new nation on the natural laws of Nature's God was much more than a justification for revolution. It was, in effect, the continuance and enlargement of Locke's natural theology as the foundation for equality, liberty, the preservation of life, and the pursuit of happiness.

9.3 JEFFERSON, THE DECLARATION, AND NATURAL THEOLOGY

Locke's ideas were ubiquitous in prerevolutionary and revolutionary America, as numerous scholars have noted.[37] Lockean natural theology was diffused through the founding-era culture – both religiously and politically. Although it is possible to make an argument for individual rights without natural theology, for example an argument from utility,[38] I suggest that the reasons for human beings' inherent equality and liberty, and the right to self-governance have much surer footing on natural theology ground. Significantly, Jefferson's view of such rights was that they are not merely secular concerns. For Jefferson they involve, essentially, theological questions, the answers to which could largely be found in Locke.

Notably, Jefferson adopted Locke's epistemology – that knowledge is gained through human beings' senses and reason. Not only would Jefferson have

---

[36] Tully, *Discourse on Property*, 54–55.
[37] See, e.g., Carl L. Becker, *The Declaration of Independence: A Study in the History of Political Ideas* (New York: Vintage, 1959), 27; Bernard Bailyn, *The Ideological Originals of the American Revolution* (Cambridge: Belknap Press of Harvard University Press, 1976), 27, 36; and Steven Dworetz, *The Unvarnished Doctrine: Locke, Liberalism, and the American Revolution* (Durham: Duke University Press, 1988), 65–96; Thomas Pangle, *The Spirit of Modern Republicanism: The Moral Vision of the American Founders and the Philosophy of Locke* (Chicago: University of Chicago Press, 1988); McGraw, *America's Sacred Ground*, 64.
[38] For a classical argument for liberty from utility, see John Stuart Mill, "On Liberty," in *John Stuart Mill on Liberty, Utilitarianism, and Other Essays*, ed. Mark Philp and Frederick Rosen (Oxford: Oxford University Press, 2015), 5–114. See also Richard A. Epstein, *Principles for a Free Society: Reconciling Individual Liberty with the Common Good* (Cambridge: Perseus Publishing, 1998).

derived this directly from Locke through his encounter with Locke's *Essay concerning Human Understanding*, but it would also have come to Jefferson through *The Philosophical Works* of Henry St. John, 1st Viscount Bolingbroke (1678–1751), who followed Locke in that regard and who was a significant influence on Jefferson.[39] Applying that epistemology in an 1823 letter to John Adams, Jefferson made clear that "Nature's God" is not merely a metaphor for reason or even for nature itself. Similar to Locke, Jefferson reasoned to the existence of God, the Creator:

> I hold (without appeal to revelation) that when we take a view of the Universe, in its parts, general or particular, it is impossible for the human mind not to perceive and feel a conviction of design, consummate skill, and indefinite power in every atom of its composition. The movements of the heavenly bodies, so exactly held in their course by the balance of centrifugal and centripetal forces, the structure of our earth itself, with its distribution of lands, waters and atmosphere, animal and vegetable bodies, examined in all their minutest particles, insects mere atoms of life, yet as perfectly organized as man or mammoth, mineral substances, their generation and uses, it is impossible, I say, for the human mind not to believe that there is, in all this, design, cause and effect, up to an ultimate cause, a fabricator of all things from matter and motion.[40]

Clearly, Jefferson's fabricator is the God of Nature, and as with Locke, Jefferson's theology was based on an understanding of Nature and God's workmanship, and that the law of nature is the law of God. It follows that the rights of humanity in that law are "sacred," as Jefferson's original draft of the Declaration stated, although in his final version Jefferson substituted Locke's "self-evident."[41] Jefferson's God is rational and benevolent.[42] Just as Locke

---

[39] There were many Bolingbroke abstracts in Jefferson's literary commonplace book from *The Works of the Late Right Honorable Henry St. John, Lord Viscount Bolingbroke*, 5 vols., which were published in London in 1754 by David Mallet. See Gilbert Chinard, ed., *The Literary Bible of Thomas Jefferson: His Commonplace Book of Philosophers and Poets* (Baltimore: Johns Hopkins University Press, 1928), 40–71, hereafter, *Jefferson Literary Bible*; and Gilbert Chinard, "Introduction," *Jefferson Literary Bible*, 20: "No single influence was stronger on Jefferson's formation [than Bolingbroke] and none was more continuous."

[40] Jefferson to John Adams, April 11, 1823, https://shorturl.at/nSByp.

[41] Thomas Jefferson, "original Rough draft of the Declaration of Independence," Library of Congress, www.loc.gov/exhibits/declara/ruffdrft.html. Some scholars have argued the change from "sacred" to "self-evident" was due to the influence of Benjamin Franklin. See, e.g., Becker, *The Declaration of Independence*, 142; John C. Fitzpatrick, *The Spirit of the Revolution: New Light from Some of the Original Sources of American History* (Boston: Houghton Mifflin, 1924), 11–12. However, John Adams later wrote that the drafting committee did not alter Jefferson's final draft, which included "self-evident." On this point, see Julian P. Boyd, *The Declaration of Independence: The Evolution of the Text* (Princeton: Princeton University Press, 1945), 24, pointing out that the handwriting for the change is consistent with Jefferson's.

[42] Jefferson referred to God as "the benevolent Governor of the world," who Jefferson "acknowledge[s] and adore[s]." "Jefferson to John Adams," April 11, 1823, in Thomas Jefferson, John Adams, and Abigail Adams, *The Adams–Jefferson Letters*, 2 vols, ed. Lester

9 A Theological Interpretation

concluded, it is fundamental to the nature of human beings that not one of us is more worthy than another – we are all God's equal creation.[43] Basing the Declaration on equal creation, Jefferson named it first among all of the ideas that derive from Locke: "We hold these truths to be self-evident that all men[44] are created equal."[45] In so doing, Jefferson rejected the doctrine of original sin, which had led to the conclusion that generally the people are not worthy, thus justifying absolute authority over them by their supposed superiors: we are not destined for the fire and brimstone of hell at God's whim, nor for heaven.[46] God does not control human beings or their destiny – nothing is predetermined.

Jefferson held that, unlike the God of biblical revelation who could be partial and unjust, thus a violator of equal creation, Jefferson's God created a justly ordered world where human beings can discover the nature of things by employing reason. What we do in the world matters for our destiny. In accord with Locke's natural theology, Jefferson maintained that human beings are created with innate reason so we can determine our duties to our Creator and each other.[47] Therefore human beings are free, even from the coercion of God. We are at liberty to do our duties, as we come to understand them, in service of God's purpose – the preservation of ourselves and each other as we strive for happiness.[48]

J. Cappon (Chapel Hill: University of North Carolina Press, 1959), 2: 591. In that letter, Jefferson also said that he "could never be" "an Atheist." See also, Jefferson to David Hartley, July 2, 1787, in *The Writings of Thomas Jefferson*, ed. Andrew A. Lipscomb and Albert Ellery Bergh (Washington, DC: Thomas Jefferson Memorial Society, 1903), 6: 151, where Jefferson reasons that God must be benevolent, otherwise if man cannot be trusted to govern himself, it would mean "either that there is no God, or that he is a malevolent being."

[43] The original draft of the Declaration used that phrase: "all men are created equal and independent; that *from that equal creation* they derive rights, inherent & inalienable, among which are ..." (emphasis added). Jefferson, "original Rough draft."

[44] There is considerable debate about whether the Declaration's reference to "men" was originally intended to include all people. We know that for some in the founding era, it was. For example, Jefferson concluded in his *Notes on the State of Virginia*: "It is civilization alone which replaces women in the enjoyment of their natural equality." And he referred to the natural "liberties" as "the gift of God," violations of which because of slavery invite God's "wrath." But see, Leslie F. Goldstein, "The Declaration of Independence and Women," Chapter 14 in this volume.

[45] Declaration of Independence, www.ushistory.org/declaration/document/.

[46] Jefferson wrote that if he were the founder of a new religion, his "fundamental principle would be the reverse of Calvin's, that we are to be saved by our good works which are within our power, and not by our faith which is not within our power." Jefferson to Thomas B. Parker, May 15, 1819, https://founders.archives.gov/documents/Jefferson/03-14-02-0292.

[47] Writing about the adoption of the Declaration by Continental Congress, Jefferson said in a letter to Judge William Johnson in 1823, "We believed ... that man was a rational animal, endowed by nature with rights, and with an innate sense of justice; and that he could be restrained from wrong, & protected in right, by moderate powers, confided to persons of his own choice, and held to their duties by dependence on his own will." Jefferson to William Johnson, June 12, 1823, https://founders.archives.gov/documents/Jefferson/98-01-02-3562.

[48] Echoing Locke, in Jefferson's original draft of the Declaration, "Life" was "the preservation of Life." Jefferson, "original Rough draft."

In the main, Jefferson's natural theology mirrored Locke's, yet Jefferson took it further. Although Locke's view was that the moral law is discernable through reason, Locke was not able to develop a full account of how moral laws are derived from the laws of nature such that they are accessible to ordinary people. Locke assumed that reason is an attribute of all human beings; yet his conception of the reasoning process required sophisticated analytical abilities. Consequently, reasoning to moral laws, even to the natural law itself, remained the purview of philosophers and theologians, and sometimes statesmen – the elite. Such reasoning was not, then, accessible to the common man (or woman). Locke lamented:

> [I]t is plain, in fact, that human reason unassisted failed men in its great and proper business of morality. It never from unquestionable principles by clear deductions, made out an entire body of the "law of nature."
>
> The greatest part of mankind want [lack] leisure or capacity for demonstration [of reason], nor can carry a train of proofs ...
>
> The greatest part cannot *know* and therefore must *believe*.
>
> I conclude, when well considered, that method of teaching men their duties, would be thought proper only for a few, who had much leisure, improved understandings, and were used to abstract reasonings. But the instruction of the people were best still to be left to the precepts and principles of the gospel.[49]

Consequently, a question presented itself: How can Locke's worthy aspirations for human beings' equal creation and innate liberty, the employment of human reason, and the right to self-governance be feasible, if they are only intelligible to an elite?

Locke's approach was to supplement reason with scripture to serve as the ordinary person's guide – "the precepts and principles of the gospel." Locke believed in the "reasonableness of Christianity,"[50] and scripture as part of the divine law, which, as noted earlier, was not contrary to reason in Locke's estimation. However, Jefferson rejected Christianity, yet he later espoused the reasonableness of Jesus, although not the Bible's account of his miracles.[51] As Bolingbroke had concluded and Jefferson concurred, biblical revelation is inconsistent with a God for all people, as it is contrary to equal creation. Instead, Jefferson adopted the view of Henry Home, Lord Kames (1696–1782),

---

[49] John Locke, *The Reasonableness of Christianity*, ed. George W. Ewing (Washington, DC: Regnery Gateway, 1965), 171, 178–179.

[50] Locke, *Reasonableness*, passim.

[51] "Of all the systems of morality ancient or modern, which have come under my observation, none appear to me so pure as that of Jesus." Thomas Jefferson to William Canby, September 18, 1813, https://founders.archives.gov/documents/Jefferson/03-06-02-0395. "[T]he Christian religion, when divested of the rags in which they [the clergy] have enveloped it, and brought to the original purity & simplicity of its benevolent institutor, is a religion of all others most friendly to liberty, science, & the freest expression of the human mind." Jefferson to Moses Robinson, March 23, 1801, https://founders.archives.gov/documents/Jefferson/01-33-02-0362.

9 A Theological Interpretation

who had expanded on Locke in his *Principles of Equity*,[52] that in addition to reason and the ordinary senses, everyone is imbued by the Creator with a moral sense or conscience. As Kames wrote,

[T]he moral sense or conscience may well be held the voice of God within us, constantly admonishing us of our duty; and requiring on our part no exercise of our faculties but attention merely. The celebrated Locke ventured what he thought a bold conjecture, that the moral duties may be capable of demonstration: how great his surprise to have been told, that they are capable of much higher evidence.[53]

For Kames, and Jefferson in turn, the moral sense or conscience is the assistance to reason that is consistent with human beings' equal creation and right to liberty and self-governance. Conscience is people's guide to what conduces to their preservation and happiness. As Jefferson said in 1817: "The evidence of … our right to life, liberty, the use of our faculties, the pursuit of happiness, is not left to the feeble and sophistical investigations of reason, but is impressed on the sense of every man."[54] Consequently for Jefferson, reason, moral sense, and conscience (in its expanded form) are capacities of every human being – high and low. As Jefferson wrote to his nephew, Peter Carr, "The moral sense, or conscience, is as much a part of man as his leg or arm."[55]

Because, in Jefferson's understanding, these capacities are available to everyone, he had great faith in ordinary people's ability to employ those capacities and therefore faith in their equal worthiness to exercise liberty to discern what is moral and to exercise self-governance: "I have no fear that the result of our experiment will be that men may be trusted to govern themselves without a master."[56]

The idea of the role of conscience was nascent in Locke, who also spoke of it. But for Locke, conscience is related more closely to the pleasure one experiences by doing right and the pain or guilt one experiences by doing wrong.[57]

---

[52] Hutcheson is often considered an influence in this regard. See, e.g., Garry Wills, *Inventing America: Jefferson's Declaration of Independence* (New York: Vintage, 1978). However, there is more evidence that this approach came from Kames to Jefferson, who included Kames, *Principles of Equity* and other works by Kames on a 1771 list sent to his brother-in-law of recommended works that Jefferson also shared with others. No works by Hutcheson are listed. See Jefferson to Robert Skipwith, August 3, 1771, https://shorturl.at/GYi7s; *Jefferson Literary Bible*, where Hutchinson is not referenced, but Kames is referenced extensively. See also, Michael P. Zuckert, *Natural Rights and the New Republicanism* (Princeton: Princeton University Press, 1994), 18–26.
[53] Lord Kames, *Principles of Equity*, 2nd ed. (Edinburgh: A. Kincaid and J. Bell, 1767), 30–31.
[54] Jefferson to John Manners, June 12, 1817, https://founders.archives.gov/documents/Jefferson/03-11-02-0360.
[55] Jefferson to Peter Carr, August 10, 1787, https://founders.archives.gov/documents/Jefferson/01-12-02-0021.
[56] Jefferson to David Hartley, July 2, 1787, https://founders.archives.gov/documents/Jefferson/01-11-02-0441.
[57] Locke, *ECHU*, Book II, chapter XX.

Jefferson had added another layer to the understanding of conscience: the perception of what God wants of us so that we can do our duty and fulfill God's purpose. Conscience, then, comes to the fore as primary. It combines reason, moral sense, intuition, and insight. It is also communication from and to God.

Jefferson regularly practiced what one scholar refers to as "private devotions" (although perhaps "contemplations of conscience" may be a better description).[58] Jefferson even entertained the possibility that there can be personal revelations – that God may communicate directly to human beings from time to time and that those messages could be different for different people. In response to Miles King, who maintained that he had received a personal revelation from God, Jefferson wrote:

> When he [God] means to make a personal revelation he carries conviction of its authenticity to the reason he has bestowed as the umpire of truth. You believe you have been favored with such a special communication. Your reason, not mine, is to judge of this: and if it shall be his pleasure to favor me with a like admonition, I shall obey it with the same fidelity with which I would obey his known will in all cases. Hitherto I have been under the guidance of that portion of reason which he has thought proper to deal out to me. I have followed it faithfully in all important cases, to such a degree at least as leaves me without uneasiness; and if on minor occasions I have erred from its dictates, I have trust in him who made us what we are, and knows it was not his plan to make us always unerring.[59]

Some scholars acknowledge Locke's influence on Jefferson. However, interpreting Locke nontheologically, their approach is one that emphasizes Locke's influence on Jefferson in a secular, rather than religious direction.[60] Further, it is common for historians, philosophers, and others to secularize Jefferson by asserting that he was a deist of the "Watchmaker God" type. Such deists professed the view that God created the universe to run as a mechanism, but that otherwise God does not intervene in people's lives or in history generally; creation runs on its own natural laws like a clock. As shown, for Jefferson (but was likely also the case for other so-called deists), that interpretation is at least very questionable.

Rather, for Jefferson, God is not absent from creation. Nor is Nature's God merely nature itself, the mechanism of natural laws, or a metaphor for

---

[58] Charles B. Sanford, *Thomas Jefferson and His Library: A Study of His Literary Interests and of the Religious Attitudes Revealed by Relevant Titles in His Library* (Hamden: Archon Books, 1977), 150, describing the recollections of Thomas Jefferson Randall in Henry Stephens Randall, *The Life of Thomas Jefferson*, 3 vols. (New York: Derby & Jackson, 1858), 3: 671–672.

[59] Jefferson to Miles King, September 26, 1814, https://founders.archives.gov/documents/Jefferson/03-07-02-0495.

[60] For a very brief discussion of this thinking, see Kody W. Cooper and Justin Buckley Dyer, "Thomas Jefferson, Nature's God, and the Theological Foundations of Natural-Rights Republicanism," *Politics and Religion* 10.3 (2017): 5–6. For depth, see Michael P. Zuckert, *Launching Liberalism: On Lockean Political Philosophy* (Lawrence: University of Kansas Press, 2002); and Matthew Stewart, *Nature's God: The Heretical Origins of the American Republic* (New York: W. W. Norton & Company, 2014).

a godless universe. Jefferson's "A Bill for Establishing Religious Freedom" (1779) makes that clear, revealing that Jefferson's view was that conscience is formed by reasoning through the "evidence" that is "proposed to their [individuals'] minds" and that God, who is "lord of both body and mind," propagates God's "plan" by "extend[ing] its influence on reason alone."[61] Clearly, Jefferson believed that God guides human beings, yet they remain free to make their own way in life. Also, it is worth noting that the final version of the Declaration adopted by the Continental Congress refers to "the protection of divine Providence." How could they have thought that God could "protect," if God were absent?[62]

It is not surprising then that for Jefferson, religious liberty is not merely a derivative liberty right or a doctrine that merely serves the utility of toleration needed for practical purposes on account of the proliferation of religious sects. Rather, religious liberty has a theological foundation just as it did for Locke. Therefore, because human beings are first answerable to God alone, not church or state, it would be an affront to God for anyone to impose uniformity, especially in religion.[63] Consequently, Jefferson recognized the rights of adherents of diverse religions, but went beyond Locke to include even those "who deny the existence of a god."[64] Further, it may well be that religious liberty was, for Jefferson, the foundation of liberty itself as he often acknowledged its central importance. For example, he stressed that "freedom of religion" is "the most inalienable and sacred of all human rights"[65] and "worship of our creator in the way we think most agreeable to his will" is "a liberty" that is "the most inestimable of our blessings."[66]

Jefferson held that equality and liberty in the preservation of self and others in the pursuit of happiness, and the right of self-governance, require a government

---

[61] Thomas Jefferson, "A Bill for Establishing Religious Freedom," (1779), in *The Complete Jefferson Containing His Major Writings, Published and Unpublished, Except His Letters*, ed. Saul K. Padover (New York: Duell, Sloan & Pearce, 1943), 946–947, 946; also found, https://founders.archives.gov/documents/Jefferson/01-02-02-0132-0004-0082 (emphasis omitted).

[62] I have argued elsewhere that most deists were not of a strict Watchmaker God persuasion. See, e.g., McGraw, *America's Sacred Ground*, 69–73. See also, Mark David Hall, *Did America Have a Christian Founding: Separating Modern Myth from Historical Truth* (Nashville: Nelson Books, 2019), 1–20.

[63] See Randall, *The Life of Thomas Jefferson*, 672, describing how sacrosanct individual conscience in religion was to Jefferson:

> If asked by one of them [his family], his opinion on any religious subject, his uniform reply was, that it was a subject each was bound to study assiduously for himself, unbiased by the opinions of others – it was a matter solely of conscience; after thorough investigation, they were responsible for the righteousness, but not the rightfulness of their opinions; that the expression of his opinion might influence theirs, and he would not give it!

[64] Thomas Jefferson, "Notes on Religion" (October, 1776?), in *The Complete Jefferson*, 945.

[65] Minutes of the Board of Visitors of the University of Virginia, October 7, 1822, https://founders.archives.gov/documents/Madison/04-02-02-0504.

[66] Jefferson to John Thomas, November 18, 1807, https://shorturl.at/AqQn4.

that is not absolute. Government is needed to recognize and preserve human beings' natural equality and liberty. It is also needed to provide a political-legal framework that creates and maintains an unbiased public space for conscience to be expressed, not only in speech but also in human beings' activities in preservation of themselves and each other. Jefferson believed that through "argument and debate,"[67] including about God,[68] we can reason to our duties to God and to each other together to serve our greater, that is, long-term, happiness. As Jefferson put it, echoing Locke, "truth is great and will prevail if left to herself."[69] In other words, the government's purpose is to make possible the discovery and operation of the natural laws which are revealed through deliberation within ourselves and in engagement with others – our deliberative capacities being central to human personhood, as Locke had concluded. Jefferson wrote:

Reason and free enquiry are the only effectual agents against error …

Reason and persuasion are the only practicable instruments. To make way for these, free enquiry must be indulged.[70]

For Jefferson, as for Locke, when government does not fulfill that purpose and "becomes destructive of these ends, it is the Right of the People to alter or to abolish it, and to institute new Government, laying its foundation on such principles and organizing its powers in such form, as to them shall seem most likely to effect their Safety and Happiness."[71]

9.4 LOCKE, JEFFERSON, AND THE AMERICAN MIND

Some scholars have considered Locke's influence on the American Founding overall to be far less than was the previously widely accepted view.[72] Yet Locke's influence on Jefferson, directly and indirectly, and therefore on the Declaration of Independence itself, has not been credibly controverted, although some have tried.[73] In Benjamin Rush's words, "Mr. Locke is an oracle as to the

---

[67] Thomas Jefferson, "A Bill for Establishing Religious Freedom," 946–947, 947.
[68] "Question with boldness even the existence of a god; because if there be one, he must more approve of the homage of reason, than that of blindfold fear." Jefferson to Peter Carr, August 10, 1787, https://founders.archives.gov/documents/Jefferson/01-12-02-0021.
[69] Thomas Jefferson, "A Bill for Establishing Religious Freedom," 946–947, 947.
[70] Thomas Jefferson, *Notes on the State of Virginia* (1781) Query XVII, "The different religions received into that State," in *The Complete Jefferson*, 675, 676.
[71] Declaration of Independence, www.ushistory.org/declaration/document/. See also Jefferson, "original Rough draft."
[72] See, e.g., J. P. Kenyon, *Revolution Principles: The Politics of Party, 1689–1720* (Cambridge: Cambridge University Press, 1977); Richard Ashcraft, *Revolutionary Politics and Locke's "Two Treatises of Government"* (Princeton: Princeton University Press, 1986), 551–601; John Dunn, "The Politics of Locke in England and America in the Eighteenth Century," in John Yolton, ed., *John Locke: Problems and Perspectives* (Cambridge: Cambridge University Press, 1969).
[73] See, e.g., Richard Mathews, *The Radical Politics of Thomas Jefferson* (Lawrence: University Press of Kansas, 1976); Mills, *Inventing America*.

9 A Theological Interpretation

principles" upon which the "*forms* of government" were to be built.[74] Jefferson acknowledged as much when he praised Locke's theory, as well as the theory's practical application in the *Federalist Papers*, stating in 1790: "Locke's little book on government is perfect as far as it goes. Descending from theory to practice, there is no better book than the Federalist."[75]

In addition to Lockean principles, which lay at the foundation of the Declaration, the Declaration itself also addresses the practical in its grounds for separation from Britain: The Declaration's list of grievances against the king tracks nearly exactly Locke's justifications for resisting tyrannous governing authority.[76] That list warranted the dissolution of the British government in the colonies and the establishment of a new and independent government that derives its "just powers from the consent of the governed."[77] Those grievances, the separation on account of them, and the establishment of a new independent nation is Locke's and then Jefferson's right of resistance put into practice at the founding.

Still, in drafting the Declaration, Jefferson was not merely reflecting his own or even only Locke's theology. Richard Henry Lee had accused Jefferson of merely copying Locke in the Declaration. But in a letter to Henry Lee nearly fifty years after the adoption of the Declaration, Jefferson wrote that his intention in drafting it was "to be an expression of the American mind" by "harmonising sentiments of the day."[78] The masses were not philosophers, prominent statesmen, or theologians. Yet through sermons and numerous pamphlets, they, too, had come to embrace what became the religio-cultural milieu of the time. In whatever way received (directly or indirectly), Lockean emphasis on individuals' capacity for reason was infused into religion, as natural theology took hold.

Influential preachers had been significant natural theology transmitters. The noteworthy Rev. John Wise of Ipswich, who opposed centralizing power, is one of numerous examples. Writing in 1717, Wise stated:

[The] original of civil power is the people ...
The end of all good government is to cultivate humanity and promote the happiness of all, and the good of every man in all his rights, his life, liberty, estate, honor, &c. without injury or abuse done to any.[79]

---

[74] Benjamin Rush, *Observations on the Present Government of Pennsylvania*, Letter III, 1777 (emphasis in original), https://shorturl.at/IGDtW.
[75] Jefferson to Thomas Mann Randolph, May 30, 1790, https://founders.archives.gov/documents/Jefferson/01-16-02-0264.
[76] For detail on this, see Allen Jayne, *Jefferson's Declaration of Independence: Origins, Philosophy, and Theology* (Lexington: University Press of Kentucky, 1998), 48–51.
[77] Declaration of Independence, www.ushistory.org/declaration/document/.
[78] From Jefferson to Henry Lee, May 8, 1825, in *The Writings of Thomas Jefferson*, https://founders.archives.gov/documents/Jefferson/98-01-02-5212.
[79] John Wise, *A Vindication of the Government of New England Churches*, chapter II, 28 and 40, respectively, https://quod.lib.umich.edu/e/evans/N09928.0001.001/1:2.8?rgn=div2;view=fulltext.

In a 1715 sermon, Benjamin Coleman wrote that, "The Law of *Nature* is a very *Sacred* Law, and the Light of Nature a very *great Light*," and his 1723 sermon stated: "Reason in us is" the "Law of God" that "is given man for his Government and Conduct."[80] Like Locke, the prominent Cotton Mather also spoke of nature and scripture in his 1721 *The Christian Philosopher* when referencing "*a Twofold Book of God*: the Book of the *Creatures*, and the Book of the *Scriptures*: God having taught first of all us by his *Works*, did it afterwards ... by his *Words*."[81] He also noted that Locke's *Essay* was "much in vogue" at the time. Others spoke specifically about religious liberty in the language of natural theology. An example is Elisha Williams, who fused Locke with Protestant individualism in "The Essential Rights and Liberties of Protestants," in which he said:

[The] rights of conscience are sacred and equal to all, and strictly speaking unalienable. This *right of judging every one for himself in matters of religion* results from the nature of man, and is so inseparably connected therewith, that a man can no more part with it than he can with his power of thinking: and it is equally reasonable for him to attempt to strip himself of the power of reasoning, as to attempt the vesting of another with this right.[82]

The theological trend was Lockean in character, embracing reason and independence of thought, rejection of the doctrine of original sin, and in general natural theology.

Influential political pamphlets reflected these views as well. Just one of many is Samuel Adams' "The Rights of the Colonists and a List of Infringements and Violations of Rights" (1772):

In regard to Religeon, mutual tolleration in the different professions thereof, is what all good and candid minds in all ages have ever practiced; and both by precept and example inculcated on mankind: And it is now generally agreed among christians that this spirit of tolleration in the fullest extent consistent with the being of civil society "is the chief characteristical mark of the true church" & In so much that Mr. Lock[e] has asserted, and proved beyond the possibility of contradiction on any solid ground, that such toleration ought to be extended to all whose doctrines are now subversive of society.[83]

---

[80] Benjamin Coleman, "A Humble Discourse on the Incomprehensibleness of God" (1715) and "God Deals with Us as Rational Creatures" (1723), quoted in Claude M. Newlin, *Philosophy and Religion in Colonial America* (New York: Philosophical Library, 1962), 42–43 (emphasis in original).

[81] Cotton Mather, *The Christian Philosopher* (1721), quoted in Newlin, *Philosophy and Religion*, 33 and 35, respectively (emphasis in original).

[82] Elisha Williams, "The Essential Rights and Liberties of Protestants" (Boston, 1744), reprinted in Ellis Sandoz, ed., *Political Sermons of the American Founding Era: 1730–1805* (Indianapolis: Liberty Press, 1991), 62 (emphasis in original).

[83] Samuel Adams, "The Rights of the Colonists and a List of Infringements and Violations of Rights" (1772), in *The Bill of Rights: A Documentary History*, 2 vols., ed. Bernard Schwartz (New York: Chelsea House Publishers, 1971), 1: 201.

9 A Theological Interpretation

During the evangelical Protestant revival period known as The Great Awakening (1730s–c. 1745), even Calvinists, who promoted the view of human nature as being inherently sinful, began to embrace human beings' natural reason and, therefore, self-reliance as against state coercion (if not with regard to their own depraved souls' need for God's grace if they were to be saved). Consistent with the views of other scholars who have studied that period, C. C. Goen credits that movement with furthering the cause of democracy.[84] However, many Calvinists eventually viewed that trend as a threat to their movement, as it tended to elevate self-reliance above dependence on God's grace. That led to a late resurgence of the emotionalism of the Awakening. Nevertheless, the Great Awakening, with its threat of hellfire and brimstone for original sinners-all, did not last, dissipating in the mid 1740s,[85] as belief in human being's inherent equal creation and innate reason took hold. The prevailing view was exemplified by Ebenezer Gay in his Harvard Dudleian lecture of 1759, entitled "Natural Religion as Distinguished from Revealed":

> Whoever observes the divine Workmanship in human Nature, and takes a Survey of the Powers and Faculties with which it is endowed, must needs see that it was designed and framed for the Practice of Virtue: That man is not merely so much lumpish Matter, or *a mechanical Engine*, that moves only in the Direction of an impelling force; but that he hath a principle of Action within himself and is an Agent in the strict and proper sense of the Word. The special Endowment of his Nature, which constitutes him such, is the Power of Self-determination, or Freedom of Choice …[86]

Even when ordinary Americans were not familiar with Locke's political writings, Lockean ideas came to the people through Locke's writings on education and through other works that echoed those writings' themes. As Jerome Huyler notes, before 1761 Locke's *Some Thoughts Concerning Education*, which was reprinted more than nineteen times, "formed the principal influence on a legion of literary transmitters."[87] Widely read bestsellers valorized themes consistent with the elevation of self-sufficiency informed by reason inherent in human beings as created by God, which shaped the culture generally.[88] Having encountered the works of Locke, Bacon, and Newton, the highly regarded,

---

[84] C. C. Goen, *Revivalism and Separatism in New England, 1740–1800* (Middleton: Wesleyan University Press, 1987), 28.

[85] Nathan O. Hatch, *The Sacred Cause of Liberty: Republican Thought and the Millennium in Revolutionary New England* (New Haven and London: Yale University Press, 1977), 28–33; Jerome Huyler, *Locke in America: The Moral Philosophy of the Founding Era* (Lawrence: University Press of Kansas, 1995), 196–199.

[86] Ebenezer Gay, *Natural Religion as Distinguished from Revealed* (1759), quoted in Newlin, *Philosophy and Religion*, 199 (emphasis in original).

[87] Huyler, *Locke in America*, 201.

[88] See discussion of the influential "literary transmitters" in Huyler, *Locke in America*, 201–203. See also Frank Luther Mott, *The Golden Multitudes: The Story of Bestsellers in the United States* (New York: Macmillan, 1947); Fliegelman, *Prodigals and Pilgrims*.

widely read, and influential Rev. Dr. Samuel Johnson wrote in 1746 in the context of the "religion of nature" (i.e., moral philosophy):

> From what hath been said, it is plain, that the first duty incumbent upon me, as a reasonable active creature, in order to answer the end of my being, is, to cultivate and improve the reason and understanding which God hath given me, to be the governing principle and great law of my nature, to search and know the truth, and find out wherein my true happiness consists, and the means necessary to it.[89]

This was the "American mind" that Jefferson was "harmonizing" when he drafted the Declaration.

Whether the founding generation was in some way employing Lockean political ideas as rhetoric to justify their previous intention to separate from Britain, as John Dunn has argued,[90] or whether the colonists were predisposed to Locke's project because of the considerable liberty they already enjoyed in America, due to being separated from the limitations of the British sociopolitical structure, as Bernard Bailyn has argued,[91] it is nevertheless the case that Lockean natural theology and the themes derived from it – interpreted, modified, and believed in by Jefferson – were the basis for the Declaration and for a wide spectrum of the population to embrace it because they believed their cause was righteousness.

9.5 CONCLUSION

We can now answer the question posed at the beginning of this chapter: Why do nearly all of us embrace liberty and equality as unquestionable facts? In the West, liberty and equality emerged as individual rights from theological speculations, derived from the application of natural reason, about the nature of God and human beings and the relationship of human beings to each other and to God. That natural theology assumes a beneficent God who glorifies in what God has created, having made a world in which it is possible for human beings to pursue happiness. That theology became the foundation for the Declaration and eventually in 1791 for the First Amendment. Today, belief in liberty and equality, though uprooted from that ground, prevails. And it can be said that, though not recognized as such, so too prevails the underlying theology that gave rise to them.

Tragically, however, the Founders who drafted the United States Constitution and its inaugural amendments known as the Bill of Rights failed to include a

---

[89] Samuel Johnson, *ETHICA: Or the First PRINCIPLES of Moral Philosophy; And especially that Part which is called ETHICS. In a CHAIN of necessary CONSEQUENCES from certain FACTS*, 2nd ed. (Philadelphia: B. Franklin and D. Hall: 1752, 1st ed., 1746), part II, chapter II, section 2, 64, https://quod.lib.umich.edu/e/evans/N05418.0001.001/1:18?rgn=div1;view=fulltext.

[90] Dunn, "Politics of Locke," 60–77.

[91] Bernard Bailyn, "Political Experience and Enlightenment Ideas in Eighteenth-Century America," in Jack P. Greene, ed., *The Reinterpretation of the American Revolution: 1764–1789* (New York: Harper and Row, 1968), 277–290.

clear statement of the central fact underlying Locke's and Jefferson's natural law theology: equal creation. And Jefferson violated his own stated principles by participating in the institution of slavery. But that does not mean that the principles themselves are not sound. In fact, any criticism of Jefferson today about slavery is really an affirmation of the principles he declared.

Still, legal recognition of that central law of human nature had to wait until after the Civil War, when the Fourteenth Amendment with its equal protection clause was ratified in 1868 – nearly a century after the Declaration of Independence. The adoption of that amendment has rightly been called the "second founding."[92] The full import of that effort has not been achieved in large part because of the legacy of slavery and continued failure to remedy injustices against Native Americans. But it is also because the struggle for constitutional recognition of everyone's fundamental equality is still ongoing.

Today, authoritarian-tending "we are better, know better, and are more deserving than other Americans" impulses abound across the political spectrum. They are echoes into our time of the "elect are more worthy than others" theology that the Declaration rejected. Yet so far, Locke's and Jefferson's natural theology still remains in the widely held belief that, as the Declaration proclaimed, there is a fundamental "self-evident" truth: equal creation. From that follows the natural unalienable rights of life (to be preserved), liberty (to be free to discern and live according to the natural laws and the virtues they anticipate, free even from the coercion of God), and the pursuit of happiness (as a means for preservation: enjoying God's earthly gifts here and now as we fulfill God's purpose).

Yet it is important to remember that for Locke and Jefferson, and for the "American mind" of the founding era, the theology underlying the Declaration implies duties. Foremost is the duty to preserve ourselves but also others in the pursuit of their own equally worthy lives. In other words, the pursuit of happiness is not only for one's own individual happiness – it is for the happiness of everyone.

I have trust in him who made us what we are ... He has formed us moral agents ... that we may promote the happiness of those with whom he has placed us in society, by acting honestly towards all, benevolently to those who fall within our way, respecting sacredly their rights bodily and mental, and cherishing especially their freedom of conscience, as we value our own.

Thomas Jefferson (1814)[93]

---

[92] See Eric Foner, *The Second Founding: How the Civil War and Reconstruction Remade the Constitution* (New York: W. W. Norton & Company, 2019). See also Derek H. Davis, "Completing the Constitution: Religion, Rights, and the Fourteenth Amendment," in Barbara A. McGraw, ed., *The Wiley-Blackwell Companion to Religion and Politics in the U.S.* (West Sussex, UK: John Wiley & Sons, 2016), 213–224.

[93] Jefferson to Miles King, September 26, 1814, https://founders.archives.gov/documents/Jefferson/03-07-02-0495.

10

The Declaration versus the Constitution

Tom Cutterham

If the Declaration of Independence set Americans at liberty, the new federal Constitution meant to shackle them again. So, at least, said some of the proposed new Constitution's enemies, during the bitter debates over ratification and the new government's establishment that took place during the late 1780s and the early 1790s. Even before the convention began in Philadelphia in the summer of 1787, voices of suspicion were raised against the secretive proceedings. Their tenor and tendency, opponents said, was contradictory to the true spirit of the revolution – a spirit they identified with ending tyranny and loosening the chains of government, not the empowerment of new authorities.

This putative dichotomy between the Declaration and the Constitution, the "Spirit of '76" and the "Spirit of '87," has remained a trope of public memory across the centuries, casting its shadows on the received meaning of both documents.[1] To understand the Declaration's afterlife and impact, we need to address its contested relationship with the Constitution. Beginning with a brief account of the Constitution's origins, this chapter sketches the interaction of the two documents through the era of the nation's founding, and through subsequent encounters up to the beginning of the twenty-first century. It shows how American publics, and individual thinkers, have both received and recast this crucial relationship. Between them, the Declaration and the Constitution bear much of the weight of the United States' founding tradition. In both their contrasts and their consonance, they reflect a complex and contested revolutionary legacy.

Of course, these were and remain fundamentally different types of documents. Each was entangled in its own complex array of contexts, meanings, and intentions. Neither was written by a single author, for a single purpose, and each is susceptible to more than one interpretation. Both documents were meant to

---

[1] The "Spirit of '76" is well known, but for the "Spirit of '87," see Joseph Ellis, "Clash of the Titans," *New York Times*, March 10, 2002, www.nytimes.com/2002/03/10/books/clash-of-the-titans.html.

mark a rupture with earlier constitutional arrangements, and to signal to both citizens and potential allies that the nation was prepared to govern and defend itself. Yet there are clear differences of function. The Declaration aimed to justify an act the Continental Congress had already taken: separation from the British Empire. The Constitution delineated the mechanisms by which the United States was to be governed. If the Declaration was a text of facts and sentiments, the Constitution was one of rules. Its political theory, or complex of theories, was implicit. Its grandeur lay not in any specific claim to moral or political truths, but in its outline of a powerful, functional structure of government, imbued with the legitimacy of popular sovereignty. The Declaration was the echoing blast of a cannon, but the Constitution was the blueprint of a fortress.

From the founding to the present, one interpretive tradition has understood the two documents as essentially compatible and complementary. As the scholar Martin Diamond put it, "these are the two great charters of our national existence, representing the beginning of our founding and its consummation."[2] In his view, the Declaration established the principle of liberty, and the Constitution built upon it by attempting to institute a form of government that would secure that liberty. Democracy or equality were merely secondary, instrumental concerns to the men who wrote them. Some authors of the Constitution, such as James Wilson, argued powerfully that their work rested upon the same political principles as the Declaration. Later interpreters, including Frederick Douglass and Abraham Lincoln, placed the two documents alongside one another in their understanding of the nation's founding.

Yet as Diamond perceived, political circumstances frequently gave life to an alternative tradition. In his own time, that alternative tradition was championed by progressive critics of the Founders' Constitution, such as Charles Beard, who had found in their commitment to equality and democracy new ways of reading, and contrasting, the two documents. Just as they had done in the era of the founding itself, many Americans in the nineteenth and twentieth centuries came to see the Declaration and the Constitution as antagonistic – representative of contrasting visions of politics, justice, and human nature. Affirming an abolitionist critique then over a century old, the historian Staughton Lynd wrote in 1965 that "the American Revolution was a revolution betrayed." Inasmuch as the Declaration promised the equality of all men and their equal rights to the pursuit of happiness, that revolutionary promise was betrayed by a Constitution which enshrined both slavery and the political arrangements necessary for its future protection.[3] Not only that, but in

---

[2] Martin Diamond, "The Declaration and the Constitution: Liberty, Democracy, and the Founders," *The Public Interest* 41 (Fall 1975): 39–55, at 45.

[3] Staughton Lynd, "The Abolitionist Critique of the United States Constitution," in Staughton Lynd, ed., *Class Conflict, Slavery, and the United States Constitution: Ten Essays* (Indianapolis: Bobbs-Merrill Company, 1967), 153–183, at 183. On the constitution's compromise with slavery, see also David Waldstreicher, *Slavery's Constitution: Revolution to Ratification* (New York: Hill & Wang, 2009).

concentrating political power in the hands of slave-holders and other elites, it also betrayed the liberty promised even to white, male citizens. On this account, the Constitution was a Hobbesian document, representing a withdrawal of the trust in human nature that the Declaration had embodied.[4]

Whatever their contradictions, the Declaration and the Constitution are bound together, both by public memory and by the legal and political practice of the United States. While the Declaration has a claim to the status of fundamental law, that claim can only be borne out through mechanisms first designed in 1787. The form of government established by the Constitution gives life to American independence. However, the Declaration's prior role in establishing the foundations of American government can only complicate the singular authority of the written Constitution. The Declaration's principles can challenge and enrich the practice of politics in the republic. These documents were never simply contradictory. They were also, from an early stage, dependent on each other.

10.1 WHAT WAS THE CONSTITUTION?

Before 1789, the governance of the United States was a ramshackle affair. From the outbreak of war in 1775, a Congress of delegates from the thirteen soon-to-be-independent states began to meet on a regular basis in order to coordinate the revolution's military and diplomatic efforts. In 1781, those delegates agreed to a more permanent instrument of collective government, the Articles of Confederation. But the Articles functioned more like a treaty between separate states than the plan of a unitary government. Crucially, the only source of revenue for the Confederation Congress was what it could extract from the state governments in the form of requisitions – in effect, voluntary contributions. It found its efforts at fiscal management and diplomacy increasingly undermined by the independent decisions of state governments, a dynamic that only grew more pronounced as the immediate threat of war faded after the victory at Yorktown.

Calls for a more powerful and centralized system of government for the United States began as soon as the Articles of Confederation were ratified. According to Alexander Hamilton, then a young aide to George Washington, "many of the fatal mistakes, which have so deeply endangered the common cause" could be traced to "A WANT OF POWER IN CONGRESS."[5] Hamilton found allies in men like the Superintendent of Finance Robert Morris and the Virginia congressman James Madison. Their movement for a stronger Congress had much of the wind taken from its sails by the advent of peace

---

[4] For the Constitution as fundamentally Hobbesian and pessimistic about human nature, see Forrest McDonald, Novus Ordo Seclorum: *The Intellectual Origins of the Constitution* (Lawrence: University Press of Kansas, 1985).
[5] Joanne Freeman, ed., *Alexander Hamilton: Writings* (New York: Library of America, 2001), 99.

with Britain. But it experienced a revival three years later due to a complicated combination of factors – a commercial downturn, elite dissatisfaction with state governments, a growing consensus among diplomats and national politicians, and finally, most dramatically, the shock of violent rebellion in Massachusetts and neighboring states beginning in the fall of 1786. Having called that summer for a national convention to deliberate amendments to the Articles of Confederation, Madison took a leading role in organizing a convention to be held in Philadelphia in 1787. By this point, nationally minded elites across the thirteen states were increasingly shrill in the condemnation of the status quo.

Working behind the scenes, Madison helped drive the Philadelphia Convention's agenda away from mere amendment and towards a total overhaul of the relationship between the states. In a set of notes on the "vices" of the existing system, he emphasized not only the Confederation Congress' incapacity to raise taxes and wage war but also its inability to exert discipline on the state governments. Madison sought a federal veto over state laws in order to suppress "wicked" policies like the issuing of paper money.[6] Although that idea was thrown out by more cautious members at the convention, many others were satisfied by the provisions in Article 1, Section 10 of the new constitution that cut off states' fiscal authority and independence. They were convinced that the newly empowered central government would pursue a more conservative economic policy.[7]

At the convention, Madison's hopes of instituting a council of revision and proportional representation by population across the federal legislature, were also both defeated – proportional representation in the senate was sacrificed to protect the interests of the small states. The new federal government would have relatively little power to intervene in the internal policies of the states. But it would have powers to tax trade and regulate commerce among the states, as well as "to make all laws which shall be necessary and proper" for the full execution of its powers and responsibilities (Article 1, section 8, clause 18). With a unitary executive, a bicameral legislature, and a powerful judiciary serving for life, the new form of government bore some resemblance to the British constitutional system. But it also emphasized popular representation through regular elections. What had the delegates designed? "A republic, if you can keep it," said Benjamin Franklin.[8]

Like the Declaration of Independence, the Constitution boasted a preamble that contained its most memorable and evocative language. It adopted the voice of "We the People of the United States." Echoing the Declaration's line

---

[6] Jack Rakove, ed., *James Madison: Writings* (New York: Library of America, 1999), 69–80.
[7] For the significance of Article 1, section 10, in particular, see Woody Holton, *Unruly Americans and the Origins of the Constitution* (New York: Hill and Wang, 2007), 228–233.
[8] Charles C. Tansill, ed., *Documents Illustrative of the Formation of the Union of the American States* (Washington, DC: U.S. Printing Office, 1927), 952.

about the institution of governments among men, the preamble declared that the purpose of the Constitution was "to form a more perfect Union, establish Justice, insure domestic Tranquility, provide for the common defence, promote the general Welfare, and secure the Blessings of Liberty to ourselves and our Posterity." Such language aimed to situate the Constitution in the tradition of Jefferson's well-remembered Declaration. From the outset, however, that effort would be fiercely contested.

10.2 BATTLE FOR RATIFICATION

Inside the state-ratifying conventions of 1787–1788, and in the broader public sphere, the Declaration quickly became a stick to beat the Constitution with. It was a symbol of the gap between what the revolution had promised and what the Constitution's advocates hoped to deliver. Anti-federalists – opponents of the Constitution, as against the Federalists, its proponents – also drew on the more general concept of a "Spirit of '76," embodied in the Declaration perhaps, but extending beyond it as well. They emphasized a narrative of revolutionary decline and betrayal that had begun to be constructed during the war itself. The Declaration was seen to embody a phase of early revolutionary purity, against a later period of corruption and decline. The Constitution, by contrast, symbolized the process of corruption and encroaching tyranny to which all republics were doomed to be subjected.

"It is my heart's wish to see a federal constitution established agreeable to the principles of republican liberty and independence," wrote one Anti-federalist, "and on the basis of a democratical government, meaning that of the people." This was the kind of government "intended by our glorious Declaration of Independence." But this was not the kind of government outlined in the Constitution. Alluding directly to the collapse of the Roman republic into tyranny and empire, as well as to the burgeoning critique of British rule in India, this writer like many others accused the Federalists of paving the way for "an ARISTOCRATICAL government, whereby about 70 nabobs would lord over three millions of people as slaves." It would be as if Americans had never won their independence at all. "I beg you," he wrote, "to call to mind our glorious Declaration of Independence, read it, and compare it with the Federal Constitution; what a degree of apostacy will you not then discover."[9] The Declaration and its principles were to be the standard by which the Constitution, like all other political measures, should be judged.

What the Declaration's principal author himself thought about the Constitution is not altogether straightforward. In France as ambassador during the drafting and ratification process, it was only when his friend James

---

[9] Merrill Jensen, ed., *The Documentary History of the Ratification of the Constitution* (Madison: State Historical Society of Wisconsin, 1978), 3: 236, 243, original capitalization.

Madison reported on his own proposal for a federal power of veto over state laws that Thomas Jefferson began to appreciate the scale of the endeavor, and to raise objections to it. The aim, he now saw, was not simply to patch up the old Articles of Confederation but to establish a new system altogether.[10] When he saw the completed document, he recognized that it contained some good and necessary measures, including fiscal independence for the central government. But he believed those "might have been couched in three or four new articles to be added to the good, old, and venerable fabrick."[11] The wholesale reform proposed in the new document was an overreaction to "the insurrection of Massachusetts," by which delegates in Philadelphia were "too much impressed."[12] It represented, in short, a reactionary swing towards more concentrated, less accountable authority.

This response did not mean Jefferson actually opposed the passage of the new Constitution. His position was a more ambivalent one. "Were I in America," he wrote, "I would advocate it warmly till nine [states] should have adopted, and then as warmly take the other side."[13] He was committed to the notion of a bill of rights that would check the potential power of both Congress and the presidency – a strategy that other moderate Anti-federalists also adopted, and a demand to which many Federalists were happy to accede. Thus, Jefferson neither promoted not disavowed the view that there was an antagonism between the Constitution and the Declaration. Leaving others to debate the spirit of the Declaration, he allowed both sides to mount their own rhetorical claims.

Anti-federalists, as Herbert Storing put it, "saw in the Framers' easy thrusting aside of old forms and principles threats to four cherished values: to law, to political stability, to the principles of the Declaration of Independence, and to federalism."[14] Like Jefferson, many were outraged that the Convention at Philadelphia had chosen not to simply put forward amendments to the Articles of Confederation, as originally mandated. Moreover, the Federalists' new Constitution seemed to undermine the legal order established by the revolution: one that had at its heart both the Declaration and the independent states. It not only paved the way for a potential aristocracy, but also sought to do so on the ruins of those republican governments that the revolution had already established.

---

[10] Thomas Jefferson to James Madison, June 20, 1787: https://founders.archives.gov/documents/Jefferson/01-11-02-0411.
[11] Jefferson to John Adams, November 13, 1787: https://founders.archives.gov/documents/Jefferson/01-12-02-0342.
[12] Jefferson to William Stephens Smith, November 13, 1787: https://founders.archives.gov/documents/Jefferson/01-12-02-0348.
[13] Jefferson to Smith, February 2, 1788: https://founders.archives.gov/documents/Jefferson/01-12-02-0590.
[14] Herbert Storing, *What the Anti-federalists Were For* (Chicago: University of Chicago Press, 1981), 7.

Anti-federalists' attachment to the governments and constitutions of their own states did, however, offer a line of attack to their Federalist opponents. A satirical list of the Pennsylvania Anti-federalists' objections made the point clear – they opposed the Constitution, it was claimed, because "by the diminution of the power of the state of Pennsylvania, we shall have fewer offices, and smaller salaries, to bestow upon our friends."[15] Pennsylvania's 1776 constitution had created one of the more radical state governments, with a unicameral legislature and relatively weak checks on democratic power. Wealthy merchants and their allies in the state had long sought to revise its constitution. So far they had failed. But both sides saw the battle over the new federal Constitution as a continuation of the same conflict, a struggle which also pitted rural and western representatives against the Philadelphia elites.[16]

What did this question of state institutions have to do with the Declaration of Independence? For James Wilson, one of the most adept and active Federalist advocates at Pennsylvania's ratifying convention, the answer was everything. The Declaration laid out "the broad basis on which our independence was based," Wilson said, and it located that foundation in the consent of the people as a whole – not of the states. "State sovereignty, as it is called, is far from being able to support its weight. Nothing less than the authority of the people could either support it or give it efficacy."[17] Wilson thus enlisted the Declaration to support his theory of popular sovereignty, and in turn to deny the sovereignty of individual states. Moreover, the new Constitution, like the Declaration, would have the consent of the whole American people. Its legitimacy would therefore trump that of the state governments.

Other Federalists, too, saw a fundamental consonance between the Declaration and the proposed Constitution. The authors of the Federalist essays identified themselves with a defence of the union from external and internal threats, including the threat of states or regional confederations breaking away from each other. By creating an energetic federal government, the Constitution would work to protect republican liberty, and American independence, from the very real dangers of insurrection and invasion.[18] Anti-federalists might argue about the impact of a powerful government and standing army on the social and political order at home, but it was harder for them to deny the utility of those measures in the sphere of foreign affairs – not to mention in the new nation's continental borderlands. Over time, the focus of the Constitution's opponents shifted from outright rejection of reform

---

[15] "The Protest of the Minority," *Pennsylvania Gazette*, October 3, 1787.
[16] For the conflict in Pennsylvania, see Terry Bouton, *Taming Democracy: "The People," the Founders, and the Troubled Ending of the American Revolution* (New York: Oxford University Press, 2007).
[17] Jonathan Elliot, ed., *The Debates of the Several State Conventions on the Adoption of the Federal Constitution* (Washington, DC: Printed by and for the editor, 1836), 2: 457.
[18] Max Edling, *A Revolution in Favor of Government: Origins of the U.S. Constitution and the Making of the American State* (New York: Oxford University Press, 2003).

towards the need for explicit protections against government encroachments on rights and freedoms. In other words, they adopted the Jeffersonian position that the Constitution was acceptable so long as it was reined in by a bill of rights. Several states, including Massachusetts and South Carolina, ratified but simultaneously recommended amendments to be sought immediately. That was not quite the same as the path Patrick Henry recommended at the Virginia ratifying convention, "to reject this government till it be amended," but it was close enough to be the basis of compromise.[19] Once the threshold of nine ratifying states had been reached with New Hampshire, the promise of substantial amendments allowed Anti-federalist delegates in Virginia and New York to swallow the bitter pill and vote to ratify.[20]

While the Federalists won the ratification battle, then, they did so on the basis of compromise. Anti-federalists succeeded in making the case that the Constitution must include specific, enumerated protections of American citizens' rights, and restrictions on the powers of the new federal government. They also achieved a broader ideological victory, which has had an important impact on American political development. By identifying the core values of the revolution with mistrust of central government power, and insisting on the necessity of explicit constitutional limits to that power, Anti-federalists – just as much as Federalists – helped define the meaning of the Constitution for future Americans.[21]

By calling on "our glorious Declaration of Independence" to bolster their case during the battle over ratification, Anti-federalists helped create the meaning of *that* document, too. The Declaration offered them a way of declaring their loyalty to the revolution, and to its resulting republican governments, without necessarily committing them to the defense of the Articles of Confederation. Moreover, unlike the Articles, the Declaration could be used to represent a set of principles rather than a particular institutional arrangement. Anti-federalists turned the Declaration into a yardstick by which any institutional design could be judged. In establishing conditions for legitimate rebellion, the Declaration demarcated a critical distance between American citizens and their forms of government – a distance which American politicians would continue to exploit, when ideals or expediency demanded.

10.3 THE CONSTITUTION IN OPERATION

Once the Constitution had been ratified, many Anti-federalists hoped for a second constitutional convention to consider the amendments they thought

---

[19] Elliott, ed., *Debates*, 3: 152.
[20] For a full narrative of the ratification process, see Pauline Maier, *Ratification: The People Debate the Constitution, 1787–1788* (New York: Simon and Schuster, 2010).
[21] Saul Cornell, *The Other Founders: Anti-federalists and the Dissenting Tradition in America, 1788–1828* (Chapel Hill: University of North Carolina Press, 1999).

they had won. These hopes went unfulfilled. Instead, when the new government began to operate early in 1789, Anti-federalists apparently dropped the issue, and Federalist legislators corralled by James Madison adopted a limited slate of amendments. while they moved on with the business of fleshing out the Constitution's framework. These amendments are what later became known as the Bill of Rights. Within a few years, the Constitution had been more or less thoroughly entrenched as the fundamental law of the United States, even as its meaning continued to be subject to political contestation.[22]

Many Americans remained suspicious of the new government. They worked to keep its powers limited within a strict construction of constitutional meaning. They also continued to look to the Declaration as a fundamental statement of American revolutionary principles. By the end of the decade, an emerging democratic movement committed to the equality of all white, male citizens had come to coalesce with a cadre of anti-administration politicians led by a perhaps unlikely duo: the father of the Constitution, James Madison, and the author of the Declaration, Thomas Jefferson.[23]

As the Virginia jurist St. George Tucker explained a few years later, in 1803, the Declaration of Independence was what secured the basic legitimacy of the Constitution as the frame of government for an independent nation.[24] But the Declaration was also an act of the several independent states that made up the union. It legitimated those states at least as much as it did the federal government. The issue arose most urgently in 1798, when John Adams' administration implemented the draconian sanctions against the opposition press and foreign residents in the United States, known as the Alien and Sedition Acts. Faced with a government that appeared to be in breach of the Declaration's basic principles, the emerging opposition sought in the states a means of challenging federal power.

The Virginia and Kentucky Resolves, drafted by Madison and Jefferson, respectively, declared those states' intention not to enforce Adams' measures. Neither referred directly to the Declaration. But the Virginia document alluded to its foundational position when it declared that it was the state legislature's duty "to watch over and oppose every infraction of those principles which constitute the only basis of that Union," in other words, the principles of the

---

[22] Lance Banning, "Republican Ideology and the Triumph of the Constitution, 1789 to 1793," *William and Mary Quarterly* 31.2 (April 1974): 167–188; Jonathan Gienapp, *The Second Creation: Fixing the American Constitution in the Founding Era* (Cambridge: Harvard University Press, 2018).

[23] For these political transformations in the 1790s, see Stanley Elkins and Eric McKitrick, *The Age of Federalism: The Early American Republic, 1788–1800* (New York: Oxford University Press, 1993); and for limited egalitarianism, Seth Cotlar, *Tom Paine's America: The Rise and Fall of Transatlantic Radicalism in the Early American Republic* (Charlottesville: University of Virginia Press, 2011).

[24] St. George Tucker, *View of the Constitution of the United States: With Selected Writings*, ed. Wilson Clyde (Indianapolis: Liberty Fund, 1999).

Declaration. "A faithful observance of them," it continued, "can alone secure [the union's] existence and the public happiness."[25] In the face of arbitrary government, the Declaration was the obvious point of reference.

Jefferson's election to the presidency in 1800 gave him the opportunity to offer a symbolic reconciliation of the two documents' principles. Indeed, the union of Declaration and Constitution gives a plausible meaning to his famous inaugural claim, "We are all Republicans, we are all Federalists." The republic instituted by the Constitution was "the world's best hope … The strongest Government on earth." Jefferson in power struggled to act within the principles of strict construction he had championed in opposition. The requirements of building an "empire of liberty" belied his imagined agrarian simplicity.[26] Yet his triumph, and the steady eclipse of the Federalist party in the following decades, allowed the opposition between Declaration and Constitution to fade from view at the dawn of the nineteenth century. It would be those excluded from the ambit of the revolution's liberty that placed it back under the spotlight.

10.4 ABOLITIONIST AND FEMINIST TRADITIONS

The Constitution did not explicitly exclude African Americans or women from the political and civil life of the nation. But nor did it offer them much encouragement. Defining the boundaries of citizenship, and controlling access to civil and political rights, was for the most part the preserve of the state governments, which almost unanimously persisted in shutting them out.[27] The Spirit of '76, however, would inspire advocates of hitherto denied equality and suffrage through the nineteenth century and beyond.

Black Americans, especially those bound in slavery, faced the dilemma of a sharp apparent opposition between the inclusive language of the Declaration – "*all* men" – and the protections that the Constitution gave to slavery. It was the Declaration, not the Constitution, that provided the model for nineteenth-century Americans' commitment to freedom, equality, and individual rights.[28] The "Declaration of Sentiments of the American Anti-Slavery Society," drafted by William Lloyd Garrison in 1833, traced its lineage explicitly to 1776 and the promise of "life, LIBERTY, and the pursuit of happiness."

---

[25] Rakove, ed., *James Madison*, 589.
[26] Merrill D. Peterson, ed., *Thomas Jefferson: Writings* (New York: Library of America, 1984), 492, 496. See Joanne Freeman and Johann Neem, eds., *Jeffersonians in Power: The Rhetoric of Opposition Meets the Realities of Governing* (Charlottesville: University of Virginia Press, 2019).
[27] For an exceptional case, see Judith Apter Klinghoffer and Lois Elkis, "'The Petticoat Electors': Women's Suffrage in New Jersey," *Journal of the Early Republic* 12.2 (Summer, 1992): 159–193.
[28] Pauline Maier, *Ratification: The People Debate the Constitution, 1787–1788* (New York: Simon and Schuster, 2010), 464; Philip S. Foner, ed., *We, the Other People: Alternative Declarations of Independence by Labor Groups, Farmers, Woman's Rights Advocates, Socialists, and Blacks 1829–1975* (Urbana: University of Illinois Press, 1976).

Of the revolutionaries, Garrison wrote, "At the sound of their trumpet-call, three millions of people rose up as from the sleep of death, and rushed to the strife of blood; deeming it more glorious to die instantly as freemen, than desirable to live one hour as slaves."[29]

At Seneca Falls fifteen years later, the delegates to a convention on women's rights, who included the self-emancipated former slave and abolitionist Frederick Douglass, issued a "Declaration of Rights and Sentiments" which echoed the language of Jefferson's original Declaration. "The history of mankind," it announced, "is a history of repeated injuries and usurpation on the part of man toward woman, having in direct object the establishment of an absolute tyranny over her."[30] By repurposing the words of the 1776 Declaration, the women of Seneca Falls implied that the United States Constitution offered no more liberty to them than had the tyranny of George III. Invoking the Spirit of '76, both they and the Anti-Slavery Society challenged the legitimacy of the constituted order in their own time.

When Garrison stood to condemn the Constitution as a "covenant with death, and an agreement with hell," he did so most famously on the 4th of July 1854.[31] There could hardly be a more potent symbol of the discordance between the Constitution and the Declaration than Garrison's act: burning a copy of one, on a day of veneration for the other. Yet the different factions of the nineteenth-century abolition movement came to disagree over their attitude to the Constitution, and they were hardly united in praise of the Declaration. As he moved away from his early Garrisonian position, Frederick Douglass sought to vindicate the Constitution, even as he denounced the hypocrisy of celebrating the 4th of July.[32] These were differences of strategy, perhaps, more than of principle. But such disagreements helped to keep alive the tangled, protean relationship between the documents.

Abraham Lincoln certainly recognized the difficulty. But as President, he emphasized consonance rather than disjunction. Lincoln's view is most concisely represented in his 1861 "Fragment on the Constitution and the Union," which compared the Declaration's principle of liberty to the "apple of gold" and the Constitutional framework to the "picture of silver" in the biblical proverb (25:11). "The picture was made, not to conceal, or destroy the apple,"

---

[29] "Declaration of the National Anti-slavery Convention," in William E. Cain, ed., *William Lloyd Garrison and the Fight against Slavery: Selections from The Liberator* (Boston: St. Martin's Press, 1995), 90–94.
[30] Elizabeth Cady Stanton et al., "Declaration of Rights and Sentiments," *Seneca Falls*, 1848.
[31] Henry Mayer, *All on Fire: William Lloyd Garrison and the Abolition of Slavery* (New York: St. Martin's Press, 1998), 444–445. Already in 1832, Garrison had condemned the Constitution as an "infamous bargain" by which the Founders "trampled beneath their feet their own solemn and heaven-attested Declaration;" *The Liberator*, December 29, 1832.
[32] Philip S. Foner and Taylor Yuval, eds., *Frederick Douglass: Selected Speeches and Writings* (Chicago: Chicago Review Press, 2000), 188–206. For the tradition of "constitutional antislavery," see Manisha Sinha, *The Slaves' Cause: A History of Abolition* (New Haven: Yale University Press, 2016), 477.

Lincoln wrote, "but to adorn, and preserve it." Rather than the two documents being at odds, it was only the Declaration that gave meaning and purpose to the Constitution. "The picture was made for the apple – not the apple for the picture."[33] This complementary view, as opposed to Garrison's oppositional one, became more or less standard in the post-Civil War era. The Union victory and the Thirteenth Amendment helped reorient the constitutional tradition, bringing it closer to the promise of the Declaration.

10.5 CONCLUSION

The Declaration of Independence continued to license radicals and revolutionaries long after peace was made with Britain in 1783, including not only the Anti-federalists but the feminists and abolitionists of a succeeding century. If the Constitution implied that the foundations of politics in the United States were now fixed, then the Declaration offered hope that transformation was still possible. The second American Revolution wrought by the Civil War and Reconstruction, while still unfinished, went some way to vindicating that radical hope.[34] In the twentieth century, progressive historians and others have maintained an emphasis on the tension between the two documents. Yet at the beginning of the twenty-first, the Declaration and the Constitution were more likely to be conflated or confused with one another, than taken as two contrasting statements about politics, justice, and human nature.[35]

Some scholars of the constitutional tradition emphasize that it relies as much upon a whole ecology of texts and concepts *outside* the written pages of the document itself, as it does upon the words agreed by the Framers in 1787.[36] They do so partly in response to the claims of legal "originalists," who seek to selectively exclude elements of the Constitution's diverse interpretative tradition.[37] Whether the Declaration ought to be granted the force of an

---

[33] Roy Basler, ed., *The Collected Works of Abraham Lincoln*, 8 vols. (New Brunswick: Rutgers University Press, 1953), 4: 168–169. See John Patrick Diggins, *On Hallowed Ground: Abraham Lincoln and the Foundations of American History* (New Haven: Yale University Press, 2000).

[34] James McPherson, *Abraham Lincoln and the Second American Revolution* (New York: Oxford University Press, 1992); Eric Foner, *Reconstruction: America's Unfinished Revolution, 1863–1877* (New York: Harper and Row, 1988).

[35] For example, "Did Obama Confuse U.S. Constitution with Declaration of Independence?" https://tinyurl.com/3kw4cky8; "Nancy Pelosi Confuses Constitution with Declaration of Independence," *Washington Examiner*, https://tinyurl.com/5b36kj95.

[36] Lawrence Tribe, *The Invisible Constitution* (New York: Oxford University Press, 2008); David Strauss, *The Living Constitution* (New York: Oxford University Press, 2010); Akhil Amar, *America's Unwritten Constitution: The Precedents and Principles We Live By* (New York: Basic Books, 2012).

[37] See Jack Rakove, *Original Meanings: Politics and Ideas in the Making of the Constitution* (New York: Alfred A. Knopf, 1996).

"act of law," as the legal scholar Charles Black argued, or considered simply as a resource for shaping political and moral debate, its place in the ongoing practice of American constitutionalism seems unimpeachable.[38] In court, and more importantly in the wider public sphere, the Declaration continues to help shape the meaning of the Constitution – and to have its own meaning remolded in turn.[39]

Historians must acknowledge that the Declaration, the product of a tiny conclave of provincial delegates, drafted by a slaveholder and amended to protect the honor of slaveholding states, is far from the apogee of American radicalism. In these respects, it bears an uncanny resemblance to the Constitution of 1787. The Declaration and the Constitution now most often appear as twin pillars in an aging republican edifice, virtually indistinguishable from each other. Yet in its function as a revolutionary document, a utopian appeal to both equality and popular sovereignty, the Declaration contributes a unique legacy to the political tradition of the whole globe.[40] From time to time, that legacy is renewed by those who take the Declaration as a symbol of their just rebellion against an unjust order, and a model for their own announcements to a candid and sometimes cynical world.

---

[38] Charles Black, *A New Birth of Freedom: Human Rights, Named and Unnamed* (New Haven: Yale University Press, 1997). For the view that the Declaration has rhetorical but not legal force, see Pauline Maier, *American Scripture: Making the Declaration of Independence* (New York: Vintage Books, 1998).

[39] There are some who invoke the Declaration and its principles in favor of a much more wholesale constitutional reform as well. See Sanford Levinson, *Our Undemocratic Constitution: Where the Constitution Goes Wrong (And How We the People Can Correct It)* (Oxford: Oxford University Press, 2006).

[40] On global echoes, see David Armitage, *The Declaration of Independence: A Global History* (Cambridge: Harvard University Press, 2008). The constitution, too, has been a model adapted by many imitators, including within the United States itself: see Robert Tsai, *America's Forgotten Constitutions: Defiant Visions of Power and Community* (Cambridge: Harvard University Press, 2014).

11

Getting "the Hang of the Declaration"
The Declaration in American Nationalism

Brian Steele

> We all know very well how quickly people recognize each other, and how unequivocally they can feel that they belong to each other, when they discover a kinship in questions of what pleases and displeases. From the viewpoint of this common experience, it is as though taste decides not only how the world is to look, but also who belongs together in it.
>
> Hannah Arendt, "Crisis in Culture" (1954)

> ... however error or passions may at times [lead] us astray, I trust that the principles of '76. will forever form a point of union round which we shall learn to rally & to recognize one another encircling them with a mass of strength which the world cannot shake.
>
> Jefferson to Fayetteville Republican Citizens, March 17, 1801

In the wake of the Dred Scott decision – which he took to be a threat not only to human equality but also to the essence of the American character and progressive political tradition – Abraham Lincoln told a crowd in Springfield Illinois that, the "authors" of the Declaration of Independence "meant to set up a standard maxim for free society, which should be familiar to all, and revered by all; constantly looked to, constantly labored for, and even though never perfectly attained, constantly approximated, and thereby constantly spreading and deepening its influence, and augmenting the happiness and value of life to all people of all colors everywhere." Against Chief Justice Roger B. Taney, who had argued that the authors of the Declaration could not have meant to include blacks in the phrase "all men are created equal," Lincoln insisted that "the Declaration contemplated the progressive improvement in the condition

---

Dedicated to the memory of Richard J. Bernstein (May 14, 1932–July 4, 2022), in democratic hope.

of all men everywhere." And against Illinois Senator Stephen A. Douglas, who insisted that the Declaration's rights claims were limited to an assertion that contemporary "British subjects on this continent" were "equal to British subjects born and residing in Great Britain," Lincoln suggested that the Declaration "promised something better than the condition of British subjects." Against Douglas' claim that the Declaration was intended merely to justify the colonists "in the eyes of the civilized world" as they withdrew allegiance to Britain, Lincoln pronounced that such a reading would turn the Declaration into "an interesting memorial of a dead past," "shorn of its vitality."[1] Celebrations of the Fourth were meaningless, by Douglas' reading, Lincoln thought, for, if Douglas was right, "the doings of that day had no reference to the present." Its "object having been effected some eighty years ago, the Declaration is of no practical use now." Lincoln conceded that "the assertion that 'all men are created equal' was of no practical use in effecting our separation from Great Britain." But, he insisted, "it was placed in the Declaration, not for that, but for future use. Its authors meant it to be, thank God, it is now proving itself, a stumbling block to those who in after times might seek to turn a free people back into the hateful paths of despotism." In Douglas' reading of the text, Lincoln said, the Declaration's promise and its standard would be "frittered away."[2]

Lincoln's use of the protean term "standard" to describe the Declaration is simultaneously Kantian and Hegelian.[3] It suggests an abstract higher – transcultural and ahistorical – authority against which our current behavior ought to be evaluated, to which it ought to conform, and, at the same time, it indicates the distinctive symbolic form of a particular solidarity, becomes emblematic of that solidarity's history, traditions, and values, and remains venerated as such, rallied around, defended, and raised – as had been the standard of a Roman legion – to distinguish that solidarity from all others. To be sure, "The principles of Jefferson," Lincoln wrote, "are the definitions and axioms of a free society" (presumably any free society worth the name), and the Declaration promised liberty "not alone to the people of this country, but hope to the world for all future time."[4] But the United States itself, he insisted, was

---

[1] For an early anticipation of this argument, see Ben Hardin's speech in the House of Representatives, February 4, 1820, cited in Philip Detweiler, "Congressional Debate on Slavery and the Declaration of Independence, 1819–1821," *American Historical Review* 63 (April 1958): 598–616, at 611.

[2] Abraham Lincoln, "Speech on the Dred Scott Decision at Springfield, Illinois," June 26, 1857, in *Lincoln: Speeches and Writings, 1832–1858*, ed. Don E. Fehrenbacher (New York: Library of America, 1989), 390–403, especially 398–400.

[3] See Richard Rorty, "Postmodernist Bourgeois Liberalism," *Journal of Philosophy* 80 (October 1983): 523–589; and "Philosophy As a Kind of Writing," *New Literary History* 10 (Autumn 1978): 141–160.

[4] Lincoln to Henry L. Pierce, April 6, 1859, and Lincoln, "Speech at Independence Hall, Philadelphia, Pennsylvania," February 22, 1861, in Lincoln: Speeches and Writings, 1832–1858, 18–19 and 213–214, respectively.

in this particular time and place, in point of fact, "the last best hope of earth," because it was there alone that those definitions and axioms were put into actual approximate practice and where they would be fiercely defended, even by the sword, precisely so that republican government itself would "not perish from the earth."[5] "The struggle should be maintained," he wrote in the midst of the war, "that we may not lose our birthright."[6]

This set of assertions about the Declaration, simultaneously insistently particular and capaciously universalistic, aware of its historicity and yet emphatic that something about the text remains alive, making continual claims on our present selves that "we" are incapable of ignoring, is perhaps the classic statement of the role the Declaration has played in our political culture and I would stop here but that Lincoln did not invent this tradition, nor is the set of truths over which he and Douglas (and Taney) argued ever not contested – or, rather, never are they entirely foreclosed – in our public life. That the speech concluded with both a rousing hostility to slavery, an insistent defense of human equality and the right of consent (in all human relations but here specifically) for black women, *and* a call for the colonization of emancipated blacks, is another testament to the complexities of the life of the Declaration of Independence in American nationalism; even in its most capacious and latest forms, it is, as Lincoln insisted, a work in progress, constantly labored for and constantly (only) approximated.[7]

11.1 ONE PEOPLE

The Declaration is both a product and progenitor of the age of nationalism. In an era in which the will of kings and priests was losing its legitimacy as a compelling foundation for political authority, in which only consent of the governed could legitimate such authority, it became imperative to not only constitute but also to define "the people" who could grant it.[8] The Declaration begins with distinctions between peoples – "one people" is deciding to separate itself "from another," it says – and provides what Rogers Smith has called an

---

[5] Lincoln, "Annual Message to Congress," December 1, 1862, and "Address at Gettysburg," November 19, 1863, in Lincoln: Speeches and Writings, 1832–1858, 415 and 536, respectively.
[6] "Speech to the 166th Ohio Regiment," Washington, DC, August 22, 1864, in *Speeches and Writings, 1859–1865*, ed. Don E. Fehrenbacher (New York: Library of America, 1989), 624.
[7] See James Oakes, "Natural Rights, Citizenship Rights, States' Rights, and Black Rights: Another Look at Lincoln and Race," in Eric Foner, ed., *Our Lincoln: New Perspectives on Lincoln and His World* (New York: W. W. Norton & Co., 2008), 109–134; Diana Schaub, "Lincoln and the Daughters of Dred Scott: A Reflection on the Declaration of Independence," in Will R. Jordan, ed., *When in the Course of Human Events: 1776 at Home, Abroad, and in American Memory* (Mercer: Mercer University Press, 2018), 189–210.
[8] Craig Calhoun, *Nations Matter: Culture, History, and the Cosmopolitan Dream* (New York: Routledge, 2007). This, and the next few paragraphs, are drawn from Brian Steele, *Thomas Jefferson and American Nationhood* (Cambridge: Cambridge University Press, 2012), chapter 1 and epilogue; and, "Inventing Un-America," *Journal of American Studies* 47 (November 2013): 881–902.

"ethically constitutive story," a narrative of "moral affirmation" justifying and constituting American peoplehood.[9] Etienne Balibar less generously calls these types of stories "fictive ethnicities" but this will do as well since nations – not to mention families, religions, individuals – "know who they are by the stories they tell" and the idea of a myth as a "story that is not true" misses the point that nations, selves, religions, families, are actually constituted by narratives told and retold and acted upon into the indefinite future.[10]

The Declaration, then, assumes American peoplehood, the "it-ness" of the national community as a sociological entity moving through time, distinct from others precisely by its history and its commitment to a particular set of cultural values. The Declaration's words, Jefferson insisted, were not intended to be original but, rather, were calculated to "command ... assent" from "a people" that already agreed with them.[11] So the people are constituted in their assent to propositions which the Declaration was merely expressing and which this people already embraced.

The Declaration's language is capacious and universalistic: "all men are created equal." But the cosmopolitanism understandably distracts us from the ways in which the Declaration asserts an American character and identity. The Declaration does not marshal an elaborate philosophical defense of its "self-evident truths"; it only asserts that Americans believe them.[12] Read this way, the Declaration is less a "foundational" document than a historical one, describing the "political history of a culture," a culture whose government would actualize the very rights the British state had failed to uphold, the only kind of government – according to the Declaration – such a people would continue to legitimize with their consent.[13] The Declaration, then, combines an anti-colonial assertion of independence with a story of peoplehood.

---

[9] Rogers Smith, *Stories of Peoplehood: The Politics and Morals of Political Membership* (Cambridge: Cambridge University Press, 2002). Also see David Miller, *On Nationality* (Oxford: Oxford University Press, 1995), 35–46.

[10] A point made clearly by Johann Neem, "American History in a Global Age," *History and Theory* 50 (January 2011): 41–70. Quotations from Robert Bellah, *Religion in Human Evolution* (Cambridge: Belknap Press, an imprint of Harvard University Press, 2011), 35, 276–280; and Etienne Balibar, "The Nation Form: History and Ideology," in Etienne Balibar and Immanuel Wallerstein, eds., *Race, Nation, Class: Ambiguous Identities* (London: Verso, 1991), 96. Also see, of course, Benedict Anderson, *Imagined Communities: Reflections on the Origin and Spread of Nationalism* (London: Verso, 1983); and William H. McNeill, "The Care and Repair of Public Myth," in *Mythistory and Other Essays* (Chicago: Chicago University Press, 1986), 23–42, at 23–24.

[11] TJ to Madison, August 30, 1823, in *The Republic of Letters: The Correspondence Between Thomas Jefferson and James Madison, 1776–1826*, ed., James Morton Smith, 3 vols. (New York: Norton, 1995), 3: 1876–1877.

[12] See Michael Zuckert, *The Natural Rights Republic: Studies in the Foundation of the American Political Tradition* (South Bend: University of Notre Dame Press, 1996), 42–46.

[13] John Dunn, "What Is Living and What Is Dead in the Political Theory of John Locke?" in John Dunn, ed., *Interpreting Political Responsibility: Essays, 1981–1989* (Princeton, 1990), 15–17.

11 Getting "the Hang of the Declaration"

Jefferson was more interested than Congress in making the cultural claims – distinguishing the "one people" from another – which may explain why his draft points its finger more sharply at the "unfeeling brethren" in England, who had forced Americans to assume their "equal & independant station ... among the powers of the earth."[14] The king may have become "a tyrant ... unfit to be the ruler of a people who mean to be free," but it was "our British brethren" who had enabled the king's behavior and that of Parliament. It was they who had been "deaf to the voice of justice & of consanguinity" and who had "by their free election re-established ... in power" those "disturbers of our harmony." Worse, perhaps, "they are permitting their chief magistrate to send over not only soldiers of our common blood, but Scotch & foreign mercenaries to invade & deluge us in blood."[15] It was this betrayal of "our common blood" that had "given the last stab to agonizing affection." "We might have been a free & a great people together," but experience had severed the connection and rendered the one people two.

The Declaration's passage through Congress was delayed, Jefferson remembered later, by the "pusillanimous idea that we had friends in England worth keeping terms with," and it was this very illusion, which led Congress to strike out "those passages" in the document "which conveyed censure on the people of England."[16] But Jefferson included them precisely because they demonstrate in a tangible way to Americans just how different their own character had become from that of the "unfeeling brethren" they were leaving behind. These passages, then, illuminate or bolster the more positive claims about American character in paragraph 2 and their exclusion from the final draft obscures the crucial place of that paragraph for the meaning of the whole.[17] The English would never again be American "brethren."[18] To be sure, American "laws, language, religion, politics and manners" were "so deeply laid in English foundations, that we shall never cease to consider their history as a part of ours, and to study ours in that as its origin."[19] But Americans should never mistake the one for the other. "Sameness of language, of manners, of appearance" might render "it impossible to distinguish us from her subjects." But "free and independent men" – the distinguishing features of American identity – would

---

[14] "original Rough draught," in Julian P. Boyd, ed., *The Papers of Thomas Jefferson*, vol. 1 (Princeton: Princeton University Press, 1950–), 423.
[15] For reflections on this effort to distinguish Americans from enemies, domestic and foreign, see Robert G. Parkinson, "Friends and Enemies in the Declaration of Independence," in Joanne Freeman and Johann Neem, eds., *Jeffersonians in Power: Ideas in Practice* (Charlottesville: University of Virginia Press, 2019), 15–37.
[16] *Autobiography*, in Merrill D. Peterson, ed., *Thomas Jefferson: Writings* (New York: Library of America, 1984), 18.
[17] Garry Wills, *Inventing America: Jefferson's Declaration of Independence* (Boston: Houghton Mifflin Co., 2002), 259–319, especially 307–319.
[18] "original Rough draught," *PTJ*, 1: 427.
[19] TJ to William Duane, 12 August 1810, in *TJW*, 1228.

never submit "to their bondage" just because "we speak English, and look like them."[20] Americans would be identified not by language and appearance, distinguished not by ethnicity or religion, but by their common adherence to what Jefferson later called the "principles of '76."[21]

11.2 "LEARN ... TO RECOGNIZE ONE ANOTHER"

Jefferson had produced a story which he assumed would continue to "command" the "assent" of all true Americans. Little wonder that the central focus of Jefferson's final substantive letter – written as a commemoration of the Declaration of Independence – was his immense satisfaction that the latest generation of "our fellow citizens, after half a century of experience and prosperity, continue to approve the choice we [the founding Congress] made." The "annual return" of the Fourth of July, he wrote, was an opportunity to "forever refresh our recollections" of the rights proclaimed in the Declaration and reinforce "an undiminished devotion to them."[22] It was by their common devotion to these "principles of '76," as Jefferson suggested to his supporters in 1801, that Americans – "we" – would "learn to rally & to recognize one another."[23]

So in the Declaration and in his later elaboration of its centrality to American nationhood, Jefferson merged the civic components of national identity – rational and volitional adherence to law and rights (not rooted in ethnicity or blood) – with the historical and emotionally resonant story of peoplehood that constituted a community of belonging and an inheritance for future generations born (or naturalized) into the community. Future Americans would be most themselves when they voluntarily reaffirmed – by their present assent – their rootedness in this past. Americans would be a people in the Augustinian sense: "united by concord regarding loved things held in common."[24] The nation's "holy purpose" from that first moment would be "adhesion to" the "principles" of the Declaration and "a sacred determination to maintain and perpetuate them."[25]

When Jefferson claimed to have expressed the American mind, then, he meant that Americans so deeply intuited what he had written that their experience of reading would not be that of revelation but of recognition and affirmation. And it would be an experience of constitution as Americans came to awareness not only of common values all Americans share, but also that the others who share them are a people with a common past and destiny. In this

---

[20] TJ to Madame de Stael, 24 May 1813, in *TJW*, 1275.
[21] TJ to Fayetteville Republican Citizens, 17 March 1801, in *PTJ*, 33: 319.
[22] TJ to Roger C. Weigntman, 24 June 1826, in *TJW*, 1517.
[23] TJ to Fayetteville Republican Citizens, 17 March 1801, in *PTJ*, 33: 319.
[24] *City of God*, epigraph in Paul A. Rahe, *Republics Ancient and Modern* (Chapel Hill: University of North Carolina Press, 1992), 2.
[25] TJ to John Quincy Adams, July 18, 1824, Thomas Jefferson Papers, Library of Congress.

sense, then, Jefferson's message is not to a "candid world" only but to the solidarity itself, a national "interpretative community" where "the only proof of membership is fellowship."[26] But because "these truths" that for Americans are "self-evident" are not in fact self-evident or "truths" out there in the ahistorical realm beyond politics but are, in fact, matters of opinion which depend upon continual "agreement and consent," Jefferson understood, with Arendt, that such opinion would be ever "arrived at by discursive, representative thinking" and "communicated by means of persuasion and dissuasion."[27] For Jefferson, those truths would manifest themselves in the political realm only when they were validated and affirmed by the judgment of others. This judgment – arrived at not by coercion but by persuasion – would constitute not only the American people but also in a very real sense, the truths themselves.

So the people were never mere spectators in Jefferson's account of the Revolution, which was never simply the work of a handful of great men. Jefferson understood that, as David Waldstreicher puts it, "the new nation could not exist until the people spontaneously celebrated its existence" and thereby "demonstrated their assent."[28] The people's continual engagement and self-constitution, rather than the text itself, was what was to be celebrated: The Declaration itself had been "their work" and, in this sense, the people became its authors.[29]

Jefferson eventually took to calling July 4th "our nation's birthday" and celebrated it rather than his own. Even the material stuff of nationhood – the writing desk on which he wrote the Declaration, for example – he hoped would accumulate significance in the nation's embrace and might one day, he imagined, be "carried in the procession of our nation's birthday, as the relics of the saints are in those of the church." However counterintuitive that might sound from one so consistently hostile to "priestcraft," Jefferson understood the power of ritual and the practices of recollection; his hope was that the relics and icons of that day's achievements would "help to nourish our devotion to this holy bond of our Union, and keep it alive and warm in our affections."[30]

---

[26] Stanley Fish, "Interpreting the *Variorium*," in *Is There a Text in This Class? The Authority of Interpretative Communities* (Cambridge: Harvard University Press, 1988), 147–173, at 173.

[27] Hannah Arendt, "Truth and Politics" (1967), in Hannah Arendt, *Between Past and Future*, ed. Jerome Kohn (New York: Penguin, 2006), 223–259, at 242–243, and "Crisis in Culture" (1954), 219–220. Also see Zuckert, *Natural Rights Republic*, 42–46.

[28] David Waldstreicher, *In the Midst of Perpetual Fetes: The Making of American Nationalism, 1776–1820* (Chapel Hill, University of North Carolina Press, 1997), 30.

[29] TJ to John Binns, August 31, 1819, LC; Waldstreicher, *In the Midst of Perpetual Fetes*, 32; TJ to Madison, August 30, 1823, in *ROL*, 3: 1876; for significant complication, see Robert M. S. McDonald, "Thomas Jefferson's Changing Reputation as Author of the Declaration of Independence: The First Fifty Years," *Journal of the Early Republic* 19 (Summer 1999): 169–195.

[30] TJ to Dr. James Mease, September 26, 1825, in L&B, 16: 122–123; TJ to Mease, October 30, 1825, in "Notes and Queries," *Pennsylvania Magazine of History and Biography* 41 (1917): 248.

Because he understood that the nation's constitution was not an event in the past merely, but a continual reaffirmation and assent, Jefferson celebrated the unbroken public celebration of that initial effusion in 1776. The revolutionary moment had itself become history, and the "one people" would, across generations, Jefferson hoped, continually reverence that moment as the shared experience that would give them a national future.

11.3 AMERICAN CREED/AMERICAN STORY

None of this is to question the crucial importance of the deeply contextualized readings of the Declaration that have so thoroughly and brilliantly returned to us its immediate meaning and purpose as distinguishable from its later significances in American political culture. Though it is perhaps worth pointing out that the wish to confine the Declaration to its historical moment has typically been associated in our political culture with efforts to deny the moral and political force of the creedal section. Jefferson Davis, for example, in his farewell speech to the Senate in January 1861, went full historicist mode, insisting that the Declaration "is to be construed by the circumstances and purposes for which it was made," and not "invoked to maintain the position of the equality of the races."[31]

But it is to suggest that what the Declaration has become is not inconsistent with its original meanings and purposes. If the people themselves – as Jefferson insisted – were in fact the authors of the Declaration, and if that Declaration was the identity statement of a political culture, we should not wonder that the people immediately made claims upon its assertions, and continually thereafter wrestled with each other over its meaning and significance, nor that they have always reread and reworked and even rewritten the text in anticipation of what it – and they – would become. The Declaration itself (as well as the people who become themselves in their continual assent to its assertions) is always in the process of *becoming* precisely because it "remains open" and, like other texts that slip out of their contemporaneity and remain always new, has "qualities not to be detected save at an appropriate moment in the future."[32] The Declaration, then, is the standard which has as often condemned as affirmed our *practices* – in those moments where and when "the declaration 'all men are

---

[31] *The Papers of Jefferson Davis*, ed. Lynda Laswell Crist and Mary Seaton Dix (Baton Rouge: Louisiana State University Press, 1992), 7: 18–23. Also see Nathaniel Macon of North Carolina, who argued during the Missouri crisis that the "clause in the Declaration of Independence" could "lead to universal emancipation" and, therefore, must not be read as "part of the Constitution." Quoted in George Dangerfield, *The Awakening of American Nationalism* (New York: Harper and Row, 1965), 114. Contrast with Lincoln, "Speech at Independence Hall, Philadelphia, Pennsylvania," February 22, 1861.
[32] Wolfgang Iser, "The Reading Process: A Phenomenological Approach," in David Richter, ed., *The Critical Tradition: Classic Texts and Contemporary Trends*, 3rd ed. (New York: Bedford Books, 2007); Frank Kermode, *Forms of Attention: Botticelli and Hamlet* (Chicago: University of Chicago Press, 1985).

11 Getting "the Hang of the Declaration"

created equal' r[i]ng[s] hollow before the facts" of American life, as SDS's *Port Huron Statement* put it – but not the national *project* itself, to which it calls us to ever-renewed commitment.[33] It is our reverberating jeremiad, preached over and again, calling us to live into its claims in new circumstances and which continually arrests us with new meanings, challenges us with new claims.

Unlike the myths of ethnically rooted nationalisms, the Declaration's role in American political culture has never tended toward a patriotism of uncritical celebration of the *volk* – "my country right or wrong" – though Americans are not exempt by any means from such sentiments. It is undeniable that the Declaration has had a redemptive effect that has sometimes allowed Americans to slough off its sins without always working through the long-term consequences of those very sins.[34] But the Declaration's function in American political culture has typically not been to reinforce self-satisfaction or to sanctify unholy acts, but mostly, rather, to set up a standard by which we have evaluated our practices, and more often than not found them wanting. As Transcendentalist and Unitarian minister Theodore Parker wrote in 1848, "if other nations wonder at our achievements, we are a disappointment to ourselves, and wonder we have not done more."[35] As an affirmation of American peoplehood, the Declaration recognizes implicitly Augustine's sense that a people is "better or worse" insofar "as it is united in loving things that are better or worse."

Frederick Douglass called the Declaration "the RING-BOLT to the chain of your nation's destiny," and encouraged Americans to celebrate it by staying true to the "saving principles" it espoused. And this in a speech roundly condemning American hypocrisy for celebrating the Declaration while tolerating slavery, a spirit hardly alien to Lincoln's disgust in the wake of the Kansas–Nebraska Act when he told a friend that "the fourth of July has not quite dwindled away; it is still a great day – *for burning fire-crackers!!!*"[36] There are things unworthy of the Declaration, in other words, and which turn its claims into lies that can be made right only with transformation of practices. Theodore Roosevelt, in his 1910 "New Nationalism" speech in Osawatomie, Kansas, put it this way: "In name we had the Declaration of Independence in 1776, but we gave the lie by our own acts to the words of the Declaration of Independence until 1865; and words count for nothing except in so far as

---

[33] *Port Huron Statement* (New York: Students for a Democratic Society, the Student Department of the League for Industrial Democracy, [1962] 1964), 3.
[34] See Nicholas Guyatt, *Providence and the Invention of the United States, 1607–1876* (Cambridge: Cambridge University Press, 2007), especially 256–258 and 290–298; and Ta-Nehisi Coates, "The Case for Reparations," *The Atlantic*, 313, June 2014, 54–77. Neither deals explicitly with the Declaration.
[35] Theodore Parker, "The Political Destination of America and the Signs of the Times" (1848), in *The Collected Works of Theodore Parker, Volume 4: Discourses of Politics*, ed. Frances Power Cobbe (London: Trübner & Co., 1863), 77–110, at 95.
[36] Lincoln to George Robertson, August 15, 1855, in *Lincoln: Speeches and Writings, 1832–1858*, 359.

they represent acts."[37] And though Roosevelt might shudder at her particular conclusions, he might agree with the broad outlines of Frances Wright's earlier suggestion that each July 4 would "stand as a tide mark in the flood of time, by which to ascertain the advance of the human intellect, by which to note the rise and fall of each successive error, the discovery of each important truth, the gradual melioration in our public institutions, social arrangements, and, above all, in our moral feelings and mental views."[38] Wright's language here is universalist but her appeal is to Americans who are, according to the Declaration, a people who measure their practices by the standards of the Declaration itself.

"For all its ambiguities," Staughton Lynd has argued, "the preamble to the Declaration of Independence is the single most concentrated expression of the revolutionary intellectual tradition. Without significant exception, subsequent variants of American radicalism have taken the Declaration as their point of departure and claimed to be the true heirs of the spirit of '76."[39] Americans have taken the Declaration as authoritative for practice, and made such claims upon the text as soon as it was printed. As Eric Slauter and Mia Bay have demonstrated, at a time when American peoplehood was constituted as white, African Americans almost immediately found in the Declaration what Bay calls "a lingua franca that could express their [long-standing] aspirations for liberty" and citizenship.[40] And because this lingua franca was understood by white Americans, too – because its claims were inescapably valid in their own continual though imperfectly realized assent to them – the African American identification of the Declaration with calls for emancipation turned it into a judgment on American slavery and racism; it became in their hands the standard for demanding that "the rulers of the land shall practice what they teach, that they 'hold these truths to be self-evident, that all men are created equal ...'"[41] In a "white republic," African Americans, in other words, kept faith with the revolutionary promise of equality and the potential for belonging envisioned in the Declaration but undermined hitherto by the preservation of slavery and racial definitions of citizenship.

---

[37] Theodore Roosevelt, *Letters and Speeches*, ed. Louis Auchincloss (New York: Library of America, 2004), 800.
[38] Frances Wright, "Fourth of July Address," New Harmony, Indiana, July 4, 1828, in Frances Wright, ed., *Course of Popular Lectures* (New York, Office of the Free Enquirer Hall of Science, 1829), 171–172.
[39] Staughton Lynd, *Intellectual Origins of American Radicalism* (Cambridge: Cambridge University Press, [1968] 2009), 4.
[40] Mia Bay, "See Your Declaration, Americans!!!" in Michael Kazin and Joseph A. McCartin, eds., *Americanism: New Perspectives on the History of an Ideal* (Chapel Hill: University of North Carolina Press, 2006), 25–52, at 27; Eric Slauter, "The Declaration of Independence and the New Nation," in *The Cambridge Companion to Thomas Jefferson*, Frank Shuffelton, ed. (Cambridge: Cambridge University Press, 2008), 12–34, especially 25–28.
[41] Committee on the Circular Address, January 15, 1806, in *Minutes of the Proceedings of the Eleventh American Convention for Promoting the Abolition of Slavery and Improving the Condition of the African Race: Assembled at Philadelphia* (Philadelphia: Kimber, Conrad, and Co., 1806), 29, cited in Slauter, "The Declaration and the New Nation," 28.

They asked, as Americans continually do, for a reconstitution of peoplehood by insisting on fuller assent to the promises of the Declaration.[42]

Thus began an American tradition of cracking open the Declaration to mine it for meaning yet to be discovered so that, in this sense, the full meaning of the text – and of American peoplehood – will not come to be known until the future. This is hardly out of step with the spirit of the text and its chief author, who insisted that laws and institutions must develop and grow "hand in hand with the progress of the human mind." and who rejected the idea that the "ark of the covenant is too sacred to be touched." As Douglass argued in his most remembered speech: With the "signers of the Declaration of independence," "nothing was '*settled*' that was not right." And so the Declaration has tended to be the essential "theory" that has continually pushed Americans throughout their history to a "practice" more consistent with a theory that itself continues to open up onto new vistas. And who is to say that the prophetic directing of our attention to what Martin Luther King, Jr., called "the gulf between promise and fulfillment" does not continually open our collective eyes to what was there all along though we knew it not?

Carrie Chapman Catt, then president of the National Women Suffrage Association, insisted, for example, that the franchise for women was "inevitable": "Woman suffrage became an assured fact when the Declaration of Independence was written." This she said some three years prior to the final ratification of the Nineteenth Amendment and in spite of the fact that "Thomas Jefferson and his compatriots" had not been thinking "of women when they wrote that immortal document." In other words, as a matter of historical record, it is abundantly clear that the imagination of the Declaration's authors did not expand widely enough to include the enfranchisement of women. But that mattered "not at all," Catt argued. Once Americans "get the hang" of the Declaration, she said, they *will* support woman suffrage. Getting "the hang" of the Declaration, for Catt, made any effort to derail the suffrage movement a contribution not to the national purpose, but rather to "the indefensible inconsistency which threatens to make our nation a jest among the onward moving peoples of the world."[43] Living in

---

[42] See Stephen Kantrowitz, *More than Freedom: Fighting for Black Citizenship in a White Republic, 1829–1889* (New York: Penguin, 2012).

[43] Chapman Catt, "An Address to the Congress of the United States" (New York: National Woman Suffrage Publishing Company, Inc., 1917), NAWSA Records, Manuscript Division, Library of Congress (092.00.00).

See also Leszek Kolakowski's description of Utopia as "born in the realm of pure spirit and not in *current* historical experience," but eventually becoming "actual social consciousness," crossing "over from the domain of theoretical and moral thought into the field of practical thinking." Utopia, he writes, is "the striving for changes which 'realistically cannot be brought about by immediate action, which lie beyond the forseeable future and defy planning" but which nevertheless is always "a tool of action upon reality and of planning social activity." Leszek Kolakowski, "The Concept of the Left," in *Toward a Marxist Humanism: Essays on the Left Today*, trans. Jane Zielonko Peel (New York: Grove Press, 1968), 69–70.

light of the Declaration's claims cultivated a capacity for shame, a visceral sense that something was not right, that our practice hitherto has been (suddenly *is*) "un-American," and hence unendurable. Catt's critique, then, "is not carping and denouncing," but rather, a keeping faith with the Declaration's imagination. So critique becomes a dismantling of the imperial consciousness that had hitherto hidden the Declaration's promise, ossified its potential.[44]

Martin Luther King was fond of calling the Declaration a "promissory note" that had yet to be fully honored."[45] King's is an apt description of the crucial significance of promises in political life, promises that create a sense of collective identity and purpose and that bind us to keep commitments when the inevitable unforeseen consequences of action bear fruit – or fail to bear fruit – and that call us to live in the promise's imagination rather than that of betrayal, which we may very well discover we have been practicing.[46] Reflecting on student sit-ins from years ago, King could look back and see the protesters as those courageous enough to live in the Declaration's alternative imagination, an imagination that would one day render reality itself – those very laws and mores – powerless against the consciousness and practices of a new story now made seamlessly continuous with the old. "As they were sitting in," King recalled in his last sermon, given on April 3, 1968, telling the tale from the perspective of the now, "they were really standing up for the best in the American dream and taking the whole nation back to those great wells of democracy, which were dug deep by the founding fathers in the Declaration of Independence and the Constitution."[47]

The Declaration's mythic role in our political culture has been to continually shape our identity – the "we" that assents – to fit the story we tell about ourselves as it unfolds in our collective memory and political action. To go back to Lincoln, the Declaration has served as both the transcultural, ahistorical standard against which we evaluate our action and as the particular story of a national solidarity that will continue to exist as long as we assent to its ever-expansive demands.

---

[44] Here I paraphrase Walter Brueggemann, *The Prophetic Imagination*, 2nd ed. (Minneapolis: Fortress Press, 2001), 9–11.
[45] Martin Luther King, Jr., "Address to the March on Washington," August 28, 1963, in *A Call to Conscience: The Landmark Speeches of Dr. Martin Luther King, Jr.*, ed. Clayborne Carson and Kris Shepard (New York: Grand Central Publishing, 2002), 81–87, at 81; "Sermon at National Cathedral," March 31, 1968, in Clayborne Carson and Peter Holloran, eds., *A Knock at Midnight: Inspiration from the Great Sermons of Reverend Martin Luther King, Jr.* (New York: Warner Books, 1998), 205–224.
[46] Here I gloss Hannah Arendt, *The Human Condition* (Chicago: University of Chicago Press, 1958), 237; and *On Revolution* (New York: Viking Press, 1963), 174; as well as Brueggemann, *Prophetic Imagination*.
[47] See Nikita Stewart, "'I've Been to the Mountain Top': Dr. King's Last Sermon Annotated," *New York Times*, April 2, 2018: www.nytimes.com/interactive/2018/04/02/us/king-mlk-last-sermon-annotated.html.

11 Getting "the Hang of the Declaration" 167

So the Declaration, as it turns out, supplies the "thick" particularist stories – and even symbols – that tend to give ethno-nationalisms their peculiar power in creating solidarity, even as the stories that provide that connective tissue for Americans are stories not of blood and soil, but of volitional allegiance to common values and principles articulated in the Declaration and made continually relevant by our assent to them in the present.[48]

William McNeill has argued that "coherent public action becomes very difficult to improvise or sustain" without believable public myths that are then "proven" true "only by the action they provoke." Such stories provide a sense of common destiny and purpose – what Benedict Anderson has called a "deep horizontal comradeship" that transcends class differences to cultivate and sustain a culture of democracy. Only in such solidarities, Richard Rorty argues, do "feelings of intense shame or of glowing pride aroused by various parts of its history, and by various present day national policies" encourage the kind of "emotional involvement ... necessary if political deliberation is to be imaginative and productive."[49]

Perhaps paradoxically, this patriotism need not be insular, in tension with cosmopolitanism or a commitment to universal human rights that transcend the material demands of national interest. Rather the opposite in this case. With "the Declaration of Independence and its large statements of the new idea," Theodore Parker argued, "the nation went behind human history and appealed to human nature."[50]

Obviously, America has always fallen short of the standard Lincoln described as "constantly labored for, constantly approximated." Even he had a great deal of difficulty imagining a democratic political community that was not exclusively white, for example.[51] None of this is to suggest that whatever gains made are consistent with some objective American character or that the struggle for such alignment as we have managed was not agonizing and costly.[52] Rhetorical uses of the Declaration have sometimes made us complacent about the seemingly easy fit between the Declaration's claims and our essential character. Like the lawn at Jefferson's University of Virginia, American memory sometimes compensates for the irregularities of elevation with an asymmetrical recollection that can create the illusion of order and obscure the fact, for example, that some of the very men who signed the Declaration itself "were trafficking in the bodies and souls of

---

[48] Michael Walzer, *Thick and Thin: Moral Argument at Home or Abroad* (South Bend: University of Notre Dame Press, 1994).
[49] Richard Rorty, *Achieving Our Country* (Cambridge: Harvard University Press, 1998), 3.
[50] Parker, "Political Destination of America," 95. Also see Parker, "Discourse Occasioned by the Death of John Quincy Adams," March 5, 1848, in *Collected Works*, 4: 147.
[51] See Eric Foner, *The Fiery Trial: Abraham Lincoln and American Slavery* (New York: W. W. Norton & Company, 2010); Oakes, "Another Look at Lincoln and Race."
[52] Rogers Smith, "Beyond Tocqueville, Myrdal, and Hartz: The Multiple Traditions in America," *American Political Science Review* 87.3 (September 1993): 549–566.

their fellow men."⁵³ Even Lincoln, who never underestimated the cost of making the union "worthy of the saving," used the Declaration to describe the revolutionary social change he oversaw as an unbroken continuity with the founding moment itself.

Historians, pledged to recover the complexities that national mythologies tend to hide, understandably find this collective memory frustrating, transforming, as it sometimes does, the terror of contingency into a coherent narrative epic consistent with the public myth of the founding.⁵⁴ But this essay is, after all, about the role the Declaration has played in American nationalism – a mnenohistory of sorts – and there is a sense in which historians challenging the national memory by calling attention to the ways Americans have always "scorned our patrimony" are but carrying on, in the guise of historiography, the national project of alignment of practice with theory, "making the invisible visible."⁵⁵

The claim, then, is not that there is some essential American character "out there" in the universe (or even in the past) that can be counted on to lead us always to progressive ends. Americans can be as boorish, materialistic, anti-intellectual, xenophobic, misogynistic, racist, violent, as other people. It is their story, rooted in the Declaration's claims about them that judges – in our continual assent – all of those characteristics incompatible with America's "better" values and ideals, reading them out of the "loved things held in common" that unite us as a people. The story the Declaration tells has always appealed to whatever "better angels" we have and constituted our peoplehood in history. Lose the story and it is hard to say what Americans will become.

It seems appropriate to end as we began, with Lincoln, whose reaffirmation and re-articulation of the national mythology reinforced and repaired and exemplifies still its capacity to create cross-class solidarity and a space for democratic politics and common public purpose without the appeal to ascriptive (non-volitional) identity that characterizes ethnonationalisms.

In a July 1858 address, Lincoln described for a Chicago audience some of what he called the "uses" of "4th of July gatherings":

---

⁵³ See Jim Cocola, "The Ideological Spaces of the Academical Village: A Reading of the Central Grounds at the University of Virginia," http://faculty.virginia.edu/villagespaces/essay/#o2e. Quote from David Walker, *Appeal to the Coloured Citizens of the World, but in Particular, and Very Expressly, to Those of THE UNITED STATES OF AMERICA* (New York: Hill and Wang, Inc., 1965), 75.
⁵⁴ With this language, I nod with appreciation to Philip Roth, *The Plot Against America* (New York: Vintage), 57. See also Aziz Rana, *Two Faces of American Freedom* (Cambridge: Harvard University Press, 2010), Rogers Smith, *Civic Ideals* (New Haven: Yale University Press, 1997).
⁵⁵ On Mnemohistory, see Marek Tamm, *Afterlife of Events: Perspectives on Mnemohistory* (London: Palgrave Macmillan, 2015). The quotation is from Danielle Allen, *Our Declaration: A Reading of the Declaration of Independence in Defense of Equality* (New York: Liveright, 2014), 23.

11 Getting "the Hang of the Declaration"

We hold this annual celebration to remind ourselves of all the good done in this process of time of how it was done and who did it, and how we are historically connected with it; and we go from these meetings in better humor with ourselves – we feel more attached the one to the other, and more firmly bound to the country we inhabit. In every way we are better men in the age, and race, and country in which we live for these celebrations. But after we have done all this we have not yet reached the whole. There is something else connected with it. We have besides these men – descended by blood from our ancestors – among us perhaps half our people who are not descendants at all of these men, they are men who have come from Europe – German, Irish, French and Scandinavian – men that have come from Europe themselves, or whose ancestors have come hither and settled here, finding themselves our equals in all things. If they look back through this history to trace their connection with those days by blood, they find they have none, they cannot carry themselves back into that glorious epoch and make themselves feel that they are part of us, but when they look through that old Declaration of Independence they find that those old men say that "We hold these truths to be self-evident, that all men are created equal," and then they feel that that moral sentiment taught in that day evidences their relation to those men, that it is the father of all moral principle in them, and that they have a right to claim it as though they were blood of the blood, and flesh of the flesh of the men who wrote that Declaration, (loud and long continued applause) and so they are. That is the electric cord in that Declaration that links the hearts of patriotic and liberty-loving men together, that will link those patriotic hearts as long as the love of freedom exists in the minds of men throughout the world. [Applause.][56]

This is Lincoln's description of Jefferson's "brethren of the same principle" who "recognize one another" by their common adherence to the "principles of '76," which principles, in turn, "form a point of union round which we shall learn to rally." One could envision a less capacious national mythology. But it would not, by definition, be American.

---

[56] Lincoln, speech in Chicago, IL, July 10, 1858, *Collected Works of Abraham Lincoln*, ed. P. Basler, 8 vols. (New Brunswick: Rutgers University Press, 1953), 2: 484–502 at 499–500.

12

Native Nations and Declarations of Independence

Jonathan Todd Hancock

In the spring of 1833, Mashpee people declared independence. Having negotiated centuries of violence and demographic disruption in New England, this Indigenous Nation on Cape Cod had carved out tribal lands that trespassers coveted for logs and hay. The Mashpees petitioned the state of Massachusetts, not only threatening to bind and expel the trespassers, but also declaring that "we as a tribe will rule our selves, and have the right to do so for all men are born free and Equal." William Apess spearheaded their cause. The Mashpees had recently adopted the Pequot tribal member and Methodist preacher, and Apess used his social standing and knowledge of the Declaration of Independence to advocate on their behalf. While the Mashpees were awaiting a reply to their petition, he encountered a pair of illegal loggers and ordered them to surrender their cart's contents. Fearing further conflict, a state representative called for the parties to resolve the dispute at a tavern the next day: July 3, 1833. But Apess wanted to delay the meeting for one more day. On the fifty-seventh anniversary of the signing of the Declaration of Independence, he arrived at the tavern to advocate for Mashpee independence and was arrested. The action became known as the Mashpee Revolt.[1]

The Mashpees' language and Apess' timing were not accidental. They reflected one of many instances in which Native Americans have appropriated the document to argue for their own independence. Characterized as "merciless Indian savages" in the Declaration of Independence, Native Americans have enacted their own agendas for maintaining their independent sovereignties in interactions with the United States since 1776. In the late eighteenth and nineteenth centuries, as the rapidly expanding United

---

[1] Donald M. Nielson, "The Mashpee Indian Revolt of 1833," *New England Quarterly* 58.3 (1985): 400–420; Philip F. Gura, *The Life of William Apess, Pequot* (Chapel Hill: University of North Carolina Press, 2015), 72–85.

States ensnared Native Nations and sought to render them dependent, these agendas followed two paths based on Native leaders' proximity to the United States and familiarity with the Declaration of Independence. Along one path, Native Americans immersed in US political culture, like Apess, made arguments based on the Declaration's highest ideals. Subjected to assimilative schooling efforts, they knew the document well. In speeches, published writings, and legal briefs, they cited it not to claim national belonging, but to argue that the United States should live up to its Declaration by respecting the independence and natural rights of the surrounding Native Nations that predated it. In taking up the language of individual rights, citizenship, and independence, they belied the merciless savagery that the Declaration of Independence ascribed to them.[2]

West of the colonies-turned-states, leaders on late eighteenth- and early nineteenth-century Native grounds sought independence through a different path. They emphasized that it was Euro-American settlers' own mercilessly savage desire for land – not independence from Great Britain – at the heart of the colonies' Declaration and subsequent founding of the United States. Through military alliances with and against the United States, treaty negotiations, and domestic legal and political transformations intended to centralize authority and to render their sovereignties and independence more legible and "civilized" to US leaders, these Native Nations consistently issued their own declarations of independence.

Over the nineteenth century, as removals and military conquests eroded their sovereignties, these two forms of Native declarations of independence began to merge. By the 1880s, treaty-making and large-scale military resistance were no longer viable strategies. The allotment of Native territory into individual plots of land, much of which was sold off to outsiders, and assimilative education posed existential threats to Indigenous lands and cultures. Still, Native Nations could point to treaties and U.S. Supreme Court decisions as legal precedents for US recognition of their sovereignties, and the children forced into residential boarding schools made connections across tribal nations there. They also learned how to effectively navigate US political, legal, and educational institutions to advocate for Native sovereignties and self-determination, as well as rights within the US legal system. With the passage of the Indian Citizenship Act of 1924 and more widespread US military service among Native Americans in World Wars I and II, citizens of Native Nations also became US citizens, acquiring new platforms from which to make claims about the Declaration of Independence and to renew their sovereign tribal nations' declarations of independence.

---

[2] *In Congress, July 4, 1776. A Declaration by the Representatives of the United States of America, In General Congress Assembled* (Philadelphia: John Dunlap, 1776).

12.1 DECLARATIONS OF NATIVE INDEPENDENCE IN THE ERA OF THE AMERICAN REVOLUTION

In the late eighteenth century, concepts in the Declaration of Independence that were familiar and important to Apess and the Mashpees did not have the same purchase across Native Nations. As foundational Indigenous political principles, reciprocity and kinship trumped the "unalienable Rights" of men. Individuals defined themselves less by their own lives, rights, and property than by their relationships. They were obligated to maintain those relationships through reciprocity and balance. Declarations and signatures were immaterial unless the obligations to which they attested were maintained and fulfilled over time. Otherwise, declarations and signatures were, as Ottawa chief Egushawa described a 1791 treaty, "pen and ink witchcraft, which they can make to speak things we never intended, or had any idea of."[3]

The Declaration's argument that it was "necessary for one people to dissolve the political bands which have connected them with another" would have been more familiar to tribal nations. Because King George III had not met his reciprocal obligations to his people, new political institutions were necessary. Native Nations ensnared in the American Revolution had their own long histories of breaking and reforming political bands. Before European arrivals on the continent, Cherokees revolted against hereditary, hierarchical leadership during the era of medieval Mississippian city-states, and the Haudenosaunee (Iroquois) Confederacy established a representative government composed of five former rival nations, gaining a sixth member in the 1720s. In addition to the Cherokees, the Muscogees (Creeks) and Catawbas were two other major Native American forces in the American Revolution that coalesced over the late seventeenth and eighteenth centuries. Beginning in the mid eighteenth-century Ohio Valley, advocates of intertribal militancy argued that separate Native Nations and confederacies were inadequate for confronting Anglo-American encroachment. They sought to dissolve specific tribal bonds altogether and unite based on Indigeneity.[4]

---

[3] [Alexander McKee], *Minutes of Debates in Council on the Banks of the Ottawa River* (Philadelphia: Printed for the Editor, 1792), 11. This phrase is used in the title of Colin Calloway's, *Pen and Ink Witchcraft: Treaties and Treaty Making in American Indian History* (New York: Oxford University Press, 2013).

[4] *In Congress, July 4, 1776*. On a Cherokee revolt against priestly hierarchy, see Raymond D. Fogelson, "Who Were the Ani-Kutani? An Excursion into Cherokee Historical Thought," *Ethnohistory* 31.1 (1984): 255–263. On the history of Cherokee political organization, see William G. McLoughlin, *Cherokee Renascence in the New Republic* (Princeton: Princeton University Press, 1986); Theda Perdue, *Cherokee Women: Gender and Culture Change, 1700–1835* (Lincoln : University of Nebraska Press, 1998); Tyler Boulware, *Deconstructing the Cherokee Nation: Town, Region, and Nation among the Eighteenth-Century Cherokees* (Gainesville: University Press of Florida, 2011). On the history of Creek political organization, see Michael D. Green, *The Politics of Indian Removal: Creek Government and Society in Crisis* (Lincoln: University of Nebraska Press, 1982); Steven C. Hahn, *The*

For those Native Nations closest to the rebellious colonies, revolutionary-era violence mattered more than revolutionary-era political ideas and reform. Historians have pointed to the escalation of violence against civilians in the aftermath of the Seven Years' War as a critical factor in shaping the increasingly antagonistic, unified, and racialized approaches of Anglo-American settlers and Native Americans to one another in mid-Atlantic colonies' western borderlands. Concerns about borderland violence, especially in the Ohio Valley, stoked both colonists' resentment about a lack of protection under British rule and Native bids for intertribal militancy, binding each group together in opposition to the other. In 1764, Benjamin Franklin decried barbarity – not of Indigenous people, but of the settlers known as the Paxton Boys, who murdered twenty Conestoga people near Lancaster, Pennsylvania. "The barbarous Men who committed the atrocious act, in Defiance of Government, of all Laws human and divine, and to the eternal Disgrace of their Country and Colour, then mounted their Horses, huzza'd in Triumph, as if they had gained a Victory, and rode off – unmolested!" Franklin recounted. "But the Wickedness cannot be covered, the Guilt will lie on the whole Land, till Justice is done on the Murderers. THE BLOOD OF THE INNOCENT WILL CRY TO HEAVEN FOR VENGEANCE." As historian Jeffrey Ostler has shown, massacres like the one committed against Conestoga people led some Native Americans in the region to believe that settlers had genocidal intentions. The resulting "indigenous consciousness of genocide" galvanized intertribal militancy, an attempted political revolution of its own that set an important precedent for future intertribal organizing.[5]

Invention of the Creek Nation, 1670–1763 (Lincoln: University of Nebraska Press, 2004). On Catawba coalescence, see James H. Merrell, *The Indians' New World: Catawbas and Their Neighbors from European Contact through the Era of Removal* (Chapel Hill: University of North Carolina Press for the Omohundro Institute of Early American History and Culture, 1989). On the development of the Iroquois Confederacy, see Daniel K. Richter, *The Ordeal of the Longhouse: The People s of the Iroquois League in the Era of European Colonization* (Chapel Hill: University of North Carolina Press for the Omohundro Institute of Early American History and Culture, 1993), 30–49; Jon Parmenter, *The Edge of the Woods: Iroquoia, 1534–1701* (East Lansing: Michigan State University Press, 2010), xxxiii–xlix. On the drive for intertribal political organization during the Revolutionary Era, see Gregory Evans Dowd, *A Spirited Resistance: The North American Indian Struggle for Unity, 1745–1815* (Baltimore: Johns Hopkins University Press, 1993). The Declaration's author nonetheless characterized Native American politics as simple and static. Jefferson wrote in *Notes on the State of Virginia* that Native Americans had "never submitted themselves to any laws, any coercive power, any shadow of government." He added, "It will be said, the great societies cannot exist without government. The Savages therefore break them into small ones." Jefferson knew better, as the nations composing the Iroquois Confederacy, as well as the Cherokees, Creeks, and Catawbas, among many others, were familiar to him. See Thomas Jefferson, *Notes on the State of Virginia*, repr. ed. Frank Shuffleton (New York: Penguin Books, [1785] 1999), 99.

[5] Benjamin Franklin, "A Narrative of the Late Massacres, in Lancaster County, of a Number of Indians, Friends of this Province, By Persons Unknown. With some Observations on the

It was in this setting of increasingly racialized violence that the Declaration leveled its complaint that King George III had "endeavoured to bring on the inhabitants of [the colonies'] frontiers, the merciless Indian Savages, whose known rule of warfare, is an undistinguished destruction of all ages, sexes and conditions." This stark rendering of colonial–Native American relations remained largely unchanged after the Continental Congress edited Thomas Jefferson's original draft of the document. Only the phrase "of existence" was removed from the line characterizing Native warfare as "an undistinguished destruction of all ages, sexes, and conditions." Historian Robert Parkinson has argued that revolutionary leaders used newspapers and other printed matter to mobilize fear that British agents were inciting Native American and African American attacks on the colonies. The Declaration was foundational to this wartime communication strategy, which helped to unify disparate colonies and to establish racial strictures of citizenship in the early United States.[6]

Alongside actual settler violence against Native Nations was a subtler threat to Indigenous territory: land speculation. Among other grievances leveled against the monarch, colonists complained that he was "raising the conditions of new Appropriations of Lands." Efforts to restrict settlement in western lands angered settlers and speculators alike. In the lead-up to the Seven Year's War, prominent Virginian families, including those named Washington and Jefferson, formed land companies that stood to gain handsomely from the western expansion of British North America beyond the Appalachian Mountains. But the Proclamation of 1763, combined with Indigenous uprisings against the presence of Anglo-American forts and settlements in the former New France, sought to stem western encroachment. Land speculators thus joined debtors and coastal merchants in seeking financial benefits from declaring independence.[7]

---

same." (Philadelphia, 1764), *Founders Online*, National Archives, https://founders.archives.gov/documents/Franklin/01-11-02-0012; Jeffrey Ostler, "'To Extirpate the Indians': An Indigenous Consciousness of Genocide in the Ohio Valley and Lower Great Lakes, 1750s–1810," *William and Mary Quarterly* 72.4 (2015): 587–622. On borderland violence and its role in forging a collective colonial and intertribal identities, see Dowd, *A Spirited Resistance*; Peter Silver, *Our Savage Neighbors: How Indian War Transformed Early America* (New York: W. W. Norton and Company, 2007); Patrick Griffin, *American Leviathan: Empire, Nation, and Revolutionary Frontier* (New York: Hill and Wang, 2007). Rob Harper has qualified this historiographical tendency to point to increasingly racialized identities and inescapable violence in the Ohio Valley by emphasizing the region's multiethnic and localistic nature in *Unsettling the West: Violence and State Building in the Ohio Valley* (Philadelphia: University of Pennsylvania Press, 2018).

[6] *In Congress, July 4, 1776*; Robert G. Parkinson, *The Common Cause: Creating Race and Nation in the American Revolution* (Chapel Hill: University of North Carolina Press for the Omohundro Institute of Early American History and Culture, 2016), 185–263.

[7] Woody Holton, *Forced Founders: Indians, Debtors, Slaves, and the Making of the American Revolution in Virginia* (Chapel Hill: University of North Carolina Press for the Omohundro Institute of Early American History and Culture, 1999), 3–38; Anthony F. C. Wallace, *Jefferson and the Indians: The Tragic Fate of the First Americans* (Cambridge : Harvard University Press, 1999), 21–49.

12 Native Nations and Declarations of Independence

Since 1776, the most consequential passage in the Declaration of Independence for Native Nations has been the principle of sovereignty explained at the end of the document's penultimate sentence: "as Free and Independent States, they have full Power to levy War, conclude Peace, contract alliances, establish Commerce, and to do all other Acts and Things which Independent States may of right do." Divided strategies for navigating the Revolution reflected Native American commitments to operating as "Free and Independent States."[8]

In certain cases, alliance with the rebellious colonies was the preferred path for maintaining independence. The Stockbridge–Mohican community in western Massachusetts took up the patriot cause. Established as a "praying town" settlement of Christian Native Americans, the community had taken up arms for the British colonies in mid eighteenth-century wars and faced a flood of settlers threatening its territory and autonomy after the Seven Years' War. Stockbridge–Mohican leaders reasoned that allying with New England colonists would ease the territorial pressure and strengthen their own independence. As soldiers and emissaries to other Native Nations during the war, they sought US support for their tribal territorial claims at war's end. But the new nation's reward for Stockbridge–Mohican loyalty came not in land protections but a meager certificate of appreciation from George Washington, and by 1783, they lost their land entirely.[9]

With a flexible plan of union that allowed member nations to chart separate paths on matters of dissension, the Iroquois Confederacy divided over the war. The Oneidas and Tuscaroras joined the colonies, while the Senecas, Cayugas, Onondagas, and Mohawks, like many Native polities, eventually decided that the rebels were a bigger threat than the British Empire. The latter nations coordinated with Loyalists to raid the outer settlements of Pennsylvania and New York, which prompted George Washington to order General John Sullivan to carry out a devastating invasion of Iroquoia in the summer of 1779. "The immediate objects are the total destruction and devastation of their settlement, and the capture of as many prisoners of every age and sex as possible. It will be essential to ruin their crops now in the ground and prevent their planting more," Washington instructed Sullivan. His name among Iroquois people became "Town-destroyer."[10]

---

[8] *In Congress, July 4, 1776*.
[9] Bryan Rindfleisch, "'Where Your Warriors Have Left Their Bones, There Our Bones Are Seen Also': The Stockbridge–Mohican Community in the Revolutionary War, 1775–1783," *Journal of the American Revolution, Annual Volume 2017*, ed. Todd Andrlik and Don N. Hagist (Yardley : Westholme Publishing, 2017), 297–309; Colin Calloway, *The American Revolution in Indian Country: Crisis and Diversity in Native American Communities* (New York: Cambridge University Press, 1995), 85–107.
[10] Calloway, *The American Revolution in Indian* Country, 108–157; "To George Washington from the Seneca Chiefs, 1 December 1790," *Founders Online*, National Archives, http://founders.archives.gov/documents/Washington/05-07-02-0005.

As his army swept through Iroquoia, burning towns and crops, Sullivan's encounter with an elderly woman named Madam Sacho captured the profound dilemmas and suffering that the Declaration of Independence unleashed on Native Nations bordering the rebellious colonies. Sacho told the invading soldiers of a debate between warriors and clan mothers about whether to flee or to defend their town. Apparently, she had encouraged the men to stay and fight. By remaining there, even amid the carnage, perhaps she sought to gather intelligence about the marauders and to demonstrate her people's continued territorial claims. This glimpse into one Indigenous woman's experience of the Revolution also points to the centrality of women in Native American politics and diplomacy, not just in the Iroquois Confederacy, but among many Native Nations in predominantly matrilineal Native North America. In these societies, an Indigenous leader's political authority stemmed from his mother's lineage.[11]

Treaty-making and internal strife over maintaining independence through peace or war were two important facets of the Cherokee Nation's experience of the American Revolution that also applied broadly across Indian Country. Cherokees confronted settlers and speculators who seized on the disruption of British imperial authority during the Revolution to pour into Cherokee territory. Land cessions to speculators and cross-border violence left the Cherokees with smoldering towns and a weak position from which to bargain with the emerging expansionist power. Militants known as Chickamauga Cherokees broke with civil authorities to continue raiding and to ally with intertribal militants further north. Having dissolved their own political bands, the Chickamauga Cherokees did not rejoin the Nation until the early nineteenth century. In exchange for further land cessions, the United States acknowledged Cherokee sovereignty and pledged to stem settler incursions in the Treaty of Hopewell of 1785. Waves of US settlers made the treaty's protections of Cherokee territory difficult to enforce, but this treaty, as well as all others concluded between Native Nations and the United States over the next century, became a powerful legal and diplomatic precedent from which to claim sovereignty. The United States also inherited treaties that the British Empire had previously concluded with Native Nations, who continue to use them as legal instruments for declaring independence.[12]

---

[11] Sarah M. S. Pearsall, "Recentering Indian Women in the American Revolution," in Susan Sleeper-Smith, Juliana Barr, Jean M. O'Brien, Nancy Shoemaker, and Scott Manning Stevens, eds., *Why You Can't Teach United States History without American Indians* (Chapel Hill: University of North Carolina Press, 2015), 57–70.

[12] McLoughlin, *Cherokee Renascence in the New Republic*, 19–32; Calloway, *The American Revolution in Indian Country*, 182–212. On Native Nations' efforts to claim sovereignty in international legal terms in the immediate aftermath of the American Revolution, see Gregory Ablavsky, "Species of Sovereignty: Native Nationhood, the United States, and International Law, 1783–1795," *Journal of American History* 106.3 (2019): 591–613. For an historical overview of the legal relationship among Native Nations, US states, and the US federal government that is grounded in political science, see David E. Wilkins and Heidi Kiiwetinepinesiik Stark, *American Indian Politics and the American Political System*, 4th ed. (Lanham: Roman and Littlefield Publishers, 2018).

During the American Revolution and its aftermath in the Gulf South, Native Nations and settlers had drastically different ideas about how to secure and maintain independence. Not unlike British colonists' relationship to empire before the 1760s, Native Americans in this region had accepted inclusion into European empires if they could remain free of undue influence and pressure. They were accustomed to imperial realignments and sought to navigate the American Revolution accordingly, but waves of settlers committed to individual land ownership as a fundamental right eroded intricate networks of interdependence among Native Nations and European empires. In seeking to unite Southeastern Native Nations to repel the early United States, Muskogee (Creek) leader Alexander McGillivray took up the rhetoric of the Declaration of Independence. In an appeal to the Spanish Empire for its assistance in upholding Indigenous territorial claims, McGillivray argued that the Creeks, Cherokees, and Chickasaws did not "forfeit their Independance [sic] and natural rights" to Great Britain, which could not then cede their land to the United States. But as indicated by the title of historian Kathleen DuVal's work *Independence Lost*, this round of imperial war was different. "The United States would be a new kind of empire, one that rejected imperial hierarchies of reciprocal dependencies and instead defined and advanced its own independence through exclusivist citizenship and military might," DuVal concludes.[13]

Left out of the Second Treaty of Paris negotiations, Native Americans continued to fight for independence by extending the war's Ohio Valley theater into the 1790s. The United States struggled to raise and finance armies that an intertribal confederacy routed in 1790 and 1791. Two years later, intertribal leaders proposed a solution to US treaty commissioners that addressed the parties' shared concern about independence. Negotiating from a position of power, they explained that the commissioners "seem to expect that because you have at last acknowledged our independence, we should for such a favor surrender to you our country." The leaders were, of course, unwilling to surrender their country, so they proposed reallocating resources spent on the US military to its poor settlers, who risked their lives encroaching on Native grounds. "We know that these settlers are poor, or they would have never ventured to live in a country which has been in continual trouble ever since they crossed the Ohio. Divide therefore this large sum of money, which you have offered to us, among these people," they suggested.[14]

---

[13] John Walton Caughey, *McGillivray of the Creeks* (Norman: University of Oklahoma Press, 1938), 92; Kathleen DuVal, *Independence Lost: Lives of the Edge of the American Revolution* (New York: Random House, 2015), 344.

[14] David Andrew Nichols, *Red Gentlemen and White Savages: Indians, Federalists, and the Search for Oder on the American Frontier* (Charlottesville: University of Virginia Press, 2008), 201. See also, James H. Merrell, "Declarations of Independence: Indian–White Relations in the New Nation," in Jack P. Greene, ed., *The American Revolution: Its Character and Limits* (New York: New York University Press, 1987), 197–223.

The confederacy's leaders found their militancy difficult to maintain, and east of the Mississippi River, legal arguments and publicity campaigns gradually replaced martial declarations of independence. Following the coalition's defeat at the Battle of Fallen Timbers, the 1795 Treaty of Greenville dramatically reduced Native territorial holdings. While younger leaders sought to renew violence, others accepted US aid, missionaries, and instruction in Anglo-American ways of farming and domestic arts to legitimize their sovereignty by projecting a "civilized" status. Federalists in the United States worked with Native leaders to promote order in the borderlands, but civil authorities could not curb settler squatting and cross-border violence. As historian David Andrew Nichols has characterized the shift in US policy, the Federalist drive for a "respectable empire" gave way to Jefferson's "empire for liberty." Educated in US law and political culture, Native leaders, in turn, appealed to US courts to recognize their sovereignties and to the US public to uphold the principles of its Declaration of Independence.[15]

12.2 THE CHEROKEE NATION'S DECLARATIONS OF INDEPENDENCE IN THE NINETEENTH CENTURY

The case of the Cherokee Nation before Removal demonstrates the melding of Native American strategies for maintaining independence. Like Apess and the Mashpees, leaders of the Cherokee Nation held up the Declaration of Independence and sought recognition of Cherokee sovereignty within US institutions, while also undertaking domestic reforms to strengthen their standing as a nation among nations in North America. Appealing to the early US republics' highest ideals and courts ultimately did not spare them from expulsion from their homelands. But in resisting US attempts to render them dependent and in transforming US assimilation policies into opportunities to strengthen their claims to sovereignty, the Cherokee Nation laid the groundwork for more contemporary Native American forms of declarations of independence.

In addition to encouraging Anglo-American lifeways and individual landholding among Native societies bordering US states, the US "civilization" plan sought to extract land by growing Native Nations' dependence and debt. The plan's architect, Washington's Secretary of War Henry Knox, argued that rather than continuing to dispatch US military forces at great expense and risk, it was more effective to send government agents, missionaries, and authorized merchants into Native communities to transform them. Framing their efforts as philanthropy, these officials encouraged Native men to head independent, Christian households as farmers, who would eventually assimilate into US

---

[15] "Journal of a Treaty held in 1793, with the Indian Tribes northwest of the Ohio by Commissioners of the United States," *Collections of the Massachusetts Historical Society* 5 (1836); repr. in Colin G. Calloway, *First Peoples: A Documentary Survey of American Indian History, Fifth Edition* (Boston: Bedford/St. Martin's, 2016), 243.

12 Native Nations and Declarations of Independence

society, or at least occupy less land as farmers than hunters. In Cherokee society, among many others that hosted US agents, women had been the primary farmers for centuries, and their social prominence stemmed in part from their roles as agricultural providers. This gendered division of labor troubled US policymakers, and they pitched their social and agricultural reforms in part as relief for overburdened Native women.[16]

As US president, Jefferson continued the "civilization" policy, and in an 1803 letter, he revealed its primary aims of nurturing dependence and dispossession. "When they withdraw themselves to the culture of a small piece of land, they will perceive how useless to them are their extensive forests," he wrote to Indiana Territorial Governor William Henry Harrison. In the same letter, Jefferson also confided that the US trading factories intended to centralize trade and promote Anglo-American material culture among Native Nations had another, more nefarious purpose. The United States "shall push our trading houses, and be glad to see the good & influential individuals among them run in debt, because we observe that when these debts get beyond what the individuals can pay, they become willing to lop th[em off] by a cession of lands," he wrote.[17]

Ironic considering Jefferson's own personal struggles with debt, the US strategy of coaxing land cessions through encouraging Native debts was successful. When Cherokee leader Doublehead received credit from a US trading factory ahead of a land negotiation in 1805, he was told that a deal favorable to the United States would cancel his debts. Doublehead and other Cherokees ultimately ceded 9 million acres of land without tribal authorization. The national trading factory system ended in 1822, but private trading factories picked up where the government left off, often in partnership with it. For instance, part of the payment that the Potawatomis received for ceding the last vestiges of their homelands was redirected to settle alleged debts with trading companies. This siphoning of treaty annuities, which were annual cash payments and supplies guaranteed to Native Nations in exchange for land cessions, constituted what historian Michael John Witgen has termed a "political economy of plunder." Witgen's study focuses on early nineteenth-century Anishinaabewaki, the region known in the early US republic as the upper Old Northwest, but the term is applicable to the trans-Appalachian West at-large. After the War of 1812, the expansion and profitability of plantation slavery had increased the potential value of Southeastern Native land, and in turn, southern US intellectuals had sharpened the blurry edges of Enlightenment thinking about the

---

[16] Theda Perdue, "Native Women in the Early Republic: Old World Perceptions, New World Realities," in Frederick E. Hoxie, Ronald Hoffman, and Peter J. Albert, eds., *Native Americans and the Early Republic* (Charlottesville: University of Virginia Press for the United States Capitol Historical Society, 1999), 105–112; Bernard W. Sheehan, *Seeds of Extinction: Jeffersonian Philanthropy and the American Indian* (Chapel Hill: University of North Carolina Press, 1973).

[17] Thomas Jefferson to William Henry Harrison, February 27, 1803, *The Papers of Thomas Jefferson*, Volume 39: *13 November 1802–1803 March 1803*, ed. Barbara B. Oberg (Princeton: Princeton University Press, 2012), 589–593. Sheehan, *Seeds of Extinction*, 170.

inherent inferiority of people not descended from Europeans. The supposed philanthropy of transforming Native societies through "civilizational" reforms accordingly gave way to US efforts to relocate Native Nations entirely.[18]

Removal advocates pitched ethnic cleansing as a humanitarian endeavor that would ensure the independence of Native Nations far from their ancestral homelands. "These untutored sons of the Forest, cannot exist in a state of *Independence*, in the vicinity of the white man," wrote Commissioner of Indian Treaties Alfred Balch to his friend Andrew Jackson in early 1830. In an address to Congress regarding the passage of the 1830 Indian Removal Act, President Jackson used the language of Declaration of Independence to cast this "benevolent policy of the Government" as a guarantor of freedom and happiness for relocated Native Nations. Living in Indian Territory would "free [Native Americans] from the power of the states" and "enable them to pursue happiness in their own way and under their own rude institutions." As it was with Jefferson's generation, land speculation was a material root of a new ideology and means of Native American dispossession.[19]

In its approaches to domestic political reorganization, diplomacy, education, and US law, the Cherokee Nation sought to declare and preserve independence from Georgia and to enlist the federal US government in recognizing and protecting its sovereignty. Doublehead was executed for his land cession as part of the drive to centralize Cherokee legal and political authority. Among a host of efforts to render the polity "civilized," legitimate, and thereby sovereign in the eyes of US authorities, the Nation adopted a written constitution and circulated news in a tribal newspaper that printed stories in the newly developed Cherokee script and English, side by side. Prominent leaders sent their children to US-sponsored schools within and beyond Cherokee territory, where they learned to speak and write in English and cohered to Anglo-American customs without renouncing Cherokee belonging and lifeways. Meanwhile, the Nation allied with US, Creek, and Choctaw military forces to put down the Redstick Creek uprising that occurred during the War of 1812. These Native allies were ultimately rewarded for their alliance with the United States with

---

[18] David Andrew Nichols, *Engines of Diplomacy: Indians Trading Factories and the Negotiation of American Empire* (Chapel Hill: University of North Carolina Press, 2016), 92–93, 170–171; Michael John Witgen, *Seeing Red: Indigenous Land, American Expansion, and the Political Economy of Plunder in North America* (Chapel Hill: University of North Carolina Press for the Omohundro Institute of Early American History and Culture, 2022).

[19] Andrew Balch to Andrew Jackson, January 8, 1830, Andrew Jackson Papers: Series 1, General Correspondence and Related Items, 1775 to 1885. Retrieved from the Library of Congress, www.loc.gov/item/majo11860/; President Jackson's Message to Congress "On Indian Removal," December 6, 1830, Records of the United States Senate, 1789–1990, Record Group 46, National Archives and Records Administration. On financial speculation on Southeastern Native American territory in Era of Removal, see Mary Elizabeth Young, *Redskins, Ruffleshirts, and Rednecks: Indian Allotment in Alabama and Mississippi, 1830–1860* (Norman: University of Oklahoma Press, 1961); Claudio Saunt, *Unworthy Republic: The Dispossession of Native Americans and the Road to Indian Territory* (New York: W. W. Norton and Company, 2020), 173–227.

more demands for their land, but like the Catawbas, Oneidas, Tuscaroras, and Stockbridge–Mohicans during the American Revolution, this War of 1812-era alliance shows that seeking to maintain independence from the United States did not always entail military opposition to it.[20]

Cherokee students enrolled in mission schools grew up to become fierce advocates for Cherokee sovereignty who employed the Declaration of Independence and declared Cherokee independence in US courts. During the 1820s, Georgia state officials did not intervene when its citizens, of their own accord, squatted, stole, and harassed on Cherokee territory. In an 1824 address to the U.S. House of Representatives, Cherokee leaders appealed for the "protection of the rights, liberties, and lives, of the Cherokee people" from these encroachments. "We expect it [protection] from them, under that *memorable declaration*," they stated, quoting the Preamble. But after the 1828 election of a US president who pledged to displace 100,000 Native Americans from their ancestral homelands east of the Mississippi River, the state began more directly attacking Cherokee independence. It nullified Cherokee law, extended state laws into Cherokee territory, and executed a Cherokee man for allegedly killing another Cherokee man in the Cherokee Nation in 1830.[21]

In this context, the Cherokee Nation's 1830 filing against the State of Georgia in the U.S. Supreme Court was also a declaration of independence from foreign interference in domestic matters. In *Cherokee Nation v. Georgia*, lawyers for the Cherokees argued that the 1785 Treaty of Hopewell demonstrated that they were:

a separate, a powerful, and a martial nation, proud and jealous of their independence; marking a boundary between themselves and the citizens of the United States; asserting an exclusive right of self government within their territory, and the lofty and decisive right of vindicating themselves by force of arms against any attempted injustice on the part of the United States themselves.

They also pointed to the recent Cherokee Constitution and aspects of the US "civilization" plan that they had adopted, including agriculture, weaving, and Christian schooling, to legitimize their sovereignty.[22]

---

[20] McLoughlin, *Cherokee Renascence in the New Republic*; Susan M. Abram, *Forging a Cherokee–American Alliance: From Creation to Betrayal* (Tuscaloosa: University of Alabama Press, 2015). On the ways in which Native American students used to elite boarding-school curricula to critique US colonialism and to advance their own ideas about time, history, and the place of Native Nations in modernity, see Christina Snyder, "The Rise and Fall and Rise of Civilizations: Indian Intellectual Culture during the Removal Era," *Journal of American History* 104.2 (2017): 386–409.

[21] *Georgia Journal* (Milledgeville), May 11, 1824, 2; Tim Alan Garrison, *The Legal Ideology of Removal: The Southern Judiciary and the Sovereignty of Native American Nations* (Athens: University of Georgia Press, 2002), 103-124; Adam J. Pratt, *Toward Cherokee Removal: Land, Violence, and the White Man's Chance* (Athens: University of Georgia Press, 2022).

[22] *The Case of the Cherokee Nation Against the State of Georgia: Argued and Determined at the Supreme Court of the United States, January Term, 1831*, ed. Richard Peters (Philadelphia: John Grigg, 1831), 10-12, 83.

In his first ruling on the question of Cherokee independence, Supreme Court Chief Justice John Marshall sought to split the difference. In depicting Native Americans as "a people once numerous, powerful, and truly independent, found by our ancestors in the quiet and uncontrolled possession of an ample domain, gradually sinking beneath our superior policy, our arts and our arms," Marshall echoed "civilization" plan architects. Also, in a famously murky formulation, he characterized Native polities as "domestic dependent nations." The Cherokees' suit against Georgia thus could not be heard in the Supreme Court because it was not a domestic Constitutional matter, but Native Nations still did not rise to status of a foreign nation. Instead, Cherokees were "in a state of pupilage. Their relation to the United States resembles that of a ward to his guardian." When Cherokees found another way to test the extension of Georgia's laws in their territory with *Worcester v. Georgia*, Marshall was less equivocal about their sovereignty. In a statement that captured the precise way in which Native Americans themselves sought to apply the language of rights and sovereignty in the Declaration of Independence to their communities, Marshall wrote, "The Indian nations had always been considered as distinct, independent political communities, retaining their original natural rights." In upholding Cherokee sovereignty, Marshall invalidated the state of Georgia's claim that it could extend its laws into the Cherokee Nation. In so doing, he substantiated the Cherokee declaration of independence.[23]

Marshall's decisions set an important legal precedent for the US recognition of Native Nations' sovereignties, but amid the larger tide of ethnic cleansing and reservations that rendered Native people dependent on the expansionist United States, the Court's rulings were little more than a legal technicality in the mid nineteenth-century United States. Marshall also had already undermined US recognition of tribal sovereignty in his 1823 *Johnson v. M'Intosh* decision, which cast Native Nations as mere "tenants" of land that the US could acquire according to a "discovery doctrine" inherited from European empires. Acting under the terms of the illegal 1835 Treaty of New Echota, an agreement brokered by unauthorized Cherokee negotiators, the U.S. Army forcibly removed about 17,000 Cherokee people to Indian Territory, where they joined tens of thousands of Native Americans from across eastern North America, who began to reconstitute their nations in unfamiliar territory.[24]

---

[23] *Cherokee Nation v. Georgia*; *Worcester v. Georgia*.

[24] Lindsay G. Robertson, *Conquest by Law: How the Discovery of America Dispossessed Indigenous Peoples of their Lands* (New York: Oxford University Press, 2005); Theda Perdue and Michael D. Green, *The Cherokee Nation and the Trail of Tears* (New York: Penguin Books, 2007), 91–140. On new scholarly approaches to the Era of Removal, as well as arguments for new terms to describe the process, see Christina Snyder, "Many Removals: Re-evaluating the Arc of Indigenous Dispossession," *Journal of the Early Republic* 41.4 (2021): 623–650.

12.3 BOARDING SCHOOLS, US MILITARY SERVICE, AND MODERN DECLARATIONS OF INDEPENDENCE

US policymakers intended for reservations across the Trans-Mississippi West to confine people and erode their economic self-sufficiency and political independence until they had to turn to US bureaucrats to avoid starvation. Those bureaucrats reestablished a "civilization" plan that targeted Native children for instruction in language, religion, and industrial arts, often in residential boarding schools that removed children from their families. US reformers hoped that boarding schools would propel Native communities into modernity by eliminating Indigenous languages, cultural customs, and other lifeways. Coupled with legislation to break up tribal reservations into individual allotments, the US assault on tribal nations' cultures and lands – the twin bedrocks of tribal sovereignty – was comprehensive in the late nineteenth century.[25]

But in certain ways, the boarding schools' assimilative aims backfired, as a generation of boarding school graduates who became professionals in medicine, education, law, and other fields used their backgrounds and elite social status to build intertribal organizations that advocated for Native American rights. In the era of World War I, two Oceti Sakowin (Sioux) educators, both early members of the intertribal Society of American Indians, continued the Native American tradition of appropriating US Founding ideals and documents. In these cases, they advocated for US citizenship rights. Zitkala-Ša, a Yankton woman also known as Gertrude Bonnin, reworked the song "My Country 'Tis of Thee" to emphasize the absence of Native American voting rights. Rosebud Sioux citizen Chauncey Yellow Robe referenced the Declaration of Independence directly, explaining, "The American Indian has helped the white man to fight for the 'Declaration of Independence' and in every succeeding war since that the Indian has sacrificed his blood under the emblem of the United States." Of course, Yellow Robe exaggerated the extent of Native American support for US military causes, but he was not wrong. Even in the American Revolution and the War of 1812, he could point to alliances between Native Nations and the early United States.[26]

---

[25] Richard White, *The Roots of Dependency: Subsistence, Environment, and Social Change Among the Choctaws, Pawnees, and Navajos* (Lincoln: University of Nebraska Press, 1983), 319–322; Frederick E. Hoxie, *A Final Promise: The Campaign to Assimilate the Indians, 1880–1920* (Lincoln: University of Nebraska Press, 1984); K. Tsianina Lomawaima, *They Called It Prairie Light: The Story of Chilocco Indian School* (Lincoln: University of Nebraska Press, 1994); David Wallace Jones, *Education for Extinction: American Indians and the Boarding School Experience, 1875–1928* (Lawrence: University Press of Kansas, 1995); Brenda J. Child, *Boarding School Seasons: American Indian Families, 1900–1940* (Lincoln: University of Nebraska Press, 1998).

[26] Zitkala-Ša, "Indians at the Front," *American Indian Magazine* 5.1 (1917): 64, cited in John R. Wunder, "'Merciless Indian Savages' and the Declaration of Independence: Native Americans Translate the Ecunnaunuxulgee Document," *American Indian Law Review* 25.1

Despite their lack of US citizenship, thousands of Native Americans fought for the United States in World War I. When they returned home to discrimination and limitations on the rights and opportunities that they fought for overseas, Native Americans and Africans American alike used their status as military veterans as a platform from which to argue and organize for citizenship rights. Recognizing Native American service in World War I, the Indian Citizenship Act of 1924 uniformly bestowed US citizenship on Native Americans, although certain states such as Maine did not abide for decades. The promise of individual rights articulated in the Declaration of Independence, and constitutionalized in the Bill of Rights and Fourteenth and Fifteenth Amendments, finally applied to Native Americans. But not all welcomed US citizenship, arguing that the law was another assimilationist measure intended to undermine tribal sovereignty.[27]

Navigating the opportunities and constraints of the overlapping forms of tribal and US citizenship became a central feature of Native political participation since the Indian Citizenship Act and the end of the Allotment Era. The Indian Reorganization Act of 1934, the centerpiece of Indian New Deal legislation, overturned Allotment and initiated an era of tribal constitution drafting that continues into the twenty-first century. In the 1930s, some tribal nations rejected the opportunity to develop constitutions because they were understandably skeptical of US officials' legally mandated involvement in the process. Nonetheless, in drafting and revising constitutions, Native Nations enshrine self-determination and re-declare independence.[28]

(2000/2001): 84; Chauncey Yellow Robe, "Indian Patriotism," *American Indian Magazine* 6 (1919): 129–130, repr. *Talking Back to Civilization: Indian Voices from the Progressive Era*, ed. Frederick E. Hoxie (Boston: Bedford/St. Martin's Press, 2001), 128. In "'Merciless Indian Savages' and the Declaration of Independence," a study of Native American "translations" of the Declaration of Independence since the late eighteenth century, Wunder also chronicles Fourth of July celebrations on turn-of-the-century reservations. On Native American patriotism and military service during and after World War I, see Paul C. Rosier, *Serving Their Country: American Indian Politics and Patriotism in the Twentieth Century* (Cambridge: Harvard University Press, 2013); Thomas Grillot, *First Americans: U.S. Patriotism in Indian Country after World War I* (New Haven: Yale University Press, 2018).

[27] Kevin Bruyneel, "Challenging American Boundaries: Indigenous People and the 'Gift' of U.S. Citizenship," *Studies in American Political Development* 18.1 (2004): 30–43; Rosier, *Serving their Country*, 42–70; Thomas Grillot, *First Americans*, 17–81.

[28] The Native Nations Institute at the University of Arizona maintains a database of tribal constitutions. See Constitutions Resource Center, Native Nations Institute, https://nniconstitutions.arizona.edu/. On the Indian New Deal, see Lawrence C. Kelly, "The Indian Reorganization Act: The Dream and the Reality," *Pacific Historical Review* 44.3 (1975): 291–312; Graham D. Taylor, *The Indian New Deal and American Indian Tribalism* (Lincoln: University of Nebraska Press, 1980); Grillot, *First Americans*, 199–211. On the drafting of tribal constitutions, see Jean Dennison, *Colonial Entanglement: Constituting a Twenty-First Century Osage Nation* (Chapel Hill: University of North Carolina Press, 2012); Keith

In 1974, Lakota legal scholar and activist Vine Deloria, Jr., declared independence once again. His book, *Behind the Trail of Broken Treaties: An Indian Declaration of Independence*, echoed centuries of Native American critiques of the US colonialism. Deloria situated the work in the context of the American Indian Movement (AIM), an intertribal body of mostly young activists who staged public demonstrations against mismanagement at the Bureau of Indian Affairs and US neglect of treaty responsibilities and tribal sovereignty. A veteran of the U.S. Marines himself, Deloria supplemented AIM's occupations of government facilities and the site of the Wounded Knee Massacre of 1890 with a prolific body of writing on law, politics, and religion.[29]

AIM developed in tandem with the broader US Civil Rights Movement, which sought to hold the United States to account for failing to live up to the nation's founding ideals. As with the drive for African American civil rights, AIM's intellectual roots and strategies were honed prior to the 1960s and 1970s. Historian Daniel M. Cobb has located the early years of the Cold War as a crucial proving ground for "translat[ing] the politics of 'cold war civil rights' into the language of tribal sovereignty." Postwar thinkers such as D'Arcy McNickle (Flathead), Robert K. Thomas (Cherokee), and Clyde Warrior (Ponca) were central figures in the intellectual and organizational ferment that preceded AIM. At the 1961 American Indian Chicago Conference, representatives from sixty-five tribal nations drafted a Declaration of Indian Purpose. This expansive document contained detailed policy proposals on economic development, healthcare, education, housing, and law in Native Nations. It opened with a series of creedal statements that included a direct reference to the Declaration of Independence: "We believe in the future of a greater America, an America which we were first to love, where life, liberty, and the pursuit of happiness will be a reality."[30]

Native Nations within the twenty-first-century United States continue to navigate opportunities to assert – and threats to undermine – their sovereignties. Tribal sovereignty was the legal basis for establishing casino gaming as a means of economic development and social service expansion in Indian Country. Just as the Declaration's signers argued, political independence could have economic benefits. What began as small bingo halls

---

Richotte, Jr., *Claiming Turtle Mountain's Constitution: The History, Legacy, and Future of a Tribal Nation's Founding Documents* (Chapel Hill: University of North Carolina Press, 2017).

[29] Vine Deloria, Jr., *Behind the Trail of Broken Treaties: An Indian Declaration of Independence* (Austin: University of Texas Press, 1974).

[30] Daniel M. Cobb, *Native Activism in Cold War America: The Struggle for Sovereignty* (Lawrence: University Press of Kansas), 4; American Indian Chicago Conference, *Declaration of Indian Purpose. The Voice of the American Indian* (Chicago: Published by the American Indian Chicago Conference at the University of Chicago, June 13-20, 1961), 3.

has developed into a transformative, if geographically uneven, multibillion industry. Still, these nations face recurring challenges to their tribal sovereignties, particularly as they seek to protect sacred sites, natural resources, and their ability to prosecute non-Native offenders for crimes committed on tribal lands. When they assert tribal sovereignty, they declare independence once again.[31]

---

[31] Jessica Cattelino, *High Stakes: Florida Seminole Gaming and Sovereignty* (Durham: Duke University Press, 2008); Peter Nabokov, *Where the Lightning Strikes: The Lives of American Indian Sacred Places* (New York: Penguin Books, 2006); Sarah Deer, *The Beginning and End of Rape: Confronting Sexual Violence in Native America* (Minneapolis: University of Minnesota Press, 2015). Indigenous legal scholars such as Sarah Deer have led twenty-first-century declarations of Native American independence. Other historically informed works by Indigenous legal scholars that address US colonialism's legal legacies on contemporary Native Nations include William Bradford, "Another Such Victory and We Are Done: A Call to an American Indian Declaration of Independence," *Tulsa Law Review* 40.1 (2004): 1–76; Robert A. Williams, Jr., *Like a Loaded Weapon: The Rehnquist Court, Indian Rights, and the Legal History of Racism in America* (Minneapolis: University of Minnesota Press, 2005); Bruce Duthu, *Shadow Nations: Tribal Sovereignty and the Limits of Legal Pluralism* (New York: Oxford University Press, 2013); Rebecca Tsosie, "The Politics of Inclusion: Indigenous Peoples and U.S. Citizenship," *UCLA Law Review* 63.6 (2016): 1694–1751; Maggie Blackhawk, "On Power & Indian Country," *Women & Law* 39.1 (2020): 39–54 (published jointly with the *Stanford Law Review*).

13

The Declaration in Anti-slavery and African American Thought

Thomas J. Davis

"We expect great things from men who have made such a noble stand against the designs of their fellow-men to enslave them." So declared Peter Bestes, Sambo Freeman, Felix Holbrook, and Chester Joie in behalf of their fellow slaves in Massachusetts. Dated April 20, 1773, their petition to the provincial legislature laid out a charge of hypocrisy. "As the people of this province seem to be actuated by the principles of equity and justice, we cannot but expect your house will again take our deplorable case into serious consideration, and give us that ample relief which, as men, we have a natural right to," the petitioners asserted.[1]

Their claim of natural rights indicted the ruling white society for its despotic double standard in subordinating blacks. Their petition displayed black Americans' early and persistent exposure of the living lie to be enshrined in the US founding document holding as universal principles "these truths to be self-evident, that all men are created equal, that they are endowed by their Creator with certain unalienable Rights, that among these are Life, Liberty and the Pursuit of Happiness."

"[W]e can feel no inspiration when we look at the American flag," declared the militant twenty-nine-year-old escaped slave H. Ford Douglas in July 1860. "[N]o colored man can feel any of this inspiration. We are denied all participation in the government; we remember that the flag only covers us as slaves," he scoffed. "[O]ur liberties are only respected and our rights only secured to us, when, escaping from the beak of the American eagle," he explained to his Framingham audience gathered for the Massachusetts Anti-Slavery Society's Fourth of July observance, as recorded in the foremost abolitionist newspaper of its day, *The Liberator*, in its July 13, 1860, issue.

---

[1] Peter Bestes, Sambo Freeman, Felix Holbrook, and Chester Joie, "Petition 'In Behalf of a Fellow Slaves in This Province'," in *A Documentary History of the Negro People in the United States*, ed. Herbert Aptheker (New York: Citadel Press, 1951), 1: 7.

"Hypocrisy is not a growth peculiar to American soil, but it has reached the most hateful development here," Douglas emphasized. For him and like-minded blacks over the centuries, glorification of the Declaration of Independence turned a blind eye to the self-evident duplicity that marked the gap between the nation's deeds and the document's pronounced philosophy. The fireworks-filled annual celebrations of flag-waving and parading bands might be appropriate for the Declaration's principles but not for its failed practices, blacks have insisted since the 1770s. The living fact of white supremacy embodied in slavery and persistent black subordination has informed every generation of African Americans since the promises of the United States of America's founding.

The theory of inalienable human rights proclaimed in the Declaration of Independence from its inception has shaped blacks' heartfelt vision of America and their place in the nation and its society. The Declaration laid the foundation for the expression of African American protest against the central paradox of US society as it touted adherence to the belief that "all men are created equal" while insistently imposing white supremacy. The Declaration has been the touchstone for blacks' demands over the centuries for America to reconcile its actual practices with its announced principles. That contradiction has marked the place of the Declaration in African American life and thought.

13.1 AMERICA'S TURNING ITS BACK

Blacks have perennially filled their rhetoric of abolition and equal rights with the fact of America's turning its back on its founding Declaration's principles. The New York black abolitionist William Hamilton early exemplified the mode of black protest. Addressing the New York African Society for Mutual Relief in January 1809 to celebrate the anniversary of the US outlawing the foreign slave trade a year earlier, Hamilton called all to notice "that while the siren song of liberty and equality was sang throughout the land, that the groans of the oppressed made the music very discordant, and that America's fame was very much tarnished thereby."[2]

More bitingly, Hamilton almost twenty years later denounced the framers of the US founding document for the "inconsistency of men holding slaves and at the same time declaring in the most solemn manner" egalitarian sentiments. Hamilton offered his remarks at Manhattan's African Zion Church to commemorate New York State's declaring complete its gradual abolition policy begun in 1799. The nation's first black newspaper, New York's *Freedom's Journal* recorded Hamilton speech and the event in its July 13, 1827, issue.

Blacks in Baltimore, Maryland, also commemorated the same July 4th New York event. *Freedom's Journal* noted in its issue of July 20, 1827, that black

---

[2] William Hamilton, "An Address to the New York African Society, for the Mutual Relief, Delivered at the Universalist Church, January 2, 1809," in *Early Negro Writing 1760–1837*, ed. Dorothy Porter (Boston: Beacon Press, 1971), 39.

Baltimoreans offered a toast that, "We hold these truths to be self-evident, that all men are born free and equal has been resounded from one end of the Union to the other by white Americans. May they speedily learn to practice what they so loudly proclaim."

Calling America to face its own self-serving creed has been a staple of black protest. Failing to be true to its own beliefs and principles demonstrated an inability or unwillingness to be more than a sham, blacks have long noted. Such self-denial created a condition akin to schizophrenia, with acknowledged fears and unacknowledged self-loathing. Also, blacks testified that such self-denial could only produce shame as the world looked upon America as the imposter it was.

The antebellum black militant David Walker illustrated the theme in his 1829 *Appeal* to the Coloured Citizens of the World. "See your Declaration Americans!!!" Walker challenged whites. "Do you understand your own language? Hear your language, proclaimed to the world, July 4th, 1776," he dared. "Compare your own language above, extracted from your own Declaration of Independence, with your cruelties and murders inflicted by your cruel and unmerciful fathers and yourselves on our fathers and on us." Mimicking the Declaration, Walker called on "the candid and unprejudiced of the whole world" as witnesses to what "the white Christians of America do to us, the blacks, or Africans. I also ask the attention of the world of mankind to the declaration of these very American people, of the United States."[3]

13.2 OUR FOURTH OF JULY COMES ON THE FIFTH

American practice made the Declaration something of a dead letter for African Americans, as many demonstrated by refusing to celebrate the Fourth of July. "On account of the misfortune of our color, our Fourth of July comes on the fifth," black abolitionist Peter Osborne proclaimed to his audience at the African Church in the City of New Haven, Connecticut, on July 5, 1832. "I hope and trust that when the Declaration of Independence is fully executed which declares that all men, without respect to person, were born free and equal, we may then have our fourth of July on the fourth," Osborne continued, as recounted in *The Liberator* on December 1, 1832.

The day's delay from the fourth to the fifth symbolized not so much despair as hope. The Declaration's promise was not lost for all time but rather was obtainable in time, Osborne insisted. Firmly staking African Americans' claim to the United States as their homeland, he urged "every colored citizen in the United States to step forward boldly and gallantly defend his rights." His was a call to action: "we must unite ... and then with the Declaration of Independence

---

[3] David Walker, *Walker's Appeal in Four Articles ... to the Coloured Citizens of the World, but in Particular and Very Especially to those of the United States of America*, rev. ed. (Boston: David Walker, 1830).

in one hand, and the Holy Bible in the other, I think we might courageously give battle," he urged. "Take courage, then, ye African-Americans! Don't give up the conflict, for the glorious prize can be won."

Frederick Douglass delivered the most famous of all fifth of July declarations. Speaking in his adopted hometown of Rochester, New York, on July 5, 1852, Douglass pointedly asked his predominantly white audience at Corinthian Hall: "What, to the American slave, is your 4th of July?" His answer eloquently encapsulated antebellum blacks' challenges to America's ignoring its principles. The Fourth of July was "a day that reveals to him [the slave], more than all other days in the year, the gross injustice and cruelty to which he is the constant victim. To him, your celebration is a sham"; Douglass charged,

> your boasted liberty, an unholy license; your national greatness, swelling vanity; your sounds of rejoicing are empty and heartless; your denunciation of tyrants, brass fronted impudence; your shouts of liberty and equality, hollow mockery; your prayers and hymns, your sermons and thanksgivings, with all your religious parade and solemnity, are, to Him, mere bombast, fraud, deception, impiety, and hypocrisy – a thin veil to cover up crimes which would disgrace a nation of savages,

he taunted. "There is not a nation on the earth guilty of practices more shocking and bloody than are the people of the United States, at this very hour."[4]

Blacks betrayed nothing by reciprocal disassociation from the political institutions and practices of a "Government of which, and the Constitution of which, is in favor of supporting and perpetuating this monstrous system of injustice and blood," Douglass declared, denouncing slavery and white supremacy. Indeed, blacks throughout the ages have insisted that in regard to the America proclaimed in its 1776 Declaration, they were ever true believers, never betrayers. Any deficit of patriotism lay elsewhere. The seventy-five-year-old Douglass reiterated the point in August 1893, speaking at "Colored American Day" at the World's Columbian Exposition in Chicago. "The problem," he explained, "is whether the American people have loyalty enough, honor enough, patriotism enough, to live up to their own constitution."[5]

13.3 LOVE IT OR LEAVE IT

To the taunt "love it or leave it," blacks often echoed Douglass' retort that African Americans had the right to criticize American institutions.[6] Indeed,

---

[4] Frederick Douglass, "What to the Slave Is the 4th of July," in *Great Speeches by Frederick Douglass*, ed. James Daley (Mineola: Dover Publications, 1852), 26–47.
[5] Frederick Douglass, "Speech at Colored American Day, 25 August 1893," in Christopher Robert Reed, ed., *All the World Is Here! The Black Presence at White City* (Bloomington: Indiana University Press, 2000), 194.
[6] Frederick Douglass, "The Right to Criticize American Institutions" (1847), in *The Life and Writings of Frederick Douglass*, ed. Philip S. Foner (New York: International Publishers, 1950), 236.

over the years, blacks created a genre of jeremiad, reciting complaints of the racial oppression embedded in America's self-contradictions. Blacks consistently insisted that they so loved America that they wanted to heal their nation not harm it. And most had no intention of leaving. Their stance as steadfast Americans emerged emphatically, for example, in response to President Abraham Lincoln's pitching black colonization to five black leaders he called to the White House in August 1862. The delegation politely listened to Lincoln repeating his views that differences between blacks and whites in the United States were such that it would be "better for us both ... to be separated."[7] Indeed, ten days before the meeting, Lincoln had appointed a commissioner of emigration to advance his project for moving blacks out of the United States. Moreover, in April 1862, when Congress abolished slavery in the District of Columbia, it appropriated $100,000 to colonize or settle blacks from the District to "such other country beyond the limits of the United States as the President may determine."[8]

News from the meeting with President Lincoln prompted resolute responses from blacks near and far. Six days after the White House talk, blacks in Queens County, New York, gathered at Newtown to denounce with emphasis Lincoln's call for separation as "a mistaken policy." They embraced the United States as "the country of our choice, being our fathers' country," and they exulted in their identity as "Colored Americans." Not only did the blacks at Newtown reiterate that "this is our country by birth," but they also professed "we love this land, and have contributed our share to its prosperity and wealth." They expressed no intention of leaving but held that they and those they represented refused to forsake their homeland. They insisted that they had at least an equal claim to all the nation's benefits and blessings. "We believe, too, we have the right to have applied to ourselves those rights named in the Declaration of Independence," they concluded.[9]

A gathering in Philadelphia later in August further pointed up the deep and everlasting roots of blacks in America. "The blood of millions of our race cries from the ground," they noted in what they published as *An Appeal from the Colored Men of Philadelphia to the President of the United States*. The meeting stressed that blacks were as American as any Americans, were part of America's foundation, and "have produced much of the wealth of this country." Moreover, the Appeal pointed out that blacks "constitute ... almost the entire wealth of the Cotton States."[10]

---

[7] Abraham Lincoln, "Address on Colonization to a Deputation of Negroes," in *Collected Works of Abraham Lincoln*, ed. Roy P. Bassler (New Brunswick: Rutgers University Press, 1953), 5: 371–72.
[8] 12 Stat. 376 (1862).
[9] Colored Citizens of Queen's County, N.Y., "Newtown Meeting," *The Liberator*, September 12, 1862, in *A Documentary History of the Negro People*, 1: 472.
[10] James Underdue, J. C. Davis, Robert Allen et al., "An Appeal from the Colored Men of Philadelphia to the President of the United States," *Documentary History* 1:473–475.

Where they were allowed to exercise the title, blacks were "respectable and useful citizens," the Philadelphia blacks declared. They asked rhetorically who would "make better citizens, prove as loyal, love the country better, and be as obedient to its laws as we have been?" Arguing what they termed "moral aspects," the group denounced the "despotism" of slavery and white supremacy and called on Lincoln as "President of the United States ... [to be] a champion, most able and willing to aid us in all that is right." They closed with a simple appeal: "We ask, that by the standard of justice and humanity we may be weighed, and that men shall no longer be measured by their stature or their color."[11]

"We pray for a more liberal and enlightened public policy," the Philadelphia black men continued. That echoed a persistent theme of African American protest centered on US founding values expressed in the Declaration of Independence. It was not simply a self-centered protest as it carried hope for America as a whole. Progressing away from the ignorance and prejudice of white supremacy afforded America the opportunity to advance toward the greater society projected in the Declaration, blacks have insisted. They have argued for America to be that special place it claimed to be in "the course of human events."[12]

13.4 A MASCULINITY THAT ELIDED BLACK WOMEN

Yet much black protest has, in fact, carried elements of exclusion as it expressed a masculinity that elided black women. Male-dominated black public leadership tended to imbibe the current American patriarchal narcotics. The Appeal from the Colored Men of Philadelphia, for example, conspicuously argued for black rights as the rights of men. As with most other black exposition of the Declaration of Independence, the authors of the Appeal embraced the phrase "all men are created equal" with considered literal emphasis. The protesting black men sought the same status as white men, which included paternal overlordship. That pervasive theme skewed universal application of rights toward a self-centered idealization of relations that accepted separate spheres of life, at least for male and female. While insisting black men could and should do whatever white men were allowed to do, black men tended also to persist in the notion that there were things men did and things women did but that men and women could not and should not do the same things. Such an approach left black women to make their own thematic connections in protesting for universal rights proclaimed in the Declaration of Independence.

And, indeed, with direct and indirect reference to the Declaration of Independence, black women connected their own universalist protest against

---

[11] Underdue, et al., "An Appeal," 473–475.
[12] Underdue et al., "An Appeal," 473–475.

rights restricted by race and gender. Their rhetoric shared elements of identity and strategy with white women. They clearly identified, for example, with the famed 1848 Seneca Falls Convention's Declaration of Sentiments, which expanded the 1776 document to proclaim "all men and women are created equal." But they pushed further in arguing against the triple bind of being black, enslaved, and female. Black women communicated early and often demands to change attitudes and behaviors for America to realize in a broader sense the words of its Declaration and be a place "among the powers of the earth" for blacks and whites, men and women, to enjoy the "equal station to which the Laws of Nature and of Nature's God entitle them."

The pioneering Connecticut-born African American lecturer Maria W. Stewart in 1833 spoke to rights of men and women "endowed by their Creator." Characteristic of her references, she reached to biblical sources, such as the image of Deborah in the Book of Judges, to declare, "What if I am a woman, is not the God of ancient times the God of these modern days?" God-given rights, she insisted, were human rights: They depended on no gender or race. Stewart voiced black women's early call for social justice that reflected a universalist understanding of the Declaration of Independence.[13]

The black abolitionist and woman's rights advocate known as Sojourner Truth further illustrated black women's drive against white supremacy, slavery, and male domination. Born enslaved as Isabella Baumfree in about 1797 among the Dutch remnant in Ulster County, New York, Sojourner Truth memorably inscribed black women's protest theme in 1851 at the Women's Convention in Akron, Ohio. Her "ain't I a woman?" refrain exhorted recognition of her proven God-given equality with any man or woman. She preached an equality of rights dependent on nothing other than being human. Dismissing any other qualifications such as intellect, she demanded "What's that got to do with women's rights or negroes' rights?" Without citing the 1776 Declaration, Sojourner Truth put in plain words her belief in universal application to hold "these truths to be self-evident."[14]

Sojourner Truth pressed further for universal human rights after the Civil War. Addressing the First Annual Meeting of the American Equal Rights Association in May 1867, she spoke of slavery's being "partly destroyed; not entirely." She told her New York City audience, "I want it root and branch destroyed." Accomplishing that required ending both racism and sexism. "I have a right to have as much as a man," she insisted. "There is a great stir about colored men getting their rights, but not a word about the colored women," she expanded. "I want women to have their rights. In the courts women have

---

[13] Maria Stewart, "What If I Am a Woman," in *Maria Stewart: America's First Black Woman Political Writer: Essays and Speeches*, ed. Marilyn Richardson (Bloomington: Indiana University, 1987), 65–74.
[14] Sojourner Truth, "Ain't I a Woman?" in *Sojourner Truth's Ain't I a Woman?' Speech: A Primary Source Investigation*, ed. Corona Brezina (New York: Rosen Publishing, 2005), 25–26.

no right, no voice; nobody speaks for them," she explained. "I wish woman to have her voice there among the pettifoggers. If it is not a fit place for women, it is unfit for men." That the rights of humanity admitted no double standard echoed in all Truth said. In her view of human equality, outlawing slavery was a start but not a place to stop. "There ought to be equal rights now more than ever, since colored people have got their freedom," she concluded.[15]

In striving to secure the blessings of liberty for themselves and their posterity, black women have struggled toward a Declaration of Independence that recognized their autonomy. They have protested to stand in their own right – free from white supremacy, male patriarchy, and white feminist sympathy. Frances E. W. Harper illustrated black women's stance in her 1869 publication, *Moses: A Story of the Nile*. Offering a revision of the biblical Book of Exodus, Harper's forty-one-page poem *Moses* set black women in a position to be judged not in relation to others but as themselves. A freeborn forty-four-year-old black from Baltimore, Harper depicted black women in *Moses* and in an accompanying four-page prose allegory, *The Mission of the Flowers*, with personal and moral capacity to navigate and negotiate life without slave masters, domineering black males, or benevolent white paternalism or maternalism.[16]

A founder of the National Association of Colored Women in 1894, Harper continued till her death in 1911 to advance black women's standing amid the social restraints of the day. Her writing illuminated black women's negotiating wretched intersections. Her much referenced 1892 novel *Iola Leroy, or Shadows Uplifted*, reflected black women's past and present challenges. From contemptible elements of racial identification twisted in miscegenation and passing to restricted schooling and limited employment, the complicated struggles of Harper's black females argued for self-determination that expressed "the consent of the governed," in the words of the 1776 Declaration.

The North Carolina slave-born Anna Julia Haywood Cooper with succinct eloquence reflected a universalist understanding of human rights. "The cause of freedom is not the cause of a race or a sect, a party or a class – it is the cause of human kind, the very birthright of humanity," she declared in her 1892 *A Voice from the South by a Black Woman of the South*. Like Sojourner Truth and others before and after her, Cooper set black women's status within the universal set of humanity. She denounced any us-against-them thinking. "It is not the intelligent woman vs. the ignorant woman; nor the white woman vs. the black, the brown, and the red, – it is not even the cause of woman vs. man," she reasoned, as she linked together all humanity. She envisioned social justice arising from what she termed "universal tolerance and its twin, universal charity."[17]

---

[15] *Proceedings of the First Anniversary of the American Equal Rights Association* (New York: Robert J. Johnston, 1867), p. 20.
[16] Alice Rutkowski, "Leaving the Good Mother: Frances E. W. Harper, Lydia Maria Child, and the Literary Politics of Reconstruction," *Legacy* 25 (2008): 83.
[17] Anna J. Cooper, *A Voice from the South by a Black Woman of the South* (Chapel Hill: University of North Carolina, 2017), 55–58.

13.5 A DECLARATION OF INDEPENDENCE FOR HUMANITY

Cooper looked forward to what she described as "the great Emancipation Day of human belief, man's intellectual Independence Day, prefiguring and finally compelling the worldwide enfranchisement." But, she noted, freedom progressed slowly as each era shook off "clamps of tradition and superstition which had manacled and muzzled it." Limited vision persistently restricted reform, as in the case of the US Founding Fathers. "They were incapable of drawing up a Declaration of Independence for humanity," Cooper said, accepting the 1776 ascription of rights to "men," rather than to humanity. "God hasten the day," she exhorted, "when 'rights' will mean the final triumph of all right over might, the supremacy of the moral forces of reason and justice and love in the government of the nation."[18]

A host of black women have shared Anna Julia Cooper's views of the limits and enlargement of the US Declaration of Independence. Even more than resisting racism and sexism, activist African American women have seized the 1776 Declaration as a pledge of progress, much as the 1788 US Constitution pledged. They have taken the founding US documents as engaging "We the people of the United States" in advancing "to form a more perfect union." And in viewing that process, they have emphasized the national purpose to "establish justice."

In her push against American apartheid in the 1950s and 1960s, Mississippi sharecroppers' daughter Fannie Lou Hamer exemplified the strong-willed selflessness of black women seeking justice to improve America. "I'm determined to give my part," Hamer declared.[19] Her work with the Mississippi Freedom Democratic Party became what some described as a call for a "new Declaration of Independence."[20] She worked "to make democracy a reality," as she put it in a speech delivered at the Vietnam War Moratorium Rally in Berkeley, California, in October 1969.[21]

Hamer's consistent theme, "nobody's free until everybody's free," echoed the all-encompassing argument of black women's ceaseless campaign to realize what they saw as the underlying values in the US Declaration of Independence.[22] Their undying call reached to the infectious roots of tyranny based on race, sex, and all else not arising from self-determination expressed in the "consent" that the Declaration asserted as the basis of all government.

Hamer also represented black women activists' radical democratic vision of pushing change from the bottom up in working to meet immediate needs.

---

[18] Cooper, *A Voice from the South*, 55–58.
[19] Earnest N. Bracey, *Fannie Lou Hamer: The Life of the Civil Rights Icon* (Jefferson: McFarland. 2011), 160.
[20] Jack Minnis, "The Mississippi Freedom Democratic Party: A New Declaration of Independence," *Freedomways* 5 (1965): 264–278.
[21] Megan Parker Brooks and Davis W. Houck, *The Speeches of Fannie Lou Hamer: To Tell It Like It Is* (Jackson: University Press of Mississippi, 2011), 98–103.
[22] Brooks and Houck, *The Speeches of Fannie Lou Hamer*, 134–139.

Ella Baker further expressed that selfless vision. One of the foremost civil rights organizers of the twentieth-century, Baker once simply explained, "I have never thought in terms of my 'making a contribution.' I just thought of myself as functioning where there was a need."[23] She demonstrated that from the 1930s through the 1970s, as a key person in the functioning of the National Association for the Advancement of Colored People, in Friendship, and the Southern Christian Leadership Conference, and in helping to create the Student Nonviolent Coordinating Committee. Baker believed in grassroots power, in what she called "community leadership."[24]

Like Baker, black women activists historically placed their faith less in any document, such as the Declaration of Independence, than in people animated by principle. They persisted in their commitment to moral behavior that valued basic humanity. And in doing so they pressed beyond legalisms and literal interpretations of documents. Their vision consistently surpassed that of even their foremost black brothers trapped in their limiting sphere of masculinity. The Rev. Dr. Martin Luther King, Jr., illustrated the persisting male confines in his 1963 March on Washington "I Have a Dream" speech. King famously invoked the Declaration of Independence as "a promissory note to which every American was to fall heir." Yet his explanation carried the restrictive rhetoric of masculinity. "This note was," King said, "a promise that all men – yes, black men as well as white men – would be guaranteed the unalienable rights of life, liberty and the pursuit of happiness."[25]

13.6 A BLACK DECLARATION OF INDEPENDENCE

While activist black women persisted in advancing universal application of equality, activist black men persisted in a literally limited masculinist rhetoric. Their speech and writing in the twentieth century appeared not so different from that of their forefathers in the nineteenth century. They remained in many instances stuck on gender-specific elements of "all men are created equal." Even when voicing the rising militancy of the 1960s, the statements of black male leaders in black male-dominated organizations lacked the comprehensive humanism characteristic of activist black women. The Black Declaration of Independence that the male-led National Committee of Black Churchmen (NCBC) issued in 1970 illustrated both the historical character of black perspectives on the US Declaration of Independence and the continuing masculinist character dominating black protest.

---

[23] Ella Baker, "Developing Community Leadership," *Black Women in White America: A Documentary History*, ed. Gerda Lerner (New York: Vintage, 1973), 345.
[24] Baker, "Developing Community Leadership," 362.
[25] Martin Luther King, Jr., "I Have a Dream," *A Testament of Hope: The Essential Writings of Martin Luther King Jr.*, ed. James Melvin Washington (New York: HarperCollins, 1986), 217–220.

Imitating the style and substance of the US Declaration that opened, "In Congress, July 4, 1776 – The unanimous Declaration of the thirteen united States of America," the NCBC's Declaration opened, "In the Black Community, July 4, 1970 a Declaration by concerned Black Citizens of the United States of America in Black Churches, Schools, Homes, Community Organizations and Institutions assembled." It followed with a similar invocation of "the course of Human Events," but it shifted the focus of "the necessity." That in 1776 had been "for one people to dissolve the political bands which have connected them with another." That in 1970 was "for a people who were stolen from the lands of their Fathers, transported under the most ruthless and brutal circumstances 5,000 miles to a strange land, sold into dehumanizing slavery, emasculated, subjugated, exploited, and discriminated against for 351 years."[26]

Both documents invoked "the Laws of Nature and of Nature's God" and "a decent respect to the Opinions of Mankind." The US document moved "to assume among the powers of the earth, [a] separate and equal station" and to "declare the causes which impelled them to the separation." The Black Declaration moved, however, "to call with finality, a halt to … indignities and genocidal practices" and to "declare their just grievances and the urgent and necessary redress thereof." In line with the long tradition of black protest referencing the 1776 document, the Black Declaration reiterated, "We hold these truths to be self-evident." It offered a twist in asserting "that all Men are not only created equal and endowed by their Creator with certain unalienable rights among which are Life, Liberty and the Pursuit of Happiness, but when this equality and these rights are deliberately and consistently refused, withheld or abnegated, men are bound by self-respect and honor to rise up in righteous indignation to secure them."

The 1970 Declaration continued to elaborate the right of rebellion centered in the 1776 Declaration. Resisting not only "any Form of Government" but also "any variety of established traditions and systems of the Majority [that] becomes destructive of Freedom and of legitimate Human Rights," the Black Declaration called for using "every necessary and accessible means to protest and to disrupt the Machinery of Oppression, and so to bring such general distress and discomfort upon the oppressor as to the offended Minorities shall seem most appropriate and most likely to affect a proper adjustment of the society." Underscoring its call for "bold tactics," the 1970 Declaration pointed to "a long train of Abuses and Violence, pursuing invariably the same Object, [that] manifests a Design to reduce them under Absolute Racist Domination and Injustice." And to the end of achieving "Legitimate Minority Power and Self Determination, for their present Relief and future Security," the 1970

---

[26] NCBC, "The Black Declaration of Independence," in *Modern Black Nationalism: From Marcus Garvey to Louis Farrakhan*, ed. William L. Van Deburg (New York: New York University Press, 1997), 225–228.

Declaration insisted that it was the blacks' "duty radically to confront such Government or system of traditions."

The 1776 Declaration of Independence expounded twenty-seven paragraphs of alleged injuries. The 1970 Black Declaration submitted twelve. It ranged from assorted acts by government "to harass our People" to "being lynched, burned, tortured, harried, harassed and imprisoned without just cause" to "being gunned down in the streets, in our churches, in our homes, in our apartments and on our campuses, by Policemen and Troops who are protected by a Mock Trial." It cited "Exploitation and Injustice" in frequent forms of "Racism and bigotry" that created "an unrelenting Economic Depression in the Black Community" and denied "to most of us equal access to the better Housing and Education of the land." It denounced "the Pretense of Urban Renewal" for "having desecrated and torn down our humblest dwelling places ... without replacing them at costs which we can afford."

The 1970 Declaration followed its litany of abuse as the 1776 Declaration had by noting tireless "petition[ing] for Redress in the most humble terms" without remedy. Similarly, it said, "nor have we been wanting in attentions to our White Brethren." In 1776, the attentions and warnings had been "to our British brethren." Both sets of "brethren" proved "deaf to the voice of Justice." As a result, both documents concluded with the necessity of re-examining allegiances. The 1776 document declared "these united Colonies are, and of Right ought to be Free and Independent States, that they are Absolved from all Allegiance to the British Crown ... and the State of Great Britain." The 1970 document declared a "Most Firm Commitment to the Liberation of Black People," who "shall be, and of Right ought to be free and independent from the injustice, exploitative control, institutionalized violence and racism of white America." But it announced no absolute renunciation of the United States. Rather, it pronounced the blacks' allegiance as conditional: "unless we receive full Redress and Relief from these Inhumanities we will move to renounce all Allegiance to this Nation, and will refuse, in every way, to cooperate with the Evil which is perpetrated upon ourselves and our Communities."

In contrast to the 1776 US Declaration that severed ties with its erstwhile government, the 1970 Black Declaration proposed allegiance only if government altered the structures and systems subjugating blacks. And while mimicking parts of the 1776 rhetorical universalism, the 1970 document pointedly focused on black people. It offered a nod to broader outreach in referring to "the Right of the Minorities" and "the offended Minorities." But such references belied the basic identification of the document with black people. It resisted the broader outreach in idioms of colonized peoples fashionable in the late 1960s and 1970s in favor of what some viewed as the blacks' group integrity. It further eschewed the universalism activist black women historically advocated. Indeed, the 1970 document persisted in a masculinist perspective. It referred to blacks as "a people who were stolen from the lands of their Fathers." It spoke of "Black sons taken captive in its Armies" and of a host of problems that "wreaks havoc upon our *men*" (emphasis added). In listing "our own Black heroes," it offered not a single black woman.

The NCBC attached its 1970 Declaration to a call for blacks not to celebrate the Fourth of July, further reaching back to antebellum black protests. In a turn toward more militancy, in the view of the *Chicago Defender* and other leading black newspapers, the NCBC urged celebrating Black Liberation Day. That alternative aimed to highlight blacks' condition, in contrast to displays in "Honor of America." The more in-your-face approach edged away from the nonviolence martyred Rev. King had championed. Coalition of Black Clergyman chairman Rev. Dr. Wendell Foster gave voice to the shift with a diverging echo of Rev. King's immortalized 1963 March on Washington address. "I still advocate non-violence, but if I see my two little daughters growing up without the same rights and privileges white people have," Foster said, "I'll burn the country down. I say let's all have freedom or let's all die."[27]

The influential *New York Times* daily newspaper acknowledged the 1970 Black Declaration, describing it in a snide July 4, 1970, editorial as "mixing doubtful analogy with some very painful truths," and saying "one may be tempted to discount the weight of a document grandly signed 'by Order and in behalf of Black People,' but one would be wrong to ignore the temper that produced it." The "temper" the *New York Times* noticed in the 1970 Declaration carried into the NCBC's joining in plans for a National Black Solidarity Day. Slated for Monday, November 2, 1970, the event called for a nationwide general work strike along with an economic boycott of all white businesses. Planners accompanied their announcement with a call for "a Congress of Black People" to carry forward the Black Declaration of Independence and advance methods for blacks to establish "new directions and effective coalitions within the liberation movement."[28]

The 1970 Black Declaration of Independence advanced an identity politics akin to that in the 1776 Declaration. It, too, aimed to engender a revolutionary political consciousness. As in 1776, in 1970 blood had already been spilled in the streets as frustration fueled black violence, beginning notably with the five-day Watts riots in Los Angeles, California, in August 1965. In 1967, more than 100 race riots erupted. The most devastating were in Newark, New Jersey, and Detroit, Michigan. The so-called Easter Week Riots that erupted in more than 120 cities in April 1968 at the assassination of King appeared to finish what the 1776 Declaration called "patient sufferance." No longer did many blacks appear to accept that America's "evils are sufferable." Rather, they appeared ready "to right themselves by abolishing the forms to which they are accustomed," as the American colonies had declared in their rebellion.

---

[27] "Against Fourth of July," *Chicago Daily Defender*, July, 17, 1970.
[28] "Black Solidarity Day Plans Made," *Amsterdam News* (New York), October 1, 1970.

13.7 MORE THAN RADICAL POSTURING

The 1970 Black Declaration of Independence was more than radical posturing. Its brooding had an immediate bloody background, and its unsatisfied grievances reached back to repeating antebellum complaints. It reflected grassroots disaffection at least as much as the 1776 Declaration had. Yet it remained relatively moderate amid the militant temper of the times. Urging reconciliation based on social justice rather than outright rebellion against state authority, the 1970 Declaration sought a fresh reconstruction in America to eliminate its systemic racism and elevate the condition of everyday black life. It demanded more than formal guarantees of equality, which many deemed achieved with the Civil Rights Act of 1964 and the Voting Rights Act of 1965. Enacting and enforcing antidiscrimination law fell short of blacks being "free and independent from the injustice, exploitative control, institutionalized violence and racism of white America" and getting "full Redress and Relief from these Inhumanities," in the words of the 1970 document.

The intense identity politics of the 1970 Declaration pursued a more democratic politics envisioned in black self-determination. Yet its self-determined containment limited its reach. It offered a politics based on injury. Some called it a politics of resentment or victimization. It clearly lacked the universalism many activist black women had been urging since at least the 1830s. US Representative Shirley Chisholm (D-NY) illustrated the difference in approach mere weeks after the July 1970 Declaration. Speaking in August 1970 on the floor of the U.S. House of Representatives against what she lambasted as the "legal expression of prejudice," the first black woman ever elected to the U.S. Congress called for the national legislature to act "to assure full equality of opportunity." She acknowledged that "laws will not eliminate prejudice from the hearts of human beings. But," she maintained, "that is no reason to allow prejudice to continue to be enshrined in our laws – to perpetuate injustice through inaction."[29] Referencing the 1776 Declaration, Chisholm argued for "the fullest expression of that equality of opportunity which our Founding Fathers professed," reiterating black activist women's push beyond race, religion, and ideology.

The outward thrust of activist black women such as Representative Chisholm and the NCBC's contrasting inward thrust nevertheless shared an unshakable core belief in the centrality of the 1776 Declaration to America's principled foundation. They reflected the persistent black vision that the 1776 Declaration has symbolized and substantiated the contradiction that white supremacy has imprinted on the United States. More than mere propaganda or anti-imperial brief, the pronouncement that "all men are created equal" has been to activist black men and women what Illinois Republican U.S. Senate candidate Abraham Lincoln in 1858 called "the great fundamental principle

---

[29] *Congressional Record*, 91st Cong., 2nd Sess., p. 28029 (10 August 1970).

upon which our free institutions rest."³⁰ The Declaration's principles, touted as America's pride, have been the touchstone of blacks' democratic aspirations. Their denial has resonated throughout the litany of blacks' grievances from slavery to segregation to persistent discrimination that has refused to acknowledge, let alone admit, blacks' equality.

President-elect Barack Obama in January 2009 repeatedly joined major elements of black Americans' conceptions and reconstructions of the US Declaration of Independence. Persisting with his campaign themes of change and hope, the man hailed as the first African American US president called for "a new declaration of independence." He echoed the universalism of activist black women's concepts with a recasting of phrasing from Abraham Lincoln's 1861 inaugural address in invoking such a declaration "not just in our nation, but in our own lives – from ideology and small thinking, prejudice and bigotry – an appeal not to our easy instincts but to our better angels." Pointing to the ongoing challenges facing Americans, as blacks throughout history had, Obama spoke to the theme of creating "a more perfect union." Without the historic biting edge of black activism, Obama appealed with some urgency for sweeping change akin to that of the American Revolution, which he called "an ongoing struggle 'in the minds and hearts of the people' to live up to our founding creed."³¹

With his characteristic cautiousness, Obama elided the facts that black and white Americans historically and persistently have disagreed on the meaning of the 1776 Declaration of Independence's place and principles in American life. Such disagreements have been reduced at times to the fact that the Declaration is not the Constitution; it is not the frame of government or a set of laws. If it has been accepted as a popular symbol of America, it has not been popularly accepted as determining the substance of America. Blacks have tended to see the Declaration as initiating a dynamic process directed toward an actual equality. Whites have tended to see the Declaration as imprinting a fresh standing fixed in its moment in time. In that sense, the Declaration has been for whites a concrete but distant symbol of past achievement, while for blacks the Declaration has been a fluid and pervasive symbol of ever-present aspirations.

13.8 THE TOUCHSTONE FOR MEASURING THE BLACK CONDITION

Blacks have consistently taken to heart the Declaration of Independence's rousing preamble, using it as the touchstone for measuring their condition and standing in the United States. Their core rhetoric has changed surprisingly little

---

[30] Abraham Lincoln, "Letter to Hon. J.N. Brown, Springfield, October 16, 1858," in *Collected Works of Abraham Lincoln*, ed. Roy P. Basler (New Brunswick: Rutgers University Press, 1953), 3: 327.
[31] Barack Obama, "Obama in Philadelphia," *The New York Times*, January 17, 2009.

over time. While adjusting for developments of the day, they have consistently used the document to call attention to the persisting gap between America's principles and practices regarding race and social justice. African Americans espousing "Black Lives Matter" demonstrated that call with the phrase and social movement that emerged with it in 2013 to protest systemic racial violence manifest in egregious examples of police killings of black men.

For advocates "Black Lives Matter" voiced a fundamental truth "self-evident" among the "unalienable Rights" proclaimed in the 1776 Declaration only to meet the backlash of "All Lives Matter" or "Blue Lives Matter." Blacks asserted their race specific statement as an accurate description of injustice, while opponents cast it as subverting universal rights. And there in large part has been the rub of blacks' embrace of the Declaration of Independence. Using the 1776 document to affirm black rights has generally produced condemnation for expressing a past-centered ideology of victimization that further stigmatizes and sets blacks apart rather than helping to eliminate discrimination or advance their exercise of rights. Using the 1776 document to affirm universal rights, however, has produced condemnation for abandoning blacks to an undistinguished status: either blacks are or are not like everyone else, "created equal."

14

The Declaration of Independence and Women

Leslie F. Goldstein

14.1 INTRODUCTION

The most well-known portion of the Declaration of Independence deploys the term "men" in an arguably ambiguous sense. The "self-evident truths" that the Document sets forth affirm that "all men are created equal" and possess God-given inalienable rights to "life, liberty, and the pursuit of happiness." "Governments are instituted among men," the Declaration continues, by virtue of the consent of the governed, "to secure these rights."

Did Thomas Jefferson use the term "men" in these sentences, and the term "mankind" in sentences immediately preceding and following these, with the sense of *humankind*, or was he, alternatively, intending to be understood as singling out male humans as the only rights-bearers? One suggestion that his intent was to allude to humankind can be inferred from his follow-up remark that when any form of government becomes destructive of these rights, it is the right of "the people" to alter or abolish it. And if he did mean to be speaking of humanity at large with these terms, what did he understand to be the place of women as natural rights-bearers, securers of rights, and as rights-holders *within* civil society, after the establishment of a government?

One way of addressing these queries would be to look at Jefferson's intellectual forebears, the philosophers whose systematic political theories undergirded these statements in the Declaration. Another is to examine Jefferson's writings or speeches that specifically address the topic of women. A third will be to look at the speeches or writings on the subject of women's rights from other leading American thinkers in the era of the Declaration in order to construct a picture of how the wording of the Declaration as it applies to women was understood in its time.

Even apart from the intent of its author, Jefferson, and even apart from the understanding of it by those who signed it and their peers, the text of the Declaration itself carried weight beyond its immediate day. The beginning of the violent revolution that the Declaration was written to justify is called "the shot heard round the world." The ideas it espoused reverberated down through the ages to inspire, among other things, a momentous women's movement of the nineteenth century, one that culminated in the Nineteenth Amendment to the US Constitution.

This first political movement for women's rights explicitly took its inspiration from the Declaration of Independence. The first Women's Rights Convention in Seneca Falls, New York, in 1848, emphasized this fact by issuing a Declaration of Sentiments that was a verbatim copy of the words of the Declaration of Independence with alterations made to specify that women too had these fundamental rights. The leaders at that convention left no doubt that they took their inspiration from the thinking espoused in the 1776 Declaration. To them, American society and law as of 1848 exposed the Declaration as having issued, in effect, an unfulfilled promissory note to the female half of the population.

In the second half of the twentieth century, however, a new women's movement burst forth in the USA, one that looked for a revolution in women's rights that went beyond the concepts of the Declaration of Independence. The goals of this second movement highlight limitations in the horizons of the thinkers who produced the 1776 document. Optimizing the potential human development of all members of society may indeed call forth more from government than the securing of equal legal rights to life, liberty, and the pursuit of happiness.

14.2 THOMAS HOBBES (1588–1679) AND JOHN LOCKE (1632–1704)

Although the phrase, "pursuit of happiness," is not to be found in John Locke's *Second Treatise of Government* (1689), there can be no reasonable denying that its basic premises undergirded the Declaration of Independence. This essay asserted that all men are by nature free and entitled to inalienable natural rights to life, liberty, and any property acquired by their own labor. Moreover, because of insecurities in the state of nature, men consent to form societies under government for the protection of these rights, and have an inalienable right to alter or abolish any government that becomes tyrannical, threatening those rights. Its resemblance to the Declaration is plain.

In contrast to Jefferson, however, both of his primary philosophic progenitors, Thomas Hobbes (1588–1679) and John Locke (1632–1704), did ponder the issue of women. Locke was immediately preceded in England by Hobbes, a philosopher widely denounced in his own day as a blaspheming atheist and defamer of human nature. During Locke's lifetime, books by Hobbes were condemned to book-burning by governmental authorities. So Locke had good reason to distinguish his thinking from that of Hobbes. Still the two agreed on certain fundamentals. Humans are born free and equal in their rights to freedom to pursue self-preservation. They also agreed that people contract to form a society with a governing authority precisely because if everyone has equal power and an equal right to self-preservation, the protection of that right outside of society, in the state of nature, is "very unsafe, very unsecure."[1] There are some differences. In contrast to Locke, Hobbes does not describe a natural right only to property mixed with one's own labor; rather, all have a right to take whatever they can get because nature implants in all people an instinct to pursue self-preservation.[2] Also, Hobbes does not endorse a right of revolution. And importantly for this essay, in setting forth the fundamentals about humans in the state of nature, Hobbes went further than Locke in describing the natural equality of men and women.

For Hobbes, because the fundamental and irresistible instinct implanted by nature in all people is the urge toward self-preservation, all humans are in the most important respect by nature equal: Each one has the ability to kill each other person. Natural differences of strength or cleverness are insignificant. Anyone can kill anyone else while the other is asleep. Prior to the establishment of governments, with their police and armies, all people are by nature free and equal. "Whereas some have attributed the dominion to the man only, as being the more excellent sex; they misreckon in it. For there is not always that difference of strength, or prudence between the man and the woman, as that the right can be determined without war."[3] Hobbes acknowledges that under most governments, civil law gives preference to men, but, he explains candidly, this is "because for the most part commonwealths have been erected by fathers, not mothers of families." "In the condition of mere nature," Hobbes posits, by contrast, that the parents either dispose of dominion over the children by contract (here in agreement with Locke), or else make no arrangement for child custody. In the latter situation, Hobbes, more naturalistic than Locke, suggests that the father is likely unaware that he has fathered any child, so the woman would remain in charge of the child when it is born. If she chooses to nourish and raise the child, then the child owes her obedience out of gratitude for life itself. If she abandons the child's care to someone else, then that person would be owed the child's obedience.[4] In sum, for Hobbes, men have no more natural right to political or domestic authority than women do. He points to the fact of queenships to buttress this assertion.[5]

---

[1] John Locke, Second Treatise of Government, in *Political Writings of John Locke*, ed. David Wootton (London: Mentor, 1993), chapter IX, para. 128. Hobbes notoriously described this condition as the war of all against all. Thomas Hobbes, *Leviathan*, ed. C.B. MacPherson (New York: Pelican Books, 1977), chapter 13.
[2] Hobbes, *Leviathan*, chapter 11, first two paras.; chapter 13; chapter 14, first four paras.
[3] Hobbes, *Leviathan*, chapter 20, fourth para.
[4] Hobbes, *Leviathan*, chapter 20, fifth para.
[5] Hobbes, *Leviathan*, chapter 20, sixth para.

Like Hobbes, and in contrast to Jefferson, Locke, too, explicitly explored the woman question. Locke broke with his fellow Whig contract theorists, Algernon Sidney and James Tyrell, in refraining from announcing that a man's consent to be governed politically automatically included his wife's consent.[6] Locke began with women as free and equal in the state of nature, and specifically limited the character of women's consent to be part of the conjugal union.[7] Men and women, he maintained, freely consent (i.e., contract) with each other for the mutual use of each other's body for purposes related to procreation and the rearing of children. They are free to limit the terms of their contract both as to its duration and nature, provided that the purpose of the contract implicitly necessitates that it endure long enough and be encompassing enough to assure that their offspring be "nourished and maintained by them, till [the offspring] are able to provide for themselves."[8] Locke took pains to emphasize that, in a conjugal unit, the husband's power "leaves the wife in the full and free possession of what by the Contract is her peculiar right, and gives the Husband no more power over her life than she has over his." He is by no means her "absolute monarch"; their contract may allow her to keep separate property, and also the right to leave when she wishes after the children's natural right to sustenance has been provided for, and even the right to custody of children.[9] Locke's depiction broke radically with the regnant Christian view of marriage, but the reticent Locke did not spell out publicly his full views on women.

Locke remained so cautious about the political persecution dominant in his lifetime that he chose to live in exile, even in hiding (in Holland), during England's time of political turbulence (1683–1689), and kept anonymous his publication of his major religious or political publications during his entire lifetime.[10] When it came to describing intramarital authority, Locke (who never married) fell back on conventional views: "[When spouses differ in their understanding related to their common project of rearing the children,] it [is] necessary that the ... rule should be placed somewhere; it naturally falls to the man's share as the abler and stronger."[11] While this was Locke's public posture, he indicated in private letters much more gender-egalitarian views: Girls' education should essentially follow the same pattern as that of boys.[12] Moreover, he described a woman with whom he was close, Damaris Cudworth Masham, as

---

[6] Melissa Butler, "Early Liberal Roots of Feminism," *American Political Science Review* 72 (1978): 135–150, 141–142.
[7] Butler, "Early Liberal Roots," 142, 144–145.
[8] Butler, "Early Liberal Roots," 144; Locke, *Second Treatise*, chapter VII, para. 78.
[9] Butler, "Early Liberal Roots," 145; Locke, *Second Treatise*, chapter VII, para. 82.
[10] Roger Cox, "Introduction," in *John Locke's Second Treatise of Government* (Wheeling: Harlan Davidson, 1982), viii–xiv.
[11] Locke, *Second Treatise*, chapter VII, para. 82; Butler, "Early Liberal Roots," 145.
[12] Butler, "Early Liberal Roots," 148. As an allowance for beauty, Locke permitted some differences in early training for "protecting the girls' complexions," 148.

"of such an original mind that you will not find many men to whom she is not superior in ... knowledge [of philosophy and theology] and ability to profit by it." He described her "judgment," "clearness of thought," and "capacity for searching through and solving the difficulties of questions" as *beyond* the range not only of most women but also beyond that of "most learned men."[13]

To sum up this section, the two main philosophic progenitors of the Declaration's pronouncements of equality in natural rights and of the idea that people leave their natural condition by consent to be societally governed in order to protect their natural rights, both included women in the natural condition of equal freedom. Hobbes was the more blunt about this sex equality than the circumspect Locke, and indeed was the first eminent philosopher to declare that women are by nature equal to men in their rights.[14] The seeds of feminism planted by these philosophers lay somewhat dormant in the Declaration of Independence, but were available to be nurtured by thoughtful readers of the document.

14.3 THOMAS JEFFERSON ON WOMEN

Whatever his awareness of the thoughts about, or implications of the discussions of, the state of nature and purposes of government in Hobbes and Locke for the status of women, Jefferson himself showed no interest in elevating their social or political status in the new republic. Jefferson appears to have believed that the idea of the rights of man applied specifically to men and not women.

When his friend Samuel Kercheval broached him by letter the question of whether women should be given the vote, Jefferson's reply, more than forty years after he had asserted the unalienable rights of man in the Declaration, was dismissive. Allowing women to mix with men in political gatherings, which would surely happen if they had the vote, would, he wrote, result in a "depravation of morals and ambiguity of issue."[15] In other words, Jefferson imagined that if women were not confined to home, they could not be trusted to avoid sexual dalliance, to the point that the "who's your daddy?" question would actually present a widespread societal problem. He wrote this at the end

---

[13] Butler, "Early Liberal Roots," 148–149.
[14] To be sure, Plato in describing an imagined perfectly just society argued that women and men deserved the same education and governing opportunities, but he ironically grounded his argument in the claim that men are superior to women in every known activity, even cooking and clothing design, so there is no such thing as properly "women's work." *Republic*, Book V, and particularly paras. 455-c-e. After Plato and before Hobbes, there were erudite women of the Renaissance and seventeenth century who defended the ideas of equal educational and professional opportunities for individual women; none of these writers attained prominence as philosophers. Miriam Schneir, "Introduction," in *Feminism: The Essential Historical Writings* (New York: Vintage Books, 1972), xii.
[15] Thomas Jefferson, Letter to Samuel Kercheval, September 5, 1816, https://founders.archives.gov/documents/Jefferson/03-10-02-0255.

of 1816, even though (unmarried) women in the state of New Jersey who met wealth and residency requirements had implicitly been allowed to vote, as of July 2, 1776 (and thereafter did vote). New Jersey made the permission explicit in 1790, only to rescind the provision in 1807.[16] Even outside of the rough-and-tumble electoral process, the idea of appointing a woman to public office also bothered Jefferson. He responded curtly when his friend Albert Gallatin suggested it in 1807: "The appointment of a woman to office is an innovation for which the public is not prepared, nor I."[17]

14.4 JEFFERSON'S PEERS: THE UNDERSTANDING OF HIS ATTENTIVE AUDIENCE

Jefferson described the Declaration as "an expression of the American mind" of "the common sense of the subject."[18] A friend of Jefferson's, Abigail Adams wrote to her husband John Adams on March 31, 1776, while both men were at the Continental Congress, and a couple of months before Jefferson began drafting the document in June, to express her own thoughts on the checking of tyrannical power within the household. "[I]n the new code of laws ... remember the ladies ... Do not put such unlimited power into the hands of husbands. Remember, all men would be tyrants if they could. [And then, apparently jokingly, she added] ... [I]f ... attention is not paid to the ladies, we are determined to foment a rebellion and *will not hold ourselves bound by any laws in which we have no voice or representation.*"[19] This emphasized passage points to one of the primary complaints against King George III that Jefferson listed in the Declaration: The King's insistence that people "relinquish the right of representation in the Legislature, a right inestimable to them and formidable to tyrants only." Another complaint listed in the Declaration – that the king "impos[ed] taxes on us without our consent" – offered a variant on this same core concern of the Declaration: Neither taxes nor other binding legislation should be imposed without representation (a mode of garnering "consent of the governed").

---

[16] Judith Apter Klinghoffer and Lois Elkis, "'The Petticoat Electors': Women's Suffrage in New Jersey, 1776–1807," *Journal of the Early Republic* 12 (1992): 159–193, correcting prior, standard historical accounts that attributed the permission to strong Quaker ideology. There were enough propertied widows and spinsters to make a political difference. One pamphleteer estimated the number to be 10,000 statewide in 1797. This fact apparently motivated the partisan-minded legislators both to grant the suffrage in 1776 and to take it away in 1807. Klinghoffer and Elkis, "The Petticoat Electors," 162–164, 166 n. 16, 167–168, 172, 177 n. 47, and on the 1807 deprivation 186–193.

[17] Thomas Jefferson, Letter to Albert Gallatin, January 13, 1807, https://Founders.archives.gov/documents/Jefferson/99-01-02-4862.

[18] Matthew Spalding, "Foreword," in *The Declaration of Independence [and] The Constitution of the United States* (Washington, DC: Heritage Foundation, 2010), 2.

[19] Schneir, "Abigail Adams, Familiar Letters of John Adams and His Wife Abigail, during the Revolution," in Feminism, 3 (emphasis added).

While Abigail's line about fomenting a rebellion was almost certainly meant as a playful exaggeration, her underlying purpose in urging her husband to use the new lawmaking power to protect women from abuse by their husbands was in earnest. Moreover, she expressed that plea within the Lockean formula of "the common sense of the subject" from the Declaration: When a tyrant abuses power, the need to check it may call forth violent rebellion.

John Adams, however, could not take any of it seriously. He replied on April 14, "I cannot but laugh."[20]

Abigail then replied on May 7, just a month before a committee was appointed to draft the Declaration, "I cannot say … that you are very generous to the ladies. For whilst you are proclaiming peace and good-will to men, emancipating all nations, you insist on retaining absolute power over wives. But you must remember that arbitrary power is … very liable to be broken."[21]

Just three weeks after Abigail's response, John seriously engaged with her idea in a May 26 letter to James Sullivan, a man who had argued for eliminating all property qualifications for voting, on the ground that such qualifications clashed with the idea of government by consent of the governed:[22]

It is certain, in theory, that the only moral foundation of government is, the consent of the people. But to what extent shall we carry this principle. … Whence arises the right of men to govern women, without their consent? Whence the Right of the old to bind the Young, without theirs …. [W]hy exclude Women [from the suffrage]? You will Say, because their Delicacy renders them unfit for Practice and Experience, in the great Business of Life, and the hardy Enterprizes of War, as well as the arduous Cares of State. Besides, their attention is So much engaged with the necessary Nurture of their Children, that Nature has made them fittest for domestic Cares. And Children have not Judgment or Will of their own. True. But will not these Reasons apply to others? Is it not equally true, that Men in general in every Society, who are wholly destitute of Property, are also too little acquainted with public Affairs to form a Right Judgment, and too dependent upon other Men to have a Will of their own? Such is the Frailty of the human Heart, that very few Men, who have no Property, have any Judgment of their own. They talk and vote as they are directed by Some Man of Property, who has attached their Minds to his Interest …

The Same Reasoning, which will induce you to admit all Men, who have no Property, to vote, with those who have, for those Laws[] which affect the Person[,] will prove that you ought to admit Women and Children: for generally Speaking, Women and Children, have as good Judgment, and as independent Minds as those Men who are wholly destitute of Property: these last being to all Intents and Purposes as much dependent upon others, who will please to feed, clothe, and employ them, as Women are upon their Husbands, or Children on their Parents.

---

[20] Schneir, "Abigail Adams," 4.
[21] Schneir, "Abigail Adams," 4.
[22] Anne M. Boylan, *Women's Rights in the United States: A History in Documents* (New York: Oxford University Press, 2016), 49. Letter of May 26, 1776, *The Adams Papers: Adams Family Correspondence*, 4: 208–213, https://tinyurl.com/5fef4zvx.

> ... [I]t is dangerous to open so fruitful a source of controversy and altercation as would be opened by attempting to alter the qualifications of voters ... New claims will arise; women will demand a vote; lads from twelve to twenty-one will think their rights not enough ... It tends to confound and destroy all distinctions ...

For John Adams, then, in contrast to Abigail, it made sense that within civil society, persons dependent on others for their sustenance could be legitimately denied the vote, since they were, for all practical purposes under the power of someone else and did not really have a free choice. This was an era in which people had not yet innovated to provide secret ballots for voting. Moreover, in assessing women's capacity to participate in political decision-making, despite having a distinguished and brilliant wife, Adams' views on women in general were not far different from those of Jefferson. As Jefferson dismissed the idea of appointing women to political office, Adams dismissed women's capacity to deal with the coarseness of political life due to their "delicacy," and to the fact that their preoccupation with household maintenance rendered them too little acquainted with questions of public policy.

As late as 1782, after the revolutionary war was successfully concluded, Abigail, for her part, had not given up her sense of justified grievance. She wrote the following to her husband, at the time Vice President of the US, complaining not only of the lack of voting power and of the lack of property rights and other rights for married women, but also of the lack of a right to hold public office:[23]

> Excluded from honours and from offices, we cannot attach ourselves to the State of Government from having held a place of eminence. Even in the freest countries our property is subject to the control and disposal of our partners, to whom the laws have given sovereign authority. Deprived of a voice in Legislation, obliged to submit to those Laws which are imposed on us, is it not sufficient to make us indifferent to the public welfare? [Yet we nonetheless exhibit patriotic virtue to a heroic degree ...]

In the US, at least, Abigail Adams' was a lone voice, and a privately expressed one, at that. No groundswell of a demand for women's rights to "government by consent of the governed" arose. New Jersey's granting woman suffrage to those women residents who had a certain minimum amount of property as early as 1776 does appear to have been somewhat influenced by the "no taxation without representation" principle espoused in the Declaration of Independence, but the drafters of New Jersey's constitution tempered that principle by extending the vote only to householders of a certain wealth, rather than to every taxpayer.[24]

---

[23] Linda Kerber, *Toward an Intellectual History of American Women* (Chapel Hill: University of North Carolina Press, 1997) 263, excerpting Letter of Abigail to John Adams of June 17, 1782, *Adams Papers*, Vol. 4, ed. L. H. Butterfield (Cambridge: Belknap Press, 1973), 328.

[24] Klinghoffer and Elkis, "Petticoat Electors."

Instead, the prominent advocates in the 1780s and 1790s for uplifting women focused not on their natural rights to form a government to secure their rights, and to throw it off, if it becomes tyrannical, but rather on the more basic need of an education that would allow women's rational faculty to flourish. Authors like Mary Wollstonecraft in England, who penned *A Vindication of the Rights of Woman* in 1792, and Judith Sargent Murray, who published "On the Equality of the Sexes" in 1790 did not demand suffrage or other political rights.[25]

14.5 DECLARATION OF SENTIMENTS OF THE FIRST WOMEN'S RIGHTS CONVENTION (1848)

Some lone public feminist voices, such as that of (the somewhat scandalous) Fanny Wright and the (quite prim and proper) Sarah Grimké attracted attention in the US in the 1820s and 1830s; neither of these relied for her arguments on the Declaration or its premises. Nor did either instigate an effective movement on behalf of women.

Not until the first Women's Rights Convention of July 19–20, 1848, in Seneca Falls, widely viewed as the launching pad of the nineteenth-century women's rights movement, did the Declaration come into the spotlight as an inspiration of the quest for women's rights. This convention, attended by 300 people, was organized by Elizabeth Cady Stanton and Lucretia Coffin Mott, who were provoked to do so in part by the exclusion of women from the World Anti-slavery Convention of 1840. For women to speak in public to mixed-sex gatherings was widely viewed as unseemly and unchaste in the early-nineteenth century. A number of women abolitionists in the US broke with this custom. Their experiences provoked them to reflect on the wider range of subjugations experienced by women, subjugations that were all itemized as grievances by the women's rights convention: their legal subordination to their husband's will once they married; the legal incapacity of a married woman to earn money or own property or make a contract or bring a lawsuit or to gain custody of her children if there were a divorce or separation; the official exclusion of women

---

[25] Despite her title suggesting a wide-ranging focus on "the rights of woman," Wollstonecraft's book is almost entirely on women's need for, and right to, an equal education, both to make them better wives and mothers and to enable them to engage in useful occupations if they choose not to marry. Her entire discussion of political rights is the following:

I may excite laughter, by dropping a hint, which I mean to pursue, some future time, for I really think that women ought to have representatives, instead of being arbitrarily governed without having any direct share allowed them in the deliberations of government. But as the whole system of representation is now, in this country [England], only a convenient handle for despotism, they need not complain, for they are as well represented as a numerous class of hard working mechanics, who pay for the support of royalty when they can scarcely stop their children's mouth with bread. (Mary Wollstonecraft, *A Vindication of the Rights of Woman*, ed. Carol Poston (New York: W. W. Norton, 1975), 147)

from higher education and from the learned professions, from the right to vote, and from the right to hold public office.

The Convention endorsed and published the Declaration of Sentiments, drafted by Mott and Stanton, who read it to the gathering, paragraph by paragraph, and some amendments to it were adopted on the first day, when it was an all-women meeting. On the second day, when men joined the meeting, the document was again read and discussed and unanimously adopted. A separate list of Convention resolutions was also adopted by a large majority. The final version of the Declaration was signed by sixty-eight women and thirty-two men and was published both in 1848 and again in 1870.

Following is a line-by-line comparison of the two foundational paragraphs of the Declaration of Sentiments with those of the Declaration of Independence. The <u>Declaration of Sentiments</u> appears in plain type with its substitute language underlined and the *Declaration of Independence* phrasing that the women omitted inserted in italics.

When in the course of human events, it becomes necessary for one <u>portion of the family of man</u> [*people to dissolve the political bands which have connected them with another and*] to assume among the [*powers*] <u>people</u> of the earth <u>a position different from that which they have hitherto occupied, but one</u> [*the separate and equal station*] to which the laws of nature and of nature's God entitle them, a decent respect to the opinions of mankind requires that they should declare the causes that impel them to such a course.

We hold these truths to be self-evident, that all men <u>and women</u> are created equal, that they are endowed by their Creator with certain <u>inalienable</u> [*unalienable*] rights, that among these are life, liberty and the pursuit of happiness; that to secure these rights governments are instituted [*among men*], deriving their just powers from the consent of the governed. [*That*] Whenever any form of government becomes destructive of these ends, it is the right of <u>those who suffer from it to refuse allegiance to it, and to insist upon the institution of a</u> [*the people to alter or abolish it and to institute*] new government, laying its foundation on such principles and organizing its powers in such form as to them shall seem most likely to effect their safety and happiness. Prudence indeed will dictate that governments long established should not be changed for light and transient causes; accordingly, all experience hath shown that mankind are more disposed to suffer, while evils are sufferable, than to right themselves by abolishing the forms to which they are accustomed. But when a long train of abuses and usurpations, pursuing invariably the same object, evinces a design to reduce them under absolute despotism, [*it is their right*], it is their duty to throw off such government and to provide new guards for their future security. Such has been the patient sufferance of [*these colonies*] <u>the women under this government, and such is now the necessity which constrains them to demand the equal station to which they are entitled</u> [*and such is now the necessity which constrains them to alter their former systems of government.*]

At this point, each declaration began a list of grievances under the current governing system. Plainly the women and men of the Seneca Fall meeting were embarking on what they understood to be a nonviolent revolution; they eschewed all talk of "abolish[ing] government." Nonetheless, their obvious verbatim copying of large portions of the Declaration of Independence made clear the point that this nation was not living up to the implied promise that the Declaration made to the female half of the population. The seeds planted by Hobbesian and Lockean principles in the 1776 Declaration had germinated and now were, if not in full bloom, certainly showing sturdy stalks.

Even prior to the Seneca Falls Convention, arguments over the legal denial of married women's property rights had prompted legislative debates invoking the assertions of the Declaration of Independence to promote women's suffrage. In the New York state legislature in 1836, Thomas Herttell first proposed that married women be granted the same property rights as single women. Arguments in the legislature suggested that letting husbands control their wives' property violated the natural rights of these wives, and then the disfranchising of all women allowed men to perpetuate the injustice. In 1846, six New York women petitioned for women's property rights and suffrage to a state constitutional convention on the grounds that their disfranchisement violated "principles of the Declaration of Independence."[26]

New York in April 1848, three months prior to the Seneca Falls Convention, did reform its marital property laws, but only to allow married women to retain real and personal property that they might bring to a marriage and any gifts or inheritance they might receive once married, not the right to earn money or make contracts while married. New York's earlier legislative and state convention discussions of more comprehensive reform, Stanton later wrote in her *History of Women Suffrage*, and New York's failure to adopt it, "at last culminated in a women's rights convention."[27]

By 1900, all the states allowed married women to earn and own property.[28] Admission to colleges and universities had slowly begun before 1848 – Oberlin Collegiate Institute had begun as a coeducational school for training missionaries in 1833. Admission to learned professions came later in the nineteenth century. Despite its obvious connection to the foundational sentences of the Declaration, suffrage was the most difficult. After the Nineteenth Amendment (of 1920) was finally ratified, a veteran of the seventy-two-year-long campaign for suffrage, Carrie Chapman Catt, summed up the efforts that had gone into the suffrage struggle as follows:[29]

To get the word "male" in effect out of the Constitution cost the women of the country fifty-two years of pauseless campaign ... During that time they were forced to conduct 56 campaigns of referenda to male voters; 480 campaigns to get state legislatures to

---

[26] Ann Gordon, ed., *The Selected Papers of Elizabeth Cady Stanton and Susan B. Anthony* (New Brunswick: Rutgers University Press, 1997), 1: 68; Boylan, *Women's Rights*, 86–87.
[27] Boylan, *Women's Rights*, 86–87.
[28] Jone Johnson Lewis. "A Short History of Women's Property Rights in the United States," ThoughtCo, August 26, 2020, thoughtco.com/property-rights-of-women-3529578.
[29] Leslie F. Goldstein, *The Constitutional Rights of Women*, 2nd ed. (Madison: University of Wisconsin Press, 1988), 84. On counting the campaign as fifty-two years instead of seventy-two years, see the explanation in Ann Gordon, ed., *Selected Papers*, 6: 281.

submit suffrage amendments to voters; 47 campaigns to get state constitutional conventions to write woman suffrage into state constitutions; 277 campaigns to get state party conventions to include woman suffrage planks; 30 campaigns to get presidential party conventions to adopt woman suffrage planks in party platforms, and 19 campaigns with 19 successive Congresses.

Two of the most prominent leaders and chroniclers of that struggle, Elizabeth Cady Stanton and Susan B. Anthony, throughout that time period turned to the Declaration of Independence to buttress women's claim on suffrage.[30] In an address on February 14, 1854, Stanton said the following to a women's rights convention, the group of which then adopted it and had it printed and mailed to every member of the New York state legislature, "[Y]ou who have declared that all men are created equal – that governments derive their just powers from the consent of the governed, would willingly build up an aristocracy that places ... sons above the mothers that bore them."[31] In the 1850s, women's rights advocates often linked their own plight to that of African American slaves, in that both groups were denied that to which the Declaration should have entitled them.[32] On the eve of the Civil War, May 8, 1860, Stanton spoke to an audience of 1,500 members of the American Anti-Slavery Society, condemning "our falsehood and hypocrisy, in the face of those grand and glorious declarations of freedom and equality which, when first proclaimed at the mouth of the cannon, raised us head and shoulders above the nations of the earth." After itemizing horrors of the slavery system, she claimed that women are more easily able to feel for the sufferings of slaves because, "She early learns the misfortune of being born ... to the crown of thorns ... For while the man is born to do whatever he can, for the woman and the Negro there is no such privilege."[33] By May of 1864, Stanton was defending the right to suffrage for both blacks and women with insistence that reconstruction must recognize "the immortal declaration, 'All men are created equal.'"[34] Throughout the 1870s, Stanton continued to invoke the Declaration in support of the suffrage cause.[35]

Similarly, with the Civil War concluded, the Women's Equal Rights Convention in New York city on December 7, 1866, prefaced their demand for suffrage for both women and blacks with the following: "whereas 'governments derive their just powers from the consent of the governed,' and 'taxation without representation is tyranny,' therefore ..."[36]

---

[30] They were not the only ones to do so; their references are cited here because of their prominence as leaders and because a comprehensive list of such citations by suffragists would require a book-length treatise.
[31] Ann Gordon, ed., *Selected Papers*, 1: 242.
[32] Ann Gordon, ed., *Selected Papers*, 1: 299–300.
[33] Ann Gordon, ed., *Selected Papers*, 1: 414.
[34] Ann Gordon, ed., *Selected Papers*, 1: 520.
[35] Ann Gordon, ed., *Selected Papers*, 1: 81 (May 1874); 3: 353 (January 1878); 3: 450 (May, 1879).
[36] Ann Gordon, ed., *Selected Papers*, 2: 3.

After the postbellum amendments had granted suffrage to blacks but not to women, suffragists continued to invoke the Declaration in promoting their cause. Anthony on October 19, 1871, addressed the territorial legislature of what was to become the state of Washington as follows:[37]

The theory of our government is embodied in the Declaration of Independence which declares that "all men are created equal; that they are endowed by their Creator with certain inalienable rights"; "that to secure these rights, governments were instituted among men, deriving their just powers from the consent of the governed." And it further declares that: "Whenever any form of government becomes destructive of these ends, it is the right of the people to alter or abolish it, and institute a new government, laying its foundation on such principles as shall secure their safety and happiness." How can this be done peaceably without giving them the right to vote?

Similarly, Anthony invoked "the principles of the Declaration of Independence" in a co-authored letter on behalf of the National Women Suffrage Association, urging the Liberal Republican Party to include women's suffrage in its 1872 platform.[38] Again, on two occasions, in 1873 and at her 1874 trial for the "crime" of voting, Anthony repeated the passages from the Declaration of Independence quoted above at note 37 as a way of asserting the propriety and moral necessity of women's suffrage. Anthony in a speech of 1887 to several hundred Kansas listeners complained, "We've waited 111 years since the Declaration of Independence was issued; we have gathered every Fourth of July and heard our statesmen and states*women* make speeches based on the Declaration of Independence as expressive of a grand and glorious truth ..."[39] She went on to point out the obvious connection between this truth and the rightfulness of granting votes to women. (Kansas granted the full vote to women in 1912.) Anthony continued through the turn of the twentieth century to advocate the women's suffrage cause and to link that cause to "the practical application of the immutable principles of the Declaration of Independence."[40]

By the 1920s, the core goals of the Declaration of Independence-inspired women's movement of the nineteenth century had been achieved via public and private reforms. To be sure, many if not most employers still discriminated on the basis of sex, as did many universities, and vestiges of discrimination lingered in a plenitude of statutes,[41] but the fundamental goals of opening up opportunities and attaining legal and political rights for women had been accomplished.

---

[37] Ann Gordon, ed., *Selected Papers*, 2: 456–457.
[38] Ann Gordon, ed., *Selected Papers*, 2: 491, published in the *Cincinnati Daily Gazette*, May 3, 1872.
[39] Ann Gordon, ed., *Selected Papers*, 5: 42–46, emphasis in original.
[40] Ann Gordon, ed., *Selected Papers*, 6: 282–283, speech of April 27, 1899. Stanton died in 1902; Anthony in 1906.
[41] Leo Kanowitz, *Women and the Law: The Unfinished Revolution* (Albuquerque: University of New Mexico Press, 1969).

14.6 THE 1960S AND BEYOND

The 1960s might be described as a decade of post-Declaration of Independence consciousness. The understanding of Locke and of the Declaration was that governments were formed to protect individual rights of life, liberty, and property from violent malefactors. The notion that one person's property could be somehow nonviolently wielded to deprive others of their liberty was beyond the horizons of conceptual framework of the Declaration of Independence.[42] The civil rights movement of the 1960s did not limit itself to attacking the use of public and private force in the South to deprive black Americans of their voting rights – a goal fully within the thinking of the Declaration's ideal of establishing government by consent of the governed. The Civil Rights Act of 1964 also targeted: (1) privately owned property, such as restaurants, hotels, gasoline stations, and so forth, which property was being deployed to impose dignitary harms on people of color by separating them off from white society; (2) private businesses across the land that deprived people of color of equal economic opportunity by refusing to hire or promote them; and (3) public schools that were refusing to desegregate under court orders, thereby continuing to impose dignitary harm on black children, hampering their psychological development in ways likely to deprive them of equal educational opportunity.

In the process of debating this bill, Southern Congressmen attempted to ridicule it by proposing that discrimination against women by employers also be banned. This tactic wildly backfired. Women members of Congress and their allies quickly supported the proposal, and it passed easily, although Congress did not set up enforcement machinery for this part of the bill until pushed to do so by a women's movement some years later.

Just as involvement in the anti-slavery movement in the mid 1800s pushed some women to begin to advocate their own rights, so involvement in the civil rights movement of the 1960s prompted some women to think about an expansion of their own rights. The federal prohibition on sex-based job discrimination came about shortly prior to the beginnings of an organized women's movement, as just described. This new women's movement, kicked off in October of 1966 with the formation of the National Organization for Women. The goals of this organization and of the accompanying women's rights movement of the nineteen sixties and seventies had two dimensions. On the one hand, both formally organized associations and informal groups of women did promote, and nearly succeeded in attaining the Equal Rights Amendment to the Constitution, which would have forbidden all remaining sex discrimination by laws – that is to say, by government – thereby reproducing in the legal system

---

[42] Of course, Jefferson knew about slave "property," but he also knew that such "property" status could be imposed on humans only by the force of the whip and guns, and law backed by guns. Enslavement is precisely what people attempt to stave off by forming governments for themselves.

the equality of natural rights acknowledged in the Declaration of Independence and in the Declaration of Sentiments. But the late twentieth-century women's movement, like the Civil Rights Act of 1964, also looked beyond formal legal equality to other sources of group subjugation. In the instance of the women's movement, both educational pressures (including not only by schools but also by depictions in media such as radio, TV, film, magazines, etc.) and economic pressures, on boys and girls that pushed each into fixed roles within the family structure came to be seen as stunting many people's full flourishing.

Changes in the family structure itself were in no way foreseen in the Declaration of Independence.[43] They were, however, in a sense presaged in the first women's movement: The Declaration of Sentiments had railed against men's (legally imposed) monopolizing child custody after a marital separation and against the double standard of sexual morality that required chastity of wives but not of husbands. And one might argue that the goal of opening up careers to married women posed at least a suggestion of upsetting the traditional, and legally sanctioned, role of woman as child-rearer and man as economic provider.[44] So one can conclude that the first women's movement did understand to some degree that the human equality proclaimed by the Declaration of Independence did need to be moved into family life itself; the second women's movement, that of the late twentieth century, can be said to have radicalized this awareness, aiming much more deeply to rearrange the fundamental structure of family life. This rearrangement was not something contemplated (except in horror) by Jefferson, author of the Declaration. It can, however, be said to have been contemplated in a way by Thomas Hobbes, the first to announce that all people by nature equally have the right to life, liberty, and the quest for comfortable self-preservation. Hobbes, after all, is the one who pointed out that the vast majority of governments were formed by men, not women, and that this is the reason that civil laws around marriage had for eons structured it in a way that favors males.

14.7 CONCLUSION

The Declaration of Independence, penned by Thomas Jefferson, sets forth the ideas that all people are by nature free and have an equal right to life, liberty, and the pursuit of happiness. These ideas produce the principle that

---

[43] Thus, it is not surprising that a comprehensive anthology of writings from the late twentieth-century women's movement, over a wide array of dozens of cultural, sociological, economic, political, and psychological topics does not contain a single mention of, or allusion to, the Declaration. Vivian Gornick and Barbara Moran, eds., *Woman in Sexist Society: Studies in Power and Powerlessness* (New York: Basic Books, 1971).

[44] Obviously, these roles were less strictly separated in self-sufficient farming families where women were economically productive in roles of raising and canning fruits and vegetables, baking bread, and preserving meats, but still, legally, the husband was required to be the provider and the wife expected to care for the household.

government must be by consent of the governed. This essay traces the sources of these ideas back to the philosophers Hobbes and Locke, and explains the ways that both of these philosophers in fact endorsed women's equality to a far greater degree than Jefferson ever did. Even the examination of other prominent voices in Jefferson's era who may have accepted that the Declaration's principles do apply to women found only that of Abigail Adams, wife of John Adams.

The nineteenth-century women's movement, however, did not only take inspiration from the Declaration, but also made its rhetoric a central part of its decades-long campaign for women's equal legal and political rights. After documenting this influence, this essay has explicated the ways that the late twentieth-century women's movement went beyond the principles of the Declaration: It exposed the multiple ways that people's equal flourishing can be stunted not just by laws and government coercion but also by economic pressures, educational pressures, and cultural pressure.

15

Aspirational Reliance on the Declaration of Independence

Labor and Woman's Suffrage

Alexander Tsesis

The Declaration of Independence remains a statement of core constitutional commitments, despite the passage of two and a half centuries since its adoption by the Second Continental Congress. Unlike other nascent statements of sovereignty, such as the Articles of Confederation, obscurity has not befallen it. The manifesto continues to influence politicians, popular constitutionalists, and ordinary people to a degree that transcends its ceremonial role at Independence Day celebrations. Its guarantees of liberty, equality, general welfare, and representative governance commit the nation to the equal treatment of each person's inalienable rights, even as its practices during the late eighteenth and early nineteenth centuries remained deeply entrenched in chauvinist and classist politics.

The document's aspirational statement has influenced popular rhetoric much more than it has judicial doctrines. The Declaration provided a variety of groups, including labor advocates and first wave feminists, with an effective aspirational and rhetorical device. For many who waged heated verbal attacks against contemporary injustices, the document was a vibrant testament. Among workers' movements, the liberty portion of the document held greatest sway, while among suffragettes most pressing was its statements of equal representation.

15.1 THE ASPIRATIONAL DECLARATION

The Declaration of Independence's opening statements embraced a vision of sovereignty that included respect for unalienable rights. Through repeated readings attended by townsmen throughout the early republic, beginning at Philadelphia on July 8, 1776, the document became a fixture in national identity. Although it was not adopted by popular vote but decreed by the representatives of the thirteen states, two days after independence was proclaimed on July 2, 1776, its stated purpose articulated core commitments in terms understandable to ordinary people. Its unified message of nationhood spoke to hearts and minds in America and abroad in a way that the British Constitution, with its diffuse laws and provisions, did not.

The second paragraph of the document is familiar throughout the world, it acknowledges the inalienability of certain rights that each person shares equally. The Declaration conceives rights in abstract terms. Life, liberty, and the pursuit of happiness are not self-definitional, create ambiguities, but also possibility of a nation committed to human dignity. Even today, parsing the meaning of these three categories of prototypical rights remain opportune for individuals and social movements to shape, define, and actuate.

The document's abstract language boded the possibility of equality – "all men are created equal" – for the disempowered and well-off, alike. It gave women reason for hope, even though they were then taxed without being granted political representation, and it offered laborers an anti-autocratic message to force through measures for ending exploitation of the workforce at exceedingly low wages and egregiously harsh hours. Rather than confine themselves to positive, existing laws and customs, feminists and labor activists parsed the Declaration to fit their political causes, emboldened generations of supporters and articulated aspirational agendas that after long advocacy elicited revolutionary changes to existing social orders, whose "long train[s] of abuses" were at least as oppressive as those the colonists in 1776 found to be intolerable. On the basis of deductive reasoning, stemming from Thomas Jefferson's grandiloquent language, they developed reform agendas, formulated demanding petitions, and articulated political platforms. The Declaration became anchor and wellspring of ideas about human equality and rights.

The Declaration of Independence's maxims have inspired generations of visionaries to advocate for the protection of natural rights and the expression of civil liberties. The document is both a concrete statement of principles and an open-ended promise of self-fulfillment in a society of equals. Its guarantee of the people's safety and happiness captured the paradoxical empowerment of society to establish just laws, which limit liberties for the sake of public safety, and of individuals, who seek an expansion of liberties to fulfill personal aspirations.

A political system whose statement of independence committed it to the well-being of the populous served as an indictment of the British monarchy but also expressed the aspirations of constituents who saw the nation as a bastion of the equal and inalienable right to human dignity. The Declaration set identifiable public ideals and broad baselines against government overreaching. But the general wording of the document also provided the latitude for each generation to reexamine the authenticity of its efforts and to evaluate the extent to which the nation's institutions reflect its statements of equality and justice.

Atop the fundamental statement of national independence was built a structure for the people to enjoy basic freedoms and the equal liberty through the election of representative government, albeit it fell short in many ways most glaringly by racist and sexist norms of private and public behaviors. Customary and positive laws – protecting slavery, retaining property qualifications on voting, and preventing married women's participation in economic life – contradicted the Declaration's statement of universal rights and political representation. The existence of ideological statements of nationhood coupled with the recognition of the people's sovereignty provided advocates with a framework for articulating demands for rights and welfare. US social movements, such as those that demanded better working conditions and equal citizenship, often drew from the principled statements of the Declaration of Independence to inspire radical change from contemporary practices.

15.2 LABOR'S DECLARATION

The labor movement of the nineteenth century was one of the most successful at formulating supportive arguments through the Declaration of Independence's aspirational statements. As with other political action groups of the early nineteenth century, trade unions latched onto the equality ideals they discovered in the founding document.[1]

The call to improve workers' conditions was part of a strategy to end labor conditions leaders regarded to resemble slavery. In the Jacksonian period of American growth, the labor movement made allusion of wage labor as the "very essence of slavery."[2] Among the most hated aspects of wage slavery was the corrosive power of monopolies on depreciated salaries, dangerous work conditions, and cramped living arrangements.[3] Conglomerations of wealth and power were thought similar to colonial aristocracies that had been ended by the Declaration of Independence's proclamation of human equality.[4] Advocates soon recognized that without the collective advancement of workers, little could be achieved against vast business agglomerations.

---

[1] See, for example, Frederick Robinson, *An Oration Delivered before the Trades Union of Boston and Vicinity, on Fort Hill, Boston, on the Fifty-Eighth Anniversary of American Independence* (Boston: Charles Douglas, 1834), appendix at 32 (writing of a Fourth of July celebration of a Trade Union celebrating the Declaration of Independence and the Declaration of Rights of the Trades Union of Boston).
[2] Quoted in Eric Foner, *The Story of American Freedom* (New York: W. W. Norton, 1998), 60.
[3] See, for example, "From the *Reformed Medical Journal*," *The Independence* (Poughkeepsie, NY), February 15, 1832, at 1 (arguing that licensing of physicians in New Jersey was a monopoly that violated the second paragraph of the Declaration of Independence); "Loco-Foco Celebration of the Fourth of July," *The Herald* (New York), July 4, 1836, at 2 (advertising a group opposed to all monopolies who would read the Declaration of Independence on the Fourth of July).
[4] "An Oration, Delivered at Rahway, N. Jersey, July 4th, 1839, by John Bently Scoles," *The Hudson River Chronicle* (Ossining, NY), August 20, 1839, at 1, 2.

This is not to imply that the pre-Civil War workers' rights movements were universalist in advocacy. To the contrary, they were exclusionary of women, foreigners, and blacks. Moreover, they tended to operate as closed guilds. On the one hand, activists subscribed to an expansive understanding of the Declaration of Independence's promises of "life, liberty, and the pursuit of happiness" for white male workers. On the other, they narrowly applied the document's principles to white male laborers, scarcely concerned or directly averse to the plight of black, Chinese, or female workers.

In the early stages of labor advocacy, benevolent societies and charitable organizations evolved at local levels. Over two decades they would become a formidable political and social force, bolstered by strikes for higher wages, reasonable working hours, and improved working conditions. Among working men, there evolved a belief in the 1820s and 1830s that the Declaration of Independence gave even the "most humble aspirant" the right to secure "the common stock of knowledge and of happiness."[5] Jackson's supporters condemned the lack of public accountability of aggregated capital. Lending a voice to the president's vigorous efforts against the Second Bank of the United States, a Philadelphia champion of the Workingmen's Movement denounced the "funding and banking systems" of the United States for being untrue to the promise that "equality of rights ... and the pursuit of happiness [were] a common boon."[6] His condemnation resonated and demonstrated the Movement's interests not only in working conditions but also in opposing chartered monopolies, demanding equal taxation, and seeking access to universal education. Furthermore, the Movement's spokesman believed the nation's sovereignty was established to deflate centralized government and, instead, to empower ordinary people to influence politics through local craft unions and democratic societies.

Worker groups' affinities to the Declaration of Independence extended to the early days of the Republic. Much of those early invocations of the document were patriotic and instrumentalist. Focus given to the exploitation of workingmen rather than to popular sovereignty. To this end, Independence Day celebrations held in cities and towns around the newborn nation offered the opportunity for various professions to exhibit their trades. Worker participation in these celebrations also demonstrated support for political parties and candidates, extolled the Revolution, and displayed the daily operation of various specialties. Their parade floats and displays also communicated how vested their achievements were in the nation's sovereign well-being and how important they were to the communities they serviced.

---

[5] *See* Stephen Simpson, *The Working Man's Manual: A New Theory of Political Economy, on the Principle of Production the Source of Wealth* (Philadelphia: Thomas L. Bonsal, 1831), 5. Simpson's stance was particularly notable since he for a time worked as a bank teller and his father was a significant figure in the First Bank of the United States. Edward Pessen, "The Ideology of Stephen Simpson, *Pennsylvania History* 22 (1955): 328, 329.

[6] Pessen, "The Ideology of Stephen Simpson."

15 Aspirational Reliance on the Declaration

The 1788 Independence Day Procession at Philadelphia was dedicated to the establishment of the Constitution, which Pennsylvania had ratified on the previous December. That year on the Fourth of July, among the procession were the manufacturing society, merchants and traders, "cordwainers, coach-painters, cabinet and chair-makers, brick-makers, painters ... watch-makers ... bricklayers, taylors, instrument makers, coopers, ... whip manufacturers, black-smiths, bell-hangers," and a variety of other guild representatives.[7] They celebrated various occupations of toilers, who from the early colonial period of the seventeenth century, in enclaves like St. Mary's County, had been of critical import to growth, development, and progress.[8]

Celebration of Independence was tied to the liberty and equality whose promises the Declaration articulated. A similar spectacle occurred in New Haven, Connecticut, and brought together persons of various backgrounds who jointly strengthened America's diversity in manufacturing:

A plough drawn by ten oxen, Sowers, Reapers with their sickles, Thrashers with their flails, Hay-makers with rakes and forks, Butchers, Cordwainers in a wagon on their benches at work, Saddlers, ... Goldsmiths, jewellers [sic], with a silver urn, beautifully engraved and bespangled with ten stars, emblematical of the Ten States which have adopted the Constitution. There too were school masters; scholars, carrying books no less; and the Mayor.[9]

A resident of Philadelphia, who had observed the Independence Day procession from the street, wrote to a friend of the cooperation of agriculture and workmen,

Farmers and tradesmen are the pillars of national happiness and prosperity. It would seem as if heaven had stamped a peculiar value upon agriculture and the mechanical arts in American, by selecting Washington and Franklin to be two of the principal agents in the late revolution. The title of farmer and mechanic, therefore, can never fail to being particularly agreeable in the United States.[10]

Behind these Independence celebrations of industry was the notion that national sovereignty raised the creative human spirit and advanced ordinary workers' social and political statuses.[11]

Festivities exalting labor went hand in hand with ceremonies remembering the signing of the Declaration of Independence. The Newark, New Jersey,

---

[7] "Philadelphia, July 4, Order of Procession," *Independent Journal* (New York), July 9, 1788, at 2; "Grand Fœderal Procession," *Pennsylvania Mercury and Universal Advertiser*, July 10, 1788, at 1–2.
[8] Bernard Bailyn, *The Barbarous Years: The Conflict of Civilizations, 1600–1675* (New York: Alfred A. Knopf, 2012), 142.
[9] "New-Haven, July 9," *Massachusetts Gazette* (Boston), July 18, 1788, at 4.
[10] "Observations on the Federal Procession, on the Fourth of July, 1788," *Columbian Herald or the Independent Courier of North-America* (Charleston), July 24, 1788, at 2.
[11] Simeon Baldwin, *An Oration Pronounced ... July 4, 1788, in Commemoration of the Declaration of Independence and Establishment of the Constitution* (New Haven: J. Meigs, 1788), 14.

Independence Day procession of July 4, 1788, likewise followed a tradition of reading the Declaration of Independence, public meals, weapons solutes, parades, and toasts to leading revolutionaries, the States, and the as-yet "New Constitution." Importantly, these events brought disparate professions together in a common cause. At the head of the Newark procession were companies of military men. After them came an array of associations inspired by the Declaration's republican message. They included, tanners, cordwainers, heel makers, carpenters, and other specialized workers like masons, blacksmiths, and hatters.[12]

In a 1788 celebration of Independence held at Hartford, Connecticut, the military and fraternal society of Society of Cincinnati, meeting in Hartford, Connecticut, toasted "Agriculture, Manufactures, and Commerce."[13] The *Philadelphia Mercury* republished the correspondence from gentleman to his neighboring state friend, expressing the unifying force of independence:

> It was very remarkable, that every countenance wore an air of *dignity* as well as pleasure. Every tradesman's boy in the procession seemed to consider himself as a principal in the business. Rank for awhile forgot all its claims, and Agriculture, Commerce, and Manufactures, together with the learned and mechanical Processions, seemed to acknowledge by their harmony and respect for each other, that they were all necessary to each other, and all useful in cultivated society.[14]

A local correspondent who witnessed this great spectacle wrote, "We have become a nation," like other powers in the world, America was now deriving benefits "from her declaration of independence."[15]

Understanding the importance of economic stability to the general welfare of the nation, celebrants of Independence Day parades in towns throughout the United States, extolled and raised toasts to commerce and manufacturing.[16] The ideals of the Declaration of Independence came to be connected in the minds of labor leaders with a free republican government's obligation to guarantee "equal protection in the pursuit of happiness" in "all the departments of industry."[17] By the nineteenth century, concern for workmen's equality was woven into the American depiction of independence. This ideal continued to be manifest throughout the country by symbolic actions. At the 1818 Independence

---

[12] "Yesterday Being the 4th July," *New-Jersey Journal*, July 9, 1788, at 3.
[13] "Hartford, July 7," *Fœderal Adviser* (Middletown, CT), July 14, 1788, at 2.
[14] "Observations on the Fœderal Procession," *Pennsylvania Mercury and Universal Advertiser*, July 15, 1788, at 2.
[15] "Observations on the Fœderal Procession."
[16] See, for example, "United States. Philadelphia, July 6," *New-York Packet*, July 11, 1789, at 2; "Boston, June 29. Address of the House of Representatives to his Excellency John Hancock ... Governour of the Commonwealth of Massachusetts," *Cumberland Gazette*, July 5, 1790, at 2; "Carlisle, July 7," *Carlisle Gazette* (Carlisle, PA), July 7, 1790, at 3; "Wilmington, July 10," *Federal Gazette* (Philadelphia), at 2.
[17] "Speech [of Massachusetts Governor John Brooks]," *Boston Weekly Messenger*, June, 8, 1820, at 552.

Day celebration in Newark, New Jersey, a diverse coterie of laborers demonstrated their support. The procession included tailors who worked even as their horse-drawn procession made its way through the parade grounds. Craftsmen followed close behind, among them were stone cutters, bricklayers, masons, and carpenters. Evidently drawn by the unity heralded by the Day of Independence, the entourage also included bakers, smiths, lace weavers, sawyers, watchmakers, hatters, cabinetmakers, candle makers, trunk makers, boat builders, and coopers. After the procession, the crowd milled about, hearing various speeches about the nation's ideals delivered by female teachers.[18]

The high praises heaped on the Declaration came at a time of labor agitation. Unrelated trade organizations joined Fourth of July celebrations, but strikes were organized by trade and craft and, even more narrowly, they typically addressed only grievances on a city-by-city basis. Strikes by the likes of journeyman tailors in Baltimore and journeyman cordwainers in Philadelphia had divergent effects, with the former achieving higher wages and the latter being taken to the mayor's court on conspiracy charges for demanding an increase in wages. Strikes gradually became regarded as indispensable to the improvement of terms and conditions of labor, as, for example, in 1809, cordwainers struck for higher wages in New York City and Albany, with little avail against conspiracy charges that yielded few successes and landed them in lawsuits charging them with conspiracy.[19]

These movements often shrouded themselves in a sense of inclusiveness and patriotism, regarding monopolies to be outliers to the norms established by the principles of independence. George Henry Evans' 1829 Working Men's Declaration of Independence best illustrates worker nostalgia for a bygone era, with much of the revolutionary generation already having passed away. The Working Men's Declaration opened with passages from the first two paragraphs of the 1776 Declaration. But unlike the original, Evans set the context of condemnations in class struggle and a demand for social justice.[20]

Two years after the nation's first labor organization was founded in Philadelphia in 1827, the Working Men's Party of New York began to agitate for equal education, equal property, and equal privileges. It also demanded a ten-hour workday, free public schools, end to monopolies, and abolition of debtor prison laws.[21] While the New York group was politically split on

[18] *Maryland: A Guide to the Old Line State*, sponsored by Herbert R. O'Conor, Governor of Maryland (New York: Oxford University Press, 1940), 78; *Trenton Federalist* (NJ), July 13, 1818, at 2.
[19] John B. McMaster, *The Acquisition of Political Social and Industrial Rights of Man in America* (Cleveland: Printed at the Imperial Press, 1903), 56–60.
[20] George H. Evans, "The Working Men's Declaration of Independence," *Working Man's Advocate* (New York) and *Mechanic's Free Press of Philadelphia*, 1829, www.trinityhistory .org/AmH/WM%20declaration.pdf.
[21] Edward Everett, *A Lecture on the Working Men's Party: First Delivered October Sixth, before the Charlestown Lyceum* [Boston] (Boston: Gray and Bowen, 1830); Victoria C. Hatta, *Labor Visions and State Power: The Origins of Business Unionism in the United*

a number of issues such as property ownership, its platform demanded a ten-hour workday as a means of preventing exploitation of labor by capital. Labor associations built on the legacy of political dissent represented by the Declaration of Independence to decry exploitation of their labors.

The Working Men's Party's Declaration demonstrated the extent to which its members thought themselves to be spokesmen of a seismic historical shift. For laborers, the Declaration of Independence was more than a patriotic statement of a bygone era. The Working Man's Declaration of 1829 began with passages from the Declaration of Independence's first two paragraphs. After setting down a statement on men's equality, it listed specific grievances against oppressive monopolies. Workers' parties, like those in Philadelphia, New York, and Cincinnati, also relied on the Declaration of Independence to formulate petitions against the opulence of the Federalists and the corporate favoritism of the Democrats.[22]

The Working Men's Party sought the "restoration of ... institutions to that primitive pureness and simplicity, from which they have unfortunately degenerated, through the intrigues of corrupt and aspiring politicians."[23] The "declaration of rights of the Trades' Union of Boston and Vicinity" appeared in 1834. It argued that the Declaration's aspirational promise to create conditions worthy of human happiness remained unfulfilled as long as "laws ... have a tendency to raise and peculiar class above their fellow citizen."[24] Even more specifically, shoemakers and mechanics wrote principles found in the Declaration into their charges, condemning employers who robbed them of their rights. Textile workers called for a general strike in 1846 to assert laborers' right to "a second Independence Day."[25]

More radically at one of its 1829 meetings the New York Working Men's Party resolved that private property interests were "eminently and barbarously unjust." They regarded part of the political disparity of politics to be the result of inheritance law, aristocratic "luxury and idleness," and the exploitation of labor.[26]

States (Princeton: Princeton University Press, 1993), 80–82; Neil A. Hamilton, *Rebels and Renegades: A Chronology of Social and Political Dissent in the United States* (New York: Routledge, 2002), 74–75; Alex Gourevitch, *From Slavery to the Cooperative Commonwealth: Labor and Republican Liberty in the Nineteenth Century* (New York: Cambridge University Press, 2015), 68–69.

[22] Philip S. Foner, ed., *We, the Other People: Alternative Declarations of Independence by Labor Groups, Farmers, Woman's Rights Advocates, Socialists, and Blacks, 1829–1975* (Urbana: University of Illinois Press, 1976), 47–49; Edward Pessen, *Most Uncommon Jacksonians: The Radical Leaders of the Early Labor Movement* (New York: State University of New York Press, 1967), 26–33.

[23] "From the [Neward] Village Chronicle Working Men's Party," *Rhode-Island Republican* (Newport), August 5, 1830, at 2.

[24] Robinson, *Oration*, 32; Gregory S. Jay, *American Literature and the Culture Wars* (Ithaca: Cornell University Press, 1997), 80.

[25] Matthew Dennis, *Red, White, and Blue Letter Days* (Ithaca: Cornell University Press, 2002), 37.

[26] "The Working Men's Party," *Richmond Enquirer*, November 19, 1829, at 2.

Other workers, led by Robert Dale Owen, Henry Guyon, and Noah Cook, argued against the hoarding of wealth by a few, but refused to altogether renounce property ownership. For its members, the Declaration of Independence's statement of equality would remain an unrealized aspiration until property was confiscated from the monied class and redistributed in equal shares to laborers. Once the state had helped people achieve financial equality, individuals would be permitted to accumulate wealth but upon death their inheritance would return to the state for further redistribution.[27] But few agreed with so radical a program. President Andrew Jackson, expressing the dominant political view, condemned any notion of property confiscation and its redistribution. In his message to the Senate, delivered upon vetoing the rechartering of the Bank of the United States, Jackson stressed that "distinctions in society will always exist under every just government. Equality of talents, of education, or of wealth cannot be produced by human institutions."[28]

The dominant strand of labor protest called for the betterment of workers' conditions and for the improvement of their families' opportunities. Demand for an end to "wage slavery" was a revisionist understanding of the Declaration of Independence, which makes no mention of class conflict. For labor, though, the document was a source of inspiration and template. An activist claimed that using private riches to pay for universal education was what "the Declaration of Independence meant when it declared all men 'to be born free and equal.'" Evolving interpretations of the document tracked social advocacy that gave it meaning to a new generation of Americans.

According to the Working Man's Party, the Declaration of Independence was, "The political textbook for republican Working Men: a practical illustration of its principles." Seth Luther, one of the Working Men's Party's most convincing orators, traveled around New England protesting dangerous industrial conditions. Luther contrasted business monopolies from labor unions, which he conceived to be lawful associations. He explained this dichotomy in terms of the distinct social function of worker's organizations for political, cultural, and civic purposes. No one argued that fire fighters are illegal, "but if *poor men* ask JUSTICE, it is [said to be] a most HORRIBLE COMBINATION. The Declaration of Independence was the work of a combination and was as hateful to the TRAITORS and TORIES of those days as combinations among working men are now to the *avaricious* MONOPOLIST and *purse proud* ARISTOCRAT." Luther analogized and related the labor movement's campaign against monopolies to the anti-aristocratic strains of American independence.[29]

---

[27] Thomas Skidmore, *The Rights of Man to Property! Being a Proposition to Make It Equal among the Adults.* New York: Printed for the author by Alexander Ming, 1829).

[28] Andrew Jackson, "Returning the Bank Bill to the Senate with His Objections," in *Annual Messages, Veto Messages, Protests, & c. of Andrew Jackson, President of the United States*, 2nd ed. (Baltimore: Edward J. Coale, 1835), 244.

[29] "The Working Men of the City of New York ...," *The Illinois Gazette* (Shawnee-town), August 7, 1830, at 4, col. B ("The political text ..."); Theodore Sedgwick, *Public and Private*

Little thought was given to actual history. Effort went into expostulations of the document's grand lessons about liberty through free labor. Similar ideas influenced the Free Soil Party, which adopted the Declaration of Independence into its 1848 Party Platform to explain the principles behind its call for "free soil, free speech, free labor, and free men."[30]

Workers' rights movements of the early nineteenth century drove home the relevance of the Declaration to the daily lives of ordinary people as they strove for collective power, heralding the Founders' ability to join against the forces of British oppression. Theirs was a creative modification of the framers' vision in proclaiming sovereignty grounded in unalienable human rights principles. The Declaration of Independence was a symbol of independence and a statement of occupational freedom.

Yet, these labor organizations missed a key component of the document. For 50 percent of the population, the Declaration was aspirational but their pursuit of personal and political happiness was stymied by cultural and legal hurdles.

15.3 FIRST WAVE FEMINISTS' ANCHOR

The nineteenth-century women's rights movement, whose bourgeoning may be traced to the first meeting between Elisabeth Cady Stanton and Lucretia Mott at the World Anti-slavery Convention of 1840, where both women were excluded from being delegates on account of their sex. From that opening conversation grew a national movement, first thriving in the western territories, such as Washington, Oregon, Utah, and Wyoming.[31] Feminists tended to focus on a aspirational interpretation, ahead of its time about the equality of natural persons averred in the Declaration of Independence. The labor movement's understanding, on the other hand, tended to focus on the document's statement of autonomy. Both movements redefined the Declaration's broad principles to meet separate rhetorical aims. The Declaration's core principles of human and political freedoms were foundational to both movements. Though they worked in different trajectories, each was inspired by the 1776 guarantees of representation, personal happiness (what today would likely be called "dignity"), and equality.

First-wave feminists demanded that the promises of the Declaration be understood inclusively of women, even though none could have participated in the debates and vote for adoption at Philadelphia. A small but vocal group of

---

Economy, Part Second (New York: Harper, 1838), 85; Seth Luther, *An Address to the Working-Men of New-England on the State of Education and the Condition of the Producing Classes in Europe and America*, 2nd ed. (Boston: Published by the author, 1833), 27.

[30] Free Soil Party Platform of 1848, www.presidency.ucsb.edu/documents/free-soil-party-platform-1848.

[31] Alexander Tsesis, *We Shall Overcome: A History of Civil Rights and the Law* (New Haven: Yale University Press, 2008), 154.

authors, journalists, and agitators understood the phrase "all men are created equal" to include males and females. They forged an inclusive understanding of the principles articulate by the second paragraph of the Declaration of Independence.

They condemned cultural stereotypes that imputed inferiority to women, characterizing them as among the long train of abuses no less harmful than had been King George's assault on the colonists. In the first decades of the nation, arguments extolling the exclusion of women from politics were often bombastic. At an 1801 celebration of independence, William Hunter delivered a speech at Newport, Rhode Island. Hunter was then a member of the Rhode Island House of Representatives and was later appointed U.S. Senate. He rationalized denying women the right to vote on the basis of "utility and expediency." At the celebration of the covenant of independence, Hunter derisively claimed women should be excluded from elective franchise because otherwise it would be they who would exclude males from the same privilege of franchise. In a society where exclusion was the norm, the paradox was lost on this spokesman for male monopoly at a festival in honor of the document that promised all members of the polity the enjoyment of life, liberty, and the pursuit of freedom.[32]

In the early years of the Nation, the incompatibility of gender oppression with representative governance often went unnoticed or, worse, was regarded as a positive good for the benefit of fragile female wards. Yet, the significance of the document's statement on natural human equality had clear implications to the representation for the entire adult population. Its meaning was not lost on the few voices who dared to advocate for its universal applicability. A woman who delivered her speech at an 1800 gathering, understood celebration of the Fourth of July not to be about military victory. To her mind, the event was a celebration of something much different than to Hunter. She extoled how "the American people have calmly, and deliberately declared, that 'all men are created EQUAL." She then mocked the notion that human equality could "embrace only half of mankind." The "half systems" that formed existing political structures at federal and state levels prevented the sons and daughters of liberty to participate in the basic elements of democracy for which the Revolution had been ostensibly fought. Likewise, the "rights of sufferages [sic]" should have been understood to be the privilege of men and women.[33] At the turn of the nineteenth century, the United States was a nation that had renounced aristocracy by birth and yet had retained the hereditary privileges of sex.

---

[32] William Hunter, *An Oration, Delivered in Trinity Church, in Newport on the Fourth of July, 1801* (Newport: Printed at the office of the *Newport Mercury*, 1801), 9–10.

[33] ["Written by a Lady"], *An Oration Delivered on the Fourth Day of July 1800 by a Citizen of the United States to which Is Added the Female Advocate* (Springfield, MA: Henry Brewer 1808), 4, 5, 11.

The Lady's speech recognized the significance of the Declaration to extend far beyond the national sovereignty it proclaimed. Put in contemporary terms, neither thought of the Declaration in originalist terms. For both, and especially the rare feminist voice of the time,[34] the document was a living instrument the embodiment of aspirations with which to indict original practices. The Declaration of Independence not only opened a window into the past but also offered a glimpse into the future, both of which were interlaced; although, the Lady could not have predicted it would take 120 years from the day she delivered her 1800 speech or 144 years from the founding document's adoption for women to gain the voting rights of citizens. Her nascent statement of sex equality was a spark in the night to shed light into how the nation's founding commitments were incompatible with sex inequality. And she made that message in the context of Independence Day solemnities. So ahead of its time was her oration that it was printed a full eight years after its recitation. One wonders whether the Lady might have mingled with the crowd afterward and discussed her meaning with them.

What at the turn of the nineteenth century had been a rare spark of insight about the Declaration's breadth of meaning had by the middle of the century become central to the advocates of woman suffrage. Suffragettes demanded that the principles of nationhood extend far beyond the horizon visible to the document's authors and signers. Adoption of the Declaration by the suffrage movement, just as with the labor movement's grafting of the document to its cause, further demonstrates the extent to which the statement of national sovereignty served to advance social causes far beyond its original purpose. A new wave of Americans sought to actualize the promises of liberty and equality. For them, the Declaration produced seeds capable of germination into a national dialogue. They developed extra-constitutional claims that were consistent with the document's broader commitments to representation and natural rights. Those who adopted its sweeping phraseology did not confine their ideals to the constraints of the Revolutionary Era's limited vision of human equality.

The blatant disconnect between national ideals and political reality continued to plague women's lives. In the years after the Revolution, male suffrage expanded in the United States. During the nation's first years, most states limited the franchise to white propertied men. Women were excluded from the franchise even in states where those free blacks who were able to meet voting qualifications were eligible to vote – including Connecticut, Delaware, Kentucky, Maryland, Massachusetts, New Hampshire, New Jersey, New York, North Carolina, Pennsylvania, Rhode Island, Tennessee, and Vermont.[35]

---

[34] Indeed, the rare female voice that was recorded to speak in public, as opposed to say a Quaker meeting of friends.
[35] Donald Ratcliffe, "The Right to Vote and the Rise of Democracy, 1787–1828," *Journal of the Early Republic* 33 (2013): 219, 232; Charles H. Wesley, "Negro Suffrage in the Period of Constitution-Making, 1787–1865," *Journal of Negro History* 32 (1947): 143, 154–155; *Cofield v. Farrell*, 134 P. 407, 416 (1913).

15 Aspirational Reliance on the Declaration

The manhood suffrage movement of the early nineteenth century turned to the Declaration's principles of equality to vindicate the right of propertyless white men to exercise the franchise and thereby to enjoy political and civil freedoms without the encumbrance of arbitrary criteria on the enjoyment of citizenship.[36] In 1792, New Hampshire became the first and in 1859 Virginia the last state to abandon property qualifications for male suffrage. Such political progress, however, left intact sex-based restrictions that attracted understandable outcries against the existence of blatant hypocrisy. In politics, women lagged even further behind than free blacks, some of whom enjoyed limited political privileges in the States of Maine, New Hampshire, Vermont, Massachusetts, Rhode Island, and New York.[37] Female suffrage, on the other hand, was virtually nonexistent outside the walls of Quaker meeting houses.

At first the call for woman's suffrage enjoyed little support among women and men. Expansion of the eligible adult voting population would require principled advocacy for which the Declaration provided the substance. Briefly after the Revolution, New Jersey granted women the right to vote, but a much contested state-wide referendum deprived them of the same in 1807. Eighty-three years passed before in 1890 the state of Wyoming granted them the right to vote by the passage of legislation. The territorial legislature of Wyoming had in 1869 already recognized their entitlement to vote and hold political office, and in 1893, Colorado became the first State to grant women suffrage by popular referendum.

Widespread political, social, and employment exclusions were masked in paternalistic rationalizations about women's role over hearth and home. Domesticity's weighty cost was exclusion from politics, contracts, or employment. For 150 years after its adoption, most Americans understood the majestic statement of all men created equal to be unrelated to women's political empowerment. At a Fourth of July 1825 celebration Huntsville, Alabama, a speaker smugly proclaimed that the home is the "best reflector of woman's brightness."[38] Prolific author and former constitutional professor, Edward Mansfield, dismissed any notion that the Declaration of Independence's

---

[36] "Letter III: From a Republican in the Country to a Federalist in Baltimore," *Baltimore Patriot*, August 3, 1820, at, col. a. ("in the year 1801 ... "); "Constitution of the State of Massachusetts," art. ix, in *Official Papers*, Printed for the Common Council of the City of Boston (1822), 23, 28; *Journal of Debates and Proceedings in the Convention of Delegates, Chosen to Revise the Constitution of Massachusetts, Begun and Holden at Boston, November 15, 1820, and Continued by Adjournment to January 9, 1821* (rvsd. & corrected 1853) (some of the references to Declaration), at 172, 483; "Town of Enfield," *Republican Chronicle* (Ithaca), April 18, 1821, at 3; "N.Y. State Constitution of 1821," art. II, in Robert C. Cumming, Owen L. Potter, and Frank B. Gilbert, eds., *The Constitution of the State of New York* (Albany: James B. Lyon, 1894), 59, 60–61; *Reports of the Proceedings and Debates of the Convention of 1821, Assembled for the Purpose of Amending the Constitution of the State of New York*, ed. Nathaniel H. Carter and William L. Stone (Albany: E. and E. Hosford, 1821), 178, 235.

[37] *Oregon v. Mitchell*, 400 U.S. 112, 156 (1970).

[38] "Ladies Celebration," *Essex Register* (Salem), August 18, 1825, at 2.

guarantees of life, liberty, and the pursuit of happiness were to be understood in universal terms as applicable to women. This perspective ruled out any notion that the Declaration's statement was consistent with female political equality.[39] He took a historicist view that disregarded the aspirational implications of the principles the framers relied on to remonstrate their grievances and statement of independence. The *Yale Literary Magazine* published an article during the same period that used hyperbole to explain away the Declaration of Independence's coverage of that "motley multitude," in which women were joined by children, criminals, insane, and slaves.[40] No statement of equality of the sexes was found in the original Constitution or the Bill of Rights, nor did the Declaration make any clear provision for sex equality. The Declaration's aspirational commitments existed, during and long after the nation's founding, side-by-side inequality, political exclusion, and innumerable legal and customary handicaps on women. With no incorporated Bill of Rights, states enjoyed virtually unlimited discretion to exclude women from the privileges of citizenship. States like Connecticut, Delaware, and Rhode Island reprinted the Declaration of Independence in the same statutory tomes that housed laws against wives' alienation of property without their husbands' countersignature.[41]

Not all was grim; help was on the horizon. Even in this period, before the 1840 meeting between Stanton and Mott, advocates of both sexes began to formulate arguments based on aspirational reasonings that they rested in part on the simple terms of the Declaration. As a literary reviewer put it in 1837, the Declaration's proclamation of self-determination was incompatible with laws that required women to obey but denied them political participation.[42]

The long-suffering movement's efforts to obtain women's political equality linked itself to Garrisonian abolitionism. Anti-slavery causes were popular with women activists of the 1830s, like Angelina and Sarah Grimké, who along with the former's husband, edited and publish *American Slavery As It Is: Testimony of a Thousand Witnesses*. Rejecting the shuddered views of historicism and textualism, by the third and fourth decades of the nineteenth century feminists conceived the Declaration's "principle that all men are born free and equal" to include interests of women, blacks, and foreigners. These early pioneers of principles that were later incorporated into the Reconstruction and Nineteenth Amendments defended what then seemed radical that "men and women [are subject to] the same duties and [enjoy] the same rights."

---

[39] Edward D. Mansfield, *The Legal Rights, Liabilities and Duties of Women* (Salem, MA: John P. Jewett & Co., and Cincinnati: William H. Moore & Co., 1845), 124–125.
[40] "The People," *Yale Literary Magazine* 9 (April 1844): 275, 276–277.
[41] *The Public Statute Laws of the State of Connecticut* (Hartford: J. B. Eldredge, Printer, 1835), 1, 351; *Laws of the State of Delaware* (Wilmington: Printed by R. Porter and Son, 1829), 1, 556; *Public Laws of the State of Rhode-Island* (Providence: Knowles & Vose, 1844), 10, 231–232, 260.
[42] *The Literary Gazette and Journal of the Belles Lettres*, book review, May 13, 1837, at 297, 298.

15 Aspirational Reliance on the Declaration

Sex stereotypes imposing unequal social station and behavioral etiquette, so proclaimed the New York Anti-Slavery Society, raised impossible barriers to occupational pursuits.[43] Along the same lines, asserted the social theorist Harriet Martineau, "one of the fundamental principles announced in the Declaration of Independence," the source of legitimate governmental authority, was consent of the governed, which was denied to them. Early feminists pointed out that as taxpayers women deserved the right to vote by the equality terms of the Declaration. They could not engage in the key purposes of independence, participatory governance. To deny women the right franchise was regarded by them as tyranny that was every bit as oppressive as was British tyranny against the American colonies. Sex inequality violated the national commitment to human equality articulated by the Declaration of Independence.[44]

15.4 THE DECLARATION AND WOMAN SUFFRAGE MOVEMENT

Group protestation lends force to an argument. In July 1848, fifty-five-year-old feminist Lucretia Mott and the thirty-two-year-old Elizabeth Cady Stanton jointly organized the Seneca Falls Convention. The results were electrifying to the cause of voter equality. Delegates to the Convention agreed that various social, legal, religious, and political reforms were essential to render the aspirations of the Declaration of Independence a reality for women. The nation's founding document became the template for the feminist meeting's written call to action, designated the Declaration of Sentiments.[45]

By linking early arguments for sex-neutral suffrage to the Declaration of Independence, feminists tapped into the same national life blood that flowed through the labor movement of the early nineteenth century. In both cases, it took decades of advocacy to convince politicians and the general public to support their causes. Progressive thought was coupled with aspirational values of the past. That pattern was widespread, partly because of the yearly Independence Celebrations and mostly because the Declaration stood for constitutional values of representative democracy. So, too, the Republican Party of the 1850s and 1860s successfully fashioned platforms that relied on the Declaration of Independence to articulate policies favorable to workers' rights and anti-slavery causes. For them as for feminists, the Declaration provided an aspirational lodestar, providing the focal purpose for movements whose aims

---

[43] *Fourth Annual Report of the Board of Managers of the New-England Anti-Slavery Society, January 20, 1836* (Boston: Isaac Knapp, 1836), 49, 52–53, comments of Professor Charles Follen.
[44] A well-known Massachusetts physician leant her voice to the growing demand that the Declaration of Independence be recognized as a statement of male and female equality. Harriot K. Hunt, *Glances and Glimpses* (Boston: J. P. Jewett & Co., 1856), 295–296, 318–319.
[45] Seneca Falls Convention, https://teachingamericanhistory.org/document/declaration-of-sentiments/.

expanded the liberal equality promised but imperfectly fulfilled in 1776. The work of the woman suffrage movement bore fruit at the national level in 1920 with the ratification of the Nineteenth Amendment. Like feminists, labors' early gains came state by state. It was only in the late 1930s that the Court recognized the constitutionality of state minimum wage laws and in the early 1940s before it confirmed the constitutionality of similar federal minimum wage and maximum hours standards.

The Declaration established promises and mandates to exercise a representative government committed to liberty and equality that activists with diverse agendas relied on to win popular opinion and to secure meaningful change. Reformers from the eighteenth through the twenty-first centuries have sought to develop the Declaration into a meaningful document. They have found in it kernels from which to grow and develop America's constitutionalism structure and reconstruction. The middle class helped to grow the political economy demanding that an increasingly industrialized nation maintained its republican character. The line was often too circuitous justifying grand injustices while supporting the nation's underlying principle. Elizabeth Bancroft Schlesinger put the point in a book review, "It seems incredible today that many of those doughty champions of the suffrage movement could take so illiberal a stand on immigration, the Negro, and organized labor, each of which they considered threats to democracy, while at same time upholding and equalitarian preamble to the Declaration of Independence."[46] Despite the tainted legacy of American democracy, the Declaration of Independence pointed a path forward. In the twentieth century its proclamations would speak to workers movements' aspirations for class equality, during the New Deal it became a vehicle for the unemployed to push for greater government engagement in the plight against poverty, and it continued to be a beacon to churchmen demanding a Declaration of Independence for Blacks.[47] Their demands were for economic stability, childcare, unemployment relief, pensions, food sufficiency, and healthcare.

15.5 CONCLUSION

Professors Joseph Fishkin and William Forbath point out that the Declaration has remained a foundational commitment to which reformers throughout the nation's history turned to develop programs that included constitutional amendments.[48] The Thirteenth Amendment is the most meaningful addition

---

[46] Elizabeth Bancroft Schlesinger, "The Ideas of the Woman Suffrage Movement, 1890–1920 by Aileen S. Kraditor," book review, *New England Quarterly*, 39.1 (1966): 102, 103.

[47] See, for example, Foner, *We, the Other People*, 151–169, containing separate a declaration of independence of the working class, workers and farmers, the unemployed, and black churchmen.

[48] Joseph Fishkin and William E. Forbath, "Wealth, Commonwealth, and the Constitution of Opportunity," *Nomos* 58 (2017): 45, 47.

15 Aspirational Reliance on the Declaration

to the Constitution, whose norms were defined by the aspirational principles of the Declaration.[49] The battles were not only national in counties around the country, like Dade County in Miami, where during the New Deal members invoked the founding document to advance populist causes.[50] On a more personal level, the document helped leaders mature, as it did with Abraham Lincoln, whose principles on labor and race were molded after the fashion of the Declaration. The document remains relevant because of its powerful message that speaks to inalienable rights while delivering an aspirational appeal for equality. As Professor Rogers Smith writes, the Declaration helps to explain the "intertwined history of labor and civil rights struggles" that "has long affirmed, policies and practices must help people acquire the economic, educational, and political resources and capabilities they need to exercise their rights."[51] Into the twenty-first century, the Declaration continues to tell a story but also offer a plan forward to a fully representative polity whose principle commitment lies in equal rights and the pursuit of happiness.

---

[49] Alexander Tsesis, *The Thirteenth Amendment and American Freedom: A Legal History* (New York: NYU Press, 2004).

[50] Thomas A. Castillo, *Working in the Magic City: Moral Economy in Early Twentieth-Century Miami* (Champaign: University of Illinois Press, 2022), 188–189.

[51] Rogers M. Smith, *That Is Not Who We Are!: Populism and Peoplehood* (New Haven: Yale University Press, 2020), 113.

16

Presidents and the Declaration of Independence

Mark A. Graber

American presidents have actively participated in the process that transformed the Declaration of Independence into a fully constitutive document. Jefferson's Declaration was partly revolutionary and partly constitutive. "We hold these truths to be self-evident" proffered a "we" who agreed on fundamental principles. In doing so, Jefferson implicitly recognized a "they" who disputed the Declaration's assertions about human equality, the purpose of government, inalienable rights, the consent of the governed, and the right to alter and abolish government institutions failing to achieve liberal purposes. Almost immediately upon promulgation, the Declaration was transformed in part into a partisan document. Proponents of racial (and gender) equality insisted that the principles of the Declaration covered all persons. Opponents, while claiming to adhere to (most of) the Declaration's principles, claimed those principles had a far narrower scope. By the end of the twentieth century, these disputes were settled. All Americans pledge allegiance to the principles set out in Jefferson's text.

This chapter surveys presidential references to and quotations from the Declaration of Independence. The essay begins by reviewing bare numbers, counting presidential mentions of and quotations from the Declaration from George Washington to Donald Trump. The numbers suggest a steady increase over time. The chapter then discusses the content of presidential citations to the Declaration. Many presidential citations are either ceremonial or express shared values. All presidents, however, claim the Declaration supports at least some of their favored policies on civil rights, governmental powers, the culture wars, and immigration. Liberal and conservative presidents dispute whether the Declaration supports regulation in the public interest or limited government. Presidents in the culture wars engage in parallel play, with more progressive presidents citing the Declaration when supporting the rights of LGBTQ persons, gun control, and liberal immigration policies, and conservative presidents citing the Declaration for bans on abortion, a greater place for religion in the public sphere and crime control measures.

The survey of presidential statements has virtues and vices. Examining all presidential references to and quotations from the Declaration avoids cherry-picking from the practically infinite number of references to and quotations from the Declaration made by all public actors in the United States. Including all presidential citations highlights the increasing banality of the Declaration. Jefferson's text is most often cited as stating basic American commitments, without much content, or in contexts completely divorced from the principles stated in that document. Nevertheless, the survey does not meet anyone's bronze medal standards for methodology. Precise numbers should not be taken seriously. The focus on the national executive misses how racists in Congress and elsewhere during the first two-thirds of the twentieth century continued claiming that the Declaration supported white supremacy.[1] If presidents ranging from Coolidge and Reagan on the right to Franklin D. Roosevelt and Obama on the left provide a fair range of mainstream conservative and liberal understandings, the focus on persons with sufficient popular support to win a national election misses how more radical movements on the left and the right have understood the Declaration during the twentieth and twenty-first centuries.

16.1 SOME NUMBERS

Presidents during the nineteenth century rarely made reference to the Declaration of Independence (Figure 16.1).[2] Presidents from George Washington to William McKinley cited the Declaration of Independence or quoted from the second paragraph only thirty-one times. Abraham Lincoln was the only president who invoked the phrase "all men are created equal."[3] John Tyler was the only president who invoked the phrase "consent of the governed."[4] Benjamin Harrison won the prize for most citations by issuing four identical proclamations declaring new state constitutions consistent with the Declaration of Independence.[5]

---

[1] Alexander Tsesis, *For Liberty and Equality: The Life and Times of the Declaration of Independence* (New York: Oxford University Press, 2012), 257–58.
[2] All documents used in this survey can be found in the American Presidency Project, hosted by the University of California, Santa Barbara, The American Presidency Project, www.presidency.ucsb.edu/. All quotations that follow are taken from that site unless otherwise indicated.
[3] Abraham Lincoln, "Special Session Message," July 4, 1861; Abraham Lincoln, "Address at the Dedication of the National Cemetery at Gettysburg, Pennsylvania," November 19, 1863.
[4] John Tyler, "Address Upon Assuming the Office of President of the United States," April 9, 1841.
[5] Benjamin Harrison, "Proclamation 291 – Admission of South Dakota into the Union," November 2, 1889. Harrison from November 2 to November 11, 1889 issued three other proclamations announcing that North Dakota, Montana, and Washington were admitted to the Union.

		Declaration of Independence	Self-evident	Created equal[a]	Endowed	Inalienable[b]	Life, liberty[c]	Consent	Total
George Washington	1789–1797								
John Adams	1797–1801								
Thomas Jefferson	1801–1809								
James Madison	1809–1817								
James Monroe	1817–1825	1							1
John Quincy Adams	1825–1829	2							2
Andrew Jackson	1829–1837	4						1	5
Martin Van Buren	1837–1841								
William Harrison	1841–1841	1							1
John Tyler	1841–1845	1						1	2
James Polk	1845–1849								
Zachary Taylor	1849–1850	1							1
Millard Fillmore	1850–1853								
Franklin Pierce	1853–1857	1					1		2
James Buchanan	1857–1861	1							1
Abraham Lincoln	1861–1865	3		2					4 (sic)
Andrew Johnson	1865–1869	2					2		3 (sic)
Ulysses Grant	1869–1877	2							2
Rutherford Hayes	1877–1881	1							1
James Garfield	1881–1881								
Chester Arthur	1881–1885								
Grover Cleveland	1885–1889, 1893–1897	1							1
Benjamin Harrison	1889–1893	5							5
William McKinley	1897–1901								

238

President	Years								
Theodore Roosevelt	1901–1909	1					2		3
William Howard Taft	1909–1913						1		1
Woodrow Wilson	1913–1921	6				1		8	14
Warren Harding	1921–1923						2		2
Calvin Coolidge	1923–1929	14		2		6	1	3	17
Herbert Hoover	1929–1933	4		1			2	2	5
Franklin D. Roosevelt	1933–1945	24	4	2	2	9	13	5	44
Harry S. Truman	1945–1953	26	2	13	2	12	5	2	40
Dwight Eisenhower	1953–1961	28	4	12	16	19	20	6	64
John Kennedy	1961–1963	10		4	3	8	7	2	21
Lyndon B. Johnson	1963–1969	30	7	15	4	18	24	11	78
Richard Nixon	1969–1974	35	1	3	2	4	10	5	46
Gerald Ford	1974–1977	53	3	12	11	13	28	6	75
James Carter	1977–1981	25	1	5	2	6	17	3	40
Ronald Reagan	1981–1989	98	9	42	43	98	57	33	200
George W. Bush	1989–1993	44	11	32	28	31	36	6	74
William Clinton	1993–2001	177	12	34	17	17	65	3	227
George H. W. Bush	2001–2009	81	7	30	9	21	23	6	112
Barack Obama	2009–2017	39	46	132	52	112	66	5	248
Donald J. Trump	2017–2021	68	7	30	18	27	24	13	97
Joseph Biden	2021–February 17, 2023[d]	10	40	90	35	34	18		94

FIGURE 16.1 Presidential references to the Declaration of Independence.
Source: The American Presidency Project.

[a] This includes "all men," "all men and women," "all people," and similar variations where the reference to the Declaration was obvious.
[b] Or "unalienable."
[c] This includes "pursuit of happiness" or "pursue happiness" when the reference to the Declaration was obvious.
[d] The last day surveyed was February 17, 2023.

Grover Cleveland made his only reference to the Declaration when issuing a nearly identical proclamation.[6]

These thirty-one citations and quotations began patterns that later solidified. Most were brief and largely symbolic. Harrison and Cleveland asserted that new state constitutions were consistent with the principles articulated by Declaration of Independence, but did not state why or elaborate on those principles. The few presidents who elaborated on those principles reached different conclusions. James Monroe and Franklin Pierce cited the Declaration as evidence that on July 4, 1776, each state became a distinctive sovereign.[7] Abraham Lincoln cited the Declaration as evidence the United States existed before any state was sovereign.[8]

With the partial exception of Donald Trump, references to the Declaration have consistently accelerated over the past 100 years. Woodrow Wilson is the first president who invoked the language of the Declaration with some frequency, quoting the "consent of the governed" eight times, mostly when fighting for his vision of the post-World War I international order. Calvin Coolidge, who cited the Declaration more often than his predecessors, is the first president to expound at some length on the meaning of the Declaration, and is the first president who quoted multiple passages in the Declaration in the same speech. Franklin D. Roosevelt is the first president who quoted the phrases "self-evident truths" and "endowed by their Creator." Truman is the first president who frequently quoted the phrase "all men are created equal," most often in speeches calling for legislation protecting persons of color. Dwight Eisenhower is the first president who frequently quoted the phrase "endowed by their Creator." William Clinton is notable for his numerous references to the Declaration. Both Barack Obama and Joseph Biden are notable for their few explicit mentions of the Declaration, but numerous quotations from the Declaration. Obama employed the phrases "truths to be self-evidence," "all men are created equal," endowed by their Creator," and "inalienable" or "unalienable rights" far more than any previous president, and quoted variations on "life, liberty and the pursuit of happiness" more than any previous president. Trump more frequently referred to the Declaration than any other president, but quoted the Declaration far less often than any other modern president.

The numbers can be deceiving. Contemporary presidents produce substantially more paper than past presidents. Some increase results from what Jeffery Tulis refers to as "the rhetorical presidency,"[9] and others speak of

---

[6] Grover Cleveland, "Proclamation 382 – Admitting Utah to the Union," January 4, 1896.
[7] James Monroe, "Special Message to the House of Representatives Containing the Views of the President of the United States on the Subject of Internal Improvements," May 4, 1822; Franklin Pierce, "Third Annual Message," December 31, 1865.
[8] Abraham Lincoln, "Inaugural Address," March 4, 1861.
[9] Jeffrey K. Tulis, *The Rhetorical Presidency* (Princeton: Princeton University Press, 1987).

as "going public."[10] The frequency with which presidents invoke or quote from the Declaration reflects greater presidential fluff and the rise of what Elvin Lim describes as "the anti-intellectual presidency."[11] Contemporary presidents issue numerous proclamations declaring Human Rights Week or German-American Month. They rely heavily on "platitudes and simplistic slogans" in more traditional fora.[12] The result is a dramatic increase in brief, usually insubstantial, references to the Declaration or pithy quotes from that text.

16.2 THE REFERENCES

Presidential references to the Declaration of Independence fall into three general categories. Presidents frequently claim that the Declaration announces the foundational commitments of the American regime. Coolidge stated, "the fundamental conception of American institutions is regard for the individual. The rights which are so clearly asserted in the Declaration of Independence are the rights of the individual."[13] Clinton maintained, "we must remember that the Declaration of Independence was written as a commitment for all Americans at all times."[14] Presidents claim the Declaration supports their distinctive policies. Obama, when calling for greater rights for LGBTQ persons, declared, "As Americans, it is our birthright that all people are created equal and deserve the same rights, privileges and opportunities."[15] "If the unborn child is a living entity," Reagan asserted when calling for pro-life legislation, "then there are two individuals, each with the right to life, liberty, and the pursuit of happiness."[16] Presidents make celebrity references to the Declaration that have little substantive content. Presidential proclamations during Irish-American Week routinely note the number of persons born in Ireland who signed the Declaration of Independence. Obama introduced the Archivist of the United States as the person who "takes care of the Constitution and Declaration of Independence."[17]

---

[10] Samuel Kernell, *Going Public: New Strategies of Political Leadership* (Washington, DC: CQ Press, 2006).
[11] Elvin T. Lim, *The Anti-intellectual President: The Decline of Presidential Rhetoric from George Washington to George W. Bush* (New York: Oxford University Press, 2008).
[12] Lim, *The Anti-intellectual President*, xii.
[13] Calvin Coolidge, "Address to the Convention of the National Education Association: Education: The Cornerstone of 'Self-Government,'" July 4, 1924.
[14] William J. Clinton, "Remarks at Georgetown University," July 6, 1995.
[15] Barack Obama, "Proclamation 8529 – Lesbian, Gay, Bisexual, and Transgender Pride Month, 2010," May 28, 2010.
[16] Ronald Reagan, "Remarks at the Conservative Political Action Conference Dinner," February 18, 1983.
[17] Barack Obama, "Remarks Honoring the NCAA Men's Basketball Champion Duke Blue Devils," May 27, 2010.

16.3 BASIC COMMITMENTS

Presidents refer to the Declaration of Independence as stating the basic commitments of the American constitutional regime. Tenses vary. Some presidents praise Americans for living up to the ideas of the Declaration. Eisenhower stated, "As we gaze back through history to that date, it is clear that our nation has striven to live up to this declaration."[18] Other presidents use the future tense. Lyndon B. Johnson said, "So the time has come in our national life when we have got to make our Bill of Rights real, when we have got to make our Declaration of Independence come true, when we have got to make our Constitution a living document."[19] Clinton declared, "I think it is obvious to anybody who even goes to the Jefferson Memorial and reads what Mr. Jefferson had to say about slavery, that when he wrote the Declaration of Independence and the Founders wrote the Constitution, they knew good and well that they were setting out perfect ideals that we were nowhere near realizing."[20]

Presidential speeches and proclamations assert that the Declaration of Independence provides the foundation for American identity. Biden insisted that Americans are "uniquely a product of a document that says, 'We hold these truths to be self-evident.'"[21] Eisenhower declared, "As Americans, we believe that all men are created equal. Our national existence began with this belief and it is the foundation of our democracy." Clinton stated, "In our country, we're not about race and religion. If you believe in the Constitution, the Bill of Rights, and the Declaration of Independence, and you're willing to show up for work tomorrow, you're our kind of person, you're part of our America, and we're going forward together. That's what we believe."[22] "The revolutionary truths of the Declaration are still at the heart of America,"[23] George W. Bush maintained.

16.4 PUBLIC POLICY

American presidents during debates over civil rights, government regulation, the culture wars, international human rights, foreign policy, and immigration claim the Declaration of Independence supports particular policy prescriptions. Presidential uses of the Declaration in different contexts vary. The Declaration in debates over the rights of persons of color was transformed

---

[18] Dwight D. Eisenhower, "Annual Message to the Congress on the State of the Union," January 10, 1957.
[19] Lyndon B. Johnson, "Remarks to Key Officials of the Internal Revenue Service," February 11, 1964.
[20] William J. Clinton, "Remarks at a Reception for Montana Gubernatorial Running Mates Mark O'Keefe and Carol Williams," October 2, 2000.
[21] Joseph Biden, "Remarks on Signing the COVID-19 Hate Crimes Act," May 20, 2021.
[22] William J. Clinton, "Remarks in Bowling Green, Ohio," August 26, 1996.
[23] George W. Bush, "Remarks at an Independence Day Celebration in Morgantown, West Virginia," July 4, 2005.

during the twentieth century from a partisan text cited only by presidents committed to civil rights legislation to a constitutive text that all presidents cited as establishing American commitments to a generalized notion of racial equality. The Declaration is also a constitutive test in presidential commentaries on international human rights and gender equality. All presidents cite the Declaration as articulating a consensus that all people throughout the world are created equal and that men and women are created equal, without connecting the Declaration to particular human rights policies or particular means for achieving gender equality. The Declaration in controversies over the role of government is cited by all parties to political debates for quite different propositions. Conservatives claim the Declaration supports limited government. Progressives insist the Declaration supports regulation in the public interest. Presidents claim the Declaration supports foreign policy goals ranging from anti-communist efforts in Europe to the invasion of Iraq. Presidents who comment on the culture wars and immigration engage in rhetorical parallel play. Both liberals and conservatives cite the Declaration for their preferred policies, but they tend to focus on different issues when doing so. With rare exceptions, presidents do not cite the Declaration when discussing controversial democratic rights.

16.5 CIVIL RIGHTS

Americans by the end of the twentieth century were committed in theory to the proposition that all persons were created equal. Presidents routinely invoked the Declaration of Independence as scorning all forms of discrimination. Clinton, after quoting the Declaration, declared, "Emancipation, women's suffrage, civil rights, voting rights, equal rights, the struggle for the rights of the disabled, all these and other struggles are milestones on America's often rocky but fundamentally righteous journey to close the gap between the ideals enshrined in these treasures here in the National Archives and the reality of our daily lives."[24] George Bush described the Americans with Disabilities Act (ADA) as "keeping faith with the spirit of our courageous forefathers who wrote in the Declaration of Independence: 'We hold these truths to be self-evident, that all men are created equal, that they are endowed by their Creator with certain unalienable rights.'"[25]

Some presidents claimed Americans needed to work continually to realize the promise of the Declaration, without specifying the nature of that work. Obama, after considering problems of poverty, hunger, poor schools, and the school-to-prison pipeline, stated, "To put up blinders to these realities or to intimate that they are inherent to a Nation as large and diverse as ours would

---

[24] William J. Clinton, "Remarks on Affirmative Action at the National Archives and Records Administration," July 19, 1995.
[25] George Bush, "Remarks on Signing the Americans with Disabilities Act," July 26, 1990.

do a disservice to those who fought so hard to ensure ours was a country dedicated to the proposition that all people are created equal."[26] Biden emphasized the forces arrayed against realizing the promise of the Declaration of Independence. His inaugural address declared, "Our history has been a constant struggle between the American ideal that we are all created equal and the harsh, ugly reality that racism, nativism, fear, demonization have long torn us apart."[27] The previous Trump administration represented the forces arrayed against realizing the Declaration's promise. "We hold these trues to be self-evident, that all men and women are created equal, endowed by their Creator with certain unalienable rights: life, liberty," Biden informed an American Federation of Labor and Congress of Industrial Organizations (AFL-CIO) Convention. "We've never met the goal, but we've never – other than the Trump administration – tried to walk away from that goal."[28]

More commonly, presidents celebrated contemporary Americans for having overcome the racial errors of the past. The second President Bush noted, "our adhering to the full extent of the liberties embedded in the Constitution and the Declaration of Independence took a while."[29] He observed how Martin Luther King "led us to see the great contradiction between our founders' declaration that 'all men are created equal' and the daily reality of oppression endured by African Americans."[30] Trump insisted, "As a Nation, we cherish and uphold the notion that all people are created with inherent dignity and entitled to life, liberty, and the pursuit of happiness."[31]

Presidential references to the Declaration on matters of gender equality take the same consensual approach. Presidents beginning with Carter routinely assert "men and women" or "all people" are "created equal." Ford declared, "all men and women everywhere are endowed by their Creator with inalienable rights of life, liberty, and the pursuit of happiness."[32] Presidents do not explore how being created equal should affect reproductive rights, sexual harassment policies, or, with one exception, working conditions. As is the case with racial equality, contemporary presidents are more inclined to praise the Declaration for motivating Americans in the past than for charting a course for

---

[26] Barack Obama, "Proclamation 9390 – Martin Luther King, Jr., Federal Holiday, 2016," January 15, 2016.
[27] Joseph Biden, "Inaugural Address," January 20, 2021.
[28] Joseph Biden, "Remarks at the AFL-CIO Constitutional Convention in Philadelphia, Pennsylvania," June 14, 2022.
[29] George W. Bush, "Remarks to Freedom House and a Question-and-Answer Session," March 29, 2006.
[30] William J. Clinton, "Proclamation 6861 – Martin Luther King, Jr., Federal Holiday, 1996," January 12, 1996.
[31] Donald Trump, Proclamation 9835 – National Slavery and Human Trafficking Prevention Month, 2019," December 31, 2018.
[32] Gerald R. Ford, "Remarks and a Question-and-Answer Session with Members of the Chicago Council or Foreign Relations," March 12, 1976.

future action. The first President Bush on Women's Equality Day declared, "the 19th Amendment offers a poignant reminder that every individual is an heir to the civil and political rights enshrined in our Declaration of Independence and Constitution."[33] Clinton observed, "The 19th Amendment did more than secure the right to vote for women. It recognized and affirmed the fundamental principle upon which this great Nation was founded – equality – 'that all [persons] are created equal, that they are endowed by their Creator with certain unalienable rights, that among these are Life, Liberty and the pursuit of Happiness.'"[34]

16.6 ECONOMIC RIGHTS

Presidents routinely refer to the Declaration as the inspiration for their economic programs, but the inspiration they draw differs. Progressives from Theodore Roosevelt to Obama interpret the Declaration as sanctioning the government regulations necessary for citizens to enjoy the pursuit of happiness. Conservatives from Coolidge to George W. Bush regard the Declaration's commitment to inalienable rights as limiting governmental regulatory power.

Progressive presidents assert that government regulations are necessary to fulfill the promise of the Declaration of Independence. Franklin D. Roosevelt described the New Deal "as new as the Declaration of Independence was new, and the Constitution of the United States; its motives are the same." New Deal measures, Roosevelt declared in another speech, were "essential to assure the continuance of the inalienable rights which the Constitution is intended to guarantee."[35] Clinton connected the Declaration and active government when he stated, "We hold these truths to be self-evident, that all men are created equal, endowed by their Creator with certain inalienable rights, and among these are life, liberty, and the pursuit of happiness. And Government was instituted to help the American people pursue those ends."[36]

Conservative presidents maintain as forcefully that the Declaration of Independence commits Americans to limited government. Coolidge linked the Declaration and property rights, declaring,

It is declared that he is endowed with inalienable rights which no majority, however great, and no power of the Government, however broad, can ever be justified in violating ... When once the right of the individual to liberty and equality is admitted, there is no escape from the conclusion that he alone is entitled to the rewards of his own industry.[37]

[33] George Bush, "Proclamation 6170 – Women's Equality Day, 1990," August 14, 1990.
[34] William J. Clinton, "Proclamation 6715 – Women's Equality Day, 1994," August 18, 1994.
[35] Franklin D. Roosevelt, "Address on Agriculture, Fremont, Nebraska," September 28, 1935.
[36] William J. Clinton, "Remarks to the Democratic National Committee" January 21, 1995.
[37] Calvin Coolidge, "Address to the Holy Name Society, Washington, DC," September 21, 1924.

Reagan called on all Americans to complete the work of the authors of the Declaration of Independence with an Economic Bill of Rights, a bill that will restore to us the freedoms that our Founding Fathers believed we should always have, a bill of rights that will protect us and future generations from the needless and wrongful encroachment of government upon our lives.[38]

"It is time," he insisted, "to check and reverse the growth of government, which shows signs of having grown beyond the consent of the governed."[39] Ford invoked the Declaration when attacking the administrative state. He asserted, "Full individual freedom in America also means freedom from intrusive, overbearing government ... As long ago as Thomas Jefferson – he sounded it in the Declaration of Independence itself, where he complained that His Majesty's Government 'has erected a Multitude of new Offices, and sent [hither] Swarms of Officers to harass our People ...'"[40]

16.7 THE CULTURE WARS

Contemporary presidents insist the Declaration of Independence supports particular positions in bitterly contested debates over the role of religion in public life, crime, gun control, sexual morality, and reproductive freedom. Democrats in the White House maintain that Jefferson's text supports gun control and the rights of LGBTQ persons, but do not invoke the Declaration when discussing public prayer exercises, abortion, and crime control. Republicans in the White House insist that the Declaration supports public prayer exercises, bans on abortion, and crime control, but do not invoke the Declaration when defending the right to bear arms or opposing same-sex intimacy.

Clinton and Obama frequently invoked or quoted from the Declaration when speaking out for the rights of LGBTQ persons. "We cannot discriminate against same-sex couples when it comes to marriage," Obama declared in 2013. He continued, "the basic principle that America is founded on – the idea that we're all created equal – applies to everybody, regardless of sexual orientation, as well as race or gender or religion or ethnicity."[41] Obama's response to *Obergefell* v. *Hodges* stated,[42] "if we are truly created equal, then surely the love we commit to one another must be equal as well. It is gratifying to see that principle enshrined into law by this decision."[43] Clinton's celebration of Gay

---

[38] Ronald Reagan, "Remarks at the Annual Convention of the National Association of Counties in Indianapolis, Indiana," July 13, 1987.
[39] Ronald Reagan, "Inaugural Address," January 20, 1981.
[40] Gerald R. Ford, "Remarks in Indianapolis at the Annual Convention of the United States Jaycees," June 22, 1976.
[41] Barack Obama, "The President's News Conference," March 1, 2013.
[42] 576 U.S. 644 (2015).
[43] Barack Obama, "Remarks on the United States Supreme Court Ruling on Same-Sex Marriage," June 26, 2015.

and Lesbian Pride Month proclaimed, "Americans have strived to make real the ideals of equality and freedom so eloquently expressed in our Declaration of Independence and Constitution."[44]

Clinton and Obama insist the Declaration supports gun control. Championing a ban on assault weapons, Clinton stated, "I think the American people have a right to be safe and secure. How can we pursue life, liberty, and the pursuit of happiness if we don't have the most elemental security?"[45] Obama declared,

That most fundamental set of rights to life and liberty and the pursuit of happiness, fundamental rights that were denied to college students at Virginia Tech and high school students at Columbine and elementary school students in Newtown and kids on street corners in Chicago on too frequent a basis to tolerate and all the families who've never imagined that they'd lose a loved one to a bullet, those rights are at stake.[46]

Republican presidents cite or quote from the Declaration when fighting on different fronts in the culture wars. Reagan and George W. Bush on an almost annual basis, and George Bush occasionally, invoked the Declaration when calling for bans on reproductive choice. "Doesn't the constitutional protection of life, liberty, and the pursuit of happiness extend to the unborn unless it can be proven beyond a shadow of a doubt that life does not exist in the unborn?"[47] Reagan asked in 1982. Reagan on National Sanctity of Human Life Day in 1988 maintained, "One of those unalienable rights, as the Declaration of Independence affirms so eloquently, is the right to life. In the 15 years since the Supreme Court's decision in *Roe* v. *Wade*,[48] however, America's unborn have been denied their right to life."[49] Five years later, George Bush on National Sanctity of Human Life Day stated,

Americans have demonstrated their commitment to the belief 'that all men are created equal, that they are endowed by their Creator with certain unalienable Rights, that among these are Life, Liberty and the pursuit of Happiness.' This tradition of generosity and reverence for human life stands in marked contrast with the prevalence of abortion in America today – some 1.5 million children lost each year; more than 4,000 each day.[50]

---

[44] William J. Clinton, "Proclamation 7203 – Gay and Lesbian Pride Month, 1999," June 11, 1999.
[45] William J. Clinton, "Remarks Honoring the 1994 Victim Service Award Recipients and an Exchange with Reporters," April 25, 1994.
[46] Barack Obama, "Remarks on Gun Violence," January 16, 2013.
[47] Ronald Reagan, "Remarks at Kansas State University at the Alfred M. Landon Lecture Series on Public Issues," September 9, 1982.
[48] 410 U.S. 113 (1973).
[49] Ronald Reagan, "Proclamation 5761 – National Sanctity of Human Life Day, 1988," January 14, 1988.
[50] George Bush, "Proclamation 6521 – National Sanctity of Human Life Day, 1993," January 4, 1993.

The Trump told participants in the March for Life, "Under my administration, we will always defend the very first right in the Declaration of Independence, and that is the right to life."[51]

Republican presidents claim the Declaration supports a greater place for religion in the public sphere. Eisenhower declared, "There is no one in the United States who needs to be told or reminded that all free civilization rests upon a base of religious faith. You can find this statement repeated in our own founding documents, in the Declaration of Independence."[52] Reagan's call for a constitutional amendment permitting voluntary prayer in schools asserted, "Our Founding Fathers weren't neutral when it came to values. 'We hold these truths to be self-evident,' they wrote in the Declaration of Independence, 'That all men are created equal,' and that they're 'endowed by their Creator with certain unalienable Rights.'"[53] Criticizing lower federal court decisions deleting "under God" from the pledge of allegiance, George Bush stated, "the Pledge of Allegiance doesn't violate rights. As a matter of fact, it's a confirmation of the fact that we received our rights from God, as proclaimed in our Declaration of Independence."[54]

16.8 DEMOCRATIC RIGHTS

Presidents over the last seventy years invoke the Declaration less frequently when staking out positions on democratic rights than when staking on positions on equality or individual rights. Presidential references to the Declaration in the years before the New Deal commonly emphasized democratic commitments. Wilson repeatedly referred to the "consent of the governed" when defending his vision of a postwar liberal world order. Championing a world league for peace, Wilson stated, "No peace can last, or ought to last, which does not recognize and accept the principle that governments derive all their just powers from the consent of the governed, and that no right anywhere exists to hand peoples about from sovereignty to sovereignty as if they were property."[55] Johnson and Reagan are the only post-New Deal presidents who quoted that phrase repeatedly. Presidential quotations express shared commitments to democracy rather than contested democratic visions. "The American heritage of individual freedom and of Government deriving its powers from the consent of the governed," Franklin D. Roosevelt declared, "has from the time of the Fathers of our

---

[51] Donald Trump, "Remarks to March for Life Participants and Pro-life Leaders," January 19, 2018.
[52] Dwight D. Eisenhower, "Remarks to the National Committee for the 1960 White House Conference on Children and Youth," December 16, 1958.
[53] Ronald Reagan, "Radio Address to the Nation on Education," August 24, 1985.
[54] George Bush, "Remarks Prior to Discussions with President Vladimir Putin of Russia and an Exchange with Reporters in Kananaskis," June 27, 2002.
[55] Woodrow Wilson, "Address to the Senate of the United States: 'A World League for Peace,'" January 22, 1917.

16 Presidents and the Declaration of Independence

Republic been proudly transmitted to each succeeding generation."[56] Clinton offered a rare instance of an argument for democratic rights when he refused to sign a bill limiting the speech rights of former public officials. Legislation that "may unduly restrain the ability of former Government officials to teach, write, or engage in any activity aimed at building public understanding of complex issues," he informed Congress, runs "risks" that are "unnecessary and inappropriate in a society built on freedom of expression and the consent of the governed." Carter's bland assertion, "the power of government is derived from the consent of the governed,"[57] is more typical of how presidents speak of the relationship between the Declaration and democracy.

16.9 CELEBRITY CITATIONS

Many presidential references and quotations trade on the Declaration's reputation rather than the Declaration's principles. Presidents make celebrity citations when they trot out the Declaration to refer to a text or phrase that is well known and valuable. Obama at a summit in the former Soviet Union made a celebrity citation when he stated, "Some have even wondered whether our Declaration of Independence may have been signed with goose quills from Russia."[58] Reagan's "Address to the Nation on the Federal Budget and Deficit Reduction" declared, "our plan recognizes that all spending is not created equal."[59] These references and quotations have rhetorical force independent of the Declaration's content. Listeners understand the reference. They can be trusted to feel positively about the Declaration or phrases in the Declaration.

Presidents rip well-known phrases from the Declaration when making policy arguments that rest on different foundations. Reagan declared, "all balanced budgets aren't created equal."[60] Obama maintained, "all nations have an 'inalienable right' to peaceful nuclear energy."[61] Presidents commonly use "pursuit of happiness" to justify particular policy commitments. Franklin D. Roosevelt promised "to speed the time when there would be for all the people that security and peace essential to the pursuit of happiness."[62] Harding asserted, "the highest function of government is to give its citizens the

---

[56] Franklin D. Roosevelt, "Proclamation 2418 – Day of Prayer," August 7, 1940.
[57] James Carter, "'Our Nation's Past and Future:' Address Accepting the Presidential Nomination at the Democratic National Convention in New York City," July 15, 1976.
[58] Barack Obama, "Remarks at the United States–Russia Business Summit," June 24, 2010.
[59] Ronald Reagan, "Address to the Nation on the Federal Budget and Deficit Reduction," April 24, 1985.
[60] Ronald Reagan, "Remarks at a Rally Supporting the Proposed Constitutional Amendment for a Balanced Federal Budget," July 19, 1982.
[61] Barack Obama, "Statement on the 40th Anniversary of the Non-Proliferation of Nuclear Weapon Treaty," March 5, 2010.
[62] Franklin D. Roosevelt, "Inaugural Address," January 20, 1937.

security of peace, the opportunity to achieve, and the pursuit of happiness."[63] Presidents find many truths "self-evident" that are far removed from "all men are created equal." Obama described as "truths that ... seemed self-evident" that "the borders of Europe cannot be redrawn with force; that international law matters; that people and nations can make their own decisions about their future."[64] Presidents issue declarations of independence. Ford issued "a declaration of independence from the needless regulations of the Government."[65] George Bush described the ADA as "a declaration of independence for millions of persons with disabilities in this country."[66]

16.10 ON THE BANALITY OF THE GOOD

Presidential invocations of the Declaration of Independence illustrate how good may be as banal as Hannah Arendt discovered evil to be in her classic account of Adolf Eichmann.[67] The Declaration's principles are noble and the rhetoric soaring, but presidential references to the Declaration are trite. Presidents trot out Jefferson's words to pursue particular policy agendas and engage in political fluff. From one perspective, this essay has documented how revolutionary sentiments may decline into political clichés. From a different perspective, the story these pages have told is how revolutionary sentiments have become so successfully integrated into the American body politic that noble commitments once thought controversial can now thankfully be taken for granted.

---

[63] Warren G. Harding, "Address at the Burial of an Unknown American Soldier at Arlington Cemetery," November 11, 1921.
[64] Barack Obama, "Remarks to European Youth in Brussels, Belgium," March 26, 2014.
[65] Gerald R. Ford, "Remarks at the National Bicentennial Salute to Small Business," May 13, 1976.
[66] George Bush, "Statement on Congressional Action on the Americans with Disabilities Act of 1990," July 13, 1990.
[67] See Hannah Arendt, *Eichmann in Jerusalem: A Report on the Banality of Evil* (New York: Viking Press, 1963).

Conclusion

Four Children, Sixteen Essays, and the Declaration of Independence

Mark A. Graber

Participants in the Passover Seder engage in a dialogue with four children.[1] The wise child asks, "What are the testimonies, the statutes, and the laws which the Lord our God has commanded you?" This child is committed to the Jewish tradition but needs instruction on the conduct and aspirations entailed by that commitment. The wicked child asks, "Whatever does this service mean to you?" This child rejects the Jewish tradition, either because the child rejects the community or because this child cannot imagine a God worth worshipping who would slay the firstborn of all Egyptians and drown the Egyptian army in the Red Sea. The simple child asks, "What is this?" This child does not understand why the Jewish community thinks the Exodus story so important and so central to Jewish identity. The last child is incapable of framing a question. That was then; this is now. Besides, we are hungry and will accomplish more of our purposes by eating dinner than engaging in political speculation.

The Declaration of Independence bears a close resemblance to the story of the Exodus that is told at the Passover Seder.[2] Both concern a people who prefer national self-determination to enduring tyranny. The Jews were slaves in Egypt. Americans declared themselves to be enslaved by Parliament and King George. The experience of slavery becomes central to the narrative of both peoples. The Passover Seder commands Jews, contrary to the policy of the current government of Israel, to treat the stranger among us with dignity and kindness, remembering that we were once slaves in Egypt. The Declaration of Independence declares that "all men are created equals," that the English, the

---

[1] The quotations in this paragraph are taken from Noam Zion and David Dishon, *A Different Night: The Family Participation Haggadah* (Jerusalem: Shalom Hartmann Institute, 1997), 58–60.
[2] For one such mediation, see Michael Walzer, *Exodus and Revolution* (New York: Basic Books, 1986).

enslaved African, and women as well as white male Americans are "endowed by their Creator with certain inalienable rights."

The essays in this volume resemble the dialogue with the four children that takes place at the Passover Seder and ought to take place at Fourth of July celebrations. The wise child asks, "How are the principles of the Declaration of Independence embedded in the constitutional law and political practice of the United States?" This child is prepared to honor the commitments and aspirations made in 1776 but needs instruction on how to do so. The wicked child asks, "Why should you care about some document penned in 1776 by people who owned slaves and wore hideous wigs?" This child refuses to identify with the commitments made in 1776, either because the child identifies with some status hierarchy or, more likely, the child refuses to take seriously the pleas of faux revolutionaries who were committed to illegitimate status hierarchies during the late eighteenth century. The simple child asks, "Why do you celebrate the Fourth of July?" This child does not understand the significance of the Declaration of Independence in 1776 or in 2026. The last child cannot figure out how to frame a question in the twenty-first century about a document written in the eighteenth century. This child may be a committed member of the Cambridge School of Political Thought, who does not think we have an adequate language for translating Jefferson's sentiments into politically meaningful commitments and aspirations,[3] or may be an aspiring business major who thinks serious political thought has little value.

Looking at the essays in this volume from the perspective of the four children, the Passover service problematizes certain features of the Seder and the Declaration of Independence. The wise child who asks how to observe the Passover and July Fourth rituals assumes without adequate reflection a commitment to the Passover story and the Declaration of Independence. Instinctive veneration of Torah structures Jewish practice as much as instinctive veneration of the Declaration of Independence and the Constitution structure constitutional politics in the United States.[4] The wicked child is quick to point out that problems exist with an unthinking commitment to either the Passover story, the Declaration of Independence, or the Constitution of the United States. God inflicts horrible evils on relatively innocent Egyptians, providing a model too often emulated by other regimes who punish entire populations for the sins of the leadership, most recently by Israel in Gaza. Slavery and violence haunt unthinking commitment to the spirit of 1776. American independence was forged on a foundation of soldiers who died for lower taxes and, arguably, more secure rights to hold others in bondage. These problems require retelling both the Passover and Declaration stories, so that the simple child

---

[3] See Quentin Skinner, *Visions of Politics: Regarding Method* (New York: Cambridge University Press, 2002).
[4] See Sanford Levinson, "Divided Loyalties: The Problem of 'Dual Sovereignty' and the Constitution," *Touro Law Review* 29.2, 3 (2013): 241, 242.

Four Children, Sixteen Essays, and the Declaration   253

can determine intelligently whether commitment to either (the same?) tradition is warranted. Once these stories are retold, asking the appropriate questions becomes complicated. How does one determine the contemporary analogies to biblical slavery or what Americans in 1776 called slavery? What does the Declaration mean in a regime in which everyone claims to adhere to the fundamental principles that Jefferson articulated more than 200 years ago?[5]

C.1 THE WISE CHILD

Many essays in this volume and much contemporary rhetoric address the wise child who wants to fulfill the commands of the Declaration but does not fully know how to do so. The authors inform the wise child that the Declaration states who Americans are. The child who wants to know how to be an American need only read the Declaration of Independence and follow the precepts there stated. "[Y]ou're our kind of person, you're part of our America," President William Jefferson Clinton declared, "[i]f you believe in … the Declaration of Independence."[6]

The Declaration is as constituent of American identity as the Seder is of Jewish identity. Brian Steele maintains that "the Declaration asserts an American character and identity,"[7] that "(t)he nation's 'holy purpose' from that first moment would be 'adhesion to' the 'principles' of the Declaration and 'a sacred determination to maintain and perpetuate them.'"[8] Alexander Tsesis begins his essay by asserting, "The Declaration of Independence remains a statement of core constitutional commitments, despite the passage of two and a half centuries since its adoption by the Second Continental Congress."[9] Read and learn your commitments as an American. The "stated purpose" of the Declaration of Independence, Tsesis continues, "articulated core commitments in terms understandable to ordinary people. Its unified message of nationhood spoke to hearts and minds in America and abroad."[10] The result is a text that "became a fixture in national identity."[11]

When Americans reason from fundamentals, they begin with the Declaration of Independence. Michael Zuckert claims that "for us as a people," the Declaration "provide[s] the first principles for our political reasoning

---

[5] See Mark A. Graber, "Presidents and the Declaration of Independence," Chapter 16 in this volume.
[6] Graber, "Presidents," 242.
[7] Brian Steele, "Getting 'the Hang of the Declaration': The Declaration in American Nationalism," Chapter 11 in this volume, 158.
[8] Steele, "American Nationalism," 160.
[9] Alexander Tsesis, "Aspirational Reliance on the Declaration of Independence: Labor and Woman's Suffrage," Chapter 15 in this volume, 219.
[10] Tsesis, "Aspirational Reliance," 220.
[11] Tsesis, "Aspirational Reliance," 219.

and acting."[12] Barbara A. McGraw agrees that, "Belief in those truths has become the foundation of American self-identity."[13] The first principles the Declaration declares are distinctively American principles that support a distinctively American political thinking. Jefferson, McGraw points out, intended his handiwork "to be an expression of the American mind."[14] Tom Cutterham channels Martin Diamond when speaking of the Declaration and Constitution as "the two great charters of our national existence, representing the beginning of our founding and its consummation."[15] The American commitment to liberty is at the core of these fundamental political truths. "According to the Declaration," Richard Newman asserts, "freedom was part and parcel of American national identity and could never be separated from it."[16]

Thomas Jefferson may be the author of the Declaration, but the essays in this volume teach the wise child that Abraham Lincoln is the patron saint whose political life and speeches best captured and advance the fundamental truths underlying the text of 1776. Steele quotes at length Lincoln's famous assertion that the Declaration "meant to set up a standard maxim for free society, which should be familiar to all, and revered by all; constantly looked to, constantly labored for, and even though never perfectly attained, constantly approximated, and thereby constantly spreading and deepening its influence, and augmenting the happiness and value of life to all people of all colors everywhere."[17] Lincoln's reference to "Four-score and seven years ago" in the Gettysburg Address, Zuckert points out, reminded Lincoln's Civil War audience that the United States was "conceived in liberty and dedicated to the proposition that all men are created equal."[18] Lincoln's Constitution may be understood correctly only in light of the Declaration. Cutterham discusses Lincoln's insistence that "it was only the Declaration that gave meaning and purpose to the Constitution."[19] The Declaration was the biblical apple of gold, the Constitution the frame, and, in Lincoln's words, "(t)he picture was made for the apple – not the apple for the picture."[20]

The wise child shares the Lincolnian understanding that slavery was incompatible with the fundamental commitments of American nationalism expressed in the Declaration. Newman reminds readers concerned with Jefferson's racism

---

[12] Michael Zuckert, "Equality, Liberty, and Rights in the Declaration of Independence," Chapter 5 in this volume, 74.
[13] Barbara A. McGraw, "A Theological Interpretation of the Declaration of Independence," Chapter 9 in this volume, 123.
[14] McGraw, "Theological," 141.
[15] Tom Cutterham, "The Declaration versus the Constitution," Chapter 10 in this volume, 143.
[16] Richard Newman, "Slavery and the Declaration: A Reinterpretation," Chapter 8 in this volume, 116.
[17] Steele, "American Nationalism," 155.
[18] Zuckert, "Equality, Liberty, and Rights," 62.
[19] Cutterham, "Constitution," 153.
[20] Cutterham, "Constitution," 153.

that Lincoln believed persons of color were "entitled to all the natural rights enumerated in the Declaration of Independence."[21] Lincoln insisted that the Declaration's commitment to "all men are created equal" provided the standard for evaluating American public policy, include the American policy on slavery that some persons in 1776 were willing to give a pass. That commitment to "all men are created equal," Lincoln insisted, entailed a commitment to putting human bondage on a "course of ultimate extinction."[22] The Civil War Amendments fulfilled the promise of 1776.

African Americans celebrate the Declaration for this reason. They were the first to insist that the American commitment to "all men are created equal" entailed the abolition of slavery.[23] The ink was hardly dry on the Declaration when enslaved persons and free blacks demanded that Americans honor their commitment to universal rights.[24] Black Americans in the antebellum period continued to mobilize for free and equal rights, as the title of Kate Masur's award winning book indicates, "until justice be done."[25] Thomas J. Davis notes how, "Sojourner Truth put in plain words her belief in universal application to hold 'these truths to be self-evident.'"[26] The Declaration played as large a role in twentieth-century African American thought. Saladin Ambar points out that W. E. B. Du Bois maintained, "[T]here are to-day no truer exponents of the pure human spirit of the Declaration of Independence than the American Negroes."[27] Even the Black Panthers adopted the Declaration's creed.[28]

Other groups rally around the Declaration when contesting status hierarchies. Leslie F. Goldstein's essay points to the central place the Declaration held in women's struggle for rights before the Civil War. "The ideas [the Declaration] espoused," she asserts, "reverberated down through the ages to inspire ... a momentous women's movement."[29] Jonathan Todd Hancock details how Native Americans' insistence on the Declaration's promise of sovereignty played a prominent role in Native American advocacy.[30] Tsesis describes how

---

[21] Newman, "Slavery," 122.
[22] Abraham Lincoln, "'A House Divided,' Speech at Springfield, Illinois, June 16, 1858," *Collected Works of Abraham Lincoln* ed. Roy P. Basler (New Brunswick: Rutgers University Press, 1953), 461.
[23] See Simon J. Gilhooley, *The Antebellum Origins of the Modern Constitution: Slavery and the Spirit of the American Founding* (New York: Cambridge University Press, 2020).
[24] Newman, "Slavery," 116.
[25] Kate Masur, *Until Justice Be Done: America's First Civil Rights Movement, From the Revolution to Reconstruction* (New York: W. W. Norton & Company, 2021).
[26] Thomas J. Davis, "The Declaration in Anti-slavery and African American Thought," Chapter 13 in this volume, 193.
[27] Saladin Ambar, "The 'Stubborn' Declaration: Less Dissent than Alienation in Black Political Thought and the Declaration of Independence," Chapter 6 in this volume, 83.
[28] Ambar, "The 'Stubborn' Declaration," 84.
[29] Leslie F. Goldstein, "The Declaration of Independence and Women," Chapter 14 in this volume, 204.
[30] Jonathan Todd Hancock, "Native Nations and Declarations of Independence," Chapter 12 in this volume.

the Declaration inspired working-class Americans to agitate for better working conditions. Groups in the United States routinely paraphrase the Declaration when making their claims against status hierarchies. The Working Men's Party Declaration of Independence,[31] the Free Soil Party's Platform,[32] the Seneca Falls Declaration,[33] the Black Declaration of Independence,[34] several claims made by Native Americans,[35] and the program of the Black Panthers,[36] are among the many documents that highlight and paraphrase the Declaration as the core commitment of American national identity, even as groups struggle for reform.

By the end of the Fourth of July service, the wise child understands that the Civil War did not mark the end of the Declaration as an inspiration for reform movements. Postbellum presidents justify their programs by pointing to the Declaration.[37] The Declaration remains vibrant for the civil rights movement and class struggle in the twenty-first century. To paraphrase Tocqueville, hardly a political movement arises in the United States that does not maintain the Declaration of Independence provides the foundation for that movement's claims. Steele details how all "variants of American radicalism have taken the Declaration as their point of departure and claimed to be the true heirs of the spirit of '76."[38]

C.2 THE WICKED CHILD

The Wicked Child at the Fourth of July celebration may invoke the Declaration for evil causes. Throughout American history, Jefferson's handiwork has not inspired only the true, the good, and the beautiful. Chief Justice Roger Brooke Taney's use of the Declaration in *Dred Scott* v. *Sandford* highlights how Jefferson's words may be used to justify the rankest injustice.[39] Hancock points out that President Andrew Jackson and Chief Justice John Marshall, respectively, employed the Declaration when justifying Native American removal and federal sovereignty over Native tribes.[40] He quotes one Native American activist who points out, "The American Indian has helped the white man to fight for the 'Declaration of Independence' and in every succeeding war since that the Indian has sacrificed his blood under the emblem of the United States."[41] "[G]enerations

---

[31] Tsesis, "Aspirational Reliance," 225.
[32] Tsesis, "Aspirational Reliance," 228.
[33] Goldstein, "Declaration of Independence," 204; "The Seneca Falls Declaration of Sentiments and Resolutions," *Documents of American History*, ed. Henry Steele Commager, Vol. 1, 7th ed. (New York: Appleton-Century-Crofts, 1963), 315–17.
[34] Davis, "Declaration," 196–97.
[35] Hancock, "Native Nations," 170.
[36] Ambar, "The 'Stubborn' Declaration," 84.
[37] Graber, "Presidents."
[38] Steele, "American Nationalism," 164.
[39] *Dred Scott* v. *Sandford*, 60 U.S. 393, 410 (1856).
[40] Hancock, "Native Nations," 180, 182.
[41] Hancock, "Native Nations," 183.

of slaveholders," Newman acknowledges, "used the Declaration's ode to personal liberty to rationalize human bondage."[42] Contemporary opponents of the civil rights movement continue to lean upon the Declaration. When challenging laws forbidding racial discrimination, Jesse Merriam declares, "There is little reason to think ... that the Declaration of Independence, by proclaiming that we 'are created equal' means that we do not have the equal right to express our 'Liberty' in associating with those of our choosing."[43]

A different wicked child points out that the grievances Americans had against England hardly justify violent revolution. This child rejects the Declaration and American political principle in the name of justice and maintaining the peace. Contrary to claims that Jefferson and his peers were protesting taxation without representation or the English denial of fundamental rights, Woody Holton's essay suggests the English laws the colonials revolted against were justifiable means for achieving the legitimate ends of the empire. England increased the tax burden on the colonies to pay for an army that would prevent violence between western settlers and Native Americans, violence that was too often initiated by the colonists. Holton points out, "Given that this peacetime army's primary mission would be to protect white Americans – essentially as a human wall – it seemed only reasonable ... to make the colonists pay for it."[44] Hancock observes how "it was Euro-American settlers' own mercilessly savage desire for land" that was "the heart of the colonies' Declaration and subsequent founding of the United States."[45] The hated Quartering Act was another measure designed "to shift the costs of feeding and housing redcoats serving in America from British to colonial taxpayers."[46] Other British policies the colonists found objectionable were directed at smuggling. Parliament, Holton notes, "cracked down on their illegal importation of molasses from French and Spanish sugar colonies in the Caribbean."[47] The British practice of trying certain offenses in London rather than in Boston does not seem unjust considering the propensities of colonial juries. Holton details how Bostonians, on the one hand, "would refuse to convict their fellow colonists for crimes such as rioting" and, on the other, sent "innocent men to the gallows" when trying British soldiers.[48] "Why should I celebrate such an illiberal people who rise up against such justices," this wicked child asks, "particularly when everyone knows that 'liberty depends on taxes.'"[49]

---

[42] Newman, "Slavery," 120.
[43] Jesse Merriam, "How Civil Rights Law Changed America," *Law & Liberty*, November 22, 2023, lawliberty.org.
[44] Woody Holton, "The Twenty-Six Grievances," 22, Chapter 2 in this volume.
[45] Hancock, "Native Nations," 171.
[46] Holton, "Grievances," 26–27.
[47] Holton, "Grievances," 24.
[48] Holton, "Grievances," 30.
[49] Stephen Holmes and Cass Sunstein, *The Cost of Rights: Why Liberty Depends on Taxes* (New York: W. W. Norton & Company, 2000).

The wicked child of the Fourth of July commemoration is arguably demonstrating virtue by refusing to celebrate the evils done by the hypocrites who professed commitment to the Declaration of Independence, while the alleged "wise" child unthinkingly accepts membership in a community constituted by those evils. Little if any reason exists to honor a culture that enslaved human beings while professing to be committed to the principle that "all men are created equal." When Jefferson's claim that "all men are created equal" is interrogated, the Declaration may function more as a ground for human bondage than as a justification for emancipation. "It would not be merely ideological or inherently cynical," Matthew Crow notes, "to read the Declaration as chiefly the authorized press release of a white settler colonialist revolt on behalf of the freedom to own other bodies and lands and things and to clear some space in which to own some more."[50] Newman details how "recent generations of both scholars and citizens see the Declaration through the prism of slaveholding hypocrisy."[51] Jefferson, he notes, was waited on by an enslaved person while he wrote, "all men are created equal."[52]

This wicked child looks elsewhere when searching for first principles. Critical race theorists point out that "'the Haitian act of independence' ... was a more powerful expression of human liberation because it 'radically upended the basic premise of white supremacy.'"[53] Enslaved persons in 1776 often looked to England for life, liberty, and the pursuit of happiness. Holton documents the many enslaved persons who sought to secure the liberties in the Declaration of Independence by fighting for the British.[54]

The Declaration of Independence this wicked child scorns is largely American propaganda. Davis speaks of "black Americans' early and persistent exposure of the living lie to be enshrined in the US founding document,"[55] and points to "the self-evident duplicity that marked the gap between the nation's deeds and the document's pronounced philosophy."[56] Ambar refers to "America's founding hypocrisies."[57] Women have similar cause for complaint. "Jefferson," Goldstein points out, "showed no interest in elevating the[] social or political status [of women] in the new republic."[58] "Blatant hypocrisy" is not limited to African Americans and other victims of status hierarchies in the United States.[59] Reformers who invoke the Declaration when reforming one status hierarchy often accept other status hierarchies. Tsesis observes that the

---

[50] Matthew Crow, "The Declaration as Political Rhetoric," Chapter 4 in this volume, 47.
[51] Newman, "Slavery," 109.
[52] Newman, "Slavery," 112.
[53] Newman, "Slavery," 111.
[54] Holton, "Grievances," 33.
[55] Davis, "Declaration," 187.
[56] Davis, "Declaration," 188.
[57] Ambar, "The 'Stubborn' Declaration," 76.
[58] Goldstein, "Declaration of Independence," 207.
[59] Tsesis, "Aspirational Reliance," 231.

labor movement did not extend the principles of the Declaration to "black, Chinese, or female workers."[60] The Black Declaration of Independence, Davis points out "in listing 'our own Black heroes,' ... offered not a single black woman."[61]

Ambar's essay plays another variation on the wicked child. Following the Seder script precisely, he points out that African American thinkers have historically asked, what is the Declaration of Independence to me? Ambar declares, "if there is a thread of discourse among black political thinkers concerning the Declaration, it is one of alienation, rather than dissent."[62] Critical race theorists do not dispute the principles of the Declaration. They point out that those principles often have little cache in the lives of persons of color in the United States. Frederick Douglass stated in his famed address, "What to the Slave is the Fourth of July,"

> (y)our high independence only reveals the immeasurable distance between us. The blessings in which you, this day, rejoice, are not enjoyed in common. The rich inheritance of justice, liberty, prosperity and independence, bequeathed by your fathers, is shared by you, not by me. The sunlight that brought light and healing to you, has brought stripes and death to me. This Fourth July is yours, not mine. You may rejoice, I must mourn. To drag a man in fetters into the grand illuminated temple of liberty, and call upon him to join you in joyous anthems, were inhuman mockery and sacrilegious irony.[63]

Douglass spoke for much of the African American community. Davis observes that: "American practice made the Declaration something of a dead letter for African Americans, as many demonstrated by refusing to celebrate the Fourth of July."[64]

African Americans have often placed far more emphasis on the Declaration's claims about the right of a distinct people to govern themselves than on colonial propaganda about life, liberty, and the pursuit of happiness. Elijah Muhammad claimed to have the vision that inspired his calls for black separatism on the Fourth of July.[65] Muhammad had little use for such phrases as "all men are created equal." Instead, when black nationalists celebrated the Declaration, they pointed to Jefferson's claim that a distinctive people is entitled to secede from a nation after suffering from "a long train of abuses."[66]

Stanford Levinson suggests the wicked child may be repelled by the nationalism strands of the Declaration that attracted Muhammad. The Jeffersonian mantra, one people/one nation, has created political havoc when applied to the United States, black separatism, or any other assemblage that invokes claims

---

[60] Tsesis, "Aspirational Reliance," 222.
[61] Davis, "Declaration," 199.
[62] Ambar, "The 'Stubborn' Declaration," 76.
[63] "What, to the Slave, Is the Fourth of July," BlackPast.org.
[64] Davis, "Declaration," 189.
[65] Ambar, "The 'Stubborn' Declaration," 78.
[66] Ambar, "The 'Stubborn' Declaration," 81.

of shared peoplehood to deprive others of fundamental rights. "The costs of nationalism," Levinson asserts, "may simply outweigh whatever putative benefits are thought to be attached to it."[67] Consider the dark side of American nationalism that Jared Goldstein lovingly documents in his study of violent fringe groups committed to racist and xenophobic principles they can plausibly trace back to 1776.[68] Many eighteenth-century Americans were not above invoking nationalism to support ethically dubious if not morally obtuse projects. Levinson observes that we might understand the Declaration as "carefully conceived propaganda to elicit support for a venture that would have perhaps appeared less enticing had it frankly been presented as an attempt to shore up the economic interests of colonial elites or, even more so, of slaveowners worried about certain trends in the mother country concerning the legitimacy of the 'peculiar institution.'"[69]

A different wicked child rejects the American political tradition by failing to identify with the Constitution of the United States in 1787, the Constitution in 2026, or the Declaration in 2026, rather than rejecting out of hand the Declaration of Independence as a statement of eighteenth-century principles. Tom Cutterham discusses the many Americans who have condemned the Constitution in the name of the Declaration. While the "Declaration of Independence set Americans at liberty," he notes, prominent political activists then and now think "the new federal Constitution meant to shackle them again."[70] Anti-federalists begged Americans "to call to mind our glorious Declaration of Independence, read it, and compare it with the Federal Constitution; what a degree of apostacy will you not then discover."[71] Both the Constitution and the Declaration may be outdated, wedded to the political principles of an earlier era.[72] Goldstein plays the wicked child when she observes, "(o)ptimizing the potential human development of all members of society may indeed call forth more from government than the securing of equal legal rights to life, liberty, and the pursuit of happiness."[73]

C.3 THE SIMPLE CHILD

The simple child's placement as third casts doubt on the wisdom of the first child and the wickedness of the second. Children should first learn the Passover

---

[67] Sanford Levinson, "'Popular Sovereignty' and the Declaration of Independence," Chapter 7 in this volume, 103.
[68] Jared Goldstein, *Real Americans: National Identity, Violence, and the Constitution* (Lawrence: University Press of Kansas, 2022).
[69] Levinson, "Popular Sovereignty," 104.
[70] Cutterham, "Constitution," 142.
[71] Cutterham, "Constitution," 146.
[72] Sanford Levinson, *Our Undemocratic Constitution: Where the Constitution Goes Wrong (And How We the People Can Correct It)* (New York: Oxford University Press, 2006).
[73] Goldstein, "Declaration of Independence," 204.

Story or study the Declaration of Independence before making firm commitments to either text or determining to abjure the community that regards the text as sacred. The wise child from the perspective of the simple child is too eager to please and the wicked child is the contrary child, destined to become an academic. The simple child is appropriately cautious, unwilling to make commitments until a fuller account of the commitment is offered.

S. Adam Seagrave provides the simple child with the intellectual background of the Declaration. He emphasizes how Jefferson merged the emphasis on natural law that structured classical political thought with the more liberal understandings that developed during the Enlightenment. Seagrave writes, "the Declaration thus echoed the united voices of the ancients and moderns on the idea of nature's relevance for politics, and highlighted the constructive character of preceding European political thought."[74] The United States, Seagrave notes, was a particularly fruitful environment for thinking about the role of nature. "The American settlers experienced and encountered nature in a way most other Europeans could only imagine,"[75] as the colonists strove to convert a wilderness into civilization and communities rose up from seemingly nowhere. The result in the Declaration is a synthesis between the communal orientation of classical natural law and the individual rights orientation of Locke. The Declaration, Seagrave observes, declares that individuals have rights as individuals but that they revolt against unjust rulers as a community. "It is not the original, equally independent, individual 'men' who have the right to alter and abolish governments, but the 'People' as a unified entity," he points out.[76] Seagrave continues, "The 'People' possess the right of revolution and the individuals composing it possess the rights to life, liberty, and the pursuit of happiness."[77]

Peter Charles Hoffer and Williamjames Hull Hoffer teach the simple child that the Declaration was "a legal document designed to place rebellion on a legal foundation,"[78] whose audience was as much the persons framing the Constitution of Virginia as other colonists, Great Britain, or nations that might support the fledging United States.[79] The Continental Congress was largely staffed by lawyers, all but one member of the committee assigned to write the Declaration were lawyers, Jefferson was a lawyer, the list of grievances resembled a bill in equity, and the signatures at the end reflect the common practice "that legal documents were always signed by the parties responsible for their

---

[74] S. Adam Seagrave, "European Antecedents to the Declaration of Independence," Chapter 1 in this volume, 18.
[75] Seagrave, "European Antecedents," 17.
[76] Seagrave, "European Antecedents," 14.
[77] Seagrave, "European Antecedents," 14.
[78] Peter Charles Hoffer and Williamjames Hull Hoffer, "The Process of Writing and Procedures for Adopting the Declaration," Chapter 3 in this volume, 35.
[79] Hoffer and Hoffer, "Process," 37.

execution."⁸⁰ Contract law provided legal grounds for American independence. If, as the Hoffers point out, "necessity was a legitimate legal ground for breaching [a] contract," then "[n]ecessity" might require "Americans to 'dissolve the bond,' that is, terminate the contract for British nonperformance of its terms."⁸¹ The last paragraph of the Declaration, the Hoffers suggest, is a mini-constitution empowering the Continental Congress to conduct American foreign policy.⁸² The Hoffers explain to the simple children why law structured Jefferson's complaint against the slave trade and provided the reason for omitting that charge. Jefferson accused King George III of piratical warfare, which was illegal under international law.⁸³ The passage was cut in large part because slavery remained legal in all the colonies.⁸⁴ Little harm may have been done from Jefferson's perspective, if, as the Hoffers suggest, Virginia was the main audience for the attack on the slave trade.⁸⁵

Holton's essay explains why the Declaration focuses on King George, rather than on Parliament. He points out that "in the delegates' view, each American colony stood in the same relation to Britain that Scotland had before the Act of Union in 1707: All they shared was a monarch."⁸⁶ While he thinks many grievances better support the wicked child's suspicion that the revolution was initiated by elites seeking power rather than by the oppressed seeking liberty, Holton suggests that Jefferson did subtly include a reference to the slave trade when condemning the Privy Council for vetoing colonial laws. He notes, "of the thirteen North American colonies that would rebel against Britain in 1776, royal officials overturned encroachments on the slave trade in eight."⁸⁷

Crow emphasizes the Declaration as a rhetorical performance that both creates American political identity and establishes a polity worthy to join the global, European family of nations. The phrase, "we hold these truths to be self-evident," implies a "we" whose existence was in doubt in 1776 and arguably remains in doubt in the polarized politics of the present. Crow reminds us that "in the 'we hold' of the Declaration, the 'we' is doing at least as much work as the 'hold.'"⁸⁸ By saying, "this is who we are," Jefferson is in part creating a "we" from a scattered people. The Declaration had to convince a skeptical world that the United States was sufficiently civilized to be a regime empowered to "do all other Acts and Things which Independent States may of right do." Throughout his career, Crow observes, Jefferson had a "felt need to

---

⁸⁰ Hoffer and Hoffer, "Process," 45.
⁸¹ Hoffer and Hoffer, "Process," 41.
⁸² Hoffer and Hoffer, "Process," 45.
⁸³ Hoffer and Hoffer, "Process," 39.
⁸⁴ Hoofer and Hoffer, "Process," 40.
⁸⁵ Hoffer and Hoffer, "Process," 39.
⁸⁶ Holton, "Grievances," 19.
⁸⁷ Holton, "Grievances," 29.
⁸⁸ Crow, "Political Rhetoric," 49.

contest the European idea of American degeneracy."⁸⁹ The legal framing of the Declaration establishes American worthiness by appealing to and demonstrating a mastery of European jurisprudence that displayed a new regime with the character necessary to take a place among the family of nations.⁹⁰

Zuckert provides a guide for the simple child who seeks to understand the ideas that animate the Declaration and, therefore, the commitments entailed by Fourth of July celebrations. Jefferson, in his view, provides a "general theory of political right that is meant to show the colonists to be justified even in the eyes of 'The Supreme Being of the world.'"⁹¹ The "first truth" of equality, Zuckert claims, is that "human beings are not *naturally* subject to the authority of any other human being."⁹² "Life, liberty, and the pursuit of happiness" follow from this principle. Zuckert writes, "(t)he three basic rights together amount to the affirmation of a kind of personal sovereignty, rightful control over one's person, actions, and possessions in the service of one's intents and purposes."⁹³ These rights belong to all human beings. Zuckert informs the simple child that "Jefferson considered the blacks to be men and thus within the meaning of the language of the Declaration,"⁹⁴ and that "it is difficult to deny that women are included, for their basic natural rights are indeed recognized in 1776."⁹⁵ The point of government is, and only is, the simple children must understand, to protect these natural rights. Zuckert insists that, following Locke, the Declaration maintains that "even though all human beings are endowed by nature or God with natural rights, these rights will tend not to be respected by others absent the existence in society of an institution armed with legitimate coercive authority."⁹⁶ Whether any particular government actually protects rights remains for the people and not the government to determine. The continued right of revolution, Zuckert explains to the simple child, follows from the constructed sovereignty of the people who acknowledge that because no natural person has the right to rule, all rule is defeasible when the rulers cease to protect the fundamental rights of the citizenry.⁹⁷

McGraw ties the Declaration closely with the Seder when she claims that "the Declaration can be ... interpreted theologically."⁹⁸ In her view, the Declaration was "the continuance and enlargement of Locke's natural theology as the foundation for equality, liberty, the preservation of life, and the pursuit of happiness."⁹⁹ She asserts that,

---

[89] Crow, "Political Rhetoric," 52.
[90] Crow, "Political Rhetoric," 52–53.
[91] Zuckert," Equality, Liberty, and Rights," 61.
[92] Zuckert, "Equality, Liberty, and Rights," 65.
[93] Zuckert, "Equality, Liberty, and Rights," 67.
[94] Zuckert, "Equality, Liberty, and Rights," 68.
[95] Zuckert, "Equality, Liberty, and Rights," 69.
[96] Zuckert, "Equality, Liberty, and Rights," 70.
[97] Zuckert, "Equality, Liberty, and Rights," 71.
[98] McGraw, "Theological," 123.
[99] McGraw, "Theological," 129.

[i]n the West, liberty and equality emerged as individual rights from theological speculations, derived from the application of natural reason, about the nature of God and human beings and the relationship of human beings to each other and to God. That natural theology assumes a beneficent God who glorifies in what God has created, having made a world in which it is possible for human beings to pursue happiness.[100]

This theological understanding of the Declaration has consequences for the Declaration's principles. McGraw explains that "liberty is not only for one's own preservation and comfort; it is also for the preservation and comfort of others."[101] The freedom of religion is particularly "sacrosanct," she maintains, because "only through free will" can "our actions" "be deemed worthy by God."[102]

The simple child's decision whether to become an American committed to the Declaration of Independence must be influenced by the role that text plays in American political and constitutional development. Just as commitments to judicial review should examine the subsequent history of *Marbury v. Madison*,[103] so no one should stop the clock in 1776 when thinking about whether the United States should continue to be constituted in part by the principles declared in the Declaration of Independence. The Declaration's central role in American abolition, as well as movements for racial, gender, and economic justice count as a reason for making a commitment to that text. That every president cites the Declaration for every cause raises the possibility that the Declaration has become is a mere celebrity citation that is trotted out on holidays but should be ignored when the real work of politics is being done.[104]

Many essays in this volume teach the simple child how the aspirational content of the Declaration of Independence saves the text from the wicked child's critique. Cutterham points to a long tradition in American politics that regards the Declaration of Independence and Constitution of the United States as "essentially compatible and complementary."[105] Each text plays a different vital function in creating a stable, just regime. "If the Constitution implied that the foundations of politics in the United States were now fixed," Cutterham concludes, "then the Declaration offered hope that transformation was still possible."[106] Other essays observe how the Declaration provides principles that enable Americans to keep revolutionary ideals alive. "Following Lincoln, Steele regards the Declaration as setting "up a standard by which we have

---

[100] McGraw, "Theological," 140.
[101] McGraw, "Theological," 127.
[102] McGraw, "Theological," 127.
[103] 5 U.S. 137 (1803).
[104] Graber, "Presidents," 249. See Mark A. Graber, "The Declaration of Independence and Contemporary Constitutional Pedagogy," *Southern California Law Review* 89 (2016): 509, 518–520.
[105] Cutterham, "Constitution," 143.
[106] Cutterham, "Constitution," 153.

evaluated our practices, and more often than not found them wanting."[107] Tsesis writes, "the Declaration provided an aspirational lodestar, providing the focal purpose for movements whose aims expanded the liberal equality promised but imperfectly fulfilled in 1776."[108]

The Declaration provides a guide for political reform as much as a statement of who Americans are in the here and now. Victims of eighteenth-century status hierarchies point to the Declaration as the foundation for their demands for equal treatment. Tsesis states that the Declaration "gave women reason for hope, even though they were then taxed without being granted political representation, and it offered laborers an anti-autocratic message to force through measures for ending exploitation of the workforce."[109] His essay details how the labor movement "was one of the most successful at formulating supportive arguments through the Declaration of Independence's aspirational statements,"[110] and how "the Declaration's breadth of meaning had by the middle of the [nineteenth] century become central to the advocates of woman suffrage."[111] Goldstein points to similar aspirations in her essay on the Declaration and women. With reference to the Seneca Falls Declaration, she writes, "their obvious verbatim copying of large portions of the Declaration of Independence made clear the point that this nation was not living up to the implied promise that the Declaration made to the female half of the population."[112] Justice was just a review of the Declaration away. Steele points out that suffragettes believed that "(o)nce Americans 'get the hang' of the Declaration ... they *will* support woman suffrage."[113]

The Declaration plays this aspirational role in much African American constitutional and political thought. "The Declaration's principles," Davis observes, "touted as America's pride, have been the touchstone of blacks' democratic aspiration."[114] Black reference to the Declaration is as old as the United States. Newman details how the Declaration inspired persons of color to challenge slavery in Revolutionary America and provided the impetus for the decision in the *Quock Walker* case[115] to declare human bondage unconstitutional in Massachusetts.[116] Abolitionist challenges to slavery were grounded in Jefferson's rhetoric. "We believe, too, we have the right to have applied to ourselves those rights named in the Declaration of Independence," African Americans stated during the Civil War.[117] Significantly, Newman notes that

---

[107] Steele, "American Nationalism," 163.
[108] Tsesis, "Aspirational Reliance," 233.
[109] Tsesis, "Aspirational Reliance," 220.
[110] Tsesis, "Aspirational Reliance," 221.
[111] Tsesis, "Aspirational Reliance," 230.
[112] Goldstein, "Declaration of Independence," 213.
[113] Steele, "American Nationalism," 165, original emphasis.
[114] Davis, "Declaration," 201.
[115] *Commonwealth* v. *Jennison* (unreported, Massachusetts, 1783).
[116] Newman, "Slavery," 119.
[117] Davis, "Declaration," 191.

Confederates repudiated the Declaration when fashioning a government explicitly for white people only.[118] "[A]ny criticism of Jefferson today about slavery," McGraw agrees," "is really an affirmation of the principles he declared."[119]

African Americans continued to lean on the Declaration after emancipation. Davis points to one of Douglass' last speeches, in which the abolitionist asked, "whether the American people have loyalty enough, honor enough, patriotism enough, to live up to their own constitution."[120] Section One of the Fourteenth Amendment reflects African American commitment to the principles stated in the Declaration. Black nationalists rallied to the Declaration when asserting sovereignty rights. Marcus Garvey's "Declaration of the Rights of the Negro Peoples of the World" justified a black separatist movement by declaring: "Be it known to all men that ... all men are created equal and entitled to the rights of life, liberty, and the pursuit of happiness."[121] The contemporary civil rights movement remains grounded in the aspirational commitment to "all men are created equal." Steele observes how "Martin Luther King was fond of calling the Declaration a 'promissory note' that had yet to be fully honored,"[122] and that the Declaration provided a "lingua franca that could express their [long-standing] aspirations for liberty."[123]

C.4 THE SILENT CHILD

The Declaration does not speak to the silent child who does not know how or does not want to ask a question. Children have many reasons to be silent during the Seder or Fourth of July celebration. They are hungry and want to eat. There may be nothing of contemporary interest to ask about an eighteenth-century document. Their questions may not be appropriate for the occasion. One cannot ask what is entailed by a commitment to the "one united people" announced in the Declaration if that one united people does not exist.

The silent child has reason to believe that eating apple pie and corn on the cob makes for a more fruitful Fourth of July than discussing philosophical questions about the Declaration of Independence. By appealing to all Americans, the Declaration may not be of much use to any American. Crow notes, "Today, the Declaration of Independence is the product of substantive and consequential reflection from many people in many different contexts on the power of language to summon available historical experience in the service of politics in the present."[124] If the Declaration can be invoked by "many people in many

---

[118] Newman, "Slavery," 122.
[119] McGraw, "Theological," 141.
[120] Davis, "Declaration," 190.
[121] Ambar, "The 'Stubborn' Declaration," 79.
[122] Steele, "American Nationalism," 166.
[123] Steele, "American Nationalism," 164.
[124] Crow, "Political Rhetoric," 46.

different contexts," children may learn more about their parents from parental lectures on the Declaration than about the Declaration. Eighteenth-century texts may be unresponsive to the problems of the present. Levinson maintains, "it should be obvious that the Declaration does not solve the problem of deep pluralism" that haunts the contemporary United States.[125] Goldstein suggests the Declaration says nothing about the changing in the structure of families that many feminists believe is central to human equality.[126] Again, that was then, this is now. Crow concludes that the "world of the Declaration is an existential one where we are left responsible for politics and justice, where no power of heaven or earth but our own can reliably promise much of anything in so far as our lives together in politics are concerned."[127] If so, let us just eat and leave speculation about the Declaration to eighteenth-century antiquarians.

The silent child may think the revolutionary force of the Declaration has been spent for at least a century. Such basic liberal commitments as "civil peace, material prosperity through economic growth, scientific progress, and rational liberty,"[128] were controversial when the Second Continental Congress was meeting in 1776. Jefferson's claim that "Governments are instituted among Men" to protect individual rights was a blow against claims that the point of government was to spread the one true religion or enrich noble families. The next 250 years witnessed the triumph of liberalism, at least in American rhetorical practice. In 2026, all parties claim to derive their principles from the Declaration. Hence, no one gains the upper hand or makes converts by appealing to the spirit of 1776. Pro-life advocates who chant "all men are created equal" to women who believe abortion rights are necessary for gender equality in contemporary polities are no more likely to be convincing than pro-choice advocates who chant the same phrase to women who believe the unborn have the same right to life as the born.

Other texts take off where the Declaration ends. A longstanding debate exists over who declared independence in 1776. Lincoln insisted the Declaration of Independence was approved by the United States as a corporate entity. Levinson observes that "the 'first Constitution' of the new country, was named the Articles of Confederation, ... announcing an alliance" of presumable independent regimes "against powerful outside threats."[129] The Declaration, which both speaks of "these united colonies" and "free and independent states," is ambiguous. The documents more worth interrogating, the silent child may think, are those associated with the Second Founding, most notably the Supreme Court's decision in *Texas* v. *White*, which speaks of

---

[125] Levinson, "Popular Sovereignty," 108.
[126] See Goldstein, "Declaration of Independence," 217.
[127] Crow, "Political Rhetoric," 56.
[128] Rogers M. Smith, *Liberalism and American Constitutional Law* (Cambridge: Harvard University Press, 1980), 18.
[129] Levinson, "Popular Sovereignty," 98.

"an indestructible Union, composed of indestructible states."[130] Such texts, however, are not up for discussion on the Fourth of July. Perhaps we need a different holiday.

The Declaration seems an exemplar of what Ian Shapiro refers to as "gross concepts,"[131] the meaning of which depend on contested value and fact judgments. Zuckert worries about gross concepts when he observes that, "ripped from its context …, the equality proposition is rendered quite indeterminate in meaning and becomes subject to this great variety of interpretive and political appropriations."[132] Douglas Rae points out the infinite number of means for implementing "all men are created equal."[133] Faced with this myriad possible interpretations of "equality," Zuckert calls for the "real work" necessary to recover the Declaration's distinctive understanding.[134] Perhaps that is too much for a family Seder or national election. The silent child's decision not to ask questions may stem from beliefs that persons and nations are often better off stumbling through life without paying much attention to first principles.

A similar concern with first principles may explain why the child who has been taught that religion, sex, and politics are not to be discussed at the kitchen table is reluctant to ask certain questions at the Seder or Fourth of July celebration for fear of spoiling the occasion. Constitutional minimalists maintain that not raising questions about first principles preserves the peace when people who disagree on fundamentals nevertheless might agree on what should be done in the immediate future.[135] Asking about the role of religion threatens an imbroglio that will undermine the atmosphere for the celebratory feast that is to follow. McGraw will explain to the children the vital role God plays in human rights. Levinson will urge the children to interpret the Declaration as substituting human for divine authority. He states, "The Declaration does … notably refer to a 'Creator,' … but, … one might believe that [this has] not been treated as its most important messages."[136] The result will be a lengthy argument, in which little progress is likely to be made other than to ruin everyone's appetite for the delicious dinner the host and hostess have meticulously cooked.

Levinson channels the silent child when claiming the Declaration provides no good answer to the identity of the "people" the Declaration purports to constitute. His essay asks, "who is imagined as part of the presumptively 'sovereign people'" that Jefferson declared to be independent and, "Does the Declaration provide a helpful answer with regard to defining the *demos* presumably

---

[130] *Texas v. White*, 74 U.S. 700, 725 (1869).
[131] Ian Shapiro, "Gross Concepts in Political Argument," *Political Theory* 17.1 (1989): 51.
[132] Zuckert, "Equality, Liberty, and Rights," 63.
[133] Douglas Rae, *Equalities* (Cambridge: Harvard University Press, 1983).
[134] Zuckert, "Equality, Liberty, and Rights," 66.
[135] See Cass R. Sunstein, *One Case at a Time: Judicial Minimalism on the Supreme Court* (Cambridge: Harvard University Press, 2001).
[136] Levinson, "Popular Sovereignty," 92.

Four Children, Sixteen Essays, and the Declaration

underlying any given democratic government?"[137] Levinson concludes the Declaration not worthy of study on this point. "At no point," he states, "does the Declaration offer any explicit description of the 'one people.'"[138] Whether and why Americans are one people is as mysterious. Levinson maintains that Jefferson's text "does not offer anything by way of argument as to why this should be thought to be true, other ... than the common oppression 'we' are said to have suffered under King George."[139] He concludes, "there was in fact no 'united people.'"[140] If so, the silent child is merely pointing out that no questions can be asked about the constitutional and political identity of that united people that might provide the wise child with the commitments entailed by the Declaration of Independence.

C.5 TELLING THE STORY

That peoples are fashioned by stories is commonplace in political science and in political theory.[141] Steele reminds all the children that "nations, selves, religions, families, are actually constituted by narratives told and retold and acted upon into the indefinite future."[142] The Declaration is as central to the American story as the Exodus is to Jewish identity. That American identity was no more firmly established in 1776 than in 2026. What the Declaration means and how American identity is constituted is always partly for the future to determine. As Lincoln hoped and Steele points out, the Declaration in the United States remains "a work in progress, constantly labored for and constantly (only) approximated."[143]

Americans without the Declaration of Independence would not be Americans. The silent child cannot ask a question about any new American identity in large part because the Declaration so constitutes Americans that imaging an American identity shorn of the Declaration is impossible. The Declaration serves as a constant rebuke to American failings while remaining the most reliable guide to redemption. Ambar rightly concludes, "(t)o remove 'all men are created equal' from the Declaration would be to remove irony from the American experience – and also, its greatest source of hope."[144] The best Fourth of July celebrations, like the best Passover Seders, are grounded in a faith that our children, wise, wicked, simple, and silent, will be inspired to fulfill the

---

[137] Levinson, "Popular Sovereignty," 93.
[138] Levinson, "Popular Sovereignty," 94.
[139] Levinson, "Popular Sovereignty," 100.
[140] Levinson, "Popular Sovereignty," 104.
[141] See Benedict Anderson, *Imagined Communities: Reflections on the Origin and Spread of Nationalism* (London: Version, 1983); Rogers M. Smith, *Stories of Peoplehood: The Politics and Morals of Political Membership* (New York: Cambridge University Press, 2003).
[142] Steele, "American Nationalism," 158.
[143] Steele, "American Nationalism," 155.
[144] Ambar, "The 'Stubborn' Declaration," 89.

promises made by the Declaration rather than engage in self-congratulatory speeches about ancestral triumphs over past evils amid ongoing present injustice. Jewish children are taught that, "it is not up to you to finish the task, but you are not free to abandon it."[145] Steele in that vein concludes, "[T]he story the Declaration tells has always appealed to whatever 'better angels' we have and constituted our peoplehood in history. Lose the story and it is hard to say what Americans will become."[146]

---

[145] Janice Prager and Arlene Lepoff, *Why Be Different? A Look into Judaism* (Springfield, NJ: Behrman House, Inc., 1986).

[146] Steele, "American Nationalism," 168.

Bibliography

Ablavsky, Gregory. "Species of Sovereignty: Native Nationhood, the United States, and International Law, 1783–1795." *Journal of American History* 106, no. 3 (2019): 591–613.
Abram, Susan M. *Forging a Cherokee-American Alliance in the Creek War: From Creation to Betrayal.* Tuscaloosa: University of Alabama Press, 2015.
Alexander, Leslie, and Michelle Wallace. "Fear." In *The 1619 Project*, edited by Nikole Hannah-Jones et al., rev. ed. New York: One World, 2021.
Allen, Danielle. *Our Declaration: A Reading of the Declaration of Independence in Defense of Equality.* New York: Liveright, 2014.
Amar, Akhil. *America's Unwritten Constitution: The Precedents and Principles We Live By.* New York: Basic Books, 2012.
Ambar, Saladin. *Malcolm X at Oxford Union.* Oxford: Oxford University Press, 2014.
Ambar, Saladin. *Stars and Shadows: The Politics of Interracial Friendship from Jefferson to Obama.* Oxford: Oxford University Press, 2022.
Anderson, Benedict. *Imagined Communities: Reflections on the Origin and Spread of Nationalism.* London: Verso, 1983.
Anderson, Mark R. *The Battle for the Fourteenth Colony: America's War of Liberation in Canada, 1774–1776.* Lebanon: University Press of New England, 2013.
The Annual Register, or, a View of the History, Politicks, and Literature for the Year 1763. London: Printed for R. and J. Dodsley, 1764.
Arendt, Hannah. "The Crisis in Culture." In *Between Past and Future*, 219–220. New York: Penguin Books, 1977.
Arendt, Hannah. *Eichmann in Jerusalem: A Report on the Banality of Evil.* New York: Viking, 1963.
Arendt, Hannah. *The Human Condition.* Chicago: University of Chicago Press, 1958.
Arendt, Hannah. *On Revolution.* New York: Penguin Books, 2006.
Arendt, Hannah. "Truth and Politics." In *Between Past and Future*, 223–259. New York: Penguin Books, 1977.
Armitage, David. *The Declaration of Independence: A Global History.* Cambridge, MA: Harvard University Press, 2008.

Armour, William. Manumission of Cudjoe Thompson. January 1, 1800. *Slavery Papers*, Delaware Public Archives. https://archives.delaware.gov/african-american-history-month/african-american-history-month-3/slavery-papers/.

Ashcraft, Richard. *Revolutionary Politics and Locke's "Two Treatises of Government."* Princeton: Princeton University Press, 1986.

Azerrad, David. "What the Constitution Really Says about Race and Slavery." *Heritage Foundation*, December 28, 2015. www.heritage.org/the-constitution/commentary/what-the-constitution-really-says-about-race-and-slavery.

Bailyn, Bernard. *The Barbarous Years: The Conflict of Civilizations, 1600–1675.* New York: Alfred A. Knopf, 2012.

Bailyn, Bernard. *The Ideological Origins of the American Revolution.* Cambridge, MA: Harvard University Press, 1967; enlarged ed., 1994.

Bailyn, Bernard. *The Ideological Origins of the American Revolution.* Cambridge, MA: Belknap Press of Harvard University Press, 1976.

Bailyn, Bernard. "Political Experience and Enlightenment Ideas in Eighteenth-Century America." In *The Reinterpretation of the American Revolution: 1764–1789*, edited by Jack P. Greene, 277–290. New York: Harper and Row, 1968.

Baker, Ella. "Developing Community Leadership." In *Black Women in White America: A Documentary History*, edited by Gerda Lerner. New York: Vintage Books, 1973.

Baldwin, Simeon. *An Oration Pronounced ... July 4, 1788, in Commemoration of the Declaration of Independence and Establishment of the Constitution.* New Haven, CT: J. Meigs, 1788.

Balibar, Etienne. "The Nation Form: History and Ideology." In *Race, Nation, Class: Ambiguous Identities*, edited by Etienne Balibar and Immanuel Wallerstein, 86–106. London: Verso, 1991.

Banning, Lance. "Republican Ideology and the Triumph of the Constitution, 1789 to 1793." *William and Mary Quarterly* 31, no. 2 (April 1974): 167–188.

Barnett, Randy E. "We the People: Each and Every One." *Yale Law Journal* 123 (2014): 2576.

Bay, Mia, Michael Kazin and Joseph McCartin eds., *See Your Declaration, Americans!* Americanism: New Perspectives, 2006.

Becker, Carl L. *The Declaration of Independence.* New York: Alfred A. Knopf, 1948.

Becker, Carl L. *The Declaration of Independence: A Study in the History of Political Ideas.* New York: Vintage Books, 1959.

Becker, Carl. *The Declaration of Independence.* New York: Harcourt, 1922.

Becker, Carl. *The Declaration of Independence: A Study in the History of Political Ideas.* New York: Alfred A. Knopf, 1942.

Beeman, Richard. *Our Lives, Our Fortunes, and Our Sacred Honor: The Forging of American Independence, 1774–1776.* New York: Basic Books, 2013.

Bell, Derrick. *The Derrick Bell Reader.* Edited by Richard Delgado and Jean Stefanic. New York: New York University Press, 2005.

Bellah, Robert. *Religion in Human Evolution.* Cambridge, MA: Harvard University Press, 2011.

Benezet, Anthony. "A Caution and Warning to the Great Britain." In the digital collection Evans Early American Imprint Collection. https://name.umdl.umich.edu/

No8023.0001.001. University of Michigan Library Digital Collections. Philadelphia, 1766.
Benezet, Anthony. *Some Historical Account of Guinea*. Philadelphia: Printed by Joseph Crukshank, 1771.
Bergh, Albert Ellery, ed. *Writings of Thomas Jefferson*. Vol. 6. Washington, DC: Jefferson Memorial Society, 1903.
Bergh, Albert Ellery, ed. *Writings of Thomas Jefferson*. Vol. 15. Washington, DC: Jefferson Memorial Society, 1907.
Bestes, Peter, et al. "Petition 'In Behalf of a Fellow Slaves in This Province.'" In *A Documentary History of the Negro People in the United States*, vol. 1, edited by Herbert Aptheker. New York: Citadel, 1951.
Bilberry, Benajmin. "To the Honorable Speaker and Gentlemen of the Assembly." November 11, 1780. Race and Slavery Petitions Project. https://library.uncg.edu/slavery/petitions/details.aspx?pid=2201.
Black, Charles. *A New Birth of Freedom: Human Rights, Named and Unnamed*. New Haven, CT: Yale University Press, 1997.
Blackhawk, Maggie. "On Power & Indian Country." *Women & Law* 39, no. 1 (2020): 39–54.
Blight, David W. *Frederick Douglass: Prophet of Freedom*. New York: Simon and Schuster, 2018.
Bloom, Joshua, and Waldo E. Martin Jr. *Black against Empire: The History of the Black Panther Party*. Oakland: University of California Press, 2016.
Boles, John. *Jefferson, Architect of American Liberty*. New York: Basic Books, 2017.
Boulware, Tyler. *Deconstructing the Cherokee Nation: Town, Region, and Nation among the Eighteenth-Century Cherokees*. Gainesville: University Press of Florida, 2011.
Bouton, Terry. *Taming Democracy: "The People," the Founders, and the Troubled Ending of the American Revolution*. New York: Oxford University Press, 2007.
Boyd, Julian P. *The Declaration of Independence: The Evolution of the Text*. Princeton: Princeton University Press, 1945.
Boyd, Julian P., ed. *Papers of Jefferson*. Vol. 1. Princeton: Princeton University Press, 1950.
Boylan, Anne M. *Women's Rights in the United States: A History in Documents*. New York: Oxford University Press, 2016.
Bracey, Earnest N. *Fannie Lou Hamer: The Life of the Civil Rights Icon*. Jefferson, NC: McFarland, 2011.
Bradford, William. "Another Such Victory and We Are Done: A Call to an American Indian Declaration of Independence." *Tulsa Law Review* 40, no. 1 (2004): 1–76.
Brewer, Holly. "Slavery, Sovereignty, and 'Inheritable Blood': Reconsidering John Locke and the Origins of American Slavery." *American Historical Review* 122, no. 4 (October 2017): 1038–1078.
Brooks, Maegan Parker, and Davis W. Houck, eds. *The Speeches of Fannie Lou Hamer: To Tell It like It Is*. Jackson: University Press of Mississippi, 2011.
Brooks, Roy L., ed. *When Sorry Isn't Enough: The Controversy over Apologies for Reparations for Human Injustice*. New York: New York University Press, 1999.
Brown, Vincent. *Tacky's Rebellion: The Story of an Atlantic Slave War*. Cambridge, MA: Harvard University Press, 2021.

Brueggemann, Walter. *The Prophetic Imagination*. 2nd ed. Minneapolis: Fortress, 2001.
Bruyneel, Kevin. "Challenging American Boundaries: Indigenous People and the 'Gift' of U.S. Citizenship." *Studies in American Political Development* 18, no.1 (2004): 30–43.
Burnaby, Andrew. *Travels through the Middle Settlements in North-America*. Dublin: Cornell University Press, 1775.
Burnard, Trevor. *Jamaica in the Age of the American Revolution*. Philadelphia: University of Pennsylvania Press, 2020.
Butler, Melissa. "Early Liberal Roots of Feminism." *American Political Science Review* 72 (1978): 135–150.
Butterfield, L. H., ed. *Adams Papers*. Vol. 4. Cambridge, MA: Belknap Press of Harvard University Press, 1973.
Calhoun, Craig. *Nations Matter: Culture, History, and the Cosmopolitan Dream*. New York: Routledge, 2007.
Calloway, Colin G. *The American Revolution in Indian Country: Crisis and Diversity in Native American Communities*. New York: Cambridge University Press, 1995.
Calloway, Colin G. *First Peoples: A Documentary Survey of American Indian History*. 5th ed. Boston: Bedford/St. Martin's, 2016.
Calloway, Colin G. *Pen and Ink Witchcraft: Treaties and Treaty Making in American Indian History*. New York: Oxford University Press, 2013.
Carbado, Devon W. "Critical What What?" *Connecticut Law Review* 43, no. 5 (2011): 1593–1643, 2011. UCLA School of Law Research Paper No. 11-28. https://ssrn.com/abstract=1919716.
Carson, Clayborne, and Kris Shepard, eds. *A Call to Conscience: The Landmark Speeches of Dr. Martin Luther King, Jr.* New York: Warner Books, 2001.
Carson, Clayborne, and Peter Holloran, eds. *A Knock at Midnight: Inspiration from the Great Sermons of Reverend Martin Luther King, Jr.* New York: Warner Books, 1998.
Carter, Clarence Edwin, ed. *The Correspondence of General Thomas Gage*. 2 vols. Hamden: Archon Books, 1969.
Castillo, Thomas A. *Working in the Magic City: Moral Economy in Early Twentieth-Century Miami*. Champaign: University of Illinois Press, 2022.
Catt, Carrie Chapman. *An Address to the Congress of the United States*. Archives of Women's Political Communication, Iowa State University. New York, 1917.
Cattelino, Jessica. *High Stakes: Florida Seminole Gaming and Sovereignty*. Durham, NC: Duke University Press, 2008.
Caughey, John Walton. *McGillivray of the Creeks*. Norman: University of Oklahoma Press, 1938.
Child, Brenda J. *Boarding School Seasons: American Indian Families, 1900–1940*. Lincoln: University of Nebraska Press, 1998.
Cicero, Marcus Tullius. *De Re Publica*. Translated by C. W. Keyes. Cambridge, MA: Harvard University Press, 1970.
Coates, Ta-Nehisi. "The Case for Reparations." *The Atlantic*, June 2014.
Cobb, Daniel M. *Native Activism in Cold War America: The Struggle for Sovereignty*. Lawrence: University Press of Kansas, 2008.
Cobb, Jelani. "The Man behind Critical Race Theory." *The New Yorker*, September 20, 2021.

Cocola, Jim. "The Ideological Spaces of the Academical Village: A Reading of the Central Grounds at the University of Virginia." http://faculty.virginia.edu/villagespaces/essay/#02e.

Colden, Cadwallader. *The History of the Five Indian Nations, Depending on the Province of New-York in America: A Critical Edition.* Ithaca, NY: Cornell University Press, 2017.

Colon-Rios, Jose. *Constituent Power and the Law.* Oxford: Oxford University Press, 2020.

Colored Citizens of Queen's County, N.Y. "Newtown Meeting." *The Liberator* (September 12, 1862). In *A Documentary History of the Negro People in the United States*, vol. 1, edited by Herbert Aptheker. New York: Citadel Press, 1951.

Commager, Henry Steele. *Jefferson, Nationalism, and the Enlightenment.* New York: George Braziller, 1975.

Constitutions Resource Center, Native Nations Institute. https://nniconstitutions.arizona.edu/.

Cooper, Anna J. *A Voice from the South by a Black Woman of the South.* Chapel Hill: University of North Carolina Press, 2017.

Cooper, Kody W., and Justin Buckley Dyer. "Thomas Jefferson, Nature's God, and the Theological Foundations of Natural-Rights Republicanism." *Politics and Religion* 10, no. 3(2017): 662–688.

Cornell, Saul. *The Other Founders: Anti-Federalists and the Dissenting Tradition in America, 1788–1828.* Chapel Hill: University of North Carolina Press, 1999.

Cotlar, Seth. *Tom Paine's America: The Rise and Fall of Transatlantic Radicalism in the Early American Republic.* Charlottesville: University of Virginia Press, 2011.

Cox, Richard. Introduction to *Second Treatise of Government*, by John Locke, edited by Richard Cox. Wheeling, IL: Harlan Davidson, 1982.

Crenshaw, Kimberlé Williams. "Twenty Years of Critical Race Theory: Looking Back to Move Forward Commentary: Critical Race Theory: A Commemoration: Lead Article." *Connecticut Law Review* 117 (2011).

Crow, Matthew. *Thomas Jefferson, Legal History, and the Art of Recollection.* Cambridge: Cambridge University Press, 2017.

Cruse, Harold. *The Crisis of the Negro Intellectual.* New York: New York Review of Books, 2005.

Cushing, William. "Legal Notes." *Massachusetts Historical Society.* www.masshist.org/database/viewer.php?item_id=630&br=1.

Dangerfield, George. *The Awakening of American Nationalism.* New York: Harper and Row, 1965.

Davis, Angela Y. *Freedom Is a Constant Struggle: Ferguson, Palestine, and the Foundations of a Movement.* Chicago: Haymarket Books, 2016.

Davis, David Brion. *The Problem of Slavery in the Age of Revolution, 1770–1823.* Ithaca, NY: Cornell University Press, 1976.

Davis, Derek H. "Completing the Constitution: Religion, Rights, and the Fourteenth Amendment." In *The Wiley-Blackwell Companion to Religion and Politics in the U.S.*, edited by Barbara A. McGraw, 213–224. West Sussex: Wiley, 2016.

Davis, J. C., et al. "An Appeal from the Colored Men of Philadelphia to the President of the United States." In *A Documentary History of the Negro People in the United States*, vol. 1, edited by Herbert Aptheker. New York: Citadel Press, 1951.

Davis, Jefferson. *The Papers of Jefferson Davis*. Vol. 7. Edited by Lynda Laswell Crist and Mary Seaton Dix. Baton Rouge: Louisiana State University Press, 1992.

Declaration of Indian Purpose. The Voice of the American Indian. The American Indian Chicago Conference at The University of Chicago, June 13–20, 1961.

Deer, Sarah. *The Beginning and End of Rape: Confronting Sexual Violence in Native America*. Minneapolis: University of Minnesota Press, 2015.

Delany, Martin R. *The Conditions, Elevation, Emigration and Destiny of the Colored People of the United States*. Amherst, NY: Humanity Books, 2004.

Deloria, Vine, Jr. *Behind the Trail of Broken Treaties: An Indian Declaration of Independence*. Austin: University of Texas Press, 1974.

Dennis, Matthew. *Red, White, and Blue Letter Days*. Ithaca, NY: Cornell University Press, 2002.

Dennison, Jean. *Colonial Entanglement: Constituting a Twenty-First Century Osage Nation*. Chapel Hill: University of North Carolina Press, 2012.

Deposition of Dr. William Pasteur In Regard to the Removal of Powder from the Williamsburg Magazine," *Virginia Magazine of History and Biography* 13 (1905), 49.

Derrida, Jacques. "Declarations of Independence." *New Political Science*, no. 15 (Summer 1986): 7–15. www-personal.umich.edu/~alisse/PDFs/Derrida.pdf.

Desjardin, Thomas A. *Through a Howling Wilderness: Benedict Arnold's March to Quebec, 1775*. New York: St. Martin's Griffin, 2007.

Detweiler, Philip. "Congressional Debate on Slavery and the Declaration of Independence, 1819–1821." *American Historical Review* 63 (April 1958): 598–616.

Diamond, Martin. "The Declaration and the Constitution: Liberty, Democracy, and the Founders." *The Public Interest* 41 (Fall 1975): 39–55.

Diggins, John Patrick. *On Hallowed Ground: Abraham Lincoln and the Foundations of American History*. New Haven, CT: Yale University Press, 2000.

Documents of the American Revolution 1770–1783. Vol. 11. Edited by K.G. Davies. Shannon: Irish University Press, 1972–1981.

Douglass, Frederick. "The Right to Criticize American Institutions" In *The Life and Writings of Frederick Douglass*, edited by Philip S. Foner. New York: International Publishers, 1950.

Douglass, Frederick. *Selected Speeches and Writings*. Edited by Philip S. Foner and Yuval Taylor. Chicago: Chicago Review Press, 2000.

Douglass, Frederick. "Speech at Colored American Day, 25 August 1893." In *All the World Is Here! The Black Presence at White City*, edited by Christopher Robert Reed. Bloomington: Indiana University Press, 2000.

Douglass, Frederick. "What to the Slave Is the 4th of July." In *Great Speeches by Frederick Douglass*, edited by James Daley, 26–47. Mineola, NY: Dover, 2013.

Douglass, Frederick. "What to the Slave Is the Fourth of July?" *Speech*, July 5, 1852. Teaching American History. https://teachingamericanhistory.org/document/what-to-the-slave-is-the-fourth-of-july/

Dowd, Gregory Evans. *A Spirited Resistance: The North American Indian Struggle for Unity, 1745–1815*. Baltimore: Johns Hopkins University Press, 1993.

Du Bois, W. E. B. *Papers*. Special Collections and University Archives, University of Massachusetts Amherst Libraries.

Du Bois, W. E. B. *The Souls of Black Folk*. New York: Norton, 2007.

Dubois, Laurent. *Avengers of the New World*. New York: Dial, 2004.

Dumbauld, Edward. *Thomas Jefferson and the Law*. Norman: University of Oklahoma Press, 1978.
Dunn, John. "The Politics of Locke in England and America in the Eighteenth Century." In *John Locke: Problems and Perspectives*, edited by John Yolton, 45–80. Cambridge: Cambridge University Press, 1969.
Dunn, John. "What Is Living and What Is Dead in the Political Theory of John Locke?" In *Interpreting Political Responsibility: Essays, 1981–1989*, 9–25. Princeton, NJ: Princeton University Press, 1990.
Duthu, Bruce. *Shadow Nations: Tribal Sovereignty and the Limits of Legal Pluralism*. New York: Oxford University Press, 2013.
DuVal, Kathleen. *Independence Lost: Lives on the Edge of the American Revolution*. New York: Random House, 2015.
Dworetz, Steven. *The Unvarnished Doctrine: Locke, Liberalism, and the American Revolution*. Durham, NC: Duke University Press, 1988.
Edling, Max. *A Revolution in Favor of Government: Origins of the U.S. Constitution and the Making of the American State*. New York: Oxford University Press, 2003.
Egerton, Douglas. *Death or Liberty: African Americans and Revolutionary America*. New York: Oxford University Press, 2009.
Elkins, Stanley, and Eric McKitrick. *The Age of Federalism: The Early American Republic, 1788–1800*. New York: Oxford University Press, 1993.
Elliot, Jonathan, ed. *The Debates of the Several State Conventions on the Adoption of the Federal Constitution*. Pub. under the sanction of Congress. (1836), 5 vols. Washington, DC, 1836.
Ellis, Joseph. "Clash of the Titans." *New York Times*, March 10, 2002. www.nytimes.com/2002/03/10/books/clash-of-the-titans.html.
Ellison, Ralph. *Invisible Man*. New York: Vintage Books, 1995.
Epstein, Richard A. *Principles for a Free Society: Reconciling Individual Liberty with the Common Good*. Cambridge, MA: Perseus, 1998.
Evans, George H. "The Working Men's Declaration of Independence." *Working Man's Advocate* (New York) and *Mechanic's Free Press of Philadelphia*, 1829. www.trinityhistory.org/AmH/WM%20declaration.pdf.
Everett, Edward. *A Lecture on the Working Men's Party: First Delivered October Sixth, Before the Charlestown Lyceum* (Boston). Boston, MA: Gray and Bowen, 1830.
Fehrenbacher, Don E. *Slavery, Law, and Politics: The Dred Scott Case in Historical Perspective*. New York: Oxford University Press, 1981.
Feldman, Noah. *The Broken Constitution: Lincoln, Slavery, and the Refounding of America*. New York: Farrar, Straus and Giroux, 2021.
Fish, Stanley. "Interpreting the Variorum." In *Is There a Text in This Class? The Authority of Interpretative Communities*, 147–173. Cambridge, MA: Harvard University Press, 1988.
Fishkin, Joseph, and William E. Forbath. "Wealth, Commonwealth, and the Constitution of Opportunity." *Nomos* 58 (2017): 45–124.
Fitzpatrick, John C. *The Spirit of the Revolution: New Light from Some of the Original Sources of American History*. Boston, MA: Houghton Mifflin, 1924.
Fliegelman, Jay. *Declaring Independence: Jefferson, Natural Language, and the Culture of Performance*. Stanford, CA: Stanford University Press, 1993.

Fliegelman, Jay. *Prodigals and Pilgrims: The American Revolution against Patriarchal Authority 1750–1800*. Cambridge, UK: Cambridge University Press, 1985.
Fogelson, Raymond D. "Who Were the Ani-Kutani? An Excursion into Cherokee Historical Thought." *Ethnohistory* 31, no. 1 (1984): 255–263.
Foner, Eric. *The Fiery Trial: Abraham Lincoln and American Slavery*. New York: Norton, 2010.
Foner, Eric. *Give Me Liberty!* 5th ed. New York: Norton, 2017.
Foner, Eric. *Reconstruction: America's Unfinished Revolution, 1863–1877*. New York: Harper and Row, 1988.
Foner, Eric. *The Second Founding: How the Civil War and Reconstruction Remade the Constitution*. New York: Norton, 2019.
Foner, Eric. *The Story of American Freedom*. New York: Norton, 1998.
Foner, Philip S., ed. *We, the Other People: Alternative Declarations of Independence by Labor Groups, Farmers, Woman's Rights Advocates, Socialists, and Blacks, 1829–1975*. Urbana: University of Illinois Press, 1976.
Forbes, Robert, ed. *Notes on the State of Virginia: An Annotated Edition*. New Haven, CT: Yale University Press, 2022.
Fourth Annual Report of the Board of Managers of the New-England Anti-slavery Society, January 20, 1836. Boston, MA: Isaac Knapp, 1836.
Franklin, Benjamin. *A Narrative of the Late Massacres, in Lancaster County, of a Number of Indians, Friends of This Province, by Persons Unknown. With Some Observations on the Same*. Philadelphia, PA: Anthony Armbrüster, 1764.
Freeman, Joanne, and Johann Neem, eds. *Jeffersonians in Power: The Rhetoric of Opposition Meets the Realities of Governing*. Charlottesville: University of Virginia Press, 2019.
Garrison, Tim Alan. *The Legal Ideology of Removal: The Southern Judiciary and the Sovereignty of Native American Nations*. Athens: University of Georgia Press, 2002.
Garrison, William Lloyd. "Declaration of the National Anti-Slavery Convention." In *William Lloyd Garrison and the Fight against Slavery: Selections from The Liberator*, edited by William E. Cain. Boston: St Martin's, 1995.
Garvey, Marcus. *Selected Writings and Speeches of Marcus Garvey*. Edited by Bob Blaisdell. Mineola, NY: Dover, 2004.
Gienapp, Jonathan. "In Search of Nationhood at the Founding." *Fordham Law Review* 89 (2021): 1783.
Gienapp, Jonathan. *The Second Creation: Fixing the American Constitution in the Founding Era*. Cambridge, MA: Harvard University Press, 2018.
Gilhooley, Simon J. *The Antebellum Origins of the Modern Constitution: Slavery and the Spirit of the American Founding*. New York: Cambridge University Press, 2020.
Goen, C. C. *Revivalism and Separatism in New England, 1740–1800*. Middleton, CT: Wesleyan University Press, 1987.
Goldstein, Jared. *Real Americans: National Identity, Violence, and the Constitution*. Lawrence: University Press of Kansas, 2022.
Goldstein, Leslie F. *The Constitutional Rights of Women*. 2nd ed. Madison: University of Wisconsin Press, 1988.
Gordon, Ann, ed. *The Selected Papers of Elizabeth Cady Stanton and Susan B. Anthony*. Vol. 1. New Brunswick, NJ: Rutgers University Press, 1997.

Gordon-Reed, Annette. *The Hemingses of Monticello: An American Family*. New York: Norton, 2008.
Gornick, Vivian, and Barbara Moran, eds. *Woman in Sexist Society: Studies in Power and Powerlessness*. New York: Basic Books, 1971.
Gould, Eliga H. *Among the Powers of the Earth: The American Revolution and the Making of a New World Empire*. Cambridge, MA: Harvard University Press, 2010.
Gourevitch, Alex. *From Slavery to the Cooperative Commonwealth: Labor and Republican Liberty in the Nineteenth Century*. New York: Cambridge University Press, 2015.
Graber, Mark A. "The Declaration of Independence and Contemporary Constitutional Pedagogy." *Southern California Law Review* 89, no. 3 (2016): 509–539.
Green, Michael D. *The Politics of Indian Removal: Creek Government and Society in Crisis*. Lincoln: University of Nebraska Press, 1982.
Greene, Jack P. *The Constitutional Origins of the American Revolution*. Cambridge: Cambridge University Press, 2010.
Griffin, Patrick. *American Leviathan: Empire, Nation, and Revolutionary Frontier*. New York: Hill and Wang, 2007.
Grillot, Thomas. *First Americans: U.S. Patriotism in Indian Country after World War I*. New Haven, CT: Yale University Press, 2018.
Grotius, Hugo. *De Jure Belli ac Pacis Libri Tres*. Translated by Francis W. Kelsey et al. 2 vols. Washington, DC: Clarendon,1913; Oxford, 1925.
Grotius, Hugo. *The Rights of War and Peace*. Translated by A. C. Campbell and with an introduction by David J. Hill. New York: Dunne, 1901. https://oll.libertyfund.org/title/grotius-the-rights-of-war-and-peace-1901-ed.
Gura, Philip F. *The Life of William Apess, Pequot*. Chapel Hill: University of North Carolina Press, 2015.
Gustafson, Sandra M. *Eloquence Is Power: Oratory and Performance in Early America*. Chapel Hill: University of North Carolina Press, 2000.
Guyatt, Nicholas. *Providence and the Invention of the United States, 1607–1876*. Cambridge: Cambridge University Press, 2007.
Hahn, Steven C. *The Invention of the Creek Nation, 1670–1763*. Lincoln: University of Nebraska Press, 2004.
Haley, Alex. *Roots*. Boston: Da Capo, 2014.
Hall, Mark David. *Did America Have a Christian Founding? Separating Modern Myth from Historical Truth*. Nashville, TN: Nelson Books, 2019.
Hamilton, Alexander. *Writings*. Edited by Joanne Freeman. New York: Library of America, 2001.
Hamilton, Neil A. *Rebels and Renegades: A Chronology of Social and Political Dissent in the United States*. New York: Routledge, 2002.
Hamilton, William. "An Address to the New York African Society, for the Mutual Relief, Delivered at the Universalist Church, January 2, 1809." In *Early Negro Writing 1760–1837*, edited by Dorothy Porter. Boston: Beacon, 1971.
Hannah-Jones, Nikole, ed. *The 1619 Project: A New Origin Story*. London: One World, 2021.
Hardt, Michael. *Thomas Jefferson: The Declaration of Independence*. London: Verso, 2007.
Harper, Rob. *Unsettling the West: Violence and State Building in the Ohio Valley*. Philadelphia: University of Pennsylvania Press, 2018.

Harrison, Hubert. *A Hubert Harrison Reader*. Edited by Jeffrey B. Perry. Middletown, CT: Wesleyan University Press, 2001.
Hartz, Louis. *The Liberal Tradition in America*. Harvest Books: HarperCollins,1991.
Hatch, Nathan O. *The Sacred Cause of Liberty: Republican Thought and the Millennium in Revolutionary New England*. New Haven, CT: Yale University Press, 1977.
Hatta, Victoria C. *Labor Visions and State Power: The Origins of Business Unionism in the United States*. Princeton: Princeton University Press, 1993.
Herzog, Don. *Sovereignty, RIP*. London: Yale University Press, 2019.
Hobbes, Thomas. *Leviathan*. Indianapolis: Hackett, 1994.
Hoffer, Peter Charles. "The Declaration of Independence as a Bill in Equity." In *The Law in America, 1607–1861*, edited by William Pencak and Wythe W. Holt Jr., 186–209. New York: New-York Historical Society, 1989.
Hoffer, Peter Charles, and Williamjames Hull Hoffer. *"The Clamor of Lawyers": The Legal Profession and the American Revolution*. Ithaca, NY: Cornell University Press, 2018.
Hoffman and Molyneaux, eds., *Lee Family Papers* [chap 2; what is this]
Holmes, Stephen, and Cass Sunstein. *The Cost of Rights: Why Liberty Depends on Taxes*. New York: Norton, 2000.
Holton, Woody. *Forced Founders: Indians, Debtors, Slaves, and the Making of the American Revolution in Virginia*. Chapel Hill: University of North Carolina Press for the Omohundro Institute of Early American History and Culture, 1999.
Holton, Woody. *Unruly Americans and the Origins of the Constitution*. New York: Hill and Wang, 2007.
Honig, B. "Declarations of Independence: Arendt and Derrida on the Problem of Founding a Republic." *American Political Science Review* 85, no. 1 (March 1991): 97–113.
Horne, Gerald, and Mary Young, eds. *W. E. B. Du Bois: An Encyclopedia*. Westport, CT: Greenwood, 2001.
Hoxie, Frederick E. *A Final Promise: The Campaign to Assimilate the Indians, 1880–1920*. Lincoln: University of Nebraska Press, 1984.
Hulliung, Mark. *The Social Contract in America*. Lawrence: University Press of Kansas, 2007.
Hume, David. "On Eloquence." In *Essays: Literary, Moral, and Philosophical*, edited by Eugene F. Miller. Indianapolis: Liberty Fund, 1985.
Hunter, Thomas. "The Teaching of George Wythe." In *History of Legal Education in the United States*, vol. 2, edited by Steve Sheppard, 138–168. Pasadena, CA: Salem, 1999.
Hunter, William. *An Oration, Delivered in Trinity Church, in Newport on the Fourth of July, 1801*. Newport: Printed at the office of the Newport Mercury, 1801.
Huyler, Jerome. *Locke in America*. Lawrence: University Press of Kansas, 1995.
Huyler, Jerome. *Locke in America: The Moral Philosophy of the Founding Era*. Lawrence: University Press of Kansas, 1995.
In Congress, July 4, 1776. A Declaration By the Representatives of the United States of America, In General Congress Assembled. Philadelphia: John Dunlap, 1776.
Iser, Wolfgang. "The Reading Process: A Phenomenological Approach." In *The Critical Tradition: Classic Texts and Contemporary Trends*, 3rd ed., edited by David Richter. New York: Bedford Books, 2007.

Bibliography

Jackson, Andrew. Andrew Jackson Papers: Series 1, General Correspondence and Related Items, 1775 to 1885. Library of Congress. www.loc.gov/item/majo11860/.
Jackson, Andrew. Message to Congress "On Indian Removal." December 6, 1830. Records of the United States Senate, 1789–1990. Record Group 46, National Archives and Records Administration.
Jackson, Andrew. "Returning the Bank Bill to the Senate with His Objections." In *Annual Messages, Veto Messages, Protests, & c. of Andrew Jackson, President of the United States*, 2nd ed. Baltimore: Edward J. Coale, 1835.
Jackson, Maurice. *Let This Voice Be Heard*. Philadelphia: University of Pennsylvania Press, 2009.
Jasanoff, Maya. *Liberty's Exiles: American Loyalists in the Revolutionary World*. New York: Alfred A. Knopf, 2011.
Jay, Gregory S. *American Literature and the Culture Wars*. Ithaca, NY: Cornell University Press, 1997.
Jayne, Allen. *Jefferson's Declaration of Independence: Origins, Philosophy, and Theology*. Lexington: University Press of Kentucky, 1998.
Jefferson, Thomas. *The Complete Jefferson Containing His Major Writings, Published and Unpublished, Except His Letters*. Edited by Saul K. Padover. New York: Duell, Sloan and Pearce, 1943.
Jefferson, Thomas. *The Literary Bible of Thomas Jefferson: His Commonplace Book of Philosophers and Poets*. Edited by Gilbert Chinard. Baltimore: Johns Hopkins University Press, 1928.
Jefferson, Thomas, *Jefferson's Legal Commonplace Book*. Edited by David Thomas Konig and Michael Zuckert. Princeton, NJ: Princeton University Press, 2019.
Jefferson, Thomas. "Notes and Queries." *Pennsylvania Magazine of History and Biography*, no. 41 (1917).
Jefferson, Thomas. *Notes on the State of Virginia*. Edited by Frank Shuffleton. New York: Penguin Books, 1999.
Jefferson, Thomas. "Original Rough Draft of the Declaration of Independence." Library of Congress. www.loc.gov/exhibits/declara/ruffdrft.html.
Jefferson, Thomas. *The Papers of Thomas Jefferson. Vol. 22, 6 August 1791–31 December 1791*. Edited by Charles T. Cullen. Princeton, NJ: Princeton University Press, 1986.
Jefferson, Thomas. *The Papers of Thomas Jefferson. Vol. 39, 13 November 1802–3 March 1803*. Edited by Barbara B. Oberg. Princeton: Princeton University Press, 2012.
Jefferson, Thomas. *Summary View*. Williamsburg, 1774.
Jefferson, Thomas. *Writings*. Edited by Merrill D. Peterson. New York: Library of America, 1984.
Jefferson, Thomas. *Writings of Thomas Jefferson*. Vol. 6. Edited by Andrew Lipscomb and Albert Ellery Bergh. Washington, DC: Jefferson Memorial Society, 1903.
Jefferson, Thomas. *Writings of Thomas Jefferson*. Vol. 15. Edited by Andrew Lipscomb and Albert Ellery Bergh. Washington, DC: Jefferson Memorial Society, 1907.
Jefferson, Thomas, John Adams, and Abigail Adams. *The Adams-Jefferson Letters*. 2 vols. Edited by Lester J. Cappon. Chapel Hill: University of North Carolina Press, 1959.
Jensen, Merrill, ed. *The Documentary History of the Ratification of the Constitution*. Vol. 3. Madison: State Historical Society of Wisconsin, 1978.

Johnson, Samuel. *Ethica: Or the First Principles of Moral Philosophy*. 2nd ed. Philadelphia: Franklin and Hall, 1752. https://quod.lib.umich.edu/e/evans/N05418.0001.001/1:18?rgn=div1;view=fulltext.

Johnson, Samuel. *Taxation: No Tyranny*. 1775. www.samueljohnson.com/tnt.html.

Jones, David Wallace. *Education for Extinction: American Indians and the Boarding School Experience, 1875–1928*. Lawrence: University Press of Kansas, 1995.

Kames, Henry Home. *Principles of Equity*. 2nd ed. Edinburgh: A. Kincaid and J. Bell, 1767.

Kanowitz, Leo. *Women and the Law: The Unfinished Revolution*. Albuquerque: University of New Mexico Press, 1969.

Kantrowitz, Stephen. *More than Freedom: Fighting for Black Citizenship in a White Republic, 1829–1889*. New York: Penguin Books, 2012.

Kateb, George. "Is Patriotism a Mistake?" *Social Research* 67 (2000): 901–924.

Keith, William. *A Collection of Papers and Other Tracts Written Occasionally on Various Subjects, to Which Is Prefixed, by Way of Preface, an Essay on the Nature of a Publick Spirit*. London: J. Mechell, 1740.

Kelley, Robin D. G., and Earl Lewis, eds. *To Make Our World Anew: A History of African Americans to 1880, Volume One: A History of African Americans to 1800* (Oxford: Oxford University Press, 2000).

Kelly, Lawrence C. "The Indian Reorganization Act: The Dream and the Reality." *Pacific Historical Review* 44, no. 3 (1975): 291–312.

Kendi, Ibram X. *Stamped at the Beginning: A Definitive History of Racist Ideas in America*. New York: Nation Books, 2016.

Kenyon, J. P. *Revolution Principles: The Politics of Party, 1689–1720*. Cambridge: Cambridge University Press, 1977.

Kerber, Linda. *Toward an Intellectual History of American Women*. Chapel Hill: University of North Carolina Press, 1997.

Kermode, Frank. *Forms of Attention: Botticelli and Hamlet*. Chicago: University of Chicago Press, 1985.

Kernell, Samuel. *Going Public: New Strategies of Political Leadership*. Washington, DC: CQ Press, 2006.

King, Martin Luther, Jr. *A Call to Conscience: The Landmark Speeches of Dr. Martin Luther King, Jr*. Edited by Clayborne Carson and Kris Shepard. New York: Grand Central, 2002.

King, Martin Luther, Jr. *A Testament of Hope: The Essential Writings of Martin Luther King Jr*. Edited by James Melvin Washington. New York: HarperCollins, 1986.

Klinghoffer, Judith Apter, and Lois Elkis. "'The Petticoat Electors': Women's Suffrage in New Jersey." *Journal of the Early Republic* 12, no. 2 (Summer 1992): 159–193.

Kolakowski, Leszek. "The Concept of the Left." In *Toward a Marxist Humanism: Essays on the Left Today*. Translated by Jane Zielonko Peel. New York: Grove, 1968.

Konig, David Thomas. "Virginia and the Imperial State: Law, Enlightenment, and 'the Crooked Cord of Discretion.'" In *The British and Their Laws in the Eighteenth Century*, edited by David Lemmings, 206–229. London: Boydell, 2005.

Kurland, Philip, and Ralph Lerner, eds. *The Founders' Constitution*. Chicago: University of Chicago Press, 1987.

Kurtz, Stephen G., and James H. Hutson. *Essays on the American Revolution*. Chapel Hill: University of North Carolina Press, 1973.

LeClerc, George Louis, and Comte de Buffon. *Natural History: General and Particular, by the Count de Buffon, Translated into English.* Translated by William Smellie. London: William Strahan and Thoams Cadell, 1781.
Levinson, Sanford. "The Confusing Language of McCulloch v. Maryland: Did Marshall Really Know What He Was Doing (or Meant?)." *Arkansas Law Review* 7 (2019): 7–33.
Levinson, Sanford. *Constitutional Faith.* 2nd ed. Princeton, NJ: Princeton University Press, 2011.
Levinson, Sanford. "Divided Loyalties: The Problem of 'Dual Sovereignty' and the Constitution." *Touro Law Review* 29, no. 2 (2013): 241–262.
Levinson, Sanford. *Our Undemocratic Constitution: Where the Constitution Goes Wrong (and How We the People Can Correct It).* Oxford: Oxford University Press, 2006.
Levinson, Sanford. "Self-Evident Truths in the Declaration of Independence." *Texas Law Review* 57 (1979).
Levinson, Sanford. "What One Can Learn from Foreign-Language Translations of the U.S. Constitution." *Constitutional Commentary* 31 (2016): 55–70.
Levinson, Sanford. "'Who Counts?' 'Sez Who?'" *University of St. Louis Law Journal* 58 (2014): 937–987.
Levinson, Sanford. *Written in Stone: Public Monuments in Changing Societies.* 2nd ed. Durham, NC: Duke University Press, 2018.
Lewis, Earl. "Revolutionary Citizens." In Robin D. G. Kelley and Earl Lewis, eds., *To Make Our World Anew: A History of African Americans to 1880, Volume One: A History of African Americans to 1800* (Oxford: Oxford University Press, 2000), 103–168.
Lewis, Jone Johnson. "A Short History of Women's Property Rights in the United States." *ThoughtCo,* August 26, 2020. www.thoughtco.com/property-rights-of-women-3529578.
Lim, Elvin T. *The Anti-intellectual President: The Decline of Presidential Rhetoric from George Washington to George W. Bush.* New York: Oxford University Press, 2008.
Lincoln, Abraham. *Abraham Lincoln: Selected Speeches and Writings.* New York: Library of America, 1992.
Lincoln, Abraham. *The Collected Works of Abraham Lincoln.* Edited by Roy Basler. 8 vols. New Brunswick, NJ: Rutgers University Press, 1953.
Lincoln, Abraham. *Speeches and Writings, 1832–1858.* Edited by Don E. Fehrenbacher. New York: Library of America, 1989.
Lincoln, Abraham. *Speeches and Writings, 1859–1865.* Edited by Don E. Fehrenbacher. New York: Library of America, 1989.
Locke, John. *The Correspondence of John Locke.* Edited by E. S. de Beer. Oxford: Clarendon, 1976–89.
Locke, John. *An Essay Concerning Human Understanding.* Edited by Peter H. Nidditch. Oxford: Oxford University Press, 1975.
Locke, John. *An Essay Concerning Human Understanding.* Edited by Peter H. Nidditch. New York: Oxford University Press, 1979.
Locke, John. *Essays on the Law of Nature.* Edited by W. von Leyden. Oxford: Oxford University Press, 1988.
Locke, John. *Of the Conduct of the Understanding.* Edited by Francis W. Garforth. New York: Teachers College Press, 1966.
Locke, John. *Political Essays.* Edited by Mark Goldie. Cambridge: Cambridge University Press, 1997.

Locke, John. *Political Writings of John Locke*. Edited by David Wootton. London: Mentor, 1993.
Locke, John. *Questions Concerning the Law of Nature*. Edited and translated by Robert Horwitz, Jenny Strauss Clay, and Diskin Clay. Ithaca, NY: Cornell University Press, 1990.
Locke, John. *The Reasonableness of Christianity*. Edited by George W. Ewing. Washington, DC: Regnery Gateway, 1965.
Locke, John. *Some Thoughts Concerning Education*. Edited by John W. Yolton and Jean S. Yolton. Oxford: Clarendon, 1989.
Locke, John. *Two Treatises of Government*. Edited by Peter Laslett. Cambridge: Cambridge University Press, 1988.
Locke, John. *Two Treatises of Government*. Edited by Thomas I. Cook. New York: Hafner, 1947.
Lomawaima, K. Tsianina. *They Called It Prairie Light: The Story of Chilocco Indian School*. Lincoln: University of Nebraska Press, 1994.
Loughlin, Martin. *Against Constitutionalism*. Cambridge, MA: Harvard University Press, 2022.
Luther, Seth. *An Address to the Working-Men of New-England on the State of Education and the Condition of the Producing Classes in Europe and America*. 2nd ed. Boston: Published by the Author, 1833.
Lynd, Staughton. "The Abolitionist Critique of the United States Constitution." In Staughton Lynd, ed., *Class Conflict, Slavery, and the United States Constitution: Ten Essays*, 153–183. Indianapolis: Bobbs-Merrill, 1967.
Lynd, Staughton. *Intellectual Origins of American Radicalism*. Cambridge: Cambridge University Press, 2009.
Mackay, R. E., and J. Feagin. "'Merciless Indian Savages': Deconstructing Anti-Indigenous Framing." *Sociology of Race and Ethnicity* 8, no. 4 (2022): 518–533.
Madison, James. *Writings*. Edited by Jack Rakove. New York: Library of America, 1999.
Maier, Pauline. *American Scripture: Making the Declaration of Independence*. New York: Alfred A. Knopf, 1997.
Maier, Pauline. *American Scripture: Making the Declaration of Independence*. 1st Vintage Books ed. New York: Vintage Books, 1998.
Maier, Pauline. *From Resistance to Revolution: Colonial Radicals and the Development of American Opposition to Britain, 1765–1776*. New York: Alfred A. Knopf, 1973.
Maier, Pauline. *Ratification: The People Debate the Constitution, 1787–1788*. New York: Simon and Schuster, 2010.
Malcolm X. *Malcolm X on Afro-American History*. New York: Pathfinder, 1990.
Mamdani, Mahmood. *Neither Settler nor Native: The Making and Unmaking of Permanent Minorities*. Cambridge, MA: Belknap Press of Harvard University Press, 2020.
Mansfield, Edward D. *The Legal Rights, Liabilities and Duties of Women*. Salem, MA: John P. Jewett, 1845.
Maryland: A Guide to the Old Line State, sponsored by Herbert R. O'Conor, Governor of Maryland. New York: Oxford University Press, 1940.
Massachusetts Historical Society. "The Legal End of Slavery in Massachusetts." www.masshist.org/features/endofslavery/end_MA.

Masur, Kate. *Until Justice Be Done: America's First Civil Rights Movement, from the Revolution to Reconstruction.* New York: Norton, 2021.
Matthews, Richard K. *The Radical Politics of Thomas Jefferson.* Lawrence: University Press of Kansas, 1976.
Matthews, Richard K. *The Radical Politics of Thomas Jefferson.* Lawrence: University Press of Kansas, 1986.
Mayer, Henry. *All on Fire: William Lloyd Garrison and the Abolition of Slavery.* New York: St. Martin's, 1998.
McBurney, Christian. "The First Efforts to Limit the African Slave Trade." *Journal of the American Revolution*, September 14, 2020. https://allthingsliberty.com/2020/09/the-first-efforts-to-limit-the-african-slave-trade-arise-in-the-american-revolution-part-3-of-3-congress-bans-the-african-slave-trade/.
McCann, Michael. "A. Philip Randolph: Radicalizing Rights at the Intersection of Class and Race." In *African American Political Thought: A Collected History*, ed. Melvin L. Rogers and Jack Turner. Chicago: University of Chicago Press, 2021.
McConville, Brendan. *The King's Three Faces: The Rise and Fall of Royal America, 1688–1776.* Chapel Hill: University of North Carolina Press, 2006.
McDonald, Forrest. *Novus Ordo Seclorum: The Intellectual Origins of the Constitution.* Lawrence: University Press of Kansas, 1985.
McDonald, Robert M. S. "Thomas Jefferson's Changing Reputation as Author of the Declaration of Independence: The First Fifty Years." *Journal of the Early Republic* 19 (Summer 1999): 169–195.
McGraw, Barbara A. "Church and State in Context." In *Church and State Issues in America Today*, 1–40, edited by Ann W. Duncan and Steven L. Jones. Santa Barbara, CA: Greenwood, 2008.
McGraw, Barbara A. *Rediscovering America's Sacred Ground: Public Religion and Pursuit of the Good in a Pluralistic America.* Albany: State University of New York Press, 2003.
[McKee, Alexander]. *Minutes of Debates in Council on the Banks of the Ottawa River.* Philadelphia: Printed for the editor, and sold by William Young, bookseller, 1792.
McLoughlin, William G. *Cherokee Renascence in the New Republic.* Princeton, NJ: Princeton University Press, 1986.
McMaster, John B. *The Acquisition of Political Social and Industrial Rights of Man in America.* Cleveland, OH: Imperial, 1903.
McNeill, William H. "The Care and Repair of Public Myth." In *Mythhistory and Other Essays*, 23–42. Chicago: University of Chicago Press, 1986.
McPherson, James. *Abraham Lincoln and the Second American Revolution.* New York: Oxford University Press, 1992.
Merrell, James H. "Declarations of Independence: Indian-White Relations in the New Nation." In *The American Revolution: Its Character and Limits*, edited by Jack P. Greene, 197–223. New York: New York University Press, 1987.
Merrell, James H. *The Indians' New World: Catawbas and Their Neighbors from European Contact through the Era of Removal.* Chapel Hill: University of North Carolina Press for the Omohundro Institute of Early American History and Culture, 1989.
Merriam, Jesse. "How Civil Rights Law Changed America." *Law and Liberty*, November 22, 2023. https://lawliberty.org/forum/how-civil-rights-law-changed-america/.

Mevers, Frank C., ed. *The Papers of Josiah Bartlett*. Hanover, NH: University Press of New England, 1979.
Mill, John Stuart. *On Liberty, Utilitarianism, and Other Essays*. Edited by Mark Philp and Frederick Rosen. Oxford: Oxford University Press, 2015.
Miller, David. *On Nationality*. Oxford: Clarendon, 1995.
Minnis, Jack. "The Mississippi Freedom Democratic Party: A New Declaration of Independence." *Freedomways* 5 (1965): 264–278.
Morrison, Toni. *Playing in the Dark: Whiteness and the Literary Imagination*. New York: Vintage Books, 1992.
Mott, Frank Luther. *The Golden Multitudes: The Story of Bestsellers in the United States*. New York: Macmillan, 1947.
Muhammad, Elijah. *The Fall of America*. Chicago: Secretarius Memps, 2006.
Murray, John Courtney. *We Hold These Truths*. Kansas City, MO: Sheed and Ward, 1960.
Nabokov, Peter. *Where the Lightning Strikes: The Lives of American Indian Sacred Places*. New York: Penguin Books, 2006.
Nash, Gary, and Jean Soderlund. *Freedom by Degrees: Emancipation in Pennsylvania and Its Aftermath*. New York: Oxford University Press, 1991.
National Committee of Black Churchmen. "The Black Declaration of Independence." In *Modern Black Nationalism: From Marcus Garvey to Louis Farrakhan*, edited by William L. Van Deburg, 225–228. New York: New York University Press, 1997.
Nederman, Cary. "Empire and the Historiography of European Political Thought: Marsiglio of Padua, Nicholas of Cusa, and the Medieval/Modern Divide." *Journal of the History of Ideas* 66 (2005): 1–15.
Nederman, Cary. Review of *The Idea of Natural Rights* and *Rights, Law and Infallibility in Medieval Thought* by Brian Tierney. *American Journal of Legal History* 42 (1998): 217–219.
Neem, Johann. "American History in a Global Age." *History and Theory* 50 (January 2011): 41–70.
Nelson, Eric. *The Royalist Revolution: Monarchy and the American Founding*. Cambridge, MA: Harvard University Press, 2014.
Newlin, Claude M. *Philosophy and Religion in Colonial America*. New York: Philosophical Library, 1962.
Newman, Richard S. "John Parrish, 'Notes on Abolition,' Circa 1805." *Quakers and Slavery*. https://trilogy.brynmawr.edu/speccoll/quakersandslavery/commentary/people/parrish_john.php
Newman, Richard S. *The Transformation of American Abolitionism*. Chapel Hill: University of North Carolina Press, 2002.
Newton, Isaac. *Philosophiae Naturalis Principia Mathematica*. Cambridge: Printed by Cornelius Crownfield, 1713.
Nicholls, Michael, and Lenaye Howard. "Slaves Freed after 1782." www.freeafricanamericans.com/virginiafreeafter1782.htm.
Nichols, David Andrew. *Engines of Diplomacy: Indian Trading Factories and the Negotiation of American Empire*. Chapel Hill: University of North Carolina Press, 2016.
Nichols, David Andrew. *Red Gentlemen and White Savages: Indians, Federalists, and the Search for Order on the American Frontier*. Charlottesville: University of Virginia Press, 2008.

Nielson, Donald M. "The Mashpee Indian Revolt of 1833." *New England Quarterly* 58, no. 3 (1985): 400–420.

Nussbaum, Martha. "Patriotism and Cosmopolitanism." *Boston Review*, October/November 1994. www.oneworlduv.com/wp-content/uploads/2011/06/patriotism_cosmopolitanism.pdf.

Nussbaum, Martha. "Patriotism and Cosmopolitanism." In *For Love of Country: Debating the Limits of Patriotism*, 2–20. Boston: Beacon, 1996.

Oakes, James. *Freedom National*. New York: Norton, 2012.

Oakes, James. "Natural Rights, Citizenship Rights, States' Rights, and Black Rights: Another Look at Lincoln and Race." In *Our Lincoln: New Perspectives on Lincoln and His World*, edited by Eric Foner, 109–134. New York, Norton, 2008.

Oakley, Francis. *Natural Law, Laws of Nature, Natural Rights: Continuity and Discontinuity in the History of Ideas*. New York: Continuum, 2005.

Onuf, Peter S. *The Mind of Thomas Jefferson*. Charlottesville: University of Virginia Press, 2006.

Ostler, Jeffrey. "'To Extirpate the Indians': An Indigenous Consciousness of Genocide in the Ohio Valley and Lower Great Lakes, 1750s–1810." *William and Mary Quarterly* 72, no. 4 (2015): 587–622.

Pangle, Thomas. *The Spirit of Modern Republicanism: The Moral Vision of the American Founders and the Philosophy of Locke*. Chicago: University of Chicago Press, 1988.

Parker, Theodore. "Discourse Occasioned by the Death of John Quincy Adams." March 5, 1848. In *The Collected Works of Theodore Parker*, edited by Frances Power Cobbe, 4: 135–83. London: N. Trubner & Co., 1863.

Parker, Theodore. "The Political Destination of America and the Signs of the Times." In *The Collected Works of Theodore Parker*, edited by Frances Power Cobbe, 4: 77–110. London: N. Trubner & Co., 1863.

Parkinson, Robert G. *The Common Cause: Creating Race and Nation in the American Revolution*. Chapel Hill: University of North Carolina Press for the Omohundro Institute of Early American History and Culture, 2016.

Parkinson, Robert G. "Friends and Enemies in the Declaration of Independence." In *Jeffersonians in Power: Ideas in Practice*, edited by Joanne Freeman and Johann Neem, 15–37. Charlottesville: University of Virginia Press, 2019.

Parkinson, Robert G. "You Can't Tell the Story of 1776 without Talking about Race and Slavery." *Time*, July 4, 2021. https://time.com/6077468/united-states-1776-racism-slavery/.

Parmenter, Jon. *The Edge of the Woods: Iroquoia, 1534–1701*. East Lansing: Michigan State University Press, 2010.

Pearsall, Sarah M. S. "Recentering Indian Women in the American Revolution." In *Why You Can't Teach United States History without American Indians*, edited by Susan Sleeper-Smith et al., 57–70. Chapel Hill: University of North Carolina Press, 2015.

Perdue, Theda. *Cherokee Women: Gender and Culture Change, 1700–1835*. Lincoln: University of Nebraska Press, 1998.

Perdue, Theda. "Native Women in the Early Republic: Old World Perceptions, New World Realities." In *Native Americans and the Early Republic*, edited by Frederick E. Hoxie et al., 105–112. Charlottesville: University of Virginia Press for the United States Capitol Historical Society, 1999.

Perdue, Theda, and Michael D. Green. *The Cherokee Nation and the Trail of Tears.* New York: Penguin Books, 2007.
Pessen, Edward. *Most Uncommon Jacksonians: The Radical Leaders of the Early Labor Movement.* New York: State University of New York Press, 1967.
Peters, Richard, ed. *The Case of the Cherokee Nation against the State of Georgia: Argued and Determined at the Supreme Court of the United States, January Term, 1831.* Philadelphia: John Grigg, 1831.
Peterson, Merrill D., ed. *Jefferson: Writings.* New York: Library of America, 1984.
Pockock, J. G. A. "Between Gog and Magog: The Republican Thesis and the *Ideologica Americana.*" *Journal of the History of Ideas* 68 (1987): 325–346.
Pocock, J. G. A. *The Machiavellian Moment.* Princeton, NJ: Princeton University Press, 1975.
Podair, Jerald. *Bayard Rustin: American Dreamer.* Lanham, MD: Rowman and Littlefield, 2008.
Prager, Janice, and Arlene Lepoff. *Why Be Different? A Look into Judaism.* Springfield, NJ: Behrman House, 1986.
Pratt, Adam J. *Toward Cherokee Removal: Land, Violence, and the White Man's Chance.* Athens: University of Georgia Press, 2022.
Proceedings of the First Anniversary of the American Equal Rights Association. New York: Robert J. Johnston, 1867.
Pybus, Cassandra. "Jefferson's Faulty Math: The Question of Slave Defections in the American Revolution." *William and Mary Quarterly,* third ser., 62, no. 2 (April 2005): 243–264.
Rae, Douglas. *Equalities.* Cambridge, MA: Harvard University Press, 1983.
Rahe, Paul A. *Republics Ancient and Modern.* Chapel Hill: University of North Carolina Press, 1992.
Rakove, Jack. *Original Meanings: Politics and Ideas in the Making of the Constitution.* New York: Alfred A. Knopf, 1996.
Rakove, Jack. *Revolutionaries: A New History of the Invention of America.* New York: Houghton Mifflin, 2010.
Rana, Aziz. *Two Faces of American Freedom.* Cambridge, MA: Harvard University Press, 2014.
Randall, Henry Stephens. *The Life of Thomas Jefferson.* Vol. 3. New York: Derby and Jackson, 1858.
Ratcliffe, Donald. "The Right to Vote and the Rise of Democracy, 1787–1828." *Journal of the Early Republic* 33 (2013): 219–254.
Reed, Annette Gordon. *The Hemingses of Monticello.* New York: Norton, 2008.
Reichenbach, Bruce. "Cosmological Argument." Revised ed., 2022. In *Stanford Encyclopedia of Philosophy.* https://plato.stanford.edu/entries/cosmological-argument.
Reid, John Philip. *Constitutional History of the American Revolution: Volume 3: The Authority to Legislate.* Madison: University of Wisconsin Press, 1991.
Reid, John Phillip. *Constitutional History of the American Revolution: Volume 1: The Authority of Rights.* Madison: University of Wisconsin Press, 1986.
Reid, John Philip. "The Irrelevance of the Declaration." In *Law in the American Revolution and the American Revolution in the Law,* edited by Hendrik Hartog, 46–89. New York: New York University Press, 1981.

Richotte, Keith, Jr. *Claiming Turtle Mountain's Constitution: The History, Legacy, and Future of a Tribal Nation's Founding Documents*. Chapel Hill: University of North Carolina Press, 2017.

Richter, Daniel K. *The Ordeal of the Longhouse: The Peoples of the Iroquois League in the Era of European Colonization*. Chapel Hill: University of North Carolina Press for the Omohundro Institute of Early American History and Culture, 1993.

Rindfleisch, Bryan. "'Where Your Warriors Have Left Their Bones, There Our Bones Are Seen Also': The Stockbridge-Mohican Community in the Revolutionary War, 1775–1783." In *Journal of the American Revolution, Annual Volume 2017*, edited by Todd Andrlik and Don N. Hagist, 297–309. Yardley, PA: Westholme, 2017.

Robertson, Lindsay G. *Conquest by Law: How the Discovery of America Dispossessed Indigenous Peoples of Their Lands*. New York: Oxford University Press, 2005.

Robinson, Cedric J. *Black Marxism: The Making of the Black Radical Tradition*. Chapel Hill: University of North Carolina Press, 2020.

Robinson, Frederick. *An Oration Delivered before the Trades Union of Boston and Vicinity, on Fort Hill, Boston, on the Fifty-Eighth Anniversary of American Independence*. Boston: Charles Douglas, 1834.

Rodgers, Melvin L., and Jack Turner, eds. *African American Political Thought: A Collected History*. Chicago: University of Chicago Press, 2021.

Roosevelt, Theodore. *Letters and Speeches*. Edited by Louis Auchincloss. New York: Library of America, 2004.

Rorty, Richard. *Achieving Our Country*. Cambridge, MA: Harvard University Press, 1998.

Rorty, Richard. "Philosophy as a Kind of Writing." *New Literary History* 10 (Autumn 1978): 141–160.

Rorty, Richard. "Postmodernist Bourgeois Liberalism." *Journal of Philosophy* 80 (October 1983): 523–589.

Rosier, Paul C. *Serving Their Country: American Indian Politics and Patriotism in the Twentieth Century*. Cambridge, MA: Harvard University Press, 2013.

Roth, Philip. *The Plot against America*. New York: Random House, 2005.

Rudolph, Julia. *Common Law and Enlightenment in England, 1689–1750*. Woodbridge, UK: The Boydell Press, 2013.

Rush, Benjamin. "An Address to the Inhabitants of the British Settlements, on the Slavery of the Negroes in America." Philadelphia: John Dunlap, 1773.

Rush, Benjamin. *Observations on the Present Government of Pennsylvania*. https://wisc.pb.unizin.org/ps601/chapter/benjamin-rush-observations-on-the-present-government-of-pennsylvania/.

Rutkowski, Alice. "Leaving the Good Mother: Frances E. W. Harper, Lydia Maria Child, and the Literary Politics of Reconstruction." *Legacy* 25, no. 1 (2008): 83–104.

Sa, Zitkala. "Indians at the Front." *American Indian Magazine* 5, no. 1 (1917).

Sandoz, Ellis, ed. *Political Sermons of the American Founding Era: 1730–1805*. Indianapolis, IN: Liberty Fund, 1991.

Sanford, Charles B. *Thomas Jefferson and His Library: A Study of His Literary Interests and of the Religious Attitudes Revealed by Relevant Titles in His Library*. Hamden, CT: Archon Books, 1977.

Saunt, Claudio. *Unworthy Republic: The Dispossession of Native Americans and the Road to Indian Territory*. New York: Norton, 2020.
Sayre, Gordon M. "Jefferson and Native Americans: Policy and Archive." In *The Cambridge Companion to Thomas Jefferson*, edited by Frank Shuffelton, 61–72. Cambridge: Cambridge University Press, 2009.
Schaub, Diana. "Lincoln and the Daughters of Dred Scott: A Reflection on the Declaration of Independence." In *When in the Course of Human Events: 1776 at Home, Abroad, and in American Memory*, edited by Will R. Jordan, 189–210. Mercer, GA: Mercer University Press, 2018.
Schlesinger, Elizabeth Bancroft. Review of *The Ideas of the Woman Suffrage Movement, 1890–1920* by Aileen S. Kraditor, *New England Quarterly* 39, no. 1 (1966): 102–104.
Schmitt, Carl. *The Crisis of Parliamentary Democracy*. Translated by Ellen Kennedy. Cambridge, MA: MIT Press, 1985.
Schneir, Miriam, ed. *Feminism: The Essential Historical Writings*. New York: Vintage Books, 1972.
Schwartz, Bernard, ed. *The Bill of Rights: A Documentary History*. 2 vols. New York: Chelsea House, 1971.
Seagrave, S. Adam. *The Foundations of Natural Morality: On the Compatibility of Natural Rights and the Natural Law*. Chicago: University of Chicago Press, 2014.
Seagrave, S. Adam. "Self-Ownership vs. Divine Ownership: A Lockean Solution to a Liberal Democratic Dilemma." *American Journal of Political Science* 55, no. 3 (July 2011): 710–723.
Sedgwick, Theodore. *Public and Private Economy*, Part Second. New York: Harper, 1838.
Shapiro, Ian. "Gross Concepts in Political Argument." *Political Theory* 17, no. 1 (1989): 51–76.
Sheehan, Bernard W. *Seeds of Extinction: Jeffersonian Philanthropy and the American Indian*. Chapel Hill: University of North Carolina Press, 1973.
Silver, Peter. *Our Savage Neighbors: How Indian War Transformed Early America*. New York: Norton, 2007.
Simpson, Stephen. *The Working Man's Manual: A New Theory of Political Economy, on the Principle of Production the Source of Wealth*. Philadelphia: Thomas L. Bonsal, 1831.
Sinha, Manisha. *The Slaves' Cause: A History of Abolition*. New Haven, CT: Yale University Press, 2016.
Skidmore, Thomas. *The Rights of Man to Property! Being a Proposition to Make It Equal among the Adults*. New York: Alexander Ming, 1829.
Skinner, Quentin. *Visions of Politis: Regarding Method*. New York: Cambridge University Press, 2002.
Slauter, Eric. "The Declaration of Independence and the New Nation." In *The Cambridge Companion to Thomas Jefferson*, edited by Frank Shuffelton, 12–34. Cambridge: Cambridge University Press, 2008.
Smith, Rogers M. "Beyond Tocqueville, Myrdal, and Hartz: The Multiple Traditions in America." *American Political Science Review* 87, no. 3 (September 1993): 549–566.
Smith, Rogers M. *Liberalism and American Constitutional Law*. Cambridge, MA: Harvard University Press, 1980.

Smith, Rogers M. *That Is Not Who We Are! Populism and Peoplehood*. New Haven, CT: Yale University Press, 2020.
Smith, Rogers. *Civic Ideals: Conflicting Visions of Citizenship in Us History*. New Haven, CT: Yale University Press, 1999.
Smith, Rogers. *Stories of Peoplehood: The Politics and Morals of Political Membership*. Cambridge: Cambridge University Press, 2002.
Snyder, Christina. "Many Removals: Re-evaluating the Arc of Indigenous Dispossession." *Journal of the Early Republic* 41, no. 4 (2021): 623–650.
Snyder, Christina. "The Rise and Fall and Rise of Civilizations: Indian Intellectual Culture during the Removal Era." *Journal of American History* 104, no. 2 (2017): 386–409.
Spalding, Matthew. Foreword to *The Declaration of Independence and The Constitution of the United States*. Washington, DC: Heritage Foundation, 2010.
Stathis, Stephen W. *Landmark Debates in Congress*. Washington, DC: CQ Press, 2009.
Steele, Brian. "Inventing Un-America." *Journal of American Studies* 47 (November 2013): 881–902.
Steele, Brian. *Thomas Jefferson and American Nationhood*. Cambridge: Cambridge University Press, 2012.
Stevens, Alexander. "Cornerstone Speech." March 21, 1861. *American Battlefield Trust*, www.battlefields.org/learn/primary-sources/cornerstone-speech.
Steward, Maria. "What If I Am a Woman." In *Maria Stewart: America's First Black Woman Political Writer: Essays and Speeches*, edited by Marilyn Richardson, 65–74. Bloomington: Indiana University Press, 1987.
Stewart, Matthew. *Nature's God: The Heretical Origins of the American Republic*. New York: Norton, 2014.
Storing, Herbert. *What the Anti-Federalists Were For*. Chicago: University of Chicago Press, 1981.
Strauss, David. *The Living Constitution*. New York: Oxford University Press, 2010.
Strauss, Leo. *Natural Right and History*. Chicago: University of Chicago Press, 1953.
Sunstein, Cass R. *One Case at a Time: Judicial Minimalism on the Supreme Court*. Cambridge, MA: Harvard University Press, 2001.
Sweet, Timothy. "Jefferson, Science, and the Enlightenment." In *The Cambridge Companion to Thomas Jefferson*, edited by Frank Shuffelton, 101–113. Cambridge: Cambridge University Press, 2009.
Tamm, Marek, ed. *Afterlife of Events: Perspectives on Mnemohistory*. London: Palgrave Macmillan, 2015.
Tansill, Charles C., ed. *Documents Illustrative of the Formation of the Union of the American States*. Washington, DC: U.S. Printing Office, 1927.
Tate, Thad. Foreword to *The Negro in the American Revolution*, by Benjamin Quarles. Chapel Hill: University of North Carolina Press for the Institute of Early American History and Culture, 1961.
Tate, Thad. "The Social Contract in America, 1774–1787: Revolutionary Theory as a Conservative Instrument." *William and Mary Quarterly, 3rd ser.*, 22 (1965): 375–391.
Taylor, Alan. *The Internal Enemy: Slavery and War in Virginia, 1772–1832*. New York: Norton, 2013.
Taylor, Graham D. *The Indian New Deal and American Indian Tribalism*. Lincoln: University of Nebraska Press, 1980.

Thom, Martin. *Republics, Nations, and Tribes*. London: Verso, 1995.
Thompson, Peter. "David Walker's Nationalism—and Thomas Jefferson's." *Journal of the Early Republic* 37, no. 1 (Spring 2017): 47–80.
Tierney, Brian. "Historical Roots of Modern Rights: Before Locke and After." *Ave Maria Law Review* 3 (2005): 23–43.
Tierney, Brian. *The Idea of Natural Rights: Studies on Natural Rights, Natural Law and Church Law 1150–1625*. Atlanta: Scholars, 1997.
Tocqueville, Alexis de. *Democracy in America*. Edited by Harvey C. Mansfield and Delba Winthrop. Chicago: University of Chicago Press, 2000.
Trenchard, John, and Thomas Gordon. *Cato's Letters: Essays on Liberty, Civil and Religious, and Other Important Subjects*. New York, 1991.
Tribe, Lawrence. *The Invisible Constitution*. New York: Oxford University Press, 2008.
Truth, Sojourner. "Ain't I a Woman?" In *Sojourner Truth's "Ain't I a Woman?" Speech: A Primary Source Investigation*, edited by Corona Brezina. New York: Rosen, 2005.
Tsai, Robert. *America's Forgotten Constitutions: Defiant Visions of Power and Community*. Cambridge, MA: Harvard University Press, 2014.
Tsesis, Alexander. *For Liberty and Equality: The Life and Times of the Declaration of Independence*. New York: Oxford University Press, 2012.
Tsesis, Alexander. *The Thirteenth Amendment and American Freedom: A Legal History*. New York: New York University Press, 2004.
Tsesis, Alexander. *We Shall Overcome: A History of Civil Rights and the Law*. New Haven, CT: Yale University Press, 2008.
Tsosie, Rebecca. "The Politics of Inclusion: Indigenous Peoples and U.S. Citizenship." *UCLA Law Review* 63, no. 6 (2016): 1694–1751.
Tuck, Richard. *Natural Rights Theories: Their Origin and Development*. Cambridge: Cambridge University Press, 1979.
Tucker, George. *View of the Constitution of the United States: With Selected Writings*. Edited by Wilson Clyde. Indianapolis, IN: Liberty Fund, 1999.
Tulis, Jeffrey K. *The Rhetorical Presidency*. Princeton, NJ: Princeton University Press, 1987.
Tully, James. *A Discourse on Property: John Locke and His Adversaries*. New York: Cambridge University Press, 1980.
Van Buskirk, Judith L. *Standing in Their Own Light: African American Patriots in the American Revolution*. Norman: University of Oklahoma Press, 2017.
Van Evrie, John. *Negroes and Negro Slavery*. New York: Van Evrie, Horton, 1861.
Waldstreicher, David. *In the Midst of Perpetual Fetes: The Making of American Nationalism, 1776–1820*. Chapel Hill: University of North Carolina Press, 1997.
Waldstreicher, David. *Runaway America: Ben Franklin, Slavery, and the American Revolution*. New York: Hill and Wang, 2004.
Waldstreicher, David. *Slavery's Constitution: Revolution to Ratification*. New York: Hill and Wang, 2009.
Walker, David. *An Appeal to the Colored Citizens of the World*. Rev. ed., edited by Sean Wilentz. New York: Hill and Wang, 1995.
Walker, David. *Appeal to the Coloured Citizens of the World, but in Particular, and Very Expressly, to Those of THE UNITED STATES OF AMERICA*. New York: Hill and Wang, Inc, 1965.

Walker, David. *Walker's Appeal in Four Articles ... to the Coloured Citizens of the World, but in Particular and Very Especially to Those of the United States of America.* Rev. ed. Boston: David Walker, 1830.
Wallace, Anthony F. C. *Jefferson and the Indians: The Tragic Fate of the First Americans.* Cambridge, MA: Harvard University Press, 1999.
Walzer, Michael. *Exodus and Revolution.* New York: Basic Books, 1986.
Walzer, Michael. *Thick and Thin: Moral Argument at Home and Abroad.* South Bend, IN: Notre Dame University Press, 1994.
Wesley, Charles H. "Negro Suffrage in the Period of Constitution-Making, 1787–1865." *Journal of Negro History* 32 (1947): 143–168.
White, Richard. *The Roots of Dependency: Subsistence, Environment, and Social Change among the Choctaws, Pawnees, and Navajos.* Lincoln: University of Nebraska Press, 1983.
Whitfield, Harvey Amani. *The Problem of Slavery in Early Vermont, 1777–1810.* Barre: Vermont Historical Society Publications, 2020.
Wilkins, David E., and Heidi Kiiwetinepinesiik Stark. *American Indian Politics and the American Political System.* 4th ed. Lanham, MD: Rowman and Littlefield, 2018.
Williams, Patricia J. *The Alchemy of Race and Rights: Diary of a Law Professor.* Cambridge, MA: Harvard University Press, 1991.
Williams, Robert A., Jr. *Like a Loaded Weapon: The Rehnquist Court, Indian Rights, and the Legal History of Racism in America.* Minneapolis: University of Minnesota Press, 2005.
Wills, Garry. *Inventing America: Jefferson's Declaration of Independence.* Garden City, NY: Doubleday, 1976.
Wills, Garry. *Inventing America: Jefferson's Declaration of Independence.* New York: Vintage Books, 1978.
Wills, Garry. *Inventing America: Jefferson's Declaration of Independence.* Rev. ed. Boston: Houghton Mifflin, 2002.
Wills, Garry. *Negro President: Jefferson and the Slave Power.* Boston: Houghton Mifflin, 2003.
Winch, Julie. *A Gentleman of Color: The Life of James Forten.* New York: Oxford University Press, 2003.
Wise, John. *A Vindication of the Government of New England Churches.* https://quod.lib.umich.edu/e/evans/N09928.0001.001/1:2.8?rgn=div2;view=fulltext.
Witgen, Michael John. *Seeing Red: Indigenous Land, American Expansion, and the Political Economy of Plunder in North America.* Chapel Hill: University of North Carolina Press for the Omohundro Institute of Early American History and Culture, 2022.
Wolf, Eva Sheppard. *Race and Liberty in the New Nation: Emancipation in Virginia from the Revolution to Nat Turner's Rebellion.* Baton Rouge: Louisiana State University Press, 2006.
Wollstonecraft, Mary. *A Vindication of the Rights of Woman.* Edited by Carol Poston. New York: Norton, 1975.
Wood, Gordon S. *The Creation of the American Republic, 1776–1787.* Chapel Hill: University of North Carolina Press, 1969.
Wood, Gordon S. "Rhetoric and Reality in the American Revolution." *William and Mary Quarterly* 23, no. 1 (Jan. 1966): 3–32.

Wright, Frances. *Course of Popular Lectures*. New York: Office of the Free Enquirer, 1829.
["Written by a Lady"]. *An Oration Delivered on the Fourth Day of July 1800 by a Citizen of the United States to Which Is Added the Female Advocate*. Springfield, MA: Henry Brewer, 1808.
Wunder, John R. "'Merciless Indian Savages' and the Declaration of Independence: Native Americans Translate the Ecunnaunuxulgee Document." *American Indian Law Review* 25, no. 1 (2000/2001): 65–92.
Yellow Robe, Chauncey. "Indian Patriotism." *American Indian Magazine* 6 (1919): 129–130. Repr. in *Talking Back to Civilization: Indian Voices from the Progressive Era*, edited by Frederick E. Hoxie, 128. Boston: Bedford/St. Martin's, 2001.
Yirush, Craig M. *Settlers, Liberty, and Empire: The Roots of Early American Political Theory, 1675–1775*. Cambridge: Cambridge University Press, 2011.
Young, Mary Elizabeth. *Redskins, Ruffleshirts, and Rednecks: Indian Allotment in Alabama and Mississippi, 1830–1860*. Norman: University of Oklahoma Press, 1961.
Zion, Noam, and David Dishon. *A Different Night: The Family Participation Haggadah*. Jerusalem: Shalom Hartmann Institute, 1997.
Zuckert, Michael. "The Fullness of Being: Thomas Aquinas and the Modern Critique of Natural Law." *Review of Politics* 69 (2007): 28–47.
Zuckert, Michael P. *Launching Liberalism: On Lockean Political Philosophy*. Lawrence: University Press of Kansas, 2002.
Zuckert, Michael. "Natural Rights and Imperial Constitutionalism: The American Revolution and the Development of the American Amalgam." *Social Philosophy and Policy* 22, no. 1 (2005): 27–55.
Zuckert, Michael P. *Natural Rights and the New Republicanism*. Princeton, NJ: Princeton University Press, 1994.
Zuckert, Michael P. *The Natural Rights Republic: Studies in the Foundation of the American Political Tradition*. South Bend, IN: University of Notre Dame Press, 1996.

Index

abolitionism, 39, 110, 115–116, 143, 211, 214, 216, 233, 255, 265. *See also* antislavery; slavery; civil rights
    Garrison, William Lloyd, 82, 106, 151, 152, 232
    Hamilton, William (Philadelphia leader), 188
    Parrish, John, 118
    state-level legislation and constitutions, 118–120
Adams, Abigail, 2, 32, 96, 112, 208–211
Adams, John, 2, 3, 35–36, 41, 50, 98, 112, 117, 130, 150, 208, 210. *See also* Continental Congress; Founding Fathers
Adams, Samuel, 35, 138
African American political thought, 76, 259. *See also* African Americans; abolitionism
African Americans. *See also* abolitionism; civil rights; racial equality; slavery
    alienation of, 89
    arguments for freedom using Declaration, 117, 164
    black political left, 84–85
        Harrison, Hubert, 77
    critiques of Declaration
        Randolph, A. Philip, 83
    emigration of, 79, 99
    liberalism, 81–84
    nationalism, 259
        Delany, Martin R., 79, 83
        Garvey, Marcus, 79, 84, 266
        Malcolm X, 80
        Muhammad, Wallace Fard, 78
    popular sovereignty, 266
    radicalism, 84–86
        Black Panther Party, 84, 255, 256
        Seale, Bobby, 84
    separatism, 78, 259, 266
    women
        struggles for equality, 192–195
Agrippa (pseud.), 98, 100. *See also* antifederalists
American colonies. *See* British policies; Continental Congress; *individual colonies by name*
Ambar, Saladin, 255, 258, 259
American exceptionalism, 107–108. *See also* American identity; nationalism
American Founding, 4, 6, 72, 78, 80, 86, 136. *See also* American Revolution; Declaration of Independence; Founding Fathers
American identity, 253–254, 269
    emergence of national identity, 100–106, 157–162
    relation to Declaration of Independence, 3, 49, 116, 158, 220
"American mind," 4, 6, 18, 116, 160–161. *See also* American identity; Jefferson, Thomas; natural rights
    philosophical sources of, 5, 136
American Revolution. *See also* Continental Congress; Founding Fathers; Loyalists; Patriots; Revolutionary War
    Declaration of Independence and, 48
    Native Americans and, 172
Americans with Disabilities Act (1990), 243

295

ancient political thought, 4
antifederalists, 260
  debate with Federalists, 98, 146–149
antislavery. *See also* abolitionism; civil rights, movement; Douglass, Frederick; emancipation; equality; Lincoln, Abraham; slavery
  and Declaration of Independence, 116–118
Aquinas, Thomas, 5, 9, 10, 12, 18
  natural law theory of, 7
Arendt, Hannah, 48, 161, 250
Aristotle, 3, 5, 6, 7, 10, 65. *See also* ancient political thought
  view of man as political animal, 12, 15, 18, 48
Articles of Confederation, 144. *See also* Constitution of the United States; Continental Congress
  state sovereignty, 98
Atlantic world. *See also* slavery
  slave rebellions in, 113
  Tacky's Rebellion, 113

Banneker, Benjamin, 77, 81. *See also* African Americans; Jefferson, Thomas; racial equality
Becker, Carl, 1, 109
Benezet, Anthony, 117. *See also* abolitionism; antislavery
Biden, Joseph, 240, 242, 244
Bill of Rights, 150, 184. *See also* Constitution of the United States; rights; *individual amendments*
  debates over ratification, 149
  natural rights and, 140
Black Americans. *See* African Americans
Black Declaration of Independence (1970, NCBC), 196–201, 256, 259. *See also* African Americans, nationalism; civil rights; racial equality
Black Lives Matter movement, 111. *See also* civil rights
  references to Declaration, 201–202
black nationalism. *See* African Americans, nationalism
black separatism. *See* African Americans, separatism
Blackstone, William, 50
British constitutionalism, 220. *See also* British monarchy; British Parliament; English Bill of Rights (1689)
  colonial interpretations of, 67
  limits of Parliamentary sovereignty, 55

Magna Carta and common law tradition, 11
British Empire. *See also* British Parliament; British policies
  colonial administration, 54–55
  Quebec, 101
British monarchy, 220. *See also* George III, King
British Parliament, 19, 43, 50, 251, 262. *See also* British parliamentary reforms
  punitive legislation (Coercive Acts, 1774), 30
British parliamentary reforms, 20–30. *See also* Townshend Duties (1767)
British policies, 257
  slave trade regulation, 115
  taxation, 34, 67, 257
Buffon, Georges-Louis Leclerc, Comte de, 52–54
Bush, George H. W., 245, 247, 248, 250
Bush, George W., 242, 243, 244, 247

Carter, Jimmy, 244, 249
Catholicism, 101, 127
Cato (pseud.), 12–13
Cato's Letters, 12
Catt, Carrie Chapman, 165
Chisholm, Shirley, 200
Chisholm v. Georgia, 102
Christianity, 11, 127
  influences on American political thought, 7
  relation to natural law and moral order, 132
Cicero, 3, 5, 6, 7, 9, 10, 15, 18
civil rights, 242
  Civil Rights Act (1964), 200, 217
  movement, 85, 185, 216, 256, 266
  uses of Declaration in protest rhetoric, 196–202
  Voting Rights Act (1965), 200
Civil War, 254, 265
  emancipation and abolitionism, 266
  right of secession, 106
Civil War Amendments, 255. *See also* Fifteenth Amendment; Fourteenth Amendment; Thirteenth Amendment
classical republicanism, 6, 12
Clinton, William Jefferson, 241, 242, 243, 245, 246, 247, 249, 253
colonies. *See* colonies, British
colonies, British. *See also* British policies; Continental Congress; Patriots; *colonies by name*
  imperial status of, 94

Index 297

colonists, 17. *See also* Loyalists; Patriots; settlers
  resistance to British rule, 112
common law. *See* British constitutionalism; natural law
Confederation Congress, 144
Connecticut, 232
conscience, 132–135
consent. *See* consent of the governed; government, legitimacy of; natural rights
consent of the governed, 148, 157, 209. *See also* Declaration of Independence; government, legitimacy of; natural rights; social contract theory; sovereignty, popular
  as foundation of legitimate government, 65, 70–71
  relation to natural rights, 208
Constitution of the United States, 144–146
  preamble, 99
  relation to Declaration of Independence, 88–89, 107–108, 142–144, 219, 242, 252, 254, 260
    in abolitionist and feminist traditions, 151
    in Early Republic era, 149–151
constitutional theory, 45, 51–55, 106
constitutional veneration, 252
Continental Congress, 208, 261. *See also* Declaration of Independence
  First, 112, 115
  Second, 2, 35, 47, 61, 111, 118, 267
Coolidge, Calvin, 241, 245
critical legal studies
  Davis, Angela, 85–86
critical race theory, 76–78, 82, 86–89, 258, 259
Crow, Matthew, 258, 262, 266
culture wars, 243
Cutterham, Tom, 254, 260, 264

Davis, Thomas J., 255, 258, 266
Declaration of Independence. *See also* consent of the governed; grievances, list of; Independence Day; natural rights; sovereignty, popular
  applications in practice, 162–168, 265
  audience of, 47, 92
  European influences on, 12
  expression of the American mind, 16, 208
  as general theory of political right, 61–62
  interpretation of
    in black political thought, 77–89
    in Black Political Thought, 265–266
    in Confederate thought, 107
    in Native American claims to independence and sovereignty, 175, 178
    in Progressive Era, 104, 243
  key phrases in
    "all men are created equal," 1, 13, 18, 37, 41, 77, 80, 85–86, 116, 131, 192, 203, 214, 220, 229, 242, 251, 255
    "consent of the governed," 63, 137, 203, 248
    "endowed by their Creator with certain unalienable rights," 13, 41, 63, 252
    "life, liberty, and the pursuit of happiness," 14, 37, 41, 63, 103, 151, 203, 222
    "our lives, our fortunes, & our sacred honor," 56
    self-evident truths, 13, 41, 48, 62, 80, 131, 197, 203, 242, 262
    "to alter or to abolish," 14, 62, 63, 66, 80, 94, 106, 203
  language and rhetoric of, 46–49, 158, 268
  legal status of, 37–40, 51–55, 261
  list of six truths, 63–64
  preamble, 40–42, 164
  as revolutionary manifesto, 55–56, 242, 264
  as syllogism, 61
  as synthesis of ancient and modern political thought, 5–6
Declaration of Independence, drafting of, 35–45
  committee of five, 3, 35–45, 111
  Jefferson's role in, 2–3, 35–45
  revision by Continental Congress, 36–45
  signing of, 45
Declaration of Sentiments. *See* feminism; women; women and the Declaration
Declaratory Act (1766), 50
Delaware, 232
democracy, 17, 47, 93, 97, 143, 229, 234, 249. *See also* consent of the governed; republicanism; sovereignty, popular
Derrida, Jacques, 48–49, 80
Dickinson, John, 39
divine right of kings, 11, 128
Douglas, Stephen A., 156
Douglass, Frederick, 59, 78, 79, 82–83, 143, 152, 163, 165, 259. *See also* abolitionism; Declaration of Independence; Independence Day
  use of Declaration in antislavery thought, 190

298   Index

Dred Scott v. Sandford, 68, 77, 122, 155.
　　See also Fourteenth Amendment;
　　slavery; Taney, Roger B.
Taney, Roger B., 68, 77, 103, 256
Du Bois, W. E. B., 83, 255. See also African
　　Americans; nationalism; racial equality
Dunmore, Lord, 39
duties, 264
　　as natural, 15, 126, 128

Eisenhower, Dwight, 242, 248
emancipation
　　uses of Declaration in arguments for,
　　164–165
empiricism, 10
English Bill of Rights (1689), 11. See also
　　British constitutionalism; Glorious
　　Revolution (1688)
English law. See common law; precedent;
　　Magna Carta
Enlightenment, 6, 11, 16, 17, 179, 261. See
　　also Locke, John; natural rights; social
　　contract theory
　　influences on American political thought,
　　4–5, 58
equal rights, 207. See also civil rights; equality;
　　natural rights
Equal Rights Amendment, 216
equality, 15, 126, 135, 140, 143, 151, 205,
　　219, 220, 221, 223, 228, 235. See
　　also equal rights; natural rights; racial
　　equality; women and the Declaration
　　in Declaration of Independence, 47, 62–66
eternal law, 7

Federalist Papers, 137
　　No. 2 (Jay), 100–102
　　No. 10 (Madison), 104–106
Federalists, 148. See also antifederalists;
　　Constitution of the United States;
　　ratification debates
feminism, 207. See also Declaration of
　　Sentiments; Equal Rights Amendment;
　　women and the Declaration
　　first wave, 228–233
Fifteenth Amendment, 184. See also civil
　　rights; Dred Scott v. Sandford
Fourth of July. See Independence Day
Filmer, Robert, Sir, 11, 13, 74, 128
Ford, Gerald, 246, 250
Forten, James, 116
Founding Fathers, 246

Fourteenth Amendment, 184, 266
　　second founding, 141
Franklin, Benjamin, 3, 35, 112, 115, 117, 173

Gage, Thomas, 116
George III, King, 11, 42, 51, 55, 102, 115, 137,
　　172, 174, 208, 229, 251, 262. See also
　　British monarchy; grievances, list of
Georgia, 31, 33, 102, 180
Glorious Revolution (1688), 11. See also
　　English Bill of Rights (1689)
God, nature's/laws of nature's God, 4, 6, 8,
　　10, 11, 12, 16, 61, 94, 130–132, 140,
　　193, 197, 268. See also Enlightenment;
　　Jefferson, Thomas; Locke, John;
　　natural law; natural rights; religion
　　concept of in Declaration's preamble, 48–49
　　relation to natural law, 9–10, 124
　　religious and philosophical traditions, 6
　　theological debates over meaning, 134
Goldstein, Leslie, 255, 260, 265, 267
government, 143. See also consent of the
　　governed; natural rights; revolution,
　　right of
　　based on consent of the governed, 13, 93
　　ends of, 135
　　just powers, 14, 63, 65, 68, 70
　　legitimacy of, 93
grievances, list of, 11, 38–39, 42, 62, 88, 137,
　　197, 212, 261. See also British policies,
　　taxation; standing armies; Tea Act;
　　Townshend Duties
Grotius, Hugo, 8, 9

Haitian act of independence (1804), 111. See
　　also abolitionism; antislavery; slavery
Hamilton, Alexander, 98, 144
Hancock, Jonathan Todd, 255
happiness, pursuit of. See Declaration of
　　Independence, key phrases in; liberty;
　　natural rights
Henry, Patrick, 58, 81, 117, 149
Hobbes, Thomas, 5, 13, 14, 70, 124.
　　See also social contract theory;
　　sovereignty
　　equality of women, 205, 217
Hoffer, Peter Charles, 261
Hoffer, Williamjames Hull, 261
Holton, Woody, 257, 258
House of Commons. See British Parliament
Hovering Act. See British policies
human dignity, 15, 220, 228, 247

Index

human nature, 7, 9, 10, 15, 39, 124, 125, 140, 144, 204
   and political philosophy, 18
human rights, 242, 243, 263. *See also* individual natural rights; natural rights
hypocrisy, charges of, 46–47, 69, 80, 109, 111, 115, 213, 221, 258
   abolitionist critique of slavery and rights, 82–83, 163, 187–189, 214
   in Founding generation, 81

immigration, 97–98, 242, 243
   naturalization, 99–100
Independence Day, 2, 104, 160, 168, 256
   compared with Passover Seder, 252
   evolution of public commemorations, 263
   origins and political symbolism, 161
   political uses of Declaration, 78, 82, 152, 229, 231
   protest and rejections of, 187–188, 189–190, 199
indigenous peoples. *See* Native Americans/indigenous peoples
individual natural rights, 8, 9, 10
individual rights. *See* equal rights; liberty; natural rights
international law, 8, 18, 39, 262. *See also* law of nations

Jackson, Andrew, 180, 227, 256
Jay, John, 105, 107
Jefferson, Thomas, 1, 2, 10, 16, 18, 49, 67, 68, 74, 80, 98, 111, 147, 158, 174, 179, 203, 204, 220, 236, 254, 262. *See also* Declaration of Independence; Founding Fathers; hypocrisy, charges of; racial equality
   equality of women, 207–208, 210, 217
   interpretation of natural rights, 129–136
   Notes on the State of Virginia, 57, 58, 121–122
   philosophical influences on, 5
   political philosophy and the American mind, 3
   response to American degeneracy thesis, 52–54, 263
   rhetoric and style in the Declaration, 46, 48, 49, 160
   tombstone, 2, 46
   views on slavery, 81–82, 112, 113–114, 121
Johnson, Lyndon Baines, 242
July 2 prediction, 2
July 4 celebration. *See* Independence Day, evolution of public commemorations
justice, 220, 264
   as moral foundation of revolution, 56, 113

Kansas, 215
Kendi, Ibram X., 110
Kentucky, 106, 121
King, Martin Luther, Jr., 46, 83, 85, 165, 166, 196, 199, 244. *See also* African Americans; civil rights; equality; Declaration of Independence

labor, 244, 256, 265
   Declaration's aspirational uses in suffrage and labor movements, 219–221, 234
   Declaration's relevance to labor rights, 219, 221–228
   strikes, 222, 225
   wage slavery comparison, 221, 227
   workers' participation in Independence Day celebrations, 222–225
   Working Men's Declaration of Independence, 225–228, 256
   Workingmen's Movement, 222
law of nations, 45. *See also* international law
laws of nature, 4, 5–11, 14, 18, 48
   classical theories of, 7, 9
   Enlightenment reinterpretations of, 6, 9
   Newtonian conception of, 9
Lee, Richard Henry, 5, 35, 36, 61, 137
Levinson, Sanford, 259, 267
LGBTQ, 236, 241, 246
liberty, 116, 126, 135, 140, 143, 205, 219, 223
limited government, 91, 93, 108, 149, 220, 236, 243, 245
Lincoln, Abraham, 2, 59–60, 62, 66, 88, 99, 107, 122, 143, 191, 200, 235, 237, 240, 267, 269. *See also* equality; Civil War, emancipation and abolitionism
   Declaration as moral touchstone, 1, 152–153, 155, 168, 200, 254
Livingston, Robert R., 3, 35, 112
Locke, John, 3, 5, 6, 8, 9, 10, 11, 18, 65, 70, 263. *See also* consent of the governed; equality; natural rights; social contract theory
   on education, 139
   equality of women, 206–207
   influence on Declaration, 129–136
   natural law theory of, 124

Locke, John (cont.)
  natural rights theory of, 13–16, 261
  Second Treatise, 8, 10, 13, 14, 18, 204
  on self-evidence, 73, 125
Loyalists, 33, 40, 94, 175

Madison, James, 104, 107, 114, 144
Magna Carta. *See* British constitutionalism
Malcolm X. *See* African Americans, nationalism; racial equality
Marbury v. Madison, 264
Marshall, John, 182, 256
Mason, George, 58
Massachusetts, 35, 116, 119, 149, 170, 187, 265
McGraw, Barbara A., 254, 263, 266
medieval Scholastics, 5, 11
Merriam, Jesse, 257
Mississippi, 195
monarchy, British. *See* British constitutionalism; George III, King
Morris, Robert, 144

Nation of Islam. *See* African Americans, nationalism, Malcolm X
nationalism, 157, 168, 254. *See also* African Americans, nationalism; sovereignty, popular; American identity
Native American lands. *See* Native Americans/indigenous peoples, land conflicts; Native Americans/indigenous peoples, treaties and land cessions; Proclamation Line of 1763
Native Americans. *See* Native Americans/indigenous peoples
Native Americans/indigenous peoples, 43, 95, 96, 127, 141, 255, 256
  American Indian Movement (AIM), 185
  Apess, William, 170
  assimilation, 172, 178, 184
  boarding schools, 183
  Cherokee Nation, 172, 176, 178–183
    Cherokee Nation v. Georgia, 180–182
  Chief Logan, 57
  declarations of independence, 170–172
    in the Nineteenth Century, 178–182
    in Revolutionary era, 172–178
  Indian Removal Act (1830), 180, 256
  Indian Reorganization Act (1934), 184
  Iroquois Confederacy, 175
  land conflicts, 96, 99, 103, 174–175
  Mashpee Wampanoag, 170–171
  military service and citizenship rights, 183–185
  Proclamation Line (1763), 174
  relations with colonists, 172
  Stockbridge-Mohican community, 175
  treaties and land cessions, 175–176
  tribal sovereignty, 178, 256
  US civilization plan, 178, 183
natural law, 8, 10, 14, 123, 261. *See also* God, nature's/laws of nature's God; natural rights; social contract theory
  classical and Enlightenment theories, 5
  and God of creation, 8–9, 124, 130, 140, 268
  as moral foundation of politics, 15, 141
  workmanship principle, 8–9, 126, 130
natural rights, 13, 14, 16, 66–67, 68, 82, 93, 141, 187, 204, 217, 219, 235, 263. *See also* consent of the governed; Declaration of Independence; equality; God, nature's/laws of nature's God; liberty
natural theology, 125, 127, 129, 140, 263
  in founding era, 137–140
nature, 7, 10, 17, 18, 261. *See also* natural law
  and politics, 17–18
New Deal, 234, 235, 245, 248
New Hampshire, 106, 149
New Jersey, 208, 210, 231
New York, 96, 98, 106, 149, 175, 213, 214, 233
Newman, Richard, 254, 257, 258, 265
Newton, Isaac, 6, 8, 9, 139
Nineteenth Amendment, 204, 213, 232, 234
nominalism, 7, 9, 10
North American political thought
  colonial and Enlightenment influences, 6
North Carolina, 33
Notes on the State of Virginia. *See* Jefferson, Thomas; racial equality

Obama, Barack, 103, 201, 240, 243, 246, 247, 249, 250
Obergefell v. Hodges, 246
Ockham, William of, 7
originalism. *See Federalist Papers*
Otis, James, 39

Paine, Thomas, 51
Passover Seder
  analogy to Declaration of Independence, 251–253
  dialogue with four children, 251

Index

Patriots, 3, 94
Pennsylvania, 35, 118, 148, 175
people, the, 3, 14, 93, 157, 161, 162, 262, 268. *See also* consent of the governed; democracy; sovereignty, popular
  description of, 94–100
Plato, 7
Potter-God metaphor, 10. *See also* Locke, John
presidents. *See also individual presidents*
  American identity and the Declaration, 242
  citations of Declaration, 236–242
  civil rights reference, 243–245
  culture wars and the Declaration, 242, 246–248
  democratic rights, 248–249
  policy claims based on Declaration, 242–243
property rights. *See* rights, to property; women, marital property and rights
Protestant Reformation, 7, 124
Providence, 56, 102. *See also* McGraw, Barbara A.

Quartering Act (1765), 257. *See also* grievances, list of
Quebec Act (1774). *See* grievances, list of

racial equality, 164, 180, 242, 244, 257. *See also* abolitionism; slavery
  Civil War-era transformations, 107, 121–122
  connection to Declaration's natural rights principles, 68–69, 187
  denial in pro-slavery constitutional thought, 88–89
  Jeffersonian legacy and limits, 120–122
ratification debates, 142
  state ratifying conventions, 146–149
Reagan, Ronald, 241, 246, 247, 249
reason, 8, 9, 10, 125, 126, 129, 131, 137, 140
  in Enlightenment political thought, 7
rebellion, 37, 261. *See also* Locke, John; revolution; resistance theory; rights, of rebellion; social contract theory; *Vindiciae contra tyrannos*
religion, 6, 21, 101, 105, 110, 137, 248. *See also* McGraw, Barbara A.; Providence
  freedom of (religious liberty), 127, 264
republican virtue
  moral requirements of self-government, 133
republicanism. *See also* Cicero; Locke, John; Trenchard, John and Gordon, Thomas
  as foundation of political community, 12

resistance theory, 137. *See also* Locke, John; rebellion; revolution; rights, of rebellion; social contract theory; *Vindiciae contra tyrannos*
revolution. *See also* resistance theory; rights, of rebellion
  Declaration of Independence as argument for, 71, 204
  philosophical traditions informing, 16
  right of, 14, 16, 63, 106–107, 199, 205
Revolutionary War, 81
  African Americans in, 113
  Loyalist participation, 258
  Native Americans in, 102
rhetoric, 140, 167, 228, 249
  of Declaration of Independence, 218, 219, 262
  as political practice, 47–49
  race and rhetoric (Native Americans, African Americans), 53, 57–60, 112
Rhode Island, 229, 232
rights, 220
  democratic, 243, 248
  to happiness, 67–68
  individual, 16, 140, 216, 267
  to liberty, 204
  to life, 66, 204, 247
  to property, 67, 204, 216, 245
  of rebellion, 112, 197, 204
  of revolution, 263
Roe v. Wade, 247
Roosevelt, Franklin Delano, 245, 248, 249
Roosevelt, Theodore, 163
rule of law, 15
Rush, Benjamin, 115, 117, 136
Rutledge, Edward, 35
Rutledge, John, 35

Sacho, Madam, 176
Seagrave, S. Adam, 261
security (safety), 10, 14, 16, 63, 69, 204
self-evident truths, 71, 141
self-preservation, 5, 9, 135, 205
settlers, 17, 96
Seven Years' War, 27, 49, 57, 101, 173, 174
Sherman, Roger, 3, 35, 112
Sidney, Algernon, 3, 5, 206
slavery, 43, 94, 103, 140, 143, 164, 253, 262, 265
  1619 Project, 104, 111
  abolitionist responses to Declaration, 151, 193, 255

slavery (cont.)
  colonization proposals/forced emigration of freed blacks, 190–192
  deleted passage from Jefferson's draft, 39–40, 52, 68, 76, 85, 115–116, 174, 262
  founders' views on, 47
  imperial slavery, 112–113, 251
  legacy in American political thought, 109–111
  resonance in civil rights movement, 110
  slave trade, 39, 40, 115
smuggling
  British response to, 257
social contract theory, 11. *See also* Locke, John; resistance theory
  classical and medieval origins of, 11–13, 15
  influence on Declaration of Independence, 5
  relation to natural rights, 15
South Carolina, 28, 30, 32, 33, 35, 53, 114, 149
sovereignty, 50, 51, 55, 56, 91, 92, 219, 221, 222. *See also* consent of the governed; people, the; sovereignty, popular
  personal, 67, 82
sovereignty, popular, 48, 90–108, 148, 222, 259
  alternative assertions of (French, Papua New Guinean, Warm Springs), 91–93
  challenged by Declaration, 45
  colonial assertions of, 36
  national self-determination, 98–99
  territory and boundaries problem, 97–98
Stamp Act (1765), 22, 23, 26, 27, 30, 31, 34, 50
state of nature, 17, 65, 205
Steele, Brian, 253, 254, 256, 266, 269, 270
Stephens, Alexander, 122
suffrage, 151, 209, 210
  Catt, Carrie Chapman, 213
  Native American, 183
  women's, 59, 207, 214

Taney, Roger B., 122
Tea Act (1773), 31, 50
Texas, 97
Thirteenth Amendment, 234
Tocqueville, Alexis de, 85, 256
Townshend Duties (1767), 27, 50
Treaty of Paris (1763), 177
Trenchard, John and Gordon, Thomas, 12
Trump, Donald J., 97, 240, 248
Tsesis, Alexander, 253, 255, 258, 265
tyranny, 142, 146, 152, 195, 204, 209, 233, 251

unalienable rights, 8, 172. *See also* Declaration of Independence, key phrases in; natural rights

Vermont
  antislavery constitution, 118
Vindiciae contra tyrannos, 11. *See also* resistance theory
Virginia, 35, 50, 98, 114, 121, 149, 174, 262
  Constitution, 37–40
  Mason, George, 3, 29, 58
virtue ethics, 15

Walker, David, 79–80
Washington, George, 102, 144, 175
Wilson, James, 35, 50, 143, 148
Wilson, Woodrow, 98, 240, 248
Winthrop, James, 98. *See also* Agrippa (pseud.)
Winthrop, John, 17
women
  in civil rights activism
    Cooper, Anna Julia Haywood, 194–195
    Hamer, Fannie Lou, 195–196
  inclusion in equality claim, 69, 193–194, 203
  marital property and rights, 216
  in political thought
    Hobbes and Locke on equality, 204–207
  in suffrage and feminism, 213, 220, 228–234, 229
    Anthony, Susan B., 214, 215
    legacy of Seneca Falls Convention, 233–234
    Mott, Lucretia Coffin, 211–212, 228, 233
    Seneca Falls Convention, 59, 152, 211–216, 265
    Stanton, Elizabeth Cady, 59, 211–212, 213, 214, 228, 233
    Truth, Sojourner, 193–194
    Wollstonecraft, Mary, 211
women and the Declaration, 208–211
  Declaration of Sentiments, 193, 204, 212–216, 217, 256
women's rights, 59, 152, 193, 203, 208–218, 210, 243, 244, 255, 265
  movement, 216–217, 228
Wyoming, 231

Yorktown, battle of, 144

Zuckert, Michael, 12, 15, 253, 254, 263, 268

For EU product safety concerns, contact us at Calle de José Abascal, 56–1°,
28003 Madrid, Spain or eugpsr@cambridge.org.

www.ingramcontent.com/pod-product-compliance
Ingram Content Group UK Ltd.
Pitfield, Milton Keynes, MK11 3LW, UK
UKHW021616130126
466887UK00018B/262